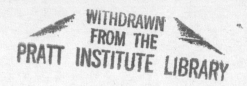

YOUR FACE HERE

BRITISH CULT MOVIES SINCE THE SIXTIES

BRITISH
CULT MOVIES
SINCE THE
SIXTIES

YOUR FACE
HERE

ALI CATTERALL & SIMON WELLS

FOURTH ESTATE / LONDON

This paperback edition first published in 2002
First published in Great Britain in 2001 by Fourth Estate
A Division of HarperCollinsPublishers
77–85 Fulham Palace Road London W6 8JB
www.4thestate.com

Copyright © Simon Wells & Ali Catterall

10 9 8 7 6 5 4 3 2 1

The right of Simon Wells & Ali Catterall to be identified as the authors of this
work has been asserted by them in accordance with the Copyright, Designs and Pat-
ents Act 1988
A catalogue record for this book is available from the British Library

ISBN 0-00-714554-3

Layout designed by M2. Typeset by Rowland Phototypesetting Ltd,
Bury St Edmunds, Suffolk
Printed in Great Britain by Clays Ltd, St Ives plc

For our parents, and for Barrie Keefe, David Sherwin and moviegoers everywhere.

YOUR FACE HERE

BRITISH CULT MOVIES SINCE THE SIXTIES

INTRODUCTION

Is THE BRITISH cult movie dead? Certainly the climate into which a 'different' sort of movie might naturally be allowed to find a cult audience has changed – perhaps for ever.

Once upon a time you knew where you were with a cult movie. A challenging, off-beat picture came out, typically (though not always) did terrible business, was left to rot by the film industry and then, kept alive by word of mouth, midnight movie screenings, and a protective circle of fans, developed an afterlife of its own. For uninitiated squares these 'cult movies' were 'the sort of movies nobody went to see'. The squares were half-right. Cult movies were the sort of films smaller, more focused pockets of cinema-goers – usually younger audiences or freer minds – went to see over and over again. As Danny Peary writes in his (very culty) *Cult Movies*, 'When you speak of cult movies you speak in extremes.' For their fans, who range from the academic to the hard-core and whose love borders on the maternal, these films are living entities. The dismay felt when the cult fan hears of the cavalier handling of their favourite film is comparable to a death in the family.

The films themselves can range from the kitsch and campy to the violent and bloody, they can be artistic masterpieces or just plain awful, but they do seem to share certain things in common. Resulting from a Faustian brew of time, place and circumstance, they are usually spun from a very personal vision that defies the commercial framework within which they're made. With production crews on the edge of bankruptcy, and in the face of studio ultimatums and mixed agendas, these films somehow break through; the wear and tear is there for all to see. And that raw and ragged quality also becomes part of their appeal.

Film-maker Chris Rodley describes *Performance* as 'one of those weird movies that continues to remake itself as if it were a jigsaw puzzle. The audience can remake the movie for themselves every time. In that respect it's truly interactive.' Umberto Eco believes it's this sense of 'glorious ricketiness . . . a hodgepodge of sensational scenes strung together' that defines the cult movie. In his essay 'Casablanca – Cult Movies and Intertextual Collage' he says it is possible 'to break, dislocate and unhinge' a cult object 'so that one can remember only parts of it, irrespective of their original relationship with the whole . . . reducing it to a series of excerpts'. An example of this is the dialogue-quoting and theme-tune humming that so often accompany the mere mention of a cult picture.

Exclusivity is a marked characteristic of cult movies, both in the kind of attraction they have for fans and in the themes they tend to pursue. Significantly, most of the twelve movies referenced here have tribal themes, whether they deal with gangsters, junkies or Mods. They also tend to involve a breaking-away from conventional society, reflecting a youthful need – and 'youth' may be the biggest cult of all – to assert a separate identity. Having tugged the rug softly or forcibly from underfoot, such movies spawn lifestyles and lifelong romances.

The history of British cinema (cult or otherwise) has, ironically, been bound up with America. It wouldn't be too sweeping a statement to say that we've never really had a wholly domestic British film industry. Encouraged by successive governments, British cinema has relied on US investment and major US studios for decades. British cult movies often arise when studios and distributors treat films made with a large degree of originality and British attitude with bewilderment or simple contempt. In times of austerity this negative reaction is magnified tenfold. Indeed, the history of British cult movies might be seen as a two-fingered salute to the crudities of mass market economics, and a heartfelt pride in one's own output. As Bob Hoskins playing Harold Shand tells wary US investors (the Mafia, in this case) in *The Long Good Friday*, 'A touch of the Dunkirk spirit, know what I mean?'

In addition, the technology through which fans might discover a cult has drastically changed. Once you could only hope to catch up with a well-loved movie by scouring the schedules of repertory cinemas and TV channels for infrequent showings. During the 1970s, for instance, fans of the TV series *The Prisoner* would travel hundreds of miles with their portable televisions, to catch local aerial signals for re-runs unavailable in their part of the country. In a time when there were only three channels to choose from and home video recorders were a rarity, there was really no other choice if they wanted to see the episodes. The rapid growth of video in the 1980s was a shot in the arm for the cult movie, not only because films that had previously been very hard to see began to become easily available, but also because the freeze-frame and the rewind afforded an in-depth appreciation that had never before been possible. Cult film fans now had the equivalent of the well-thumbed paperback that could be read over and over again. And today we are in the midst of a new revolution. Sponsored promotions like Stella Screen, and the rise of DVD and the Internet, have encouraged 'cult' to spread like wildfire. Just as today Napster-style websites enable music fans to download their favourite tracks, it is not unlikely that soon even the most obscure cult movies might be found on the Net and downloaded as easily as an MP3 file. And from the vantage point of this book's second edition, in 2002, this is now technically possible, thanks to a broadband connection. At the same time the Net affords a new creative freedom to talented film-makers who have previously struggled within the restraints of mainstream commercial cinema. It is not far-fetched to suggest that the cult movies of the future will be born and bred on the Internet.

Your Face Here traces the history of a dozen British cult movies, chronicling their inside stories, their shooting locations, their cross-cultural appeal, their afterlives, and their often belated but massive pulling power – to the point where the market has taken on the term 'cult' as a serious selling point.

Our initial list of likely contenders ran to over a hundred movies, including *Bedazzled*, *Kes*, *McVicar*, *Scum*, *Straw Dogs*, *Theatre of Blood* and *Witchfinder General*. Once you start making lists like these, it's very hard to stop. Other films up for consideration were *The Bed Sitting Room*, *Blood on Satan's Claw* and *Privilege*. We had to settle on certain (relatively) objective criteria, so we chose only those films that had had a British theatrical release, that had imaginatively exploited their British locations, and that had made an undeniable impact on audiences and on the cultural landscape. As it is impossible to write about such films in isolation, we have, where relevant, also given page space to other great movies denied chapters of their own. For, as Eco acknowledges, a cult film is not one film but many films, trading on an audience's grasp of recognisable archetypes and knowing cinematic references. *Withnail & I*, for example, offers a vaudeville echo of *Performance*, just as *Trainspotting* pays loving homage to *A Hard Day's Night* and *A Clockwork Orange*.

Finally, a word or two about the locations. To dedicated fans, a pilgrimage to the original shooting locations is a must. So strong is their desire to savour any residual energy left over from the shoot that they will travel from all points of the globe to claim brief ownership of some sacred celluloid turf. To run down the same street as the Beatles did in *A Hard Day's Night*, or to stand where the Wicker Man burned thirty years ago, is akin to visiting Jerusalem or Mecca – a truly religious experience. Over the years devotees have collected leftover props from the shoot, hanging them on their walls and mantelpieces like trophies from a big game hunt. Others so completely enter into the 'Your Face Here' philosophy that they re-enact scenes from the film on the exact spot where they were shot, videoing themselves to compare their exploits with the originals.

We, too, have been there, be it on Scottish clifftops, in London parks, or down obscure back alleys, and to help fans track down the settings for their favourite movies we have detailed as many of the original shooting locations as possible. Some proved easier to find than others. The history of the Beatles, for example, has been thoroughly picked clean over the years and their movements during the making of *A Hard Day's Night* can be easily traced. But often memories have faded or locations have changed beyond recognition. *Get Carter*, for example, serves as a unique record of the old industrial city Newcastle-upon-Tyne and today fans of the movie battle to save one of its key settings – an old multistorey car park in Gateshead – from demolition. Such is the power of these movies that they can change our perception of even the most banal surroundings. With a steady stream of tourists flocking to their favourite film locations, the British Tourist Authority has now produced a map of famous British film sites to help boost trade. Cult has come overground.

We have had enormous pleasure in tracking down these sites, but implore location hunters to treat them with respect. If you've seen the inside of Uncle Monty's remote Lake District cottage recently, you'll know what we're talking about. For those wishing to follow the location trail further, we thoroughly recommend Brian Pendreigh's *On Location* (Mainstream, 1995), Mark Adam's *Britain Through the Lens* (Boxtree, 2000), Allan Foster's *The Movie Traveller* (Polygon, 2000) and Tony Reeves's *The Worldwide Guide to Movie Locations* (Titan, 2001).

This book has been written for fans by fans. Fans often come in for pretty heavy criticism, but without them there would be no cult films. It is the diligent work of these admirers that offers hope that these treasures will continue to enjoy a life of their own. Be seeing you. Live long and prosper. Viddy well.

Ali Catterall and Simon Wells, Good Friday, 2001

ACKNOWLEDGEMENTS
For this book, we have conducted dozens of interviews with directors, stars, studio heads, industry insiders, marketing chiefs and fans, and sourced hundreds of publications. Where appropriate we have credited those books and publications that have been most useful.

So many people to thank, all of whom gave up their time one way or another to help us out. Thanks to Andy Miller, our commissioning editor, for giving us the gig in the first place, and to Charles Drazin, our line editor, for showing us where we were going wrong (and right). Thanks also to Mike Leigh for the lovely foreword. So many people to thank – why not thank them all?

Staff at Aldenham School, Hertfordshire; Lindsay Anderson (RIP); Mitzi Angel; Gail Ashurst; Chris Bailey; Andrew Bainbridge; Tim

Beddows; the Beehive Social Club, Gatwick Airport; Jonathan
Benton-Hughes; Brooke Berry; Isla Blair; Bob and Mel; Stuart
Bolton; Brian Bovell; Eric Boyd-Perkins; Mickey Bray; Brighton
Reference Library; British Library; Michael Brooke; Anthony
Brown; James Brown; Ralph Brown; Tim Brown; Paul Buck; Adam
Buxton; Café D'Jaconneli, Glasgow; David Cammell; Helen
Catterwell; John Castle; Michael Challenger; Paul Chamberlain
and the staff of Cheltenham College; Charlton Local Studies
Library; Cheltenham Library; Glenda Clarke Rose Clarke; Terence
Clegg; Cliff at Repton Boy's Club; Colin and Marco (and Mao the
Cat); Matthew Collin and staff at the *Big Issue*; Michael Collins;
Clark Collis; Dave Courtney; Simon Coward (for the videos); Alex
Cox; Crosslands bar, Glasgow; Richard Dacre; Robin Davies; Roz
Davies at the Edinburgh Film Office; Laura De Casto; Michael
Deeley; Vincent De Ritas; Doug and 'Moonie' from *Who's Who*; Paul
Douglas; Thalia Droussioti and the Big Listings guys; Harvey
Edgington and the London Film Commission; the Ellengowan
Hotel, Creetown; Firhill Health Sports Complex, Glasgow; Alan
Fletcher; Nicole Fries; Julie Freedman; Marcel Galvan; security at
Gateshead's car park, Newcastle; Estitxu Garcia; Richard E. Grant;
Christopher Gibbs; Jane Giles; Glasgow Film Office; the manager,
staff and Charlie O'Hare at the Grand Hotel, Brighton; Steve Green;
Shani Grewal; Roberto Gomez; Richard Griffiths; Mike Hall; Peter
Hannan; Robin Hardy; Frank Harper; Andy Harrison; Simon
Hattenstone at the *Guardian*; David and Joanne Healey; Jocelyn
Herbert; John Heron; Paolo Hewitt; Paul Hills; Mike Hodges; Holly;
Leo Hollis; Brian Hovmand; Bob How; Lisa Honeywell; House of
Commons Information Centre, London; Joss Hutton; Independent
Working Class Association (Hackney Branch); all at the Internet
Movie Database; staff at the ITC library; Robert Irwin; Anita
Jackson; Jane Jackson; Sarah Jenkin; Joe and Perri; Sandie
Johnson and the staff of Penrith Tourist Information Office; Barrie
Keeffe; Ken (from Texas); Roz Kidd; Daren King; Scott King; Mike
Knowles and Barry Davis of Blandfords, Newcastle; LA Fitness
Centre, Southgate; Trevor Laird; Dave Lally; Ulla Larson;
Christopher Lee; Neil Lee; Mike Leigh; Richard Lester; Sandy
Lieberson; London Borough of Greenwich Press Office; Owen Luder;
'Irish Jack' Lyons; Tony Lyons; Roger McGuinn; Leonie Macdonald;

Marilyn MacMillan; David Mapstone; Michael Medwin; Meg and Jane at Penny Lane; Ed Miles; Iain Miller at Wills & Co. Factory, Glasgow; Ralph Mulford and the gardeners of Maryon Park, Greenwich; Michael Moorcock; Alan Moore; Chris Moore; Paul Morley; Peter Mullan; Ian Nathan; National Sound Archive; Kim Newman; Ciara Nolan; Robert Oates; Matt Owen; Barrie Pattison; Brian Pendreigh; Mr and Mrs Pepper at the Old Schoolhouse, Amworth; Mark Perry; Brian Pettifer; Paul Phillips of North West Water; Ingrid Pitt; Richard Porter; Tim Poulter; Clive Priddle; Alex Quine; Ian Rakoff; Deborah Reade; Nick Reynolds; Rick and Jo; Chris Riley and members of the *Get Carter* Appreciation Society; Jane Robertson; Franc Roddam; Chris Rodley; 'Rose'; Jonathan Rutter; Dave Sharp; Julia Short; Adrian Sherwood; David Sherwin; Caroline J. Simpson; Iain Sinclair; Six of One Appreciation Society; Adam Smith; Bryan Smith; Peter Snell; Barry Spikings; Eddie Standish; Carolyn Starren and staff of Kensington and Chelsea Local Studies Library; Ralph Steadman; Kate Stretton; Harriet Sutcliffe; Peter Sutton; David Thewlis; Anthony Thomas; Paul Tickell; Topsy Cat; Paul Tunkin; Carlos Ulla at El Blason, Chelsea; Tom Vague; Austin Vernon; Richard Vine at the *Guide*; Reg Vivash; Sheila Wakeling; Alexander Walker; the family Walsh; Wandsworth Local Studies Library; David Ward; Barbara Watson and staff of Newcastle-Upon-Tyne Central Library; Phillip Watson; Paul Weller; George Wells; Westminster Central Reference Library; Phil Wickham and Ian O'Sullivan at BFI Information; Jeremy Wilton; Ray Winstone; David Wood; Matt Worley; Paul Worts; Duncan Youel. Thanks again, and if we have unwittingly missed anybody, sincerest apologies: we truly couldn't have done it without you.

Thanks must also go to Stephen Woolley, who, with two films in production, still found time to share his thoughts with us. Thanks also to Terry Jeffery and Julia Raeside, whose assistance has gone above and beyond. Much love and thanks, too, to Sian Rider who, as the 'third partner' in this book, has provided more than just tea and sympathy, being a real rock in the sometimes troubled waters of cult appreciation.

YOU CAN'T DO THAT

It's one of the most instantly recognisable openings in the history of cinema: three smartly dressed young men, barely out of their teens, running for their lives from a pack of rabid girls. And from beginning to end *A Hard Day's Night* is *busy* – these Beatles pack more into thirty-six hours than most of us do in a lifetime. The landmark movie captures a period of time that John Lennon would later recall as like 'living in the eye of a hurricane', and director Dick Lester enters the mouth of that storm to catch an animated Polaroid of Beatlemania.

'Let's get something very clear about the Beatles deal. We made the deal for one reason . . . we were expanding our music recording company so we were going to get publishing rights and a soundtrack album . . . I'd never even seen them perform.'

David Picker, head of production, United Artists

A Hard Day's Night is an eighty-five-minute scream of orgasm. As Tommy Steele tickled and Cliff Richard teased, the four-headed, eight-legged hydra called JohnPaulGeorgeAndRingo brought teeny-boppers to a shuddering climax. The groundswell of interest that grew as the Beatles toured the UK ensured that by the time they headed the bill at the Royal Variety Performance on the evening of 4 November 1963 they had become the newspapers' darlings. The press did not 'invent' Beatlemania – they just rode the train. That night, the 1960s took a left turn, left the tracks and never looked back. The screams that accompanied the Beatles carried, in the same breath, a release from the past.

In the scheme of things it was obvious the Beatles were going to make a film. Following Elvis the Actor's lead, pop stars (possessed of an indeterminate life expectancy) were now expected to provide evidence of thespian ability – however dire – alongside their musical exploits. The first generally acknowledged UK pop film was *The Tommy Steele Story* in 1957. Cliff Richard's ersatz Beach party flicks would soon follow – *Expresso Bongo* (1959), *The Young Ones* (1961) and *Summer Holiday* (1962) – hardly innovative, but faring well enough at the UK box office. There was a smattering of British jukebox movies, mostly dreadful – little more than promotional pieces (*Just for Fun, Live it Up, It's a Mad, Mad World*), save for a notable exception – the Adam Faith vehicle *Beat Girl* (1960), which would paint a more truthful vision of music-led teenage rebellion. At the same time a new school of realist film-making had emerged.

Jack Clayton's *Room at the Top* (1959) had demonstrated that gritty Northern accents could break through class and social barriers to grab a wider audience. *A Taste of Honey* and *Saturday Night, Sunday Morning* followed. But by the time *This Sporting Life* (1963) hit the screens the 'kitchen sink' genre was becoming a miserable cliché. The early 1960s now found the British film industry in typically bifurcated form: on the one hand, still plumbing the sink for more grime, on the other, exploiting a pop renaissance. In the midst of all this United Artists, under the leadership of George Ornstein, set up a London office in 1961, launching James Bond's first outing in *Dr No* (1962). With homegrown cinema more dependent on foreign investment than ever, serious British film-makers were now encouraged to celebrate a new, commercially viable, user-friendly 'classlessness', as television was doing. *A Hard Day's Night* was about to transcend its origins: not so much a movie as a news report, a visual diary of Beatlemania, the biggest cult in the world.

Previously, moving pictures of the Beatles had been rare. Their appearances on at least a dozen TV pop shows during 1963 had been mainly restricted to musical interludes. In a hitherto unthinkable nod to Northern soul, the BBC had commissioned a half-hour profile of the Beatles and their home town, *The Mersey Beat*, broadcast on 9 October 1963. It portrayed the quartet as thoughtful, ambitious young men, the musical equivalents of the Liverpool poets.

The band always claimed they'd refrained from making a vehicle movie – the sort they hated so much in other pop films – and that they had turned down all offers until the right script was found to showcase their unique appeal and musical expertise. As John Lennon told *Rolling Stone* in 1970: 'We didn't want to make a fucking shitty pop movie.' In reality the Beatles diary was full for 1963 and, given their massive recording commitments – two albums, four singles, plus an almost daily ritual of stage, radio and TV appearances – there was no way they could have set aside the six weeks required for filming. Furthermore, the only space available was after their first sortie into America.

Walter Shenson was an American independent producer living and producing films in London. At that time, he was best known for the 1959 Peter Sellers comedy, *The Mouse That Roared*, a quirky low-budget sleeper hit. United Artists told Shenson they wanted to make a 'low-budget comedy' with the express purpose of gaining exclusive rights to a soundtrack album. In something of an oversight, Capitol – the Beatles' record label in the United States – hadn't included the option of covering movie soundtracks in their contracts with the band, a decision United Artists quickly capitalised on, drawing up plans for a three-picture deal (and swiftly renegotiating the boys' contract to plug the leak). If the film stiffed in the States at least, United Artists stood to reap dividends from the record sales, no matter what. Director Richard Lester recalls 'United Artists' attitude was: "If it's cheap and it's quick, we are not in any danger because, if we get it out in time, we don't think the bubble will burst before the summer." And that was October of 1963.'

The Beatles were set to scoop £25,000 in appearance fees and a percentage of the profits. The Beatles' manager Brian Epstein was still naïve as far as business dealings went. The manager's usual cut would have been a clear 25 per cent, but he informed the group that he wasn't prepared to accept anything more than 7.5 per cent. Intoxicated by his love for the boys, Epstein now proceeded to shoot his remaining toes off, agreeing that all movie rights would revert back to Shenson after fifteen years, a decision that would cost the group millions. Shenson, a generation older, and no fan, first met the boys during a crowded, chaotic taxi ride. 'It was like being in a Marx Brothers picture,' he recalled. 'They were crawling all over the place.' When asked if he had a director in mind for them, Shenson suggested Richard Lester.

'David Picker [UA's production head] was a fan of mine,' says Lester. 'He knew what I liked and he thought, because of having seen my first film, 1962's pop music anthology *It's Trad, Dad*, that I could probably get away with it and pull it off.' Lester was another American, living and working in London since 1955. He'd come from live television, 'doing serious comedy – and I was also making documentaries. I wasn't a cineaste particularly, and came ill-equipped to judge a mass of material. My influences were more Ernie Kovacs – a master of televised surrealist gags, Jacques Tati, and Spike Milligan.' At this time Lester was best known in movie circles for the Goons' Oscar-nominated *Running, Jumping and Standing Still* film and the Shenson-produced *Mouse on the Moon* (1963). It was the Goons connection, however, that really appealed to the boys, with Lennon in particular a lifelong fan (both outfits had also shared the same producer in George Martin). 'I knew their music by accident,' says Lester. 'I was a jazzer – that's what I liked. Most of my ABC television art director mates were also jazz enthusiasts, and had brought back some of the first discs from Liverpool. I heard the Beatles at parties rather early and liked their energy. I remember taking their first album home and playing it to my wife, and saying "I think I could do something with this."'

Lester first met the group that October at London's Playhouse Theatre while they were rehearsing a radio show. 'We were asked to sniff round each other like dogs to see whether we would get on,' Lester recalled for the BBC. 'What came out was that we knew the kind of film we didn't want to make and, mercifully, we coincided.' While the Beatles were conquering Europe during autumn 1963 Shenson and Lester searched for the scriptwriter who might best realise their anarchic vision. Kitchen-sink playwright Alun Owen was suggested.

McCartney and Epstein had seen Owen's Liverpool-based TV play *No Trams to Lime Street* and remembered his name. And, of course, he was from Liverpool, with an acknowledged ear for the rhythm and nuance of the Liverpudlian dialect and put-down – though this didn't stop Lennon later slating him as 'a bit phoney . . . a professional Liverpudlian'. The playwright initially envisaged 'an airy, fairy theme' for the boys, a million miles away from the finished product. As Owen told *Rave* magazine in 1964, 'I wanted the boys living it up in fancy costumes, but quickly realised that nothing could compare with their own fantastic lives.'

To become more acquainted with the boys' daily lifestyles and routine, during November 1963 Owen was dispatched to Dublin where the Beatles were performing. The meeting was important, since it would determine whether the leads could meet the demands of a full-blown production. For the actor-turned-playwright, the Beatles were born to tread the boards: 'John, in particular, is great. In all the years I've been connected with the theatre, I've never known anyone do an audition at first sight the way he did. He didn't just read the script the first time he saw it ... he acted it all over the floor.' What Owen witnessed that weekend both shocked and exhilarated him. 'We went right through the hotel, straight to a press reception, straight to the theatre, and at no time were they actually allowed to enjoy what was supposed to be their success.'

Owen felt the Beatles paid a terrible price for their popularity and was determined to 'compress this claustrophobia' for his script. 'The only freedom they ever get,' he observed, 'is when they are playing their music. That's when their faces light up. I had to get to know them pretty well to write the film, and that's what really made my mind up how to write it.' Ultimately, the writer would simply take an aspect from each and exaggerate, with McCartney presented as the romantic, Starr the lonely loveable runt, Lennon the sardonic sybarite and Harrison an anchor of unknown quantity, who tethered the others down.

Before filming began, the Beatles had another little gig to attend to. Their first tour of America, charmingly recreated by Robert Zemeckis in *I Wanna Hold Your Hand* (1978), was an overwhelming success, Ed Sullivan's bemusement notwithstanding. 'Once *The Ed Sullivan Show* had happened nobody was talking abut bubbles bursting any more,' says Lester.

Their airliner touched down at 1 p.m. on 7 February 1963 at New York's Kennedy airport to be greeted by 3,000 teenagers waving placards (many astutely handed out by Capitol Records). The fans had travelled from all over the States, skipping school or risking the sack. Despite Lennon's later claim that Owen's screenplay had merely caricatured the band, a little-seen documentary from the period, *What's Happening? The Beatles in New York*, shot by the Maysles Brothers, who would later make the Rolling Stones concert movie, *Gimme Shelter*, captures real-life Beatlemania, and bears an uncanny resemblance to *A Hard Day's Night*, so close that Epstein demanded that the documentary only be released after its fictional counterpart. 'I've read that I chose to do this because of the Maysles' documentary,' says Lester. 'But none of us had seen it, and didn't know anything about it until our script was written and the film was completely in position.'

Having successfully conquered the world superpower, the Beatles returned home on 22 February to start work on the movie soundtrack. They already had one song in the can, 'Can't Buy Me Love', which they had recorded some weeks before in Paris, and a week later the remaining songs had been recorded. As legend has it, the title, *A Hard Day's Night*, sprung fully formed from a classic comment of Ringo's to describe a marathon recording session that had lasted well into the next day. Shenson seized upon the phrase, instructing Lennon to go and write the song immediately. The finished song would play over the opening sequence, which was originally to have consisted of pre-pubescent screaming. Yet the phrase can be found in a line of Lennon's short story 'Sad Michael' from *In His Own Write*, published in 1964 but written well before filming began.

Shot in black and white, mainly for budgetary and technical reasons, under Lester's direction *A Hard Day's Night* would exploit every cinematic trick in the book: *cinéma vérité* borrowed from Truffaut, stunningly stylised shots swiped from Fellini (most evident in the closing scenes, a nod to *La Dolce Vita*, in which the Beatles replace Christ as the icon of the day), a substantial dollop of Free Cinema's unsentimental framing, Marx Brothers-variety romps, Keaton pastiches and Mack Sennett-style tomfoolery. The wilfully deranged surrealist passages and dizzying variations in pace might have eclipsed lesser personalities, but the Beatles were weighty enough to carry it off, wisecracking and poncing about in a London both familiar but oddly compressed, as if they were cavorting in a huge back garden of their own. 'We didn't have time to sit back and think about what we were doing,' Lester said. 'We just did it by instinct.' As delinquent Jean-Pierre Léaud is whirled around a fairground's centrifugal contraption during Truffaut's *Les Quatre Cents Coups*, he somehow performs a miraculous physical feat within its spinning walls, encapsulating most of what is right about Lester's film. Lester's direction expertly caught a sense of the four as being prisoners of their own success: it was clear that these girls meant business, that if they were to catch up with the boys they would rip them limb from bloodied limb. Here was the quintessential come-on: 'catch us if you can'.

Shooting commenced at 8.30 a.m. on 2 March 1964, continuing on the tightest of schedules for the next seven weeks. It had a minuscule budget – £189,000. On the very first day of shooting it was discovered that the Beatles were not Equity members, so they were hurriedly nominated and seconded by co-stars Wilfred Brambell and Norman Rossington. Shenson instructed a second crew to shadow the shoot, filming behind-the-scenes footage, with an eye for further exploitation.

Various locations were kept under wraps to avoid crowds. 'This whole picture is wrapped in secrets!' a production executive protested. The script would have us believe the group is leaving Liverpool's Lime Street Station, bound for London, although all departure sequences were shot at Marylebone; the Beatles had forsaken Liverpool culturally and literally. They belonged to London now. Marylebone Station, sitting elegantly off Grand Central Street, was chosen for the boys' departure because it was so quiet on a Sunday. Lester had taken the precaution of employing a posse of extras at the agreed daily Equity fee of £7.10s. He needn't have worried. London's Beatlepeople – 'the eyes and ears of the world' said Harrison – were one step ahead and an enormous crowd turned up. No one had any idea who was being paid or not; it didn't matter – all produced the same amount of enthusiasm.

The opening sequence, that unforgettable image of John, George and Ringo running from a pack of baying fans, was filmed on Sunday, 5 April in a street next to Marylebone Station called Boston Place. And yes, George really did take an unscheduled tumble here as the boys approached the station entrance. The detail so impressed Lester, ever the opportunist when mixing real life with fantasy, that he decided to keep it in. The boys must have felt a sense of *déjà vu* when in 1968 they purchased 34 Boston Place as the base for their ill-fated Apple Electronics venture.

Entering the station from Melcombe Street, John, George and Ringo hurried round the concourse while Paul, in disguise (something he routinely adopted as an aid to getting around London unimpeded) sat blissfully undisturbed with Wilfred Brambell. At one point, the boys hid in three public telephone boxes in what was the old ticket hall before running the length of platform 1 for their waiting train.

News footage of the station filming, which surfaced later in America in 1964, revealed the chaos Lester had to contend with that Sunday, struggling with a megaphone to direct the group against the sheer weight of fans, press and police. Lester recalls the shoot as 'total madness. I just saw them coming and I thought, "This is the film!" I grabbed the camera, which was loaded, and hand-held it out the window as they came on board. The script girl was saying, "Nobody knows what's going on. Nobody's got release forms. If this is the way this film is going, my notice is being given at the end of the week."' The crew would have to make a return trip to Marylebone the following Sunday to fill in some of the gaps. 'Not a bad way to get through an afternoon,' thought Paul.

The scenes on board the train were shot between 2 and 6 March on a specially hired train that ran the Beatles and crew between Paddington and the West Country. Settling in their first-class compartments, they are introduced to Paul's goatish grandfather, played by Wilfred Brambell, star of the enormously popular TV comedy series *Steptoe and Son*. Brambell would be constantly referred to throughout the film as a 'clean old man'. Oddly enough, this wasn't actually a jokey reference to Steptoe's 'dirty old man': the part had originally been written for another elderly Irish character actor.

'Johnson', played by Richard Vernon, the very model of the uptight upper class city gent, enters and is immediately pitched into a battle of wills with the four, John in particular giving it all he's got ('Gie's a kiss'). With Paul's dismissive 'Ah, come on . . . Let's leave the kennel to Lassie', two taboos – class deference and respect for the elderly – are given a good kicking. Having generated a sense of *vérité* by using a hand-held wide-angled lens for the train journey, Lester now jettisoned all realism for the next shot as the Fabs further torment the commuter with John and Paul (and George on a bicycle) running alongside the moving train from the platform at Crowcombe Station, Somerset. Unlike the rest of the other train sequences, the 'I Should Have Known Better' interlude was filmed in a mock-up at Twickenham Studios. These scenes had to be re-shot when it was discovered that the crew, shaking the carriage to simulate a real train, were rocking it in time to the music. During the song they are watched by moon-faced fans, who ghoulishly poke their fingers through the chicken wire that separates the mortals from the gods, like the frustrated flesh-tearing zombies from George A. Romero's *Night of the Living Dead*. As an introduction to the performing Beatles, this is a strange choice of song, jarring against the pace of the journey, further removed from reality by cross-cutting between their performance and a simultaneous hand of cards.

Says Lester: 'The film people I admired weren't making Presley movies. My interest was more on the Continent and therefore my heroes were Truffaut and *400 Blows*. Also *Shoot the Pianist*, where there are those little surrealist touches that come out of nowhere. It was that which led me to alter some of the early musical numbers, so that we got two realities bumping against each other. It seemed to me that if you were going to play those games, you'd need to prepare the audience for it. That's why we had them sitting in the train car and then suddenly outside banging on the windows, trying to get noticed. It was just saying to the audience, "Don't make much of this, there isn't anything to be worried about, but things may not be totally as they seem."'

Another stone through the palatial greenhouse saw the boys relaxing in the relative tranquillity and splendour of their hotel suite – in reality, a set at Twickenham studios. For all interiors, the boys used the Surrey-based studios, conveniently tucked away in what is still primarily a residential area. Ringo, an almost silent presence from the off, is roundly insulted for having a big nose and receiving more fan mail than the rest of the group put together. Ringo's magnificent hooter had first come to prominence when the boys' February trip to the States had drawn hate mail referring to the 'English Jew' (later, the basis of a death threat).

The casino and discotheque sequences were held in a real club, at Les Ambassadeurs, 5 Hamilton Place, in London's Mayfair. A couple of years previously a film crew had visited the staid establishment to film the casino sequences for James Bond's début in *Dr No* (1962). The ornate staircase served as a perfect red carpet to the Beatles as they entered the club. The Beatles regularly visited all London's 'in' spots so it's no surprise that they look pretty relaxed in this sequence. Norman Rossington and John Junkin, who played road managers Norm and Shake, the fictional counterparts to roadies Neil Aspinall and Mal Evans, couldn't have been further from the truth. 'Honestly, I know what they'd say if I tried that lark on them,' Aspinall chuckled to the *Beatles Monthly* magazine, referring to Rossington's demands that the boys knuckle down to answering their fan mail.

At the time of filming, McCartney was romancing the young Jane Asher, Lennon was attached to Cynthia, with whom he was living in a top-floor flat in London's Kensington, while Ringo was secretly seeing old Liverpool flame Maureen Cox. But in the film none of the group is shown to have a girlfriend – every girl is their girlfriend. As Owen explained, 'There isn't time for romance.' This was only half the story. Years later Lennon summed up their touring days to *Rolling Stone* magazine in a single, leering phrase: '*Satyricon.*' Epstein's PA, Peter Brown, in his candid memoir, *The Love You Make*, describes the boys entertaining groupies and extras during the filming, but Lester, who shadowed the boys throughout the shoot, is keen to downplay this: 'There was no time. They were with us all the time.'

One thing the audience certainly noticed was that the boys smoked like chimneys, making no effort to hide their dependency. Shenson later told a US film crew, 'I knew most of the fans were youngsters and I thought their idols shouldn't set a bad example. I never told them not to smoke, but whenever I possibly could, I would take the cigarettes out of their hands.' Says Lester: 'Well, Walter had to have something to do . . .' According to Lennon (and unknown to Shenson) all four were consuming vast quantities of drugs during the shoot – a habit that had begun in their Prellie-driven Hamburg days. 'Thanks for the Purple Hearts,' Lennon quipped when the band interrupted filming to pick up silver heart-shaped Variety Club awards.

Lennon was certainly off his rocker on the night of Friday, 20 March, when the boys appeared on ITV's *Ready Steady Go* after a gruelling day's filming. The surviving footage shows an out-of-control rhythm guitarist, barking like a dog and feverishly scratching his face, as he mistimes his chords. When the band mimed to Lennon's own song, 'It Won't Be Long', Lennon could barely voice-synch his own lyrics without visibly drooling down his velvet collar. The producer, noticing his state, concentrated the cameras on the other members, while the Beatles' early 'official' photographer, Dezo Hoffman, received a speed-fuelled, post-performance tongue-lashing. As he recalled in his memoir *With the Beatles*, 'John and I had an argument which meant I saw less and less of them. He began not to trust anybody, believing they were being fleeced by everybody. And because he was taking drugs, his paranoia was worsened. That day he actually accused me of making a fortune out of the Beatles, while they saw nothing.' Somehow, Epstein's diplomatic spin-doctoring managed to keep all the sexual and chemical shenanigans out of the papers and away from the ever-present paparazzi, who swarmed like flies looking for new angles on the boys. The nearest they came to anything resembling a scandal was the re-emergence of Fred Lennon, John's wayward sailor father who'd come home looking for gravy; Lennon simply slammed the door in his face.

A scene showing the boys on their way to a press conference, which featured the future *Are You Being Served* star, Frank Thornton, as the group's chauffeur, was cut from the final picture. Stuck in a traffic jam (at the junction of Arlington Road and Rosslyn Road, Twickenham), the group is overtaken by a company director's Rolls. Lennon lowers his window and all four let fly an imaginary hail of bullets at the executive in the back seat. He shouts back, as Paul and Ringo tumble out of the car to further take the piss. There are numerous jibes at the 'bourgeoisie' throughout the movie, but perhaps the backers felt this one crossed the line.

The press conference contains the familiar stream of irreverent one-liners. 'The reason that press conference scene worked so well,' says Lester, 'was because we were creating a disturbance and the police told us to stay off the streets. We knew we had a press conference scene to shoot, but didn't have any actors to do it. We called upon actual journalists, or roped in our mates. Nobody was really prepared. So that scene has a very extemporaneous feel about it, even to the extent of taking answers from one question and cutting them into somebody else. Anything to make it crazier and crazier. It was almost an afternoon of ad-libs.'

For well over two hundred years there stood at 58 Scala Street a grand tiered auditorium, the Scala. Well tucked away from the lights of Shaftesbury Avenue, the obscurely positioned theatre, which has since been demolished, was perfect for crew and Beatles alike, the narrow streets that surrounded it easy to seal off and quick to exit from. The boys filmed the entire press junket and TV concert sequence here between 23 March and 2 April. The short-fused television director was played by Victor Spinetti. He was personally invited to appear in the film by the boys, who had seen him in a production of *Oh What a Lovely War*. Spinetti, who formed a close bond with the group, especially with John, has the honour of being the only actor to have reappeared in the other Beatles' films *Help!* (1965) and *Magical Mystery Tour* (1967).

A liberating device was needed to transport the boys from stuffy studio to the grass arena. The twisting iron fire escape at the rear of the Hammersmith Odeon (now the Apollo) performed this function on 22 April. Although the Hammersmith Odeon was a popular venue at the time, the Beatles had surprisingly yet to play the 3,500-seater auditorium. The field the boys enter is actually an amalgam of two different locations. On 13 March, aerial shots had been taken of the group cavorting on a helicopter launch pad at Gatwick Airport, thirty miles south of London. Filming was held up as Lennon's leather Breton cap, which he wore through the film, had been left back in town and had to be retrieved. A small crowd gathered to watch the boys run, in stage costume, from an old station building at the airport to a waiting helicopter, which then lifted off as a confetti of signed photographs scattered over the field. The crew then pretended to pack up and the crowd were told that the day's filming was over. But after lunch the boys were then filmed larking about on the old part of the airfield around the helicopter launch pad for one of the most memorable sequences of the picture.

Finally, they posed for promotional photographs at the nearby derelict Gatwick Railway Station. The station was still derelict in early 1999 when a band of gypsies removed the final fragments of the terminal for their own use. The launch pad itself was still there but some ominous-looking demolition equipment occupied the path the boys had once run down, ready to demolish the last memories of the Beatles' trip to the airfield.

The aerial sequences at Gatwick were interpolated with footage shot on the ground at Thornbury Playing Fields in Isleworth, Middlesex, with the boys horse-playing on a mocked-up launch pad. As John was tied up at a Foyles literary lunch to mark the publication of his first book, *In His Own Write*, Lester literally stepped into John's shoes for knee-high close-ups.

'I had this idea of them all suddenly wandering off by themselves,' said Owen. 'Ringo going out to prove he's The Man. Lennon going out just to annoy people, and I thought George could take a wrong turning.' Owen had written individual sequences for each of the Beatles to build their 'personalities'. 'They were playing themselves,' says Lester. 'They were pretty good at that. In retrospect, we felt that the person who attempted least and achieved most was George. With John, it would either be spectacularly right or spectacularly wrong. And I think John was instinctively the most talented actor. George was the least demonstrative as an actor, but whatever he did he nailed.' Harrison was still a bit of a dark horse. Audiences could easily recognise Ringo's clown, Paul's Lothario and John's acid-tongued anarchist, but had difficulty pigeon-holing the reserved, slightly sombre George.

In the sequence Owen wrote for him, George's detour takes him to an advertising agency, promoting shirts for teenagers, where fashion director 'Simon Marshal' mistakes George's 'adenoidal glottal stops and carry-ons' as a pose designed to sell an image – the very business he's involved in (the business, of course, of the pop and movie games, as Owen well knew) – and attempts to hire George as an influential clothes horse for the 'kids'. In a razor-sharp, bitterly funny send-up of the fashion and media industries – also incorporated by Bob Rafelson in the Monkees' 1968 classic *Head* ('We're made of tin!') and in Peter Watkins' darker *Privilege* (1967) – Marshal tries to ingratiate himself while George dismisses his proposed new clothes as 'Grotty', a word often incorrectly attributed to Harrison himself. 'I didn't invent the word,' said Owen. 'Liverpool did. There's a famous character in Liverpool called "Grotty Jean" and the word itself is an abbreviated version, like so many Liverpudlian words, of grotesque. George hadn't even heard of it, and it eventually wound up with Princess Margaret at the premiere saying, "Where's this wonderful word 'grotty' coming from?"'

There are more heated exchanges and Marshal meditates on how best to manipulate the swinging scene in terms that nearly forty years on have a strangely familiar ring – 'the new thing is to care passionately, and be right wing'. He then dismisses George from his sight and, consulting his marketing calendar, decides the new image 'isn't due for another three weeks'.

Paul's 'solo' was to be cut from the final film. While he is looking for Ringo, he meets a dancing girl, Isla Blair, who is rehearsing her lines in a TV rehearsal room. The scene was shot in Jack Billing's TV School Of Dancing at 2 Goldhawk Road, Hammersmith, over 20–21 April. According to those few who have seen the sequence, Paul couldn't carry the long dialogue scene. 'They told me they felt it was not appropriate for any of the Beatles to have a love scene,' says Blair. 'But we were probably both very bad.' Lester, however, gives a different version. 'Because we had the rather lethargic scene with Ringo coming up, I felt we couldn't have two rather gentle scenes going on, that it would slow the tempo and the energy of the film up too much. Of the two scenes, we kept Ringo's and sacrificed Paul's. It wasn't that it wasn't that good.'

Today, all that remains of the sequence are a couple of production shots of McCartney entering the rehearsal studios. The only sustained solo effort that Paul would subsequently make before the cameras was *Give My Regards To Broad Street* (1984), for which he received the worst reviews of his career. Since then, Paul has shied away from any further attempts at screen acting.

Ringo's sequence has him wandering through Notting Hill Gate. 'We wanted a place where there was not that much through traffic,' says Lester. 'Because after you did a take, there'd suddenly be 2,000 kids and a policeman would say "Piss off. You're creating a disturbance." So most of the locations you see in the film were not chosen, they were sort of "Oh, Christ. Where are we going to go now?"'

Ringo was filmed strolling down Lancaster Road, pausing to take a photograph of milk bottles at No. 2. After being chased by two fans, he pops into a second-hand shop at 20 All Saints Road (at the time of writing, a vacant bookmaker's). Owen's first draft, which would not be filmed, had originally seen the drummer talking with a 'typical Jewish' proprietor, then walking behind his counter and selling a top hat and tails to some East Indian seamen – a sequence Ornstein ordered out as he felt the dialogue inferred that they looked like 'stupid niggers'. Ringo then heads off in the direction of McGregor Road. As he stops to chat up a young girl, he is watched by a suspicious policeman.

Ringo is given the brush-off and, in another amalgamation of two settings, wanders disconsolately along a towpath by the river. The towpath sequence was filmed in Ferry Lane near Kew, West London, after a hard day's night partying. 'I arrived on set straight from a nightclub,' Ringo recalled in 1982, 'and we had a lot of dialogue in those scenes. I couldn't even speak, but we had a whole crew so we had to do something.' Lester remembers having to bark orders at him that morning. 'Go here, stand there.' Mooching along the towpath, he encounters a young truant (David Jaxon), who tells Ringo about his mates 'Ginger, Eddy Fallon and Ding Dong'. If they seem oddly familiar it's because Owen has almost certainly modelled them on the Fab Four. 'Ginger's mad, he says things all the time [George]. And Eddy's good at punching and spitting [John]. Ding Dong's a big head and he fancies himself with it but it's all right cos he's one of the gang [Paul].' This leaves Ringo in the Jaxon role, another deserter who should be 'in school'. With the Beatles' fan letter duties described as 'homework', Owen is going for all-out identification here.

Ringo then wanders into a pub and manages to upset everyone in it, disrupting board games, accidentally smashing glasses, and misthrowing darts. The scene was shot on 10 March, close to Twickenham Studios, in the Turk's Head public house in Winchester Road. Ringo leaves the pub and walks past a street market. His calamitous sojourn finally comes to a halt when a misplaced act of chivalry – laying his coat, Walter Raleigh-fashion, over a puddle for a young woman, accidentally tipping her down a hole at a building site – leads to his arrest. This was the very last scene of the film to be shot. Its location was a new housing estate at Edgehill Road, West London. The manhole, now resplendent with a wrought-iron lid, still exists today for any intrepid Beatle fans who may wish to emulate Ringo's efforts that day.

Ringo is taken to a police station, where he is joined by Paul's grandfather, who has been hauled in for peddling faked autographed Beatles photographs without a licence. 'There's a great tradition of autograph faking,' laughs Lester. 'In fact, John used to do it deliberately. He gave me one of his books, and it said, "To Walt Disney, with thanks – George Harrison."' St John's Secondary School at 83 Clarendon Road, Notting Hill (soon afterwards demolished to make way for a housing estate) served as the exterior for the police station and was filmed on the afternoon of 16 April.

Paul's grandfather escapes, informs the other Beatles that Ringo has been arrested, and they set out to rescue him. A mad Keystone Kops chase ensues, taking the boys into Heathfield Street, off Portland Road, then past St Luke's Church, St Luke's Road, Notting Hill. On 16 April, a brief sequence was filmed of the boys being chased by police in and out of the Portland Arms at 119 Portland Road. This scene was to be cut from the finished film although Lester revisited the location for his next film, *The Knack* (1965). The Fabs then return to the TV studios where a large crowd has gathered, including the Milky Bar Kid of the day. They hare down Charlotte Mews into Scala Street and back into the theatre to perform their concert. Lester recalls, 'One of the six camera operators got some terrific material for the final sequence but then went to the dentist because the sound level had loosened his molar teeth and his teeth fell out.' The show over, the boys race to a waiting helicopter and take off, scattering *faked* autographed photos from the skies and, by extension, into cinemagoers' laps everywhere. Owen had the last laugh.

All that remained to be filmed were two trailers, which showed the Beatles sitting in baby carriages against a wall in Twickenham studios, Ringo cradling a telephone and John a typewriter, as all four babbled inanities into the camera. Quickly dubbed and edited, the film had its premiere at the London Pavilion on 6 July 1964, a mere three months after the first day of shooting. A crowd of over 5,000 waited outside to see the boys arrive. 'Because it was a Royal premiere,' remembers Lester, 'they had an organist, playing his version of Beatles hits on the mighty Wurlitzer as the audience came in. We'd been up day and night trying to get this thing done in time, and we knew that the one thing that really worked was that chord and those opening shots. The lights went down, and they started to roll the film. But he hadn't finished. They turned the film's sound off, so on the first chord on the first three shots, there he was, slowly going down, waving and smiling, still happily playing some other Beatles song. You could see the film through the curtains. I was so angry and frustrated. Later, Shenson decided in his wisdom that he would add a bit to the front of the film ("I'll Cry Instead") and ruin the opening again, and it has taken me something like twenty years to get that off.'

The Liverpool premiere took place four days later. The Beatles' jet landed at Liverpool Airport to be greeted by 1,500 screaming fans. The boys were then driven to the centre of Liverpool for a full civic reception. Lennon was unable to resist giving the crowd of civic dignitaries a Nazi salute from the Town Hall balcony. Wilfred Brambell stormed out of the reception, alleging that police had shoved him from a staircase where he was signing autographs, saying, 'This is not your night, it's the Beatles'.' Later, the Beatles were introduced by David Jacobs on to the stage of the Liverpool Odeon to a tumultuous welcome. Afterwards, the group wasted no time leaving Liverpool, boarding a plane bound for the capital at 1.30 a.m.

Critical reaction was mostly positive. Ann Pacey of the *Daily Herald* recognised that the film had 'nothing whatever in common with the standard British Pop musical'. Cecil Wilson of the *Daily Mail* 'marvelled that Mr Epstein's nervous breakdown [was] such a long time in coming'. The *Daily Mirror*'s Dick Richards was an overnight convert: 'Has the film clicked? "Yeah Yeah Yeah" and I was never a founder member of the Beatles admiration society. They're cheeky, irreverent, funny . . . irresistible.' *The Times* praised the freshly observed London locations and realised it was not 'by any manner of means the usual sort of thing British film-makers come up with to exploit the latest show business sensation'. But *Film Daily* pithily disagreed: 'Noisy, confused, weak, shoddily acted, poorly recorded . . .'

On the other side of the pond the highest praise came from Andrew Sarris, who, writing in the *Village Voice*, famously called it 'the *Citizen Kane* of jukebox movies'. From the underground, the American Communist Party's youth magazine praised the band as 'the true and unique voice of Liverpool's working class', and with the film as demonstrating their 'refreshing, light-hearted contempt for the very society that had made them what they are'. Many critics compared the boys to the Marx Brothers. Groucho thought otherwise: 'The Marx Brothers were different. The Beatles are the same.'

United Artists got what they wanted. Advance US album sales ensured the film was in profit before it hit the cinemas. 'The Beatles got practically no money, and practically no profits from it, and I got nothing,' says Lester. With both soundtrack and script nominated for Academy Awards, it smashed box office records worldwide, grossing $5.6 million, setting the record for a rock movie until *Woodstock* dwarfed that figure six years later.

The film had an immediate impact on fans and film-makers, inspiring many to form bands of their own or to shoot similar films. John Boorman's *Catch Us If You Can* (1965) steered the Dave Clark Five down a similar route, while Gerry and the Pacemakers' sole excursion into cinema, *Ferry Across the Mersey* (1964), all but sounded their death knell. Roger McGuinn of the Byrds remembers: 'We'd done quite a bit of research on the Beatles before we saw the film, so it wasn't that big a revelation. I'd say it was pure fun! One major thing we learned was that the Rickenbacker George was playing was a 12-string. When we walked out of *A Hard Day's Night*, [David] Crosby swung around a lamp post like Gene Kelly in *Singin' in The Rain* and said, "That's what I want to do!"'

A decade later, Wolverhampton's wanderers Slade followed the now familiar trail of fronting their own movie. Richard Loncraine's *Flame* (1975), originally conceived as a sci-fi spoof called 'The Quite A Mess Experiment', featured the Boys from the Black Country in a rags-to-Glam-rags tale, battling against unwelcome attention and mismanagement. Uncharacteristically bleak, it hardly endeared the non-Slade fan to the group – especially potential overseas audiences, who, unfamiliar with rich Brummie accents, would have been alienated from the start. (It was hugely to his credit then that Shenson had insisted the Beatles' accents remain intact and undubbed for US cinemagoers.) Madness's *Take it or Leave It* (1981) borrowed some of the imagery of *A Hard Day's Night*, but mostly lacked the infectious humour or directorial confidence of the Beatles' début. More recently, Beatles fan Danny Boyle would pay homage to Lester's film in his frenetic reading of Irvine Welsh's *Trainspotting*, and Bob Spiers' Spice Girls vehicle *Spice World* (1997) so closely appropriated Lester's original that Lester was bemused to be called up one day and to be asked by a national newspaper about what it was like to direct the Spice Girls. The movie's working title, after all, had been 'It's Been a Hard 15 Minutes'.

The Beatles' next offering, *Help!*, was a Beatle-ised travelogue in which the Fabs played extras to their own star. The group's self-financed, self-indulgent *Magical Mystery Tour* showed what happened when the boys were let off the directorial leash. The fifty-minute, made-for-TV effort, screened on Boxing Day 1967, married the group's Goonish madcap capers to a synthetic psychedelic vision that pleased neither a mainstream audience nor members of the counter-culture, who might reasonably have expected something a little more far out. Seen today, it remains somewhere between curio and crap, though it has picked up its fair share of cult followers along the way. It has a few saving graces: Lennon's quintessentially English 'I Am the Walrus', very much the LSD in the vicar's tea, and the inclusion of the Bonzo Dog Doo-Dah Band performing 'Death Cab for Cutie' – a very British coup. The animated *Yellow Submarine* (1968) revealed how, for all the inner space traversed, the Beatles never veered too far from Blighty, culturally or artistically. By the time *Let it Be* (1970) emerged, the carefree years of *A Hard Day's Night*, made just five years before, seemed like a distant dream.

Given the group's legendary status, it was only a matter of time before they would be the subject for a pastiche. Eric Idle's and Neil Innes' wonderfully accurate *The Rutles* (1978) would chronicle the rags-to-riches tale of the pre-Fab Four, with none other than George Harrison as its co-sponsor, programme consultant and participant. The mischievous Harrison sneaked a very early print of the Beatles' *Anthology* (then known as 'The Long and Winding Road') out of Apple for Idle and producer Gary Weiss to fillet for references.

Naturally *A Hard Day's Night* was paid homage to, becoming *A Hard Day's Rut*, in which the pre-Fabs are shown running around various locations, including an iron staircase. Lennon, never entirely happy with the way the group had been canonised, reportedly idolised the film on its release. McCartney, allegedly none too pleased that the Rutles' album was released on the same day as his solo effort *London Town*, has yet to go public on it.

The film's locations are still regularly visited by Beatles' fans under the expert guidance of Richard Porter, president of London's Beatles Fan Club. Known as the 'pied piper of Beatlemania', twice a week Porter carefully steers a pack of tourists from all nations around London's Beatles sites. The locations of *A Hard Day's Night* remain particularly inviting, especially Boston Place, the site of the opening sequence, where you're likely to find many a lens pointed up the street. Richard recalls that visitors from the former Iron Curtain countries, where Beatles music had been forbidden, would burst into tears as they stumbled on some of the locations.

Shenson – 'a man who didn't know who the Beatles were,' sniffs Lester – had the film rights returned to him after fifteen years, but he shrewdly waited until the film reached its twentieth birthday before launching it on video. Prior to this the film had been doing brisk business in bootleg sales to fans desperate to acquire the picture, its limited distribution practically guaranteeing a cult renaissance. A further thirty-five-year anniversary re-release – this time with some of the behind-the-scenes footage as a bonus – was mooted for 1999, although this was scotched following the hype surrounding the re-release of *Yellow Submarine*. In spring 2001 it had a limited relaunch, taking reasonable returns – about £50,000 in UK cinema receipts at the time of writing – not a bad showing.

For contemporary audiences the film probably seems a bit of a lark, at best an historical footnote – certainly much too popular to be classed as a 'proper' cult movie. But movies do not necessarily have to be initial failures in order to be cult objects, and the generations of nostalgic, often hardcore fans who have dissected and picked over Lester's movie are ample evidence of its cult status. This film brings distant people together in act of worship. Above all, the

Beatles' début picture – a film about, and starring, the biggest cult in the world – is important because Lester rewrote the rules in this film. As Danny Peary remarks, 'It is because of Lester that *A Hard Day's Night* bears no resemblance to the cheap exploitation picture United Artists expected to distribute.' The personality of the Beatles, and Lester's vision, gave the film an artistic credibility. Cheekily mixing and matching techniques from the great directors of the cinema's past, *A Hard Day's Night* carved out a hip new youth-oriented lifestyle and post-modern template that has become cult movies' stock in trade.

Its huge success meant that the youth market – a once largely dismissed sector – would now be taken with the utmost seriousness by the industry. And it's youth, or youthful exuberance, that turns pop stars into icons and movies into cults. As Lester recalls, 'While filming Paul's concert tour, *Get Back* (1991), half the audience were hearing those songs for the first time. But, among older audiences, there was a mass outpouring of love, which had overtones of "Do you remember when we first heard this?" The sense that this was a great sing-along. The film has that innocent quality. My aim was that in no way would it be manipulative, or at least in no way seen to be. And I tried not to let anything else get in the way of that. Because its cynicism, for all of it, is controlled and it's aiming at things that are not dangerous. Youthful exuberance lasts much better than most things in the ephemera of film.'

There was a flip side to such integrity. The innocence of *A Hard Day's Night* was going to be defiled once the enormous returns on UA's paltry investment became public. If such an offbeat, potentially unintelligible film could win the hearts and minds of the world, surely the same formula, however contrived, might just work again, exploiting the youth dollar further. Arguably, the first victim of this cash cow was the Beatles' second feature *Help!*, awash with Technicolor, dope and James Bond posturing. Donald Cammell's Mick Jagger movie *Performance* (1970), though hardly in the same groove, would be given the green light on the same premise – studio heads still saw the money-spinning potential in a pop-star-driven vehicle, however obscure. While Antonioni's unfathomable *Blow-Up* (1966) could be similarly embraced as a 'flick about trendy Swinging

London'. After *A Hard Day's Night* studios were going to make sure they would never be caught on the hop again.

SHE'S OLDER THAN the others, fifteen or sixteen perhaps, and, very possibly, it's her first pop concert. Dressed in a kind of sailor-suit get-up, she's exceptionally neat and tidy, with bobbed blonde hair framing her shoulders. Lester calls her 'the White Rabbit'. She looks like she comes from a fairly well-to-do family, with the sort of parents who have only allowed her to attend tonight's performance because she's finished all her homework and household chores. She stands in the aisle, slightly apart from the others, the howling, ravenous rabble, and she stares at the stage. That's all she does, she just stares at the four, she's got her own personal gig going on. She's hardly there at all. But the camera loves her. It keeps coming back to her, teasing her into focus, a second, third, fourth time, once every number.

At the show's finale, split seconds before the Beatles launch into the first bunch of 'She Loves You's, Yeah Yeah Yeah's, the camera suddenly swoops upward, like a vulture heading for a high ledge, returning for the crumbs. You see, it hasn't forgotten her, even if we have. There she stands, ice-cool as ever, the Lady of Shalott, but now she only breaks your heart. Lost, hopelessly, horrifyingly lost, presumed missing, her glazed eyes brim with glycerine and a brand new set of emotions she can barely articulate, barely bring herself to admit. You want to look away, the mind recoiling at such base voyeurism, but the camera's timed it just right, just so, there's no escape, no emotional safety net, and just before she completely dissolves into milk and sugar she sobs his name.

WE'RE NOT IN KANSAS
ANY MORE

**In a world recently departed from black and white, *Blow-Up*'s
Thomas cuts a velvet dash against the mid-1960s London skyline.
Arrogant, independent and successful, he leads a charmed life as a
fashion photographer, treating all the ostentatious trappings of
'Swinging London', girls, wealth, music and success, with a disdainful
sneer. A chance encounter in an obscure London park results in an
unremarkable set of photographs; but on closer inspection Thomas
discovers a dark secret, which takes him on an odyssey of intrigue
and ultimate self-discovery. Probably.**

'London was special, it had a kind of mystique. But what prompted the
bloody cover story was not a fascination with a socio-cultural phenomenon, it was the fascination among senior editors for mini-skirts.
There was no more depth of emotion than that.'

Andrea Adam, Editor, *Time*, 1966

One morning in early 1966 the Italian film director Michelangelo
Antonioni took his dog Aristotle for a walk along the Woolwich
Road, in South London. For his latest project, set in 'Swinging
London', the director had cooped himself up in a local bed and
breakfast, the better to get a feel for the area and its ambience.
Such was the detail Michelangelo demanded in his films that he
readily pitched camp in one of the least salubrious parts of the
capital to familiarise himself fully with the psychoscape. Taking a
left turn off the main road, the Italian found himself standing outside a pair of wrought-iron gates, the entrance to an unnamed park,

fronted by four impassive sentry-like trees. There was something so weird about the place, so devastatingly lonely and still yet so profoundly enchanting, he couldn't help but enter. Oddly, the sounds normally associated with the area – traffic, trains, everyday hubbub – seemed to have been switched off, replaced by an overwhelming natural soundtrack, an organic tinnitus of wind rustling through the trees, as if the leaves were gossiping to one another about the new intruders. The interior was stranger still. Plants grew out of season here – in some places overblown and grotesque, in others, microscopically intricate as if a gigantic reduction lens had been thrown over them. Deeper into the park pitch-black paths like veins of tarmac appeared to lead nowhere, disappearing into the heavens like well-trod Jacob's Ladders, giving the impression they had been laid out in a deliberately random fashion in order to confuse and lead the unwary traveller into the upper reaches of the wood. Michelangelo took a wander. Up here, on the highest point, he'd find the heart of the place and the heart of his film.

ANTONIONI WAS BORN on 29 September 1912 in northern Italy. As a boy, he used to make puppets, inventing little stories around them, and paying particular attention to their habitats, and in his teenage years he began to paint. He took a degree in Economics and Commerce at the University of Bologna, but still found time to form a theatre company, staging his own plays alongside those of Ibsen's and Pirandello's. A keen moviegoer, he also began to submit film criticism to his local newspaper.

After graduation in 1939, he toyed with experimental film-making, later becoming a staff writer for *Cinema* – the official film magazine of the Italian Fascist party – before he was fired for making anti-Fascist editorial comments. He then trained at the renowned film school, Centro Sperimentale Di Cinematografia, where he made his first tentative steps towards film production. Stints as a script collaborator and production assistant followed, and he began directing documentaries of his own. In 1942, he was conscripted into the army, but covertly continued to shoot films at night, an experience that left him 'completely stupefied with fatigue'. On leaving the army, he resumed full-time film-making, gaining a reputation as a highly idiosyncratic, neo-realist director through such works as *L'Avventura* (1959), and *Il Deserto Rosso* (1964).

As a young man, he'd been rather ashamed of his comfortable, middle-class background and, having been raised a Catholic, would continuously suffer pangs of guilt. He'd later suggest that these two factors played a determining part in his creative outlook. Antonioni's particular speciality lay in portraying psychologically fucked-up, alienated middle-class characters, beset by what he called 'spiritual aridity' and 'moral coldness', fruitlessly searching for meaning in a world where images and icons reigned supreme. By the mid-1960s he'd pushed the subject as far as it could go and began to be assailed by self-doubt. Had he really discovered something profound about the human condition? Or was it just him? Could one ever, in fact, through the creative act, capture any sort of objective reality?

While Michelangelo feared he might have reached the end of the road, in England new opportunities seemed to be opening up. A land forever set in sepia, a constipated nation of terraced houses and ageing industrial edifices, had begun to pulsate with vivid colours, the blood and guts of childbirth. In March 1965, following the phenomenal success of, among other things, the first three Bond flicks, *Tom Jones* and *A Hard Day's Night*, United Artists was declaring record profits. American money now poured into the British film industry and all the Hollywood majors and some independents set up production arms in London, which was fast superseding Rome as the world's trendiest capital.

In late 1965 Michelangelo arrived in England. Ostensibly he had come to visit his protégée Monica Vitti, then shooting Joseph Losey's *Modesty Blaise*. But perhaps also, as *Blow-Up* star David Hemmings believes, he wanted to attain some international recognition, as Fellini had done before him. While there, he found the perfect setting for his next film treatment (working title: 'The Story of a Man and a Woman on a Beautiful Autumn Morning'), which concerned a jaded fashion photographer. 'I think that London is, right now, the city that offers the right background,' he'd tell the Italian TV station RTE in 1966. 'There is a freer atmosphere here, a sort of turmoil which is much livelier than anywhere else. London offers the best and worst in the world.'

Antonioni had loosely adapted a short story, 'Las babas del Diablo' ('The Devil's Spittle'), by the celebrated Argentine writer Julio Cortazar. The title was a Spanish colloquialism for 'a narrow escape' ('I was so close, the Devil could have spat on me'). In Cortazar's story a Paris-based translator, who takes a photograph of a teenage boy and an older woman talking intimately together, concocts his own fantasies about the pair. A moment after the snap is taken, the boy scurries away and the woman demands that the translator hand over the negative. While a mysterious man in a waiting car ('a flour-powdered clown') becomes enraged for no apparent reason, the photographer laughs in their faces and flits away, refusing to hand over the negative. A few enlargements later, he convinces himself that he has interrupted a sleazy transaction – the woman was the boy's pimp, the man her 'john'. But now he realises to his horror that 'the abusive act had certainly already taken place'. Antonioni would change the transaction to an apparently adulterous, aborted tryst and hide a 'gunman' in the bushes, who only becomes visible through a series of increasingly ominous blow-ups (perversely, the most humdrum yet thrilling sequence in his film).

A willing backer for the project was soon found. Born on 11 December 1910 in Magenta, Italy, Carlo Ponti was one of cinema's heavyweights, having worked with such acclaimed directors as Fellini and Godard. A prolific producer, the cinema was his life – and love: he'd married Italian screen diva Sophia Loren in 1957. Ponti, who had a production deal with MGM, heard that Antonioni wanted to make his next film in London and asked him if he could produce it. He'd already produced David Lean's enormously successful, Oscar-nominated *Dr Zhivago* (1965) for MGM, and would have no difficulties getting another film off the ground with the same studio.

Coincidentally, Ponti was already *in simpatico* with Antonioni. Back in May 1964 the *Sunday Times Magazine* had run an article by the well-connected journalist Francis Wyndham called 'The Modelmakers', featuring profiles of such trend-setting photographers as David Bailey and Terence Donovan. Ponti thought the article would make a great little film – he'd call it *The Photographer* – and met Bailey that year with a view to hiring him as the director. Bailey had wanted to make movies – he'd already planned a film version of Anthony Burgess's *A Clockwork Orange*, but seen his script rejected by the censors at the starting gate. For various scheduling reasons, the Ponti/Bailey project was nixed and lay dormant until Antonioni showed up a year and a half later talking about 'photographers' and 'London'.

Having noticed how fashionable London had become, Ponti correctly assumed that an English-language film set among Swinging London's sexy snapper set, and made by a critically revered, trendy Italian director would be a commercial success. But Antonioni's film was going to be rather different from the one Ponti had anticipated – not that he'd mind, once the returns came through.

Contrary to received wisdom, *Blow-Up* is not a film about Swinging London. It took an American magazine editor to coin *that* term when in April 1966 *Time* devoted an issue to London, which it dubbed the 'city of the decade'. 'Youth is the word – and the deed – in London,' it reported. 'The London that has emerged is Swinging.' A once class-ridden city had shed its smugness, becoming 'alive with birds (girls) and Beatles, buzzing with mini-cars and telly stars, pulsing with half a dozen separate veins of excitement'. Even the notoriously intellectual Antonioni, the magazine revealed, was currently 'prowling the streets of London, looking toward making a film on – of all things – the Swinging London scene'.

Hardly. What Antonioni had realised, with the benefit of an outsider's viewpoint, was that 'Swinging London' was in itself a misnomer. What the vast majority of the Great British public bought into swung several hemlines below. Behind the palm fronds of Biba and lacquered coifs of Mary Quant lay possibly the most exclusive, snotty, class-ridden members' club of the second half of the twentieth century. Here, thought Michelangelo, with pangs of middle-class guilt, were his favourite bugbears – 'spiritual aridity' and 'moral coldness' – writ large. Exactly the sort of shallow, alienated people, craving style over substance, he was determined to expose in his movie.

The scene's core members, for all their 'come and join us' rhetoric, jealously protected their little world, as had their forerunners, the

Bloomsbury set and the Romantics – their principal ammunition a cultural canon and a loaded trust fund. Occasionally the gilded catflap was raised to admit a Kray for tea or a Beatle for breakfast, but outside a very small and exclusive area of the capital 'Swinging London' was a fairytale, to be prettified on TV and in the cinema or to be bitched about in the *News of the World*. Only when the stale hash fumes seeped from the bedrooms and apartments of SW3 did the masses follow their noses to Carnaby Street, snapping up dandified imitations to squirrel back to the suburbs.

North of Watford, poverty was still a very real and immediate concern: the swingers' studied decadence, a natural extension of the midnight feast in a public school dormitory, hurt. Liverpool, once considered London's rival in the style stakes, died a death the day the Beatles fled town, leaving fellow bands and dreamers to return to the shop floor and factory bench. The flip side of Swinging Britain was the BBC's twin sticks of dynamite, *Up the Junction* and *Cathy Come Home*, which exposed a side of Britain its politicians had long tried to pretend wasn't there.

But for that very small and privileged metropolitan crowd, the negatives that had languished in the darkroom for years were finally developing and bursting into colour for a belatedly realised Oz. Amid a confetti of marijuana and with LSD the laced icing on the wedding cake, Antonioni, an honorary if deeply sceptical wedding guest, was there to take the photographs.

After reading Francis Wyndham's article, Antonioni prepared a questionnaire for him about the lifestyle of the photographers that had featured in the piece. He also consulted directly with Bailey and Donovan. Wyndham was very helpful, but neither photographer was too forthcoming. 'I never talked to Antonioni,' Bailey recalled later. 'He didn't like me because he thought I was after his girlfriend.'

Antonioni next scouted out a location base for his leading character, Thomas the photographer. Rather than build a film set, he wanted to use a real photographic studio and had visited several potentially suitable ones in and around London. Finally he chose the studio of *Vogue* fashion photographer John Cowan, at Princes Place, West London. With its multi-levelled interior, its numerous nooks, walkways and galleries, the white-fronted building was perfect. It had originally been designed as an abattoir, then served time as a fire station, before finally being converted into a photographic studio. Next to the building was a charming ivy-clad cottage, where Cowan lived.

But for the exterior of Thomas's studio Antonioni chose a residential property at the less salubrious 77 Pottery Lane, on the fringes of Notting Hill and a stone's throw away from the Princes Place Studio. He painted a bogus number 39 on its garage because that had been the number of Cowan's home. In the late nineteenth century the area had been a slum in which pig farmers allowed their animals to wallow. The result was a mass epidemic of cholera and typhoid, which caused the authorities to implement a policy of urban renewal. As the pig farmers retreated to the country, bohemians began to move in, keen to take advantage of the cheap rents and a thriving community was soon established.

If you visit Cowan's old studio in Princes Place today, you'll find it occupied by a thriving multimedia company. On the ground floor the staff tap feverishly away on laptops, apparently unaware of the building's place in cinema. Upstairs, the managing director has his office where once Hemmings held court to Redgrave. The cottage is unoccupied, although the ivy still clings to its walls.

Ponti set up a production office above a bookies called Mack's in nearby Princedale Road, where daily production schedules would be pinned up on the wall. On the other side of the street, a few doors down, at number 74, was the headquarters of the British National Socialist Party, where a Swastika flew above the building in defiance of the times. Aptly, the Prince of Wales pub in the adjacent Pottery Lane also featured in Kevin Brownlow and Andrew Mollo's mini masterpiece *It Happened Here* (1963), a brilliantly realised Nazi invasion of Britain. Later, the drug advice agency RELEASE would set up home in the street.

Originally Terence Stamp was chosen to play Thomas. 'He wrote *Blow-Up* for me,' Stamp told the BBC's *Hollywood UK* in 1993. 'He changed his screenplay from an Italian fashion photographer in Milano to a kind of a David Bailey portrayed by Terence Stamp in London.' In a piece of casting that would have rivalled the screen partnership of Richard Burton and Elizabeth Taylor, Stamp's then girlfriend, the model Jean ('the Shrimp') Shrimpton, was offered the part of Jane, the girl at the heart of the film's 'murder' plot.

Stamp had little trouble acquainting himself with his character's lifestyle. His brother co-managed The Who and his association with Jean Shrimpton brought him into almost daily contact with Swinging London life. He could not have been better placed to observe the scene, but just a fortnight before shooting was due to commence, he received a phone call from assistant director Claude Watson. Antonioni, Watson told him, had decided to drop him, along with Jean Shrimpton, in favour of a virtual unknown. An outraged Stamp ('he might have treated me to a cappuccino and told me to my face') immediately issued writs on Antonioni, Ponti and MGM for breach of contract and defamation of reputation – a case he won. 'I never saw Antonioni again. There was not a word of apology or anything.'

To this day Stamp has no idea exactly what happened. From a visual point of view both Stamp and Shrimpton were – and remain – extraordinary presences, on screen and off. Their screen lives and real lives were said to be indivisible. If you take the argument that *Blow-Up* is a canvas, requiring only a couple of subtle brush strokes for balance, it becomes obvious why the director's first choices would not have worked. Stamp and Shrimpton – Pluto and Aphrodite in looks and temperament – would have blown the vision out of all proportion. The director's next choice of leads worked so well precisely because their relative newness to the screen allowed them to assume impenetrable mask-like visages through most of the movie.

David Hemmings, who had starred in a handful of undistinguished 'B' features and TV dramas (*Live It Up*, *Be My Guest*, and the BBC's sci-fi series *Out of the Unknown*) was hardly a household name. Born in the Surrey stockbroker town of Guildford in 1941, Hemmings was the son of a biscuit salesman, who had at the age of nine begun to tour with the English Opera Group as a boy soprano. After his voice broke at fifteen, he fell back on his second love, painting, and in 1956 had his own exhibition. But he was soon drawn to showbusiness again, and stints as a cabaret singer in West End nightclubs led to theatre work. Antonioni first saw him in a production of Dylan Thomas's *Adventures in the Skin Trade* at the Hampstead Theatre Club; he decided to try him out.

Hemmings went to meet the director at the Savoy. 'You look

wrong, you're too young,' Antonioni said. But Hemmings assured him that he'd gladly dye his shock of blonde hair to age himself for the role. They then repaired to John Cowan's studio for a screen test. As Hemmings later recalled for *Hollywood UK*, the Italian still had his guard up. 'Out of the corner of my eye I saw him underneath the camera, shaking his head. I thought "I'd better stop this right now." And I went home despondent. I then had a call saying: "Come to the office and meet Antonioni." I walked in, Antonioni walked towards me, leant ahead, put out his hand and said "I'm so pleased you've got the role."'

Vanessa Redgrave was born with a silver script in her mouth, on 30 January 1937. The daughter of Sir Michael, she made her stage début at the age of twenty. Film roles quickly followed, including a small part alongside her illustrious father in *Behind the Mask* (1958). But word soon spread that she was a genuinely gifted actress and in 1961 she joined the Royal Shakespeare Company. Her appearance in *Morgan, A Suitable Case for Treatment* won her the 1966 Cannes Best Actress Award and also an Academy Award nomination. It was soon afterwards that Antonioni got in touch and offered her the part of Jane. At the director's request, she would dye her hair black and shave an inch off her hairline to give her a higher forehead.

Sarah Miles was cast as Patricia, Thomas's lonely and frustrated neighbour. Born to wealthy parents in December 1941, she enrolled in RADA and, after initial training, landed a plum role alongside her childhood idol Laurence Olivier in the 1962 classic, *Term Of Trial*. It was a dream come true for Miles, who had been infatuated with Olivier's portrayal of Heathcliff in the 1939 version of *Wuthering Heights*. Miles's fantasies liquid-dripped into the waking world, as she went on to become Olivier's mistress, while walking out with James Fox. She continued to play a number of appropriately seductive roles on screen, most notably in Joseph Losey's *The Servant* (1963), which brought her to Antonioni's attention.

Blow-Up's original script, by Antonioni and writer-collaborator Tonino Guerra, contained no camera directions and was just thirty-two pages long. It had been translated into English by playwright Edward Bond, whose distinctively halting patches of dialogue would contribute to the picture's almost lazy sense of menace. But 'the dialogue was of no great significance, or certainly of secondary importance,' recalled Redgrave. Two other cast members, Jane Birkin and the real-life *Vogue* model Countess Veruschka von Lehndorff, hardly said a word, their roles mostly requiring them to writhe around on Thomas's studio floor as a model and wannabe model respectively. 'Vanessa and I talked at great length about our roles,' Hemmings recalled, 'but in the end it made no difference. [Antonioni's] directions were so specific that any ideas we had were not even remotely considered. He would say, "You lean forward, you pick up the glass, you put it up to your eyes and you take a sip and you put it down." And I'd say, using actor's licence, "OK, I'll pick up the glass, I'll do this, take a sip and put it down." He'd say, "No. You take it like this, you take a sip and you put it down." When people ask me about my performance I always say, "Saying you like my performance in *Blow-Up* is a bit like saying you like the colour yellow in a Van Gogh."'

Filming began on May Day 1966 and lasted five weeks. The first shots in the can were of Hemmings driving around Pottery Lane in a convertible Rolls-Royce with the director strapped to the back. During lunch breaks, Antonioni would distance himself from cast and crew, retiring to a private office he had created in one of Cowan's rooms above the studio – dubbed 'Heaven' – and Antonioni couldn't have failed to hear their giggles as the specially ordered lunch from Fortnum & Mason, complete with a bottle of champagne, was brought up to him each day. Every now and then Antonioni, who was usually rather quiet and shy, would disappear into an ante-room and have a blazing row with Carlo Ponti (known to the crew as 'Charlie Bridges', the English translation of his name). Sunny days would also cause him to lose his temper as the Italian members of his crew would stop shooting to play football.

At the beginning of the film Thomas wearily emerges from a doss-house, having spent a sleepless night taking gritty photos of tramps. The scene was shot at the Camberwell Clinic in Peckham, nicknamed the 'Spike' after the protruding metal spikes overhanging the building. Although it has long since ceased to be a shelter for male down-and-outs and has been converted into residential housing, it retains an almost palpable stench of misery. An attempt has been made to gentrify the place but, walking up towards the housing complex, a sense of sadness overwhelms you. Underneath the tarmac of the road lie the remains of the workhouse dead, ignobly dumped in makeshift graves. Thomas then chats with a group of homeless men underneath a railway arch. This sequence was shot at the junction of Consort and Copeland Road, SE15.

Back at his studio Thomas figuratively seduces Veruschka during that morning's fashion shoot and treats a team of models like shop window dummies. He then drives in his open-top Rolls into Woolwich, South London. Fittingly, for a movie drawing inspiration from the catwalk, the director would dress his production with an almost feminine regard for *haute couture*: *Blow-Up*'s art director Assheton Gorton painted entire stretches of shopfronts and mid-Victorian terraced houses along the Woolwich Road deep crimson. 'Antonioni wasn't at all worried that he was likely to go "over-schedule" by stopping filming for a few hours while he had a wall repainted the colour he wanted,' recalls actor John Castle (who played Bill, Patricia's lover).

The antique shop in which Thomas buys a propeller had been a grocer's, on the junction of Clevely Close and Tamar Street. Today it is home to a derelict camping shop called 'Best In Tents'. In the film a pub called the White Horse is seen across the road. It is still there today. During shooting an upstairs room was hired as a canteen in which, one rainy afternoon, the crew took time out to toast Vanessa Redgrave's Cannes award for *Morgan*. Prior to filming, a reporter from the local Mercury newspaper had visited Tamar Street to gauge the local residents' responses. They were less than forthcoming, although the reporter did collar one man cleaning his car: 'We're all looking forward to this. There's supposed to be plenty of birds in the cast.'

Walking up Clevely Close, Thomas comes across an obscure London park. The real star of the film, Maryon Park was founded in 1889, when Sir Spencer Maryon Wilson, a Charlton landowner, presented to the London County Council land that had served for many years as a chalk, sand and gravel pit. In 1915 excavations revealed a Roman British settlement occupying some 17 acres, and in 1966 the Romans, in the shape of Antonioni and crew, paid a return visit. They quickly began to paint the park's paths jet-black, and its fences a darker shade of green, and might even, Assheton Gorton later mused, have painted the grass green.

As you walk through Maryon Park today, you become curiously aware that something has happened here – perhaps something not altogether happy. The Hanging Woods that surround the park were so called after the many executions that took place there, and Samuel Pepys often spoke of his fear of the place whenever he visited the area. Grazing the mystical Meridian line where time both ends and begins, it's a fantastical, primordial place – and largely deserted. When the authors last visited it, one of us saw a ghost, a translucent, rather sorrowful apparition hunched by the top path. In 1966 strange runic symbols and other cabalistic insignia started to appear in Greenwich parks, much to the bemusement of the local authorities.

The houses next to the park which Antonioni had whitewashed are now hidden by trees. Dominating the lower part of the amphitheatre are two tennis courts, like two large unspotted dominoes, an incongruous intrusion from the outside world. The park has its own microclimate; in freezing November you can stand in certain parts of it and feel a great warmth emanating from the earth. The chalk-based soil provides a rich diet for plants while the park remains an area of outstanding biological and geological importance; as such it may never be interfered with. A team of Greenwich Borough gardeners pass through once a week on a rota with other plant maintenance companies to ensure appearances are kept up, and that the grass never grows too high – grass so dense it can only be cut with a Flymo.

The topmost part of the park is called Cox's Mount, named after a local who took it upon himself to plant poplar trees here. The park-keepers call the place the 'Top Lawn', and it is where Thomas first spots Jane with her lover. He photographs them and then refuses Jane's demand that he hand over the negative. The tree under which Gorton strategically placed foliage, and where Thomas later discovers a corpse, has long gone, but a hole remains, waiting to be filled.

Thomas leaves the park and lunches with his agent Ron (Peter

Bowles) in a restaurant. Then known as Andreas, it was renamed the El Blason in 1990 and is still to be found at 8 Blacklands Terrace, Chelsea, off the King's Road. The restaurant has undergone some restoration, but there's still the table where Thomas and Ron had their lunch, as they pored over the photographs that Thomas had taken in the Spike, as well as other distressing images from war-torn parts of the globe (in real life the photographs were taken by Don McCullin, who had been hired as set photographer).

Back at the studio, Thomas is visited by Jane, who is still intent on retrieving the photographs. He gives her a fake roll of film to take away and begins to develop the genuine roll that he shot in the park. Through a series of blow-ups, he discovers that he has disturbed a murder: Jane had been luring her 'lover' towards a gunman, hidden in the bushes. Just as Thomas is on the verge of putting another jigsaw piece in place, he is interrupted by two young aspiring models looking for work. The girls, played by Jane Birkin – then married to soundtrack composer John Barry – and the twinkle-eyed Gillian Hills wind up frolicking naked with Thomas on his studio floor.

After more blow-ups, Thomas spots a corpse – Jane's 'lover' – lying underneath a tree on Cox's Mount. He returns to the park and finds the dead man, lying in the moonlight. Back in his studio, he observes Bill and Patricia making love in the adjacent cottage. According to his usual practice, Antonioni gave Sarah Miles no script and no inkling of what was to ensue. It was only when she turned up on set that she discovered that she was expected to appear in the love-making scene with John Castle, whom she hadn't met before. Remembering her agent's advice that on no account was she to argue with Antonioni, she unhappily acquiesced and took off her clothes.

According to Miles, Antonioni then revealed that he wanted her character Patricia to reach an orgasm while Thomas looked on. Through waves of nausea, Miles was forced to reshoot the scene a second and then a third time. Finally she cracked and cried, 'Cut!', pre-empting the director's instruction.

'Why?!' thundered Antonioni. No one had ever dared interrupt him before.

'May I ask you something, Antonioni?' ventured Miles.

The director cocked a gold-ringed forefinger at her: 'Don't call me Antonioni,' he growled. Then he momentarily softened: 'Call me Michelangelo . . .'

He brought over a towelling robe and escorted Miles to a secluded corner of the set. 'What's your problem, Sarah?'

Under the patrician's level gaze, Miles broke down, confessing her anxiety about her role, the lack of continuity, the lack of anything resembling a plot.

Antonioni simply shrugged his Burberry-covered shoulders and looked away. 'It doesn't matter,' he said and gently told her that in future she should just listen to his directions.

He was back among his childhood puppets. 'The director owes no explanations to the actor,' he had once said, 'he must not compromise himself by revealing his intentions.' '*Blow-Up* wasn't easy,' the puppet master explained to the Italian film magazine *Cinema Nuovo* in 1967. 'I was working without my usual team – except for the director of photography – subject to timetables, working methods and mentalities completely different from our own, so I was working in a state of continual tension.'

Thomas discovers his studio has been ransacked. Determined to find Ron, he drives into the West End, in the direction of Oxford Circus, where he spies a suspiciously familiar woman queuing outside a doorway. On seeing Thomas, she darts into an alleyway. In pursuit he leaps out of his Rolls, rushes past the clothes shop Permutit at 151 Regent Street and stops at the entrance to Heddon Street, later made famous on the cover of David Bowie's 1973 album *Ziggy Stardust and the Spiders From Mars*. The iconic red telephone box can be glimpsed in the background. He then turns back and heads down the narrow alleyway of New Burlington Mews, off Regent Street, in pursuit. The director cheated here a little: if you were to veer to your left, as Thomas does at the end of the alleyway, you'd end up sprawled on the ground with concussion. Turn right, however, and you'll find a small car park with iron steps leading up to a locked door in the foreground. In the film it is these steps that Thomas dashes up to get into the Ricky Tick Club.

It was inevitable that Antonioni would bring Thomas into London's vibrant music scene, aware that significant changes were taking place in pop. He originally wanted to film in the Marquee, in Soho's Wardour Street, but it was not available for a long enough period. So he opted instead for Windsor's Ricky Tick, one of the many 'in' venues on the club circuit. But there was a snag. The ceiling was too low to accommodate the enormous arc lights required for the production. So instead the interior of the club was recreated at Elstree Studios for a three-day shoot.

Antonioni had wanted the band performing in the club to be The Who. Townshend's guitar-wrecking routine, which was still a trademark of the band's performances in late '66, fascinated the director. But the group declined the invitation. Perhaps co-manager Chris Stamp was angry about the way his brother Terence had been cast aside. After considering a number of other groups – including The Lovin' Spoonful and the Velvet Underground – Antonioni had the group Tomorrow, who regularly gigged at Tottenham Court Road's UFO, record two songs for the soundtrack. But they would soon be discarded in favour of a group just breaking across the UK, the Yardbirds. The director wanted them to perform 'Train Keep a Rollin' from their live repertoire, but the song couldn't be used in the film due to copyright restrictions. So the group rewrote it, kept the structure and renamed it 'Stroll On'.

The Yardbirds were a strictly cool, no moves band, not given to smashing their instruments, but Antonioni was adamant that there should be a guitar-trashing sequence, and so Jeff Beck was called upon to give what turned out to be a not very convincing display of pique.

Thomas eventually finds Ron at a party in Chelsea. So familiar had Antonioni become among the 'scene's' core members that one of them, Christopher Gibbs, lent his wood-panelled first-floor flat at 100 Cheyne Walk to the crew for five days' filming. Its windows offered a view of a sumptuous garden, in which grew the oldest mulberry tree in the country. Built in 1647, the flat was originally part of Lindsay House, which sprawled between 95 and 101 Cheyne Walk, before being split up into individual properties in 1775. Cheyne Walk has long been associated with artists and writers. Thomas Whistler lived at 101, Hilaire Belloc at 104, and J. M. W. Turner at 119. During the 1960s Mick Jagger and his then girlfriend Marianne Faithfull had a pad up the road at number 48.

Gibbs was a choice contact as he knew and belonged to the 1966

Chelsea set, who were more than happy to accommodate what was to be a week-long happening, financed by MGM, with drink and drugs on tap. It must have been one hell of a party. Gibbs, now a successful antique dealer, who went on to dress another 'Turner' House at 15 Lowndes Square for Roeg and Cammell's *Performance*, recalled the scene for *Sight and Sound* in 1996: 'I had a part in making the party scene look the way it did, and a lot of the people who came were my friends. If I looked at it today I could probably point out twenty of them. Half of them might still be alive.'

The party was presided over by an MGM catering crew, who handed out endless rounds of drinks and steaks to the assembled guests. Antonioni preferred to crunch his apples. One partygoer, old Oxfordian Kieran Fogerty, brought along his beautiful girl-friend, Didi Verschoyle, who so impressed Ponti that he arranged an extra scene of Didi sashaying down the stairs like some Sixties siren. But it would be left on the cutting-room floor after her father refused permission for his daughter, not yet twenty-one, to appear in the film. Fogerty, who had been despondent at the amount of attention his girlfriend was receiving, cheered up when he was picked out by the casting director to enter the exclusive perfumed garden of the back bedroom. As he recalled for Jonathon Green's *Days in the Life*, 'I was flung into this bedroom, plonked on the front of this bed with about nine people on it as Antonioni tossed a couple of kilo-bags of grass on the bed and said "Right, get on with it." It took five days. It just went on and on. Nobody wanted to stop . . . people would stumble out going "yeeeaahhh" and go gibbering back.'

Also hired for the party scene was Veruschka, at the time playing an intricate game of deception with Antonioni, flying to and from Paris to maintain an affair. According to Fogerty she was heavily stoned for her minuscule appearance in the sequence, though still managed to blurt out the required dialogue. The rest of the time she really was 'in Paris'. Meanwhile, the inscrutable director, puffing away on Toscano cheroots, held silent sway like some mildly disapproving exchange student. 'I go to these parties,' he would later comment, 'and the atmosphere is . . . empty. There they are, all these young people, so beautiful in their velvet and ruffles and lace. They are sitting around the room in little groups, without talking, without moving . . . I think emotions will get more and more feeble in England. They are already more feeble here than anywhere else.'

After a night at the party, Thomas returns to the park to find the corpse missing. In the final scene he watches a couple of ragweek students play an imaginary tennis match. He retrieves their imaginary 'ball' and throws it back to them. He watches as they continue their imaginary game, switching his eyes from player to player, as if he can see a ball for real. Our sense of reality is further challenged as we begin to hear the sound of racket on ball, and finally Thomas himself vanishes as the closing credits run.

For the soundtrack Antonioni typically passed over the big guns among soundtrack composers in favour of the gifted, twenty-six-year-old jazz pianist, Herbie Hancock. It was the first time he had composed for a motion picture. Although Hancock's eclectic, funky score was heavily pruned by Antonioni, the superb soundtrack was none the less a major factor in *Blow-Up*'s cult appeal. In 1989 part of Hancock's score, 'Bring Down the Birds', was appropriated by US dance ensemble Dee-Lite, courtesy of a now instantly recognisable bassline. It was fitting. The late 1980s' Vogueing craze among New York's clubbers, combined with a *fin de siècle* decadence, echoed the period *Blow-Up* had cruised through some twenty-five years before. In 1993, on the cusp of the Britpop wave, DJ Paul Tunkin changed the name of his easy listening/Sixties soul and R'n'B nights above the Laurel Tree pub in London's Camden to 'Blow-Up' (both 'Swinging London' and 'Londinium' had been considered and rejected). The renaissance had arrived. Since relocating to London's West End Metro club, on Saturday nights, Blow-Up also has its own record label, intermittently releasing club classics compilation albums.

The film received its world premiere at London's Coronet Theatre, Notting Hill, on 18 December 1966. The then powerful National Catholic Office for Motion Pictures in the United States requested that the two nude scenes in the film be cut, prior to approving a rating. When Antonioni refused, they issued an edict forbidding Catholics to see the film. Antonioni dug his heels in but after careful diplomatic work by Ponti in Italy (where a ban would have spelt trouble for the director) the film was eventually passed, though it was still banned in Buenos Aires.

Perhaps inevitably the popular press showed little regard for the film's artistic merits, but homed in on the fact that for a blink-and-you'll-miss-it moment, there is a tantalising glimpse of the pubic hair of *Blow-Up* dolls Jane Birkin and Gillian Hills. Cinema staff reported huge exoduses from their auditoriums immediately following the scene. According to MGM, at the time of the movie's initial distribution, prints of the film were being returned with complaints that Birkin's and Hills' sequence was missing, having been pruned by rampant projectionists for later, more private use. MGM were forced into the unprecedented position of warning all cinemas that the film would be 'inspected' on return for 'missing parts' (*sic*).

The *News of the World* made the most of an opportunity for an exposé. '*Blow-Up* exposes the shallow, sex-crazed world of a fashion photographer in so-called Swinging London,' ran an introduction. 'Girls are shown in some of the most eyebrow-raising scenes ever screened.' Whetting the appetites of the hairiest-handed voyeurs, the reporter Weston Taylor was charged with sorting out the smut from the style with the help of an interview with the twenty-two-year-old Gillian Hills.

'I didn't see anybody for two months because I felt so ashamed of being in the nude,' said Hills, who'd later pop up for another nude scene in Stanley Kubrick's *A Clockwork Orange*. 'I felt so ugly, I didn't want to see my friends any more. But it's simply awful to call it an orgy.' Weston argued it was the simplest description for two girls prancing naked around a photographer's studio, nothing less. Treating Taylor as a trusted confidant, Gillian babbled candidly on: 'I've needed protecting so much. All kinds of film men have wanted me to undress in films and I've had to refuse them because I'm not that kind of girl. But Antonioni's different, isn't he?' Gillian left the caring hack in no doubt about her future. 'I've decided to become a very serious girl. I'm studying for my GCE in French – I've just got to complete my education.' Interview completed, Weston Taylor couldn't help but add a postscript: 'This film will be a swinging finishing school for her.'

The Times's John Russell Taylor peered a little closer, but saw very little: 'It seems to offer much, to say something, without ever actually delivering. It is ideally a film to talk about at smart parties; but when the party is over, disappointingly little remains.' The *Daily Express*'s Peter Evans regarded the film as a cynical exposé of the 'scene': 'Like an eggshell delicately tapped to disclose the emptiness inside without disturbing the finish ... Nevertheless, the emotional freeze is necessary on an unpleasant orgy of self-glorification.' The *Guardian*'s Richard Roud disagreed: 'If you make a film about essentially shallow people, you risk making a shallow film.'

Stateside, the reaction was rather more extreme. The film was shown in Hollywood the day before Walt Disney's death and roused its audience to new levels of bemused irritation. Critic Arthur Knight reported the packed cinema house appeared to hate what it saw – 'almost as if Antonioni had insulted them personally'. Celebrity guests scratched their heads over its precise meaning – but answers came there none. Richard Goldstein reported that the film had 'a lack of understanding that can only be called Parental'. But it was Pauline Kael who delivered the most brutal dismissal. '*Blow-Up* is the perfect movie for the kind of people who say "now that films have become an art form ..." and don't expect to understand art.'

Variety magazine predicted losses all round. But to everyone's astonishment *Blow-Up* Stateside grossed $30,000 in its first week. The French journal *Postif* observed that it was 'not unusual to see Americans freezing in line for over an hour'. The film went on to win the Golden Palm at Cannes, while the script was nominated for an Oscar the following year.

The unexpected studio hit caused things to get a little out of hand. The new breed of late Sixties movies executives may have had no idea what Antonioni's picture was about, but its huge returns caused them to look for similarly 'challenging' or 'groovy' stories from Britain and Europe. Such cynicism resulted in some truly horrendous dogs – Peter Hall's *Work is a Four Letter Word* (1968) for Universal, starring a 'magic mushroom'-munching David Warner, being one of the worst. By 1967, Swinging London had become a royal pain in the arse. For all the careful brushstrokes Antonioni had applied to *Blow-Up*, Desmond Davis's *Smashing Time* (1967), was an appalling Pollock of a movie. Again produced by Ponti (who obviously saw mileage in a more mainstream flick about the scene), this featured two stereotypical Northern lasses (Lynn Redgrave and Rita Tushingham) coming down to London to experience it for themselves. This slapstick tabloid view of the era had the appeal of 'Laurel and Hardy go to Carnaby Street', but failed to present any true picture of the time.

Other imitations and homages followed. John Lennon and Yoko Ono's short *Rape* (1968) saw an attractive woman hounded through a secluded London park and the City by an unseen film crew. Francis Coppola's *The Conversation* (1974), in which surveillance expert Gene Hackman projects his own fears on to a taped conversation, offered an aural counterpart to Thomas's darkroom enlargements. Hal Ashby's *Shampoo* (1975), penned by Warren Beatty and Robert Towne in London in 1967, starred 1960s' icons Julie Christie, Goldie Hawn and Beatty himself. In place of Maryon Park were the tennis courts of Beverly Hills, where Beatty's hairdresser supplanted the fashion photographer as the ultimate in 1970s' cool, in *Time* magazine's words, 'the last shabby survivor of the age of grooviness'. Brian De Palma's *Blow Out* (1981) offered a virtual parody, Hemmings's icon of fashion being replaced by John Travolta's lowly sound engineer. More recently, Mike Myers's *Austin Powers* movies, with their joking references to Thomas's writhing phallocentric stance atop pouting studio models, have satirised the self-conscious grooviness of the era.

If any one film truly reveals 'Swinging London', it is Peter Whitehead's little-seen documentary *Tonite Let's All Make Love in London* (1968). Beautifully shot, with a Syd Barrett-led Pink Floyd supplying the soundtrack, it is perhaps the only true masterpiece of the period, offering a visually captivating window on the 'in' crowd. Revealing, often very personal interviews with the era's prime movers – Michael Caine, Julie Christie, David Hockney and Mick Jagger – are interspersed by dazzling images of the 'dedicated followers of fashion', patronising the clubs and discotheques of the day. As a trusted confidant of the Rolling Stones, who had filmed their first US tour, and a member of the inner circle, Whitehead was able to give an unusually free rein to his eye for detail.

Over thirty years on, *Blow-Up* continues to baffle and frustrate those viewers and critics determined to decipher Antonioni's celluloid Morse code – the seeming lack of plot, stilted dialogue, symbolism. Part of its cult status (aside from its period iconography, attitude and style) surely lies in its inscrutability – those who 'get it', and these for who it remains a gorgeous/irritating enigma. The real charm of this film lies in the fact that, beyond such worthy meditations on the nature of perception and urban alienation, it isn't really about 'anything'. Ambience is all. Like the rolling frescos of the other Michelangelo back in Italy, *Blow-Up* is a roving landscape of colour, in which a telephone box or flashing neon sign plays just as important a role as an actor.

With *Blow-Up*, Antonioni opened up European art to the masses. He then followed the *zeitgeist* to San Francisco for his next picture, *Zabriskie Point* (1969), but his take on the US campus counterculture dive-bombed into a critical dry canyon. The soundtrack, featuring Pink Floyd and the Grateful Dead remains a redeeming factor for a very pretty but otherwise terminally tedious film. His status, however, as one of the great European film-makers was reaffirmed by both *The Passenger* (1974) and *Beyond the Clouds* (1995). He was awarded an honorary Academy Award for Services to Cinema in 1995. He still lists 'ping pong' as one of his main interests.

TODAY MARYON PARK remains as empty as ever, save for the odd tourist or student from nearby Goldsmith's College. So Harvey Edgington, formerly Greenwich Council's film officer, was baffled by the interest that the film continued to excite. 'I was amazed at how many people would phone me about *Blow-Up*. There's no other film which attracts this amount of interest, despite *Four Weddings and a Funeral* and the Bond film *Tomorrow Never Dies* being partly shot in Greenwich.' One person was so obsessed by the movie that he would film himself with a camcorder in the same places as Hemmings and attempt to buy the park's green bollards. In 1996, as part of the celebrations to commemorate the centenary of cinema, the British Film Institute wrote to all London boroughs looking for possible sites to commemorate a century of film. On Harvey

Edgington's insistence, Greenwich Council convinced the BFI to put up a plaque to the film on a wall opposite Maryon Park's tennis courts. Given local authority budgets, a novel idea to reform the Yardbirds for the event failed to come off, as did plans to attract Hemmings and Redgrave. Nonetheless, a small ceremony took place on a midweek afternoon with a few councillors and school children roped in to make up the twenty or so heads who listened to Harvey's speech as the plaque was unveiled by the top brass from the BFI. The plaque was soon smothered in incomprehensible graffiti and in 1999 vandals prised the heavy plaque off the wall. On closer inspection, they decided to leave it on the ground. It is now under lock and key in the gardeners' tea hut, a curio for the park-keepers, most of whom have no idea what all the fuss is about. Perhaps, they venture, it's a porn movie that was filmed in the park's bushes. Today, as the curtain of darkness falls over central London, the park comes alive once more, to be taken over by wild nature fairies and spirits from an ancient Roman settlement who dart, chuckling, in and out of trees, playing psychic hide and seek with their lost souls.

WILL THEY CARE IN WIGAN?

'Which side are you on . . . ?' ran the provocative slogan of the poster for *If . . .* Schoolboy rebellion has never been so succinctly captured on celluloid. Bathed in nostalgia and surrealism, *If . . .* charts the rise of a small band of public school dissidents as they struggle to escape the narrow confines of their establishment college. Ridicule, exclusion and a final, bloody thrashing by their anachronistic peers proves the last straw, resulting in an explosive climax.

'You are listening to the legal free radio station of Czechoslovakia. We appeal to all radio stations . . . please let the whole world know the truth . . .'   Anonymous broadcaster, Radio Free Europe, 1968

If . . . began life as the fevered brainchild of two disaffected school-boys, the deeply sensitive David Sherwin and his childhood friend John Howlett. Both had attended the traditionally English Tonbridge public school during the 1950s, enduring what Sherwin was later to describe in his diaries as 'the nightly beatings and buggery. No mother. No father. A diet of cabbage and watery stew.' Experiences that would plague Sherwin for years afterwards.

Although both boys distinguished themselves academically, taking the traditional route to Oxford, they much preferred to wallow in the new wave of European cinema tangoing across the screen. Inspired by the films they were watching, they decided to write their own screenplay, vowing to gain a belated revenge on the system they despised. Employing William Wordsworth's dictum, 'Poetry is experience recollected in tranquillity', as their motto, the eighteen-year-olds, over three days and nights, poured out the pain of their schooldays on to paper. There was a lot to get through. The finished product, a brutal diatribe on the English public school system, was christened 'Crusaders', evoking lost dreams of justice and nobility. They showed it to their girlfriends, who just adored it. And, with passionate naïveté, they sent copies of their hastily completed first draft to everyone they had heard of in the movie industry.

Interest was swift, but short-lived. Ian Dalrymple of the Crown Film Unit suggested the boys be summarily 'horse-whipped', while on the basis of a single previous encounter they were invited to meet Lord Brabourne, film producer and son-in-law of Lord Mountbatten. Choking on his heritage, he declared the work to be the most 'evil and perverted script' he'd ever read. Top literary agent Margaret 'Peggy' Ramsay was impressed enough with the idea, but unconvinced it would make a feature film, and advised the boys to turn it into a documentary instead. Legendary *auteur* Nicholas Ray made an initial fuss of Sherwin, to the extent of promising him an assistant's position, but suffered a nervous breakdown soon afterwards, leaving the boys back at square one. As Sherwin recalled in his published diaries: 'We leave our last copy of "Crusaders" in a crummy city bus station waiting room . . . I write "Great film available" across the cover, you never know . . . Lady Luck may strike.'

In a last-ditch bid to sell the script the boys sent their masterpiece to the maverick Ealing studios director Seth Holt, who replied in early 1963 – a languid eighteen months later. He liked the script, although he felt he wasn't the right person to direct it. But he was happy to help find someone else to do so, and in 1966 passed it on to Lindsay Anderson. Attracted by the title, with its overtones of what he called 'idealism, struggle and the world well lost', Anderson took on the project.

At this stage, John Howlett bowed out to work on another script for Seth Holt, while Sherwin went on to forge a fellow traveller's bond with Anderson that would last until the director's death nearly thirty years later. Anderson seemed to have much more to say about the script's failings than its strengths, but, taking on the role of mentor and midwife, encouraged Sherwin to rework it. Sherwin, said Anderson, should be thinking of 'the image of a world; a strange sub world, with its own peculiar laws, distortions, brutalities and loves'. In what was to become their regular working routine, more often than not holed up in Lindsay's beloved seaside retreat,

Fuchsia cottage in Rustington, the pair tossed ideas around and improvised, until they were both happy.

David and Lindsay now hawked the script around Soho's film distribution companies throughout 1967, but met with almost universal disapproval. One response was, 'Shapeless . . . No story line . . . Will they care in Wigan?' Another, 'There are no parts for Julie Christie or Mike Caine. What about Sir Laurence as the Headmaster? Or Sir John, or Sir Michael, Sir Alec or Sir Ralph?' And, 'Can you shoot it in six weeks?' With Lindsay reduced to casting a despondent Sherwin in vacuum-cleaner commercials to stay afloat, help arrived in the shape of Albert Finney, who had made the role of the Angry Young Man all his own in the 1961 kitchen-sink classic *Saturday Night and Sunday Morning*. An important box-office star, Finney would acquire a reputation in the industry as a kind of hairy godmother, later also setting Mike Leigh and Stephen Frears on their way. His company Memorial Films, which was run by actor Michael Medwin, took on the project. Medwin brokered a deal with CBS, who had just set up a film division. In his diary, Sherwin recalled wandering round Memorial's offices looking at wall-to-wall sheets with scene numbers, characters and shooting dates. 'After seven years, it's really happening.'

Just when all seemed to be going well at last, there was a hitch. CBS pulled out. The box office returns from Hollywood's British ventures had finally begun to shrink. Takings were down to £289 million, £37 million less than in 1966. 'Swinging London' was in its death throes and film-makers and executives were fleeing the scene of the crime. Fox had already packed its bags in 1966 following the dud that was *Modesty Blaise*, and US fiscal policy changes to help fund the war in Vietnam were further discouraging US investment abroad. Tired of pouring money into a sieve, the Americans began to inspect their own front doorstep, where the likes of *Bonnie and Clyde* and *The Graduate* were cleaning up at the box office. The youth focus and dollar were doubling back.

If . . . was off. It looked like years of Sherwin's life had been utterly wasted. But wait a minute: Paramount had just been taken over by oil billionaire Charlie Bluhdorn, possibly Albert Finney's greatest fan. Clutching at the last remaining branch, Medwin rang Bluhdorn. *If . . .* was on again, with the budget set at £250,000.

Pre-production began with adverts placed in the *Stage*, *Melody Maker*, *NME*, *The Times* and the *Telegraph*: 'Do you want to be a star? Boys – 12–19, this is your chance.' Reportedly, over 5,000 hopefuls turned up at Marylebone Town Hall on 1 January 1968, but only one, Phillip Bagnell, 'gangly and tusk-toothed – a savage mated with a scholar', was eventually cast in the role of the maniacal stargazer Peanuts.

An audition of professional actors was held four days later on the stage of a Jimmy Edwards' farce at the Shaftesbury Theatre to determine the main cast. Sherwin later called it 'the best audition in the world'. Among them was twenty-four-year-old David Wood, who would take the role of Crusader Johnny. As Wood recalls: 'I remember a circular revolving bed in the centre of the stage – not quite the atmosphere that perhaps Lindsay had wanted. Half a dozen of us at a time were reading scenes. I remember Robin Askwith was there, as was David Dundas. Lindsay came up to me and asked, "What do you understand by the word 'epic'?" I didn't know what he was talking about really, so I said, "It suggests to me something quite long." But I felt that there was a certain quality that he was after, something lasting, heightened and better than most things.'

On casting director Miriam Brickman's advice a pugnacious little chap, who had had a bit part in *Dixon of Dock Green*, was called to read. Malcolm Taylor had been born in 1943 in Liverpool, and worked as a waiter in his father's pub before becoming a coffee salesman (an experience that later found its way into Anderson's and Sherwin's follow-up to *If . . .*, *O Lucky Man!*). His interest in acting had been sparked by an octogenarian teacher, one Mrs Harold Attlee, during visits to an elocution class with Malcolm's then girlfriend. Mrs Attlee encouraged him to take acting lessons. Borrowing his mother's maiden name (there was another Taylor working as an actor in the 1960s), Malcolm McDowell launched himself into the fray: his first job was a stint with a rep theatre on the Isle of Wight at £8 a week. An unhappy period with the RSC would follow. 'Just like being in the civil service,' recalled McDowell.

'I . . . just went into another dimension,' McDowell said of his *If . . .* audition in an interview with *Rolling Stone* magazine in 1973. 'It was electric! I'll tell you this, I have never experienced such elation or joy.' In the red corner McDowell, blessed and damned with that extraordinary visage, part Archangel, part Anti-Christ. In the blue, twenty-two-year-old Christine Noonan, the perfect Picture of Lily from a schoolboy's wet dreams: McDowell, cocky, under-rehearsed, and 'in one hell of a temper'. Noonan: raw, gypsy, fractious. McDowell glances at his lines for the first time. 'This is much more my cup of tea,' he thinks. 'It's like a Western.' He lurches towards Noonan, forcing a scripted predatory kiss, thrusting his tongue down her throat. A shocked Christine returns his advances with a crack around the head, bringing tears to McDowell's eyes and sending him reeling across the circular scuff-marked stage. What follows is not in the script. Noonan tears into McDowell, caterwauling and catapulting the pair across the stage. A frightened McDowell retaliates, ripping her bra and pulling the curtain down on the shocked on-lookers. 'I wouldn't bother to go on auditioning,' an ecstatic Sherwin says to Anderson. 'You've got Mick and the girl.'

The Beatles' anthem, 'Hey Jude' (itself born out of regret and emotional starvation), filled the airwaves that long hot summer, but it was now clear that people were fed up with taking a sad song and making it better. John Lennon was sufficiently moved to plead on 'Jude's B-side, 'Revolution', that they should 'free their minds instead' – hollow homilies, half believed. If the baby boomers had relaxed for a couple of years in lysergic-tinted spectacles, there was now a sense of being at the barricades. The assassination of Martin Luther King, who campaigned for change through pacifist means, sent a bullet-riddled telegram to students everywhere that pacifism wasn't working. Enoch Powell was expelled from the Cabinet after making his infamous 'Rivers of Blood' speech, and Smithfield meat market traders took to the streets in his support. Psychic cowboys turned militant frontiersmen, demanding change by any means necessary, bringing the war home.

Watching from the sidelines, Anderson could barely contain his delight, although he'd later deny that he had sought to exploit the chaos at large. 'We were very lucky with *If* . . . ,' the director recalled for the BBC shortly before his death. 'The interesting thing is that it was not designed to echo what was going on in the world. *If* . . . is anarchistic because I'm anarchistic.' Nevertheless, as assistant editor Ian Rakoff recalls, 'It was deeply unnerving . . . I'd come into the cutting-room and Lindsay was standing there with the *Daily Telegraph*. There was a giant picture, half a page, of rebellion on the rooftops of Paris. It looked as if it had been taken from the final sequence of *If* . . . , which we'd already shot. Just extraordinary.' David Wood remembers, 'One of us said it was a shame that the film wasn't already out, but I remember him being quite pleased they were rioting.' (Lindsay, the left-wing humanist, carried the *Daily Telegraph*. 'If I read the *Telegraph*, I don't expect to agree with it. If I read a liberal paper, I'm supposed to agree with it and it just makes me annoyed.')

Anderson had secured use of the 150-year-old Cheltenham College, some 200 miles from London, for the main exterior shooting. It was an apt setting, not least because Lindsay had distinguished himself there as a student, becoming a head of house. Far from 'paying off old scores' the director had 'very fond memories of my schooldays', as he told the *Sunday Telegraph*. Assuring Cheltenham's headmaster David Ashcroft that the film was to be a 'bit like *Tom Brown's Schooldays*', Lindsay went so far as to provide the school with a hastily drawn-up dummy script, which omitted any references to beatings, buggery or armed insurrection, on the correct assumption that these would have led to permission to shoot there being hastily withdrawn. Here's an extract from that dummy script, faithfully preserved by David Wood:

The film is intended to be a poetic, humorous view of life seen through the eyes of the boys. The film will show the general life of the school into which will be woven the lives and also the adventure fantasies of three particular boys – Mick, Johnny and Wallace. The overall effect of the film is to show the reality of the world and its innate lyricism. To achieve this, and because we are working outside the commercial framework of studio production, the film will be improvised. The following rough notes are an outline to aid the budgeting and the logistical problems of the production . . .

So ran its deceitful introduction. A description of the Whips beating the boys was changed to them ordering the boys to go on 'Barnes's afternoon runs for a week'. Any mention of homosexuality was suppressed. Here was a clue to the real dynamite that lay beneath the public school system: shootings, explosions and bombings were deemed acceptable, but any mention of Wilde's 'deep, spiritual affection' was summarily castrated. The bogus script deceptively hinted at the finale with the following description: 'A fantasy scene follows where Mick and Johnny mimic Al Capone, Humphrey Bogart, Marlon Brando, and Bonnie and Clyde.'

While the authorities at Cheltenham were making their minds up, another dummy was presented to the sixth-formers at Charterhouse School in Surrey, which was chosen as a possible back-up location. As producer Michael Medwin recalls: 'Lindsay and I went to dinner with the sixth form's geniuses and the boys started saying that the script was the greatest piece of rubbish they'd ever read. I think we'd just got through the soup when Lindsay snorted, "I'm not coming here to listen to the criticism from these young men."' On hearing the cries of laughter from the assembled diners, Anderson 'made his excuses and left'. Once the film was released, however, Lindsay, who wore grudges like Victoria Crosses, took perverted pleasure in pointing out that he had subsequently rejected the college as the base for the film. Medwin recalls, however, that when pupils at Charterhouse saw the finished film, they loved it.

During production the film was known variously as 'Crusaders' (its original title), 'Come the Revolution', Lindsay's preferred sobriquet, and, at times, 'Stand Up, Stand Up', after an article Anderson had written for *Sight and Sound*. But all would be outlasted by *If...* Albert Finney's secretary Daphne Hunter had been asked to think of something old-fashioned and corny to call the dummy script, and came up with the title of Kipling's famous poem. Previous British films had tended either to romanticise or to demonise the public school system. *Goodbye Mr Chips* (1939) and *Tom Brown's School Days* (1951) had represented the two extremes. A decade and a half after *If...* another movie would expose the cabalistic rituals that lurked in the corridors and dormitories of the British public school system but, for now, that was *Another Country* away.

In the published screenplay Anderson was quick to credit Jean Vigo's *Zéro De Conduite* (1933) as a source of inspiration. 'We especially saw *Zéro*... again before writing started, to give us courage.' Set in a repressive French boarding school, *Zéro De Conduite* employs a European surrealism to question the pedestrian, conservative reality of the establishment. 'I never bought that thing about Vigo,' says Rakoff, undermining subsequent schools of film theorists who would lump the two together. If nothing else, it inspired the poetry of the film. Much of this poetic vision may be attributed to veteran Czech cameraman Miroslav Ondricek, head-hunted and dragged through the Home Office's red tape by Anderson for his ability to 'just get on with it', without bogging Lindsay down in the mechanical details of film-making, which he loathed. To further alienate the technical crew, the shooting script contained no descriptions of camera angles or movements, all of which were worked out on the spot between Sherwin, Anderson and Ondricek, Anderson huddling with the Czech and conversing through an interpreter.

It was a bizarre sight, this bear-like, six-foot-plus émigré towering over the diminutive director, both gesticulating wildly in the common language of film. Twenty-five years later, BBC2's *Hollywood UK* took Ondricek back to the Cheltenham locations. 'Although I'd seen some films and books on the British school system, when I arrived, the whole traditional thing here amazed me,' the cameraman recalled. 'It was intriguing to read inscriptions naming where various people had sat. I soon realised that the public school system had a vicious element from which the children were trying to free themselves.'

On arriving at the shoot, Miroslav quickly recognised the limitations of the budget, especially the expense of lighting some of the larger interiors at Cheltenham (notably the vast chapel), so that scene, and others, were shot in monochrome. In fact, the often pondered-over black-and-white sections of the film were entirely a result of budgetary limitations, despite Rakoff's assertions that they had been deliberately inserted to jar the viewer. To this day, when *If . . .* is shown on television, continuity announcers pre-warn viewers not to adjust the colour on their sets during the black-and-white sequences. Nevertheless, Rakoff may have a point. In Anderson's brilliant, but little seen *The White Bus* (1966), a surreal precursor to *If . . .* , colour filmstock cuts into what is essentially a black-and-white film.

Fantasy sequences, often invented on the spot – the chaplain in the bureau, the headmaster's Pinteresque, sexually repressed wife wandering naked throughout the boys' deserted dormitory – served to confirm the director's aesthetic belief that there ought to be no distinctions between reality and fantasy. 'The trouble is', Lindsay once told Sherwin, 'I don't believe in naturalistic cinema. People being boring in front of the camera.' Art, thought Lindsay, was 'an experience, not the formulation of a problem'. As McDowell told *Premiere*'s John Naughton in 1995, '[Lindsay] said to me "Malcolm. In *Cinderella* when the clock strikes 12, why does the carriage turn back into a pumpkin?" I said, "I don't know." He said, "It just does." It was my first taste of surrealism.'

The plot of *If . . .* is built around a series of eight vignettes, each preceded by a title, as in *Zéro de Conduite*. The first instalment, *College House . . . Return*, sees the young boys return to school from their holidays, the heaving spiral staircase filling the viewer with the feeling that all childhood is returning to school. For Brian Pettifer (the luckless Biles), then seventeen, the sights that greeted him on his first day on set were virtually indistinguishable from the real thing just along the corridor: 'For someone like me, who had been to an ordinary school, it was very unusual to see boys wandering about in army fatigues, and being ordered to "Run in the corridors". My eyes nearly popped out of my head.'

Jute, the innocent new boy, is really our guide, the lamb to the slaughter, leading us through the closeted corridors of tradition and up the hierarchical ladders. We soon discover there are two distinct camps at college: the Whips, those who follow in the well-trodden footsteps of their predecessors (their very dead predecessors, as frequent cuts to World War memorial plaques remind us); and the Crusaders, Mick Travis (McDowell) and fellow conspirators Johnny Knightly (Wood) and Wallace (Richard Warwick). Travis returns late. A hat and scarf cloaking his features make him look like Guy Fawkes (Hitchcock's *Lodger* too), and conceals a symbol of juvenile defiance, a moustache which he has grown in the long summer holiday. Travis, we learn, has spent his holidays chatting up working-class girls in East End pubs, while his crony Johnny, in urban guerrilla style, has been camping out in the woods for six weeks.

The boys' heady tales of freedom are jarringly brought back to reality by the school bell. For all his adolescent rebellion we soon discover that Travis is no intellectual slouch, thereby remaining a conundrum that his establishment peers find impossible to deal with. 'It was just to show that he wasn't a thug,' explains Sherwin. 'He's an intelligent romantic . . . an idealised version of myself.' Travis and his friends aren't prefects; they are not afforded the same privileges as those who have followed the correct path. Their accommodation, cramped and dingy, is adorned with clashing images of sleeping lions, establishment and revolutionary figures, cut the night before from Anderson's own *Paris Match* magazines. The record on their turntable, 'Sanctus' from the *Missa Luba*, is appropriately elegiac and primitive.

The gymnasium, toilet and shower scenes were filmed at Aldenham public school in Hertfordshire. The day's call sheet contained a request for a reinforced tie with which to hang the unfortunate Biles. 'What a way to spend Good Friday,' observed a crew member perched on top of a urinal. 'That shocked me,' said Sherwin, recalling the way Biles had been bullied in the gym before being hung upside down in the loo. 'It was so violent. But Lindsay had this quality in him that he could make things cruel and he did not flinch.'

The shower scene was similarly fraught. Wood remembers a long cold day at Aldenham. 'It went on all day. And between takes, in order to dry our hair, they had this huge industrial heater, a vast machine to put our heads in front of. We were meant to have a cold shower, but Malcolm had done some sort of a deal with the props people and his shower, although there wasn't any steam coming out, wasn't that cold. But Lindsay got his own back in the end.'

The latrines have since been demolished and the gymnasium redeveloped beyond all recognition. The dining-room remains, although the distinctive portraits that adorned the walls were stolen in 2000. Dormitory interiors were shot at Aldenham during the Easter holidays. To reach the set a visitor had to pass the ever-watchful Medwin, positioned sentry-like on the door. Given that many boys were chaperoned by their parents, one particular scene required a great deal of careful planning, lest one mother discovered her son in bed with a leading man. As Wood remembers, 'They were shooting the scene with Rupert Webster in bed with Richard [Warwick]. Webster's mother, the actress Heather Chasten, was coming to pick him up that day, and everyone was terribly worried she would be shown on to the set, up the stairs into a real dormitory . . . There was a certain amount of subterfuge, with people saying, "Take her to the tea tent!"'

Sherwin's original text, later published in book form, would make the finished film seem like an abridged novel. Scattered throughout this highly idiosyncratic script, which reads more like an annotated diary than anything else, are perverse, often charming asides:

During one lunch Peanuts announces that the world will end at 1.30. Everybody in India, he says, is kneeling in prayer as they wait for the prophesied moment. He asks to be excluded in order to say goodbye to one of the Spanish kitchen girls. He is upset to think that she is sweeping the floors downstairs in the kitchens totally unaware of what is about to take place. He wants to kiss her goodbye and hold her hand as the world blows up. Rowntree refuses him permission.

Unfilmed scenes include a poltergeist turning the boys' beds upside down ('it is exorcised by the chaplain who rides through the grounds on a bicycle and feels a sudden wall of evil'), and Biles receiving a correspondence course on 'How to Paralyse your Friends'.

Filmed, but later removed, was a harmonious slow-motion sequence shot in monochrome, in which the boys – the youngest just fifteen years old – fly across the school quadrangle and over a prone and naked matron. As Robin Davies, who played Machin, one of the Juniors, remembered: 'She was lying on the ground with this stuffed alligator, crying: "Come on then boys . . . !" I didn't know what was going on, but when Lindsay said do it, you just did it.'

For Anderson, actors were 'just children'. If they couldn't be put in their place, what was the bloody point? On his regular trips to the theatre, if Lindsay didn't like the way the performance was going, he'd announce in a loud voice, 'It's not very good, is it?' So loudly, both audience and cast, wincing on stage, would hear every word. 'Lindsay liked being a little bit superior,' says Wood. 'He was an arrogant man, and certainly a great self-believer in what he was doing . . . He was an intellectual and therefore one couldn't get terribly near to him.' Wood recalls that after a few days' filming, 'he came up and said, "What's the matter with you? You're wandering around with a long face looking as miserable as sin." I said, "Quite honestly I never know what I'm doing is right . . . I find it very difficult to know or judge whether I'm giving you what you want." At which point his eyes blazed and he thundered, "Listen! I've taken six months to cast this film!"' And that was that.

Where Anderson and Sherwin were totally simpatico was in their abhorrence of paternal authority. The character of the headmaster was painstakingly researched, anticipating the epic insincerity of a New Labour spin doctor. 'He is cool Britannia in 1968!' spits Sherwin thirty years later. 'He puts a spin on everything. He knows perfectly well what's going on. The speech he gives to the Whips, Tony Blair could have uttered every single word of this!' One has only to recall the headmaster's confab with the prefects to appreciate Sherwin's sentiments: 'Britain today is a powerhouse of ideas, experiments, imagination on everything from pop music to pig-breeding . . . That's the challenge we've got to meet. We must not expect to be thanked. Education in Britain is a nubile Cinderella, sparsely clad and much interfered with.' As Sherwin says, 'He's sophisticated. He's selling the school to the world. The headmaster fits in totally as the super-salesman/spin doctor/Prime Minister running this Belsen. He's presiding over this place, which is totally elitist, so of course the Crusaders blow the place up.'

The production continued at a frenetic pace. While Lindsay was busy filming, Medwin was smoothing plumes at Cheltenham by hosting interminable cocktail parties for the staff. 'There was a kind of secrecy at Cheltenham,' says Brian Pettifer. 'I don't know what the staff had seen, but they weren't idiots.' For his part, Lindsay always treated the authorities at Cheltenham with immense courtesy. On one of his regular chats with headmaster Ashcroft, Lindsay had turned on the usual charm and reminisced about his days as a student at Cheltenham. The headmaster, suddenly cutting through Lindsay's waffle, cocked his head and said quietly: 'You know, Lindsay, I do know what's going on . . .'

One weekday afternoon the crew ventured out to the nearby town. In line with Sherwin's original script, McDowell and Wood paraded through the traffic, bound together by toy handcuffs, unwittingly dragging a couple of Cheltenham's residents into the proceedings. Wood recalls: 'We were going to pretend to have a fight, and just see what happened. There's a little old lady in the film who comes up – well, she was real – and she says, "Stop hitting this man!" Malcolm whines, "Well he started it, he hit me first," and Lindsay's shouting, "Keep going, keep going!" Suddenly I'm lying on the ground and there's a screech of brakes ... It's a lorry driver, wielding a hammer, who comes at Malcolm, shouting: "What do you think you're doing?" Malcolm, fronting it out, just says, "This bloke, he attacked me first!" Lindsay's loving it, shouting "Keep it up, Keep it up!" When the lorry driver turned around and saw the camera and this huge crowd of people behind it, he sort of blushed and turned away, and this huge cheer went up.'

Liberated, the boys wander into a motorcycle shop (located in South Wimbledon), stealing a bike and taking off through Cheltenham's country lanes. 'Riding on that motorbike was one of the most terrifying moments of my life,' says pillion rider Wood. 'We were on a public road, and to my knowledge the bike wasn't even taxed. Malcolm had never driven a motorbike and during the shooting there were the odd moments where this putt-putt would be brought up for him to have a little ride on. When it came to the actual thing the bike was enormous, an 800cc contraption, but Malcolm was full of bravado. I was a bit worried when I overheard stunt arranger Peter Brayham saying to Lindsay and Michael Medwin that he would not take any responsibility for the shot. So off we went, with Malcolm not going particularly fast. But Lindsay wanted us to go faster. It was terrifying because Malcolm really didn't know what he was doing. There was this feeling that, because it was the last day of filming, if there had been a fatality, the film was in the can.'

Following the Crusaders' repeated rebellions, they are ritually beaten – sound effects supplied by slapping an animal carcass. The scene was filmed in one uninterrupted take up until the moment McDowell makes his insouciant entrance. 'It was all acted out for real in there,' says Wood. 'Lindsay didn't really direct – the little looks we gave each other in the ante-room, occasionally peering through the glass, trying to see through, that was all improvised, we didn't rehearse that at all.' As McDowell later told film writer Peter Matthews, the scene 'was marvellous to do, because I was really living it. If I relax and watch it, I end up in tears. The scene was the ultimate in the picture for me.'

Anderson and Sherwin deliberately held back the details of some of the more surreal imagery they were intending to weave into the story. For most of the cast stuffed alligators, torches shone on genitals and group showers had become familiar sights on set. But many sensibilities were stretched to breaking point when an uncredited cast member made a cameo appearance. 'Originally,' says Sherwin, 'I had the idea of a skeleton in the cupboard with clothes on, something from the Crimean or the First World War, but Lindsay didn't like the idea of that. It would have been too realistic for the dream.' Wood recalls: 'Christine, Malcolm and I looked at each other as if to say, "Is that a real one? And if so what's it doing there?"'

The 'It' in question was a real foetus, suspended in a jar in the cupboard underneath the stage. Says Sherwin, 'He [Mick] looks at it in wonderment and she [the girl] comes into the scene, takes it from him, as sort of a sacred mummy and it must go back into its tomb. It's very much part of the girl, she's a sort of a Madonna cum lover. Of course they don't say a word of dialogue, which was my intention, and I got wigged by Lindsay: "Do you realise that from the moment they go under the stage there isn't a single word of dialogue?" I said, "No, Lindsay, that's poetry, the poetry of the cinema."'

Poetry and symbolism were the last thing on the minds of the technical crew, more used to the dry, genteel humour of the Ealing comedies, or the bawdy *double-entendres* of the *Carry Ons*. The exhausting shooting schedule, combined with Anderson's improvisational style, abrasive manner and selective on-set secrecy, led one crew member to explode. Sherwin recalls, 'One of the assistant cameramen said, "You must have an evil mind to think of a thing like that, you bastard," and it was then that I was asked to leave the set very quickly.'

The end-of-term assembly was filmed at St John's Church, Albion Street, Cheltenham, disused then, now demolished. Lindsay had wanted the penultimate scenes to look 'natural and fantastic at the same time', and with fifty-six Cheltenham-recruited teachers and pupils in attendance the crossover was complete. Many had no idea who was real and who wasn't, but the general consensus was that the shabbily dressed teachers were the real ones. Extra Reg Vivash, the man in the suit of armour, threw himself into his role with such enthusiasm he damaged himself in the ensuing mêlée. 'Someone trod on my coat and brought me down and I broke my arm,' Vivash recalls. 'And when I fell they were actually filming it. Lindsay came up to me and said, "What a pity you fell." I said, "Do you want me to do it again?" "Oh, no no *no!*" said Lindsay.' Later, the real-life pupils of Cheltenham would be unimpressed when their fictitious headmaster was shot. 'Surely there'd be some brains coming out as well,' mused one of the boys as they gazed at the unlikely scene unfolding over the quadrangle. The final shots, in which a rabid McDowell straddles the rooftops toting a Sten gun, hadn't caught the sort of image Anderson was looking for. Rather than return to Cheltenham and risk damaging sensitivities even further, a mock-up of the roof was built at Twickenham Studios. When results from that shoot were still not satisfactory, Rakoff put together a foot of out-takes from the initial shoot and ran it through on a continuous loop to everyone's delight.

It is fitting that the girl shoots the headmaster. The public school system represented much that was anti-women. But Christine Noonan's film career halted on top of the Cheltenham College roof. Forever after she would be referred to as 'that naked bird in the café'. 'Oh God,' her drama-teaching husband had muttered at the time. 'You're going to be one of those titty actresses.'

'I'm out of work, and I'm broke,' Christine told the *Sunday Telegraph* from the wool counter of the Army and Navy Stores, where she was working as an assistant after filming finished. Anderson brought her down from the roof and on to the factory floor for a tiny role in *O Lucky Man!*, but ironically she was to find more security in the system her character did so much to usurp, as a teacher. As for Miroslav, he returned to Czechoslovakia to find his country overrun with Russians in the midst of an invasion. This was real life.

'I don't know if Lindsay ever intended to suggest that we won,' reflects Wood. 'There was very much a suggestion that the system would defeat us in the end. It's very noticeable right at the end when on the very final shot before it fades out, Mick is crying, and

I never felt that was clear enough, I never felt people quite got that.' As Sherwin told reporters during the shoot, 'This is what society really does to good people and people who want to be free. Mick becomes as evil and as terrible at the end as the headmaster or the general.' For McDowell, at least, the revolution was far from finished: 'There is a lot of Travis in me,' he told Peter Matthews. 'I wouldn't have the guts to get up there and shoot all those lovely people, but after the film I took a holiday in Cannes and looked around me at all the people on the beach and imagined myself with that machine-gun and the bullets flying. They were all there with their yachts and expensive cars, while the peasants in the field were hardly scraping a living.'

Anderson said his sympathies were always with the revolution-aries. 'Fighting means commitment,' Lindsay once trumpeted in *Sight and Sound*. 'It means believing what you say and saying what you believe.' As Sherwin says, 'Lindsay would have loved to be on the roof. Although he'd been in the army, he'd never seen a shot fired in anger. He was young at heart when he wasn't being the pompous one. His nickname was "Lord God Almighty", you know.'

If . . . was released in February 1969 at the same time as *The Italian Job*, Franco Zeffirelli's opulent *Romeo and Juliet* and the whimsical *Yellow Submarine*. As Lindsay was obsessed with getting *If . . .* across to as many people as possible, obtuse logic led him to arrange a special preview for an audience of hairdressers, since he was convinced that they could spread the word better than any two-page advertisement in the *Evening News*. The official premiere was held at the Piccadilly Plaza in London's West End. Typically, Lindsay shunned the offer of Albert Finney's chauffeur-driven limousine and took the tube to Piccadilly, bumping into Robin Davies. 'I was going to the premiere, and who got on but Lindsay. He had all these little stickers with "*If . . .* Which Side Are You On?" written on them. He said, "Don't get caught with these, but stick them everywhere," which we did, on the doors, on the ceiling, all over the place. But when I got to the cinema, they turned me away because I was too young and I didn't get to see it.'

The British press was virtually unanimous in its praise. The *New Statesman* hailed it 'a masterpiece', the *Daily Mail*'s Cecil Wilson felt the general effect was 'to make you rock with laughter and then send you away for some very serious thinking'. Nina Hibbin of the Communist *Morning Star* urged 'every reader to make a special effort to see it . . . the best and most significant film of the 1960s'. The *Guardian* reported 'cheers and clapping and furious arguments breaking out between patrons and usherettes'. But Eric Rhode in the *Listener* lambasted the climactic scenes as 'a clear embodiment of homosexual violence . . . Why does [Anderson] loathe the system so much?' Were its targets 'Buckingham Palace, the Tory Party, the City, our dwindling army – or even the Church?' And he concluded, '*If* . . . is the most hating film I know of.'

If . . . went from strength to strength that year, winning the Grand Prix at Cannes, against the wishes of the British ambassador who declared it an insult to the British nation. Anderson revelled in being shown the door at one screening for not wearing a black tie, screaming 'Stop, listen everybody! We are being treated like animals!' Marketing the film in the UK was always going to be difficult. Many nationwide cinemas, flummoxed with an array of unknown leading actors, fell back on the new *Dad's Army* favourite, presenting *If* . . . 'starring Arthur Lowe'. Wood remembers: 'It had far, far more of an impact abroad. A friend of mine who was in France said, "If you were to go down the Champs-Elysées now you would be mobbed because it's on at about six cinemas simultaneously."' New York's art-house brigade lapped it up, as did Stanley Kubrick, who loved Anderson's work (and vice versa). Further afield, South Africa classed *If* . . . for 'Whites Only', and all sexual references and nudity were excised. Back home, posters for the film were banned from several sixth-form common rooms.

As Stephen Frears reflected for the BBC, 'The country was arthritic in a sense and there was, particularly among film people, a desire for change. A public school would be precisely where you would set the metaphor, in that it was both traditional and yet somehow training people who were discontented. *If* . . . was so successful because it offered the possibility of change from the old class-ridden system.' Bryan Smith, a contributor to the 'Genius of Lindsay Anderson' website, says, 'Most films that rail against social schemes and traditions have very little heart, and can be perceived as heavy-handed "message" films. *If* . . . somehow works in both the personal and the political, keeping it from being a "time capsule"

like so many of the other "quirky" movies of the 1960s.' As Brian
Pettifer says: 'Alan Parker could make a Ken Loach film and vice
versa. But only Lindsay could have made *If . . .* and those that
followed.'

If . . . awoke some sleeping lions. Barrie (*Long Good Friday*)
Keeffe's play *Gotcha* from 1977's *Gimme Shelter* trilogy, starring a
pre-*Quadrophenia* Philip Davis, took from *If . . .* the struggle of the
individual to be heard amid a hypocritical, uncaring school system.
In *Gotcha* the significantly unnamed 'Kid' takes two adulterous
teachers and one patronising headmaster hostage on his last day
of school, dangling a cigarette over the open petrol tank of his
brother's motorcycle. Keeffe recalls: '[*Gotcha*] was written during
the time of what was then called the Great Education Debate, about
Comprehensive school education, during the early 1970s. I noticed
that teachers, politicians, local authorities, education committees,
and the National Union of Teachers were all involved in it. But
there seemed one voice lacking, someone on the receiving end of it,
the actual pupil. I wanted to give a voice to the kids on the block.'
Gotcha has since been performed in twenty-six countries. 'The best
one was when they did it in Moscow, during the late 1970s. It was
seen as a metaphor of capitalist society, and that this situation
could not possibly happen in the Soviet Union. Discussing the
production, I was told that the young actor playing "Kid" totally
identified with the part, that it was his "life story". So I said, "Excuse
me, if this can't happen in the Soviet Union . . . ?" They said, "Oh,
yes, he has mental problems."'

Lindsay's mob remained fiercely loyal. His stock cast were to follow
him through his Travis trilogy, reprising their roles, often playing
several 'Brechtian social types' at once. And Malcolm, especially,
would always go that extra 200 miles for Anderson. *If . . .* , said
McDowell years later, was the best film he'd ever made.

A rambling road movie from an idea by McDowell, *O Lucky Man!*
(1973) was less focused than its predecessor, and at nearly three
hours long tested the patience of even Anderson's most dedicated
fans, but it too has a hard-core following. It does have its moments
– Graham Crowden's horrifying genetic-hybrid; Ralph Richardson's
admonishing of McDowell not to 'die like a dog'; the wonderful Alan
Price score. One of its admirers was Martin Scorsese, who named

his taxi-driver anti-hero after McDowell's character. Says Rakoff, who also worked on the picture, 'Without being too derogatory, Malcolm's an actor. He's wonderful, but not a thinker. *If* . . . came out of schoolboy dreams of anarchy and revolution. What did *O Lucky Man!* come out of? It came out of Malcolm having spent time as a coffee salesman, wanting to construct something out of it and do a *Candide*-like odyssey. But it didn't have the same motivation behind it, a flaw from the beginning.'

Rakoff had first-hand experience of how sensitive Anderson was to criticism of *O Lucky Man!*. 'We were sitting in a pub, about ten or twenty of us (there always seemed to be a lot of people around Lindsay) and Lindsay was talking about *If* . . ., saying how economically he'd shot it, how he'd done this, how he'd done that, turning to me for confirmation and I'd nod in agreement. Then he said: "And of course in *O Lucky Man!* I've been just as economical and just as controlled. Isn't that so, Ian?" "Well . . . no," I said. Lindsay lurched up and slapped me, really hard, in front of the assembled drinkers. Then he pulled me into a waiting chauffeured car and shouted, "How could you do that to me?"'

The critics gave *O Lucky Man!* a lukewarm reception ('all puff and no thought . . . confused, long-winded, self indulgent'), but they crucified Anderson for his follow-up. *Britannia Hospital* (1982) presented a savage satire of a fragmented and strife-ridden country. British critics attending its screening in Cannes stormed out of the cinema, hurling abuse at the screen. The film was withdrawn from cinemas a month into its release by Thorn-EMI. It virtually killed Anderson's film career in Britain. Yet it did go down very well in Argentina, where it won film of the year in 1982.

Like a kite cut free, Anderson was in limbo. He briefly flirted with pop videos, directing Carmel's 1983 jazz-tinged 'More, More, More', going on to film Wham's tour of China. The experience was an unhappy one. Lindsay broke his leg during filming and later removed the film from his CV. He courted Hollywood, briefly. Actors were very keen to work with him and Mia Farrow, in particular, pursued him for some time. But the scripts he was offered were awful, he said, and Anderson, who did not take easily to being a hired director, detested compromise. So he whiled away his days, channel surfing, singing ballads in the bathtub from his beloved

John Ford films and dashing off film criticism to any paper willing to indulge him, in raptures over the latest Scorsese, Kieslowski or his perennial Saturday night favourite, *The Texas Chainsaw Massacre*.

A characteristically restless and eccentric self-portrait, the award-winning *Is That All There Is?* for the BBC's Directors series, caught him in full rancorous flow, re-enacting meetings with old partners, barking questions framed as statements. The film ended with a memorial service aboard a Thames river boat for Anderson cohorts, Rachel Roberts and Jill Bennett, their ashes cast into the River Thames making a moving climax. The old trooper could still pull it out of the hat when it mattered. *Whales of August* (1987), starring Bette Davis and Lillian Gish, offered another reflective swan song for both leads.

The Class of '68 never forgot Lindsay. For most, he was the house-master they never had. Towards the end of his life, Lindsay's Finchley Road flat resembled the chaos of College House. Daily, it seemed, a steady stream of lost souls, old scholars and admirers would beat a path to his door and up the imperial staircase that led to Lindsay's inner sanctum to receive the customary abuse Lindsay dealt to those he cherished. Here an alcoholic actor, there Lindsay's mad, wayward nephew Sandy, or a despondent David Sherwin, plucking through the pile of rejected manuscripts that tumbled from his plastic bags. As Brian Pettifer frequently witnessed: 'There were always people coming and going – and Lindsay was forever making dinner for them, dressed in a little pinny. Someone would knock on the door and Lindsay would say: "I suppose you haven't eaten either. I suppose Joe Cunt here will have to do the cooking as usual."'

There were plans for a school reunion. Sherwin had written a sequel to *If . . .* which centred on an unlikely meeting between the main protagonists some twenty years on. But, like so many of Anderson's projects in the last years of his life, it was to remain a dream. Of those five Crusaders on the rooftop that spring, one of them (Noonan) left the industry as quickly as possible, another (David Wood) has become one of Britain's most prolific and success-ful children's writers, McDowell – well, you know the story – and two are now dead. Rest in Peace Richard Warwick, the beautiful boy on the parallel bars, who died from a form of dementia, brought on by AIDS in 1997. Rest in Peace Rupert Webster, who took a line from his character Bobby Phillips ('If I pass all the tests I'm definitely going to California. I'm going to be a criminal lawyer') and made it a reality, becoming a criminal lawyer in New York. He was knifed to death on a New York subway in the 1980s.

Today, David Sherwin has found peace among the Gloucestershire hills, more often than not indulging his passion for flying model aeroplanes. Recently he was moved to reply to a derogatory statement Lindsay had made some years ago about him to Ian Rakoff: 'I had to smile at Lindsay's remark to you that I hadn't written a line of *If . . .* and shouldn't have a credit. After I'd written the script he told me I was the only genius and poet he'd met. He told me after *O Lucky Man!* that Malcolm was a saint. Later, when black-mouthing him, I reminded him of this. He called me a fucking liar, and then the monster mellowed until the decay of his last year.'

Anderson died from a heart attack on 30 August 1994. As Sherwin recalls in his diaries – which he confesses he could never have had published while Lindsay was alive – McDowell said the director's death had been 'a tragic mistake. Some idiot gave him Prozac to cure his depression, one thing you never take with a heart condition.' Such dreadful, cackling irony could have come straight from the script of *Britannia Hospital*; the system claimed its trophy. As Brian Pettifer says: 'He made lots of enemies, never won a BAFTA – people have long memories. He alienated people – he was never short of saying what he thought of David Lean, for example . . . It doesn't help to make enemies in this business.'

Says Rakoff: 'He could be absolutely charming – speak to anybody on any level of society. He was certainly one of the most intelligent people I've ever worked with, with a clarity of intellect that was very unusual, unpretentious – and he frightened the hell out of people. Never suffered fools. He was always trying to get me to do dodgy things, in a way . . . He often couldn't be bothered to sign things. We'd have tremendous arguments: "I'm not going to learn how to forge your signature!" But I did one criminal thing, on his behalf, on *O Lucky Man!* He was the only director I knew of who didn't get a print of his movie. Reel by reel I stole an entire copy of the film from the lab. In many ways Lindsay was my teacher. He was a great person for encouraging and inspiring, and also for undermining people – and yet I came back for more. Anyone would think I was mad . . .'

Today, Cheltenham College looks exactly as it did in 1968, at least from the outside. The building's exteriors are as vivid as they appear in the film. Wandering around the manicured quadrangle, your eyes are drawn to the rooftops of the chapel and the stone-clad classrooms. But the remoteness the movie afforded the school is a cleverly filmed lie; it's located directly opposite a busy main road leading into Cheltenham's town centre. The authors' overtures to Cheltenham College brought an initial response from the school's registrar of 'We're trying to forget *If* . . .' This attitude soon softened, however, and the staff were perfectly accommodating when we visited the school. Present Headmaster Paul Chamberlain was surprised that anyone would still try to associate *If* . . . with his school. 'Everyone's totally relaxed about *If* . . . ,' he said. 'Because it's so far in the past, any sensitivities that were bruised at the time are now so far behind us.' Cheltenham's glossy prospectus is a million miles away from the movie's monochromatic vision, Chamberlain's preface promising 'the security of a caring and close community in which support and a sympathetic ear are always at hand'.

The school is now fully co-educational, with a 'lively cosmopolitan atmosphere', including a College drama society. Spring 1999's prospectus even raves about a recent production by the Lower Sixth of Dario Fo's *Accidental Death of An Anarchist*. A number of traditions apparent in *If* . . . are maintained. The daily pilgrimages to chapel, the military presence, and competitive edge in all fields, while the prospectus boasts established links with a good number of local companies. Today's alumni would rather participate in 'national fantasy share competitions' suggested by the FTSE index than overthrow their masters. 'The cats become fatter . . .' runs the seemingly irony-free caption beneath a staged photo of young teens scrutinising the *Financial Times*.

THIRTY YEARS ON, at our request, David Sherwin, who had not seen
the film for over twenty years, sat down to watch a video of *If*...
'Well, I watched it, and naturally I was shattered, because the whole
of my life from the age of thirteen to when I made the film and for
many years after came flooding back ... it's truly cathartic. The
film terrorises me, as I was terrified in that Belsen. People still
hate their public or comprehensive schools, there's still as much
bullying and that whole ethos of school hasn't really changed. In
fact it's even more squalid in terms of an authoritarian regime, be
it the army or school or whatever ... I would say Lindsay understood my original vision to 200 per cent perfection. There's not one
single piece of décor, of painting of corridors, of atmosphere, or any
part of term I hadn't experienced. All was straight from my school.
The horror of the beating. I can still smell the bleach they used to
clean the concrete floors and the lino in my schoolhouse, the biggest
and the most horrible in Tonbridge. He realised it totally.'

'I believe every few years I can make a film that can change the world.
And if it doesn't – it isn't my fault.'

Lindsay Anderson, 1923–1994

THE NOTTING HILL FILM

Turner through the looking glass, Chas through a glass darkly, where Ronnie Kray meets Jorge Luis Borges and Thomas De Quincey en route to the Garden of Earthly Delights. What *Blow-Up* merely hints at, *Performance* explodes, an acid-dipped bullet aimed at the third eye, as directors Donald Cammell and Nic Roeg take scarlet spray cans to a 'back-to-front house' in Notting Hill Gate, and harvest mushrooms in the dark.

> 'Quam bonum in unum habitare'
> ('What a good thing it is to dwell together in unity')
>
> The Royal Borough of Kensington and Chelsea motto

By the end of the 1960s British cinema was in freefall. In the face of some spectacular flops, such as MGM's *Alfred the Great* and United Artists' *The Charge of the Light Brigade*, Britain's Labour government was expressing concerns that US investment in the film industry was significantly declining. Universal was the worst casualty, having spent $30 million on a baker's dozen of British pictures, most of which had curled up and died. Cinema attendances dipped further with the arrival of colour television, while, saddest of all, in 1969 MGM pulled the curtain down on Borehamwood Studios – Britain's own Hollywood.

Such was the atmosphere of pessimism and neglect that greeted *Performance*, Donald Cammell's and Nicolas Roeg's acid-fried antidote to Swinging London. While remaining very much a film of its time, employing practices then common in European neo-realist cinema, *Performance* would subvert and transcend its origins, presenting something uniquely British in the process: homegrown counter-culture, unflinching violence and a labyrinthine, mindblowing plot. Simply, there's really nothing else quite like it.

Attempting to nail the real story behind *Performance*, however, is a maddening exercise. Reports, dates and chronologies often differ – wildly so – from source to source. If a large part of cultdom's appeal lies in the propagation of myth, then *Performance* can be said truly to be the dark prince among cult movies. To quote the movie, 'Nothing is true: everything is permitted . . .'

Performance's co-creator, Donald Seton Cammell, was born on 17 January 1934 beneath the lens of the Camera Obscura in Edinburgh's Outlook Tower, later moving to Richmond, Surrey. His father Charles was a noted writer and poet, whose circle of friends ensured a heady bohemian atmosphere permeated Donald's childhood. As Donald later boasted, the house was 'filled with magicians, metaphysicians, spiritualists, and demons'. Aleister Crowley lived across the green. The family's association with the Beast would later become part of the rich tapestry of myth and legend surrounding the director and *Performance* today.

'One of the absolute red herrings that had dogged Donald is this association with Crowley,' says Donald's younger brother David. 'My father, who had never really emerged from the seventeenth century, wrote one of the first books on Crowley following his death. He had certain points in common with my father; they were both literary figures, they played chess together, he'd come over and have dinner. And that was the extent of the relationship. But when Crowley became a cult figure and was taken up by Jimmy Page and a few others, Donald occasionally claimed he was his godfather. I occasionally claimed I was his godson too, and it's just a sort of fantasy. We both knew who our godfathers were. The idea that he had a sort of profound influence on Donald is absolute rubbish. He didn't believe in religion, he didn't believe in Black Magic – other than the effects it can have on people.' His brother may be right, yet the director would tell friends towards the end of his life, 'I wish I'd never got involved in magic. It fucked everything up.'

Like many brothers, the Cammell boys revelled in a secret world, building makeshift dams, and gleefully conjuring up a gallery of characters and situations. David remembers, 'I had this guy I'd invented who was, I guess, in retrospect, the exact antithesis to

Mickey Mouse – a rather sinister character called Jackie Mouse, who had a private island and was a sort of fascist dictator. Donald drew maps of the island and designed all the uniforms for Jackie Mouse's army. And I'd come up with new adventures which Donald would illustrate.'

But a real war had begun. Around 1942 the boys were evacuated to the relative sanctuary of the Scottish Highlands – David to his grandmother, Donald to a monastery school in Fort Augustus. According to David, Donald became 'almost clinically homesick. I don't know what had happened, but I remember him coming back at half term pleading with me to tell our mother to come and rescue him. I remember that very clearly, his sensitivity, and feeling desperate that there was nothing that I could do to help.'

After attending Westminster School, Donald, who'd been a gifted illustrator since childhood, won a scholarship to London's Royal Academy, going on to study in Florence at the feet of Annigoni, the celebrated portrait painter. Returning to London during the 1950s he established a studio in Flood Street, Chelsea, and soon became a noted portraitist himself – his portrait of the Marquis of Dufferin and Ava was hailed by *The Times* as *the* society portrait of 1953.

In Chelsea he'd experience his carnal awakening, in an era of druggy, sexually promiscuous open house parties. According to friends and acquaintances, Donald was magnetic, a highly intelligent, hugely sexual mesmerising force, able to charm almost every nubile young woman he came across into bed; they'd have to be democratic, however – Donald was heavily into threesomes. In 1954 he married Greek actress Maria Andipa, but it didn't last. A resulting unplanned pregnancy and the thought of domesticity drove him to New York, where he took up with model Deborah Dixon and numerous other lovers.

The couple moved to Paris, Donald supported in his artistic pursuits by Dixon's modelling contracts. Around the mid-1960s, he hit a creative block. Figurative art, he thought, was a dead medium, portraying just one fixed version of reality. For a control freak like Donald, this was completely unacceptable. As David Cammell told the *Guardian*'s Tom Dewe Mathews in 1998, 'He realised that the mental process involved in observing shouldn't necessarily be linear, that what you are actually observing is a whole series of events at the same time. It's like a Picasso. You have to include several viewpoints, all within one frame.' Having determined that he might best achieve this through film-making, Donald destroyed all the paintings in his studio and moved back to London, then at the height of the Swinging Sixties.

He soon resumed his pioneering status among the Chelsea set's networking entourage, 'a strange mixture of aristocrats and gangsters, politicians, creative people, destructive people, all in a kind of exciting mélange,' says David. It was here that he first hooked up with the Rolling Stones and their circle of friends, including the Beatles, Brian Jones's girlfriend Anita Pallenberg and the art dealer Christopher Gibbs.

In 1967 Donald collaborated with his brother David (who by this time had started his own company producing short films and commercials) on his first script. *The Touchables* told the story of a pop star abducted and tortured by female fans. Ian La Frenais ultimately received the writing credit, and in 1968 it emerged as a dire Swinging Sixties flick, directed by Robert Freeman.

Around this time Cammell hooked up, via Rolling Stones confidant Robert Fraser, with the American agent Sanford ('Sandy') Lieberson, then working for the Creative Management Agency (CMA). Sandy, who was as much at home with artists as businessmen, was fascinated by Donald, and the pair soon formed a close friendship. 'Donald was very much an individual, not really part of any group or movement,' says Sandy. 'He kind of typified what was happening in England in the Sixties, as somebody who was outside the system but had the opportunity to come inside it and make a mark in it. This had never really happened before.'

Sandy agreed to act as agent for Donald's next screenplay, co-written with a Hollywood producer's son, Harry Joe Brown, Jnr. The story, encompassing Donald's fascination with sex, drugs, rock 'n' roll and violence, concerned a criminal hippie dropout collaborating with two young men to fleece their millionaire father. Donald's script was sold to Columbia without much difficulty – Sandy also represented its leading man James Coburn – and director Robert Parrish turned it into *Duffy* (1968), a 'Swinging Europe' romp. Having seen his vision unravel before his eyes, Donald vociferously complained and was fired halfway through shooting, accused of harbouring 'Independent thought'. Determined to have more control the next time round, Donald was able to use his connections with Sandy and Mick Jagger to make this a reality.

Sandy happened to represent the Rolling Stones' film and television interests. Jagger, who had dilettantishly toyed with the idea of a variety of spin-off careers, including acting, had already been offered a number of scripts, but felt none of them had been quite right for him. These included a treatment of writer/musician Michael Moorcock's *Final Programme*, with Jagger mooted for the part of Moorcock's time-travelling hero Jerry Cornelius. According to Moorcock, Mick thought the part 'too freaky . . . I guess you can only be a bad white boy singing old Chicago blues songs for so long. That's the Willie Dixon of the south-eastern London suburbs for you. Those LSE boys were always a bit cautious, as we've since discovered.'

Donald and Jagger, who'd both been looking to break into movies, and enjoyed similar arcane interests and arcane friends (notably, the Crowley student and film-maker Kenneth Anger), had discussed various Cammell film projects over the years with a view to getting them off the ground. They now had their chance. By 1967 CMA, which represented Warner Brothers television interests in America (Seven Arts having bought out Warner Brothers that year), had been looking to move into film production in order to create complete packaged deals around their stars. Sandy invited Donald to create a cinematic vehicle around Mick and another of Donald's long-time friends, Marlon Brando. The deal would be a move to establish CMA as an agent for Warners in packaging film productions.

Warners genuinely believed *Performance* was going to be another *Help!* or *A Hard Day's Night*, as opposed to the long dark night of the soul it turned out to be. The great attraction was Jagger, whom Warners had already approached to be their 'youth advisor'. It was only when the studio saw the first rushes that they began to regret their decision.

Donald wrote a treatment which played on some of the themes explored in *Duffy*. 'The Liars' concerned a Brooklyn gangster called Corelli, who holes up with a reclusive rock star named Haskin in West London's Earls Court, then possessing a kind of seedy cosmopolitan charm. Haskin's runaway girlfriend Simon falls in love with Corelli and they embark on a tour of Swinging London, along the way picking up a European groupie called Pherber, with whom Corelli winds up sharing a bath.

It was envisaged that Brando would play Corelli and Jagger Haskin. But Brando turned his part down. Without Brando to play Corelli, Donald decided to jettison the character's Brooklyn roots and looked closer to home – to homegrown gangster culture – for inspiration. As Donald told Chris Rodley and Kevin MacDonald for *The Ultimate Performance*, their 1998 BBC documentary, 'We had to have a gangster world, an underworld – a necessary ingredient of any society. The Krays happened to be there and the Richardsons and a few others, sort of ready made, really British, really wicked.' The Krays – then part of the new working-class aristocracy of pop stars, footballers and photographers – had been at their most powerful during the Sixties, their reign of terror paralleling their induction into glamorous society. Never ones to buck a photo opportunity or turn down an invite, they carried their notoriety well beyond the boundaries of their East End domain into the highest circles.

One of the figures who regularly flitted between the Chelsea set and the underworld was a puckish, scar-faced Polish Jew called David Litvinoff, who was able to claim such disparate figures as Charles Richardson, Francis Bacon and Brian Jones among his contacts. When he wasn't flogging paintings or second-hand books to the Chelsea set, he'd be fishing for boys with Ronnie Kray, who was later to slash his throat. David Cammell, for one, had been 'absolutely dazzled by him. Such a chat artist, and highly intelligent. He loved young people, adored London – and certainly opened my eyes to all aspects of it. But he did have this craving for *nostalgie de la boue*, and was fascinated by criminality. He never did anything "official". He'd always be doing odd jobs. Once, when winter was coming on, he asked me, "Haven't you got an overcoat?" He came around to my parents' house a few days later with a cashmere coat with very fancy lining. I wore it for about five years until I was at a party one day and somebody said to me, "Oh, gosh, I had a coat just like that."'

During the summer of 1967, with Litvinoff's first-hand knowledge of the gangster world, Donald reworked 'The Liars' into what was to become *Performance* – 'a poetic treatise on violence'. The collaboration transformed what had been a crude Swinging London story into a work of almost documentary realism. Chas Devlin, a vicious hood – a real 'performer', in gangster slang – has become a public liability to his boss Harry Flowers (almost certainly based on Ronnie Kray), having murdered bookie Joey Maddocks in an inferred homosexual grudge killing. A marked man, Chas holes up in a Notting Hill flat belonging to Turner, a rock star gone to ground. Turner – a 'performer' of another kind – has lost his 'daemon', the wildness that made his name in the first place. Recognising the very qualities he's lost in Chas's personality, Turner attempts to extract Chas's primal wickedness for himself with mind games, polymorphous sex and psychedelics. The masks upon masks that both parties have been creating throughout are finally stripped away – an 'exegesis' through 'play'. By the time Chas's bosses catch up with him, the two superficially different performers, opposite sides of the same coin, have merged identities.

This was the version Donald presented to Jagger, who readily accepted. Such was his faith in Donald that Sandy encouraged the scriptwriter to direct the vehicle himself. He also decided to produce the movie, despite the fact that he'd never produced a film before. The likelihood of such an extraordinary arrangement occurring these days is close to zero. But in 1967, the decade's most easy-going, accommodating year, anything seemed possible.

Donald asked Nic Roeg if he would be director of photography. But Roeg, who was about to begin *Walkabout*, his first film as a director, refused unless he was able to direct. Roeg's credentials were impressive: as a cinematographer, he'd brought a stylish visual finish to Roger Corman's *Masque of the Red Death* (1964) and Truffaut's *Fahrenheit 451* (1966), among others. When Donald immediately suggested that they should make it together, Roeg stalled for a few weeks, but accepted the offer after *Walkabout*'s production was delayed. Finally, Ken Hyman, Warner–Seven Arts' production chief, approved the project. The budget was set at £1.1 million, and Donald's brother David became the associate producer.

As upset as Donald had been by the experience of *Duffy*, the film had reunited him with an old Chelsea acquaintance, the troubled young leading man, James Fox. Donald offered him the part of Chas.

Anita Pallenberg was picked to play Turner's girlfriend Pherber, a part originally earmarked for Tuesday Weld until Deborah Dixon accidentally broke the actress's shoulder through New Age therapy. Anita's most notable role up to that point had been as the lesbian Black Queen in Roger Vadim's *Barbarella* (1967). She'd first met Donald and Deborah Dixon in Paris. Following a Stones concert in Munich, she'd ingratiated herself into their inner sanctum, becoming Brian Jones's girlfriend, later transferring her favours to Keith Richards.

Marianne Faithfull had originally been considered for the role of Pherber, but she was pregnant with Jagger's child and withdrew under doctor's orders. Aware that she might get in the way, Mick happily acquiesced to her staying in Ireland for a few weeks. Pallenberg had also become pregnant with Keith Richards' child, but on being offered the part of Pherber had an abortion.

Mia Farrow had been cast as Lucy, Turner's other live-in girlfriend but, in a curious coincidence, broke her ankle just before she was due to fly to London. So the part was given to seventeen-year-old Michèle Breton, a girlfriend of Donald's, then sharing his bed with Deborah Dixon as one third of a sleeping partnership.

'Baby faced' John Bindon was cast as Harry Flowers's henchman, Moody. He was a face in both the underworld and the acting communities, but also regularly featured in the gossip pages, which chronicled his encounters with Princess Margaret. He was also famed for being able to carry six half-pint beer mugs by their handles on his erect penis. He loved wagging it about, did John. During Lord Longford's inquiry into pornography in the early 1970s, Bindon thought it tremendously funny to expose himself in all his glory to the lord in the middle of the King's Road, Chelsea. Following an acclaimed début in Ken Loach's *Poor Cow* (1968), he went on to make guest appearances in *The Sweeney*, *Minder*, *Get Carter*, *Quadrophenia* and *Softly, Softly*, almost always playing the same role – that of a laddish crook. Fellow actors would laugh indulgently at his jokes, which weren't really jokes, and at his frightening stories, which weren't really stories, and privately they were terrified of him.

Both for the sake of authenticity and to avoid Warners breathing hotly down their necks, David Cammell suggested that the film be shot entirely on location. The setting Donald had specified for Turner's house was perfect. West London's Notting Hill was exactly the sort of place a dissolute rock star could disappear into without leaving a trace. For writer Jonathan Raban, the Notting Hill of the late 1960s and early 1970s was 'a ruined Eden, tangled, exotic and overgrown, where people see signs in scraps of junk and motley'. Home to the silt and chaff of West London, anything and everything could happen here. It was a teeming bohemian Petri dish, with London's grooviest bus route, the number 31, linking Hampstead's liberals and Chelsea's style gurus via Notting Hill's hippie radicals. Ploughing further through the perfumed smoke, a network of Satanists, dabblers and occult chroniclers could be discovered at work – the likes of Kenneth Anger, Colin Wilson and Bill Hopkins. 'These people at the Gate have clearly embraced the idea of a magical city,' wrote Raban. 'Here magic flourishes, and everywhere one can see evidence of a growing devout irrationalism.' From the arcane to the mundane, then as now, a 'Phantom' number 7 double-decker bus circled the Cambridge Gardens area in the dead of night at breakneck speed – the supernatural legacy of a tragic 1930s road accident.

Once it was established that the film would be set in Notting Hill, location scouts turned up a property at 25 Powis Square to serve for the exterior shots of Turner's house (in the film it's 81 Powis Square, as the production team needed a number which didn't exist in the Square). Built in the 1860s, Powis Square was unique, home to unaltered 'back to front houses', where the design called for a reverse view of the property opening onto the street, affording the Square an architectural perversity and cussedness, wholly in keeping with its rich diversity of tenants.

The Turner house had previously been owned by Peter Rachman, a larger-than-life figure who had bought up huge tracts of Notting Hill during the 1950s and 1960s. He then took advantage of the influx of immigrants from the Commonwealth by converting town houses into flats. Rachman would provide Black Power leader Michael X – aka Michael De Freitas aka Michael Abdul Malik – with a basement flat in Powis Square, while the Square also housed

David Hockney for a stretch during 1968. As 25 Powis Square was one such property, interiors for Turner's house had to be found elsewhere. David Cammell recalled a miserable weekend some years previously when he had visited an illegal gambling club in a 'decaying mansion' at 15 Lowndes Square, Knightsbridge, and lost a potload of cash. He was now determined that his loss should be the production's gain and got in touch with the owner, Captain Leonard Plugge. Plugge was a heavily-titled ex-MP, well-known for raising in Parliament – during the Second World War – issues such as mail delivery by rocket and the use of lipstick in the army. He was also an ice-skater, inventor of numerous electrical contraptions, among them, 'television glasses', the two-way car telephone, and his own patented 'autocircuit'. In 1968 Plugge was in the midst of a romantic liaison, requiring him to reside elsewhere, leaving the Lowndes Square property vacant.

David and Sandy met Plugge at the house. 'He opened the door, and there was this overwhelming smell of dog shit,' Sandy recalls. 'There were probably half a dozen dogs roaming the house.' David thought it was wonderful, later recalling the 'faded splendour of its cavernous reception rooms, the ancient lift jammed in the basement, the stone staircase curling up to impenetrable gloom. On the walls hung innumerable paintings in various stages of disrepair, their cracked canvases bulging, their faded nameplates announcing such artists as Rubens, Rembrandt (some signed), Velasquez, Bernini and other familiar names.' For a ridiculously small sum 15 Lowndes Square was handed over to the film-makers on the understanding that the rent was paid weekly, in cash. The famous Plugge art collection was insured for £2 million. Not wishing to blow the entire film budget on an insurance premium, a compromise was reached: the paintings would be stored in the top half of the building under the watchful eye of a neck-braced caretaker, armed with a Luger gun and a flea-ridden mongrel dog.

Deborah Dixon and Christopher Gibbs dressed Turner's flat with silks, Persian carpets, tapestries, Japanese plates and Moroccan artefacts. Jagger's friend John Lennon donated Apple recording equipment for further embellishment, and fellow Chelsea-set member Ulla Larson provided silks from her King's Road antique market stall – at one point during the film there is an affectionate nod to her when Michèle Breton's character suggests a visit 'to Ulla's'.

The actors prepared themselves for filming, to various levels of commitment. Reportedly, Jagger's girlfriend Marianne Faithfull told Mick he was 'too straight' to play the role, and encouraged him to draw a composite picture from fellow Stones Keith Richards and Brian Jones for Turner's personality. Ultimately, Jagger's portrayal would owe more to the latter, who had by 1968 become an overfed decadent dandy, gone to seed.

James Fox's part was going to be harder to train for. Having picked up rave notices for mostly upper-class roles in films such as *The Servant* (1963), *Thoroughly Modern Millie* (1967) and *Isadora* (1968), he now had to transform himself into a vile South London gangster. But Donald had glimpsed something wild in Jimmy, something violent and angry, and was convinced he could pull it off.

Fox took Roeg's instructions to 'go away and come back as Chas' to obsessive extremes. He booked himself into a cheap hotel room in Brixton, pared back his golden locks and wore nothing but Cecil Gee. Through David Litvinoff, he met Johnny Shannon, a part-time boxing trainer, who moved in many of the same circles as the South London criminal fraternity. As Shannon told *Neon*'s Rebekah Wood, 'Tommy Gibbons, who ran the Thomas A Becket on the Old Kent Road, rang me to say he'd got some film guys that wanted someone to meet up with this actor. My brief was simply to take Jimmy round South London to meet some of the "chaps". Jimmy started to get himself very, very fit. I made sure he worked the bag, did a bit of skipping and some sparring. Obviously he was an actor, so you couldn't bash him up. Jimmy took it dead serious . . . He kept catching one bloke, who ended up smothered in his own blood. Jimmy loved that.' And for their part, the chaps loved him to bits: nobody messed with Jimmy. So successful had Shannon's tutelage been that Fox had no qualms about recommending him to Donald for the role of Harry Flowers.

The writer Francis Wyndham introduced Fox to Ronnie Kray, so that the actor could hear gangland recollections of revenge killings first hand. 'I became almost completely taken over by the role,' Fox later wrote in his 1983 autobiography *Comeback*. 'It even affected my choice of girlfriend; Donald had cast Ann Sidney, who had been a recent Miss World, as my girl in the film, and we went out for a bit . . . I spoke, thought and ate like Chas.' On one occasion he'd stormed into Sandy's office in character, terrorising the secretaries and tipping over desks, insisting Johnny Shannon was properly paid for his screen time. 'He was so built up and puffed up, and boxing every day in order to be this character, he could have carved up anybody on the set,' said Donald.

Filming at 15 Lowndes Square began in late July 1968, and continued for the next dozen weeks. Nic Roeg's practice of handpicking broad-minded crew, like cinematographer Tony Richmond (later to shoot *Let it Be*), would ensure few eyebrows were raised around set. The two directors discussed everything, from casting, to script changes and visual style. So successful and fluid was the partnership that people would muse that the two-director scene was obviously the future of film-making.

The exterior of the Black Swan public house at Effingham Junction, Surrey, served as the country pub spotted at the beginning of the film. We first encounter Chas dressing himself smartly in his flat, in readiness for a day of racketeering. The movie then cuts back and forth between Chas threatening the proprietors of a viewing theatre in Soho's Wardour Street and a barrister in court (shot in Chelsea Old Town Hall's function room) threatening to name Harry Flowers as the person really responsible for his 'respectable' client's crime. The worlds of big business, politics and crime are seen to be, in keeping with the movie's themes, two sides of the same coin, as corrupt as one another.

A garage in Queensgate Mews, near Hyde Park, next provides a backdrop as Chas and his mob warn the barrister off the case by burning his Rolls with acid and shaving his chauffeur. For this scene, Donald drew directly on one of Litvinoff's more hair-raising experiences. 'He'd had a terrible falling out with the Krays,' says David. 'One day he woke up seeing upside down – there was a vast procession of banners and music in the air. It turned out he'd been tied naked to a kitchen chair and suspended upside down over Kensington High Street, with the Aldermaston CND march passing down below. He'd pulled himself together, realising something odd had happened, but couldn't quite remember what. Having untied himself and hauled himself over the parapet, he went back into his apartment to find out it had been completely trashed – to the extent that someone had even boiled kettles to strip the wallpaper off. Then he went into the bathroom to clean up – and he realised he'd been shaved.'

Having wrecked Joey Maddocks's 'betting shop', situated opposite Chelsea Football Ground at 469 Fulham Road (strangely enough, a newsagent's two doors down at 473 was at that time called Turner's), Chas is ambushed and brutally beaten by Maddocks whom Chas overpowers and shoots dead. Fox later recalled in his autobiography that the fight scene in Chas's flat hadn't been stage-managed. 'Tony Valentine [Joey Maddocks] and his two mates held back their punches, but we threw ourselves around in a room with spectators hanging from the walls to see it.' In the event, Valentine sustained a swollen cheekbone, while Fox received a black eye.

Back in his boudoir – a tenth floor suite of the Royal Garden Hotel off Kensington High Street – Harry Flowers orders Chas's immediate termination. Chas goes on the run, stopping off at a telephone box outside Wandsworth Town railway station to call his mother. At first he plans to leave for Barnstaple, but in a café at Paddington Station he overhears a conversation about a vacancy in Turner's house. British Rail refused to allow the production crew to film inside Paddington, so the crew took over a waiting-room at the minuscule Kensington Olympia station for a day.

Arriving at the Powis Square house, Chas notices two Mars Bars left by the milkman outside the front door – a joking allusion to a notorious Rolling Stones party the previous year. In February 1967 Keith Richards's West Wittering home in West Sussex was busted, and Jagger and Richards arrested for possession of drugs. The tabloids made much of the fact that Marianne Faithfull had been caught naked in a rug and the rumour went round that Jagger had been performing oral sex on Faithfull with a Mars Bar. According to Faithfull the story was completely untrue. Jagger himself heard it from a fellow inmate while on remand.

Having successfully hustled his way into Turner's house, Chas hunkers down in his basement flat, while Pherber climbs into bed with Turner for an early morning sex session. To get as close as possible to the action, Cammell insisted on filming under the covers: Donald ducked. Rather than hump huge 35mm lenses into the huge double bed, Roeg used a 16mm camera, offering a grainy Oriental peep show. 'How was it for you?' Donald asked Nic, lifting up the bed sheets.

But the material still had to be processed. This dubious honour was passed to David Cammell. The personnel at Humphries, the developing lab, had seen many things but drew the line at this. David was already aware that one female technician in particular was going to take offence, and phoned the lab in advance, pleading that she should not be allowed anywhere near the rushes. Too late, on seeing the material, she complained to the managing director, who quickly telephoned David: 'Look, Mr Cammell, you know we can be prosecuted for this. You've sent us questionable material of a possibly pornographic nature.' David tried to placate the man, but he was adamant. When David and Sandy arrived to collect the processed material, the managing director gathered together as many witnesses as he could and destroyed the footage before their eyes with a hammer and chisel on the concrete floor. But afterwards he quietly slipped them the negatives, which Roeg later had printed through contacts at Technicolor.

In 1970, the fifteen minutes of footage surfaced at a pornographic film festival called 'The Wet Dream Festival', where Jagger's uplifting cameo brought the house down. For years a question hung over who provided the festival with the footage. The mystery is solved. Lieberson still owns the out-takes to this day. As Sandy observes, although Jagger is not actually *in flagrante*, 'he's up and ready'.

The movie's next scene, in which Jagger, Breton and Pallenberg relax in a bathtub, caused even further commotion back at Warners HQ. Up till this point, a few weeks into shooting, the executives had daily sat through hours of chronologically shot film. Having mostly slept through the previous rushes after lavish lunches, they were now startled to discover images of nudity and unrestrained violence flitting across the screen. Production chief Ken Hyman was appalled and, according to rumour, would even later attempt to bury the negative. How could Lieberson, somebody he'd considered a friend, have done this to him? 'If he'd have bothered to read the script he would have known it was not *A Hard Day's Night*,' says Sandy. Anticipating a dreaded 'X' rating, Warners suspended the shoot over a weekend, and Sandy had to persuade them to allow the directors to finish the movie.

It was not only the Warners executives who were causing the film crew problems. As David Cammell recalls, 'One morning, three weeks into shooting, I was phoned by a grand lady who asked me if I realised that "there are more titled people living in Lowndes Square than in any other Square except Eaton Square". She understandably objected to what she described as the "ice cream vans" parked opposite her flat next door and to the loud banging on her communal wall, and she was going to put a stop to it.'

David and Sandy arranged for her and her husband to go off on a protracted cruise in the Caribbean at the production company's expense until filming was finished. That should have been the end of the matter, but she had already informed Sun Life, mortgagors of the property, that it was being used for illicit filming. 'Lenny Plugge had mortgaged this house up to the hilt and of course he hadn't got permission to use it as a film location,' says David. 'Given the lease, they had a perfect right to say that he'd defaulted on the contract.' Sun Life immediately took out an injunction to stop the filming. David recalls, 'I remember sitting in court and dozing off while the prosecutor for Sun Life dug up some precedent of Gordon Selfridge, of Selfridge's, when suddenly our QC, Anthony Lincoln, came up ashen face and said, "My God we're going to lose this case." I said, "Well, it's the end of the film if we lose, we've got to settle." Plugge's solicitor was a dwarf, a hunchback, like something out of a Gothic horror, and there was a lot of going backwards and forwards. Eventually Lincoln said, "OK, we've got a deal. You can finish shooting providing you behave yourselves."'

Meanwhile, Plugge began to call round on regular visits, 'always supported by two young ladies on either side wearing these enormous beaver-lined overcoats,' David recalls. The diminutive old boy still managed to maintain a champagne lifestyle on his dwindling income, sending his Man Friday to collect the rent from the film-makers every week. After filling Plugge's ageing Buick with petrol, the good Captain would be driven to see ballet in Covent Garden. Plugge's trademark gesture of throwing flowers at the feet of the young ballerinas was slowly coming to an end, as most of his bouquets landed in the orchestra pit. Some weeks after filming was completed David was contacted by the police to see if he could shed any light on the 'missing Plugge collection'. It transpired that the once loyal caretaker had walked off with the paintings and, unaware of their value, had sold them at a provisional auction house for £1,200. When the culprit was picked up by police at Paddington Station, David was surprised to receive a call from the man's solicitor wondering if he would stand bail.

Back at Lowndes Square, dark alchemy was being brewed. As the focus switched from gangster scenes to cloistered bohemian decadence, the script was all but flung out of the window. 'Donald wanted to actually create an atmosphere so that the film itself would evolve, with its own momentum,' says David. 'Once the cast were installed on the set they did begin to play off against each other both behind and in front of the camera. And that's what gives it that authentic quality.' In her biography, *Faithfull*, Marianne describes the on-set atmosphere as 'a psychosexual lab . . . a seething cauldron of diabolical ingredients: drugs, incestuous sexual relationships, role-reversals, art and life all whipped together into a bitch's brew'. Roeg encouraged this atmosphere of both intimacy and claustrophobia by shuttering all the windows, shrouding in darkness a flat that was already filled with a febrile smog of dope smoke. The crew had only to walk through the door to be knocked off their feet.

For her part, Michèle Breton was off her head on dope and other psychedelics for most of the shoot. Doctors were often called round to calm her down with Valium. 'I didn't know what I was doing and they used me,' she later told author Mick Brown. 'It was a very spaced-out atmosphere. There was no love there, no understanding between people.'

Meanwhile, Anita Pallenberg had begun taking heroin to relieve on-set boredom, the drug reputedly supplied by the Stones' dealer, 'Spanish' Tony Sanchez. Often to be found glowering outside in a parked blue Bentley was her other half, Keith Richards. At first, he had found the idea of Pallenberg being involved in an orgiastic tryst with Jagger and the teenage Michèle Breton a gas, but once filming began his own chemical intake only further fuelled his paranoia. His spy in the house of love was Robert Fraser, who would report back from the set. Fully aware of what was going on, Donald eventually banned Fraser from the house.

Faithfull, who was regularly sent flowers by Jagger during her sojourn in Ireland, recalled she'd 'never imagined Mick would be fucking Anita'. Like some one-man Interflora, Jagger had also been showering Pallenberg with roses. 'We're all one big family,' he leered to bassist Bill Wyman. But at the same time Jagger and Richards were both being duped by Pallenberg, who was said to have been having an affair with sexual Olympiad Donald – a real love quadrangle.

Relations between James Fox and Mick Jagger were also under strain. Fox, the consummate professional, would turn up every morning on set, having memorised the lines of a now completely redundant script, and then demanded take after take. Affecting annoyance Jagger would flounce off set, slamming doors behind him like a little girl. As Donald told Chris Rodley and Kevin MacDonald, 'Mick was constantly trying to do James Fox in, because that's the only way Mick can operate. Mick is a ruthless tease and he worked on Jimmy for two or three days before Jimmy had a complete crack-up.'

When Stanley Meadows and Tony Morton discovered that Donald wanted them to strip off for a group nude sequence towards the end of the film, in which Turner 'becomes' Chas, they refused point blank. Well, argued Donald, what if Fellini had requested the same thing? Donald wasn't Fellini, said Stanley. Shannon refused point-blank: 'Imagine, round Lambeth, people saying, "Seen Johnny Shannon's fat arse up there?" Didn't want none of that.' John Bindon, on the other hand, was well up for it. Donald took Morton for lunch and plied him with red wine. By the time they got back on set, Morton was suggesting better ways to shoot the scene.

'I didn't mean it to be in any way mocking,' Donald told the BBC. 'It was a mark of respect for the gay world that they had so much influence and control in the underworld. My access to that world was through Lucien Freud, Francis Bacon. A number of them happened to be gay, and the overlap between the underworld and the artistic world was what I was showing in *Performance*. The image of four or five naked men lying around in [Harry Flowers'] office was intended to be a sort of Baconesque homage.'

The 'Memo From Turner' song accompanying the scene – shot in a boardroom above the Chuen Cheng Ku Chinese restaurant in Wardour Street – was originally going to have been a Jagger/ Richards collaboration. Due to the on-set shenanigans, however, a sullen Richards refused to complete the co-writing or to co-operate during the recording session itself. Donald dragged Jagger into a Soho pub and pleaded, 'Mick, for God's sake, what about the song?' At this point, as if the pressure had become too much, Jagger promptly burst into tears. 'It was a thing he could always do for maximum effect,' Donald recalled. Tears dried, Jagger returned to the studio with a clutch of the country's top session musicians, including Traffic's Steve Winwood and Jim Capaldi.

One myth that has circulated for years is that the psychedelic 'bullet hole in Turner's head' sequence was achieved by inserting a microscopic camera into Pallenberg's vagina. 'Another red herring,' laughs David. 'In fact it was shot at the Cancer Research Centre. There was a guy there who was into microscopic photography and I got him to shoot it through a cadaver's tubing.' As Turner fades into death, a portrait of Jorge Luis Borges momentarily fills the screen – a nod to one of Donald and Nic's favourite writers, quoted in *Performance*, and whose magic realist stylings inform much of the film. The final scene sees Chas/Turner leaving Powis Square, *en route* to oblivion through Richmond Park in a white Rolls Royce; the loan of the car a final gift from John Lennon.

Filming over, a drained, disillusioned Anita Pallenberg left for South America in October with Mick, Keith and Marianne to look for flying saucers. A few months later they'd have to face the death of Brian Jones and, soon after that, the tragedy of Altamont. Marianne Faithfull, who had miscarried Jagger's child on her return from Ireland, slid head first with Pallenberg and Richards into heroin addiction. James Fox's life had also gone haywire, and, in 'absolute denial' about the film, he renounced screen acting for the next ten years to become a Christian missionary in the north of England. Michèle Breton returned to Paris where she fell in and out of drug addiction, psychiatric care and anonymity. A year after being cursed by Kenneth Anger, David Litvinoff killed himself in Christopher Gibbs's house.

That the film had been completed pretty much on schedule and on budget impressed Warner Brothers not a jot. They hated the picture; it was a total embarrassment to them, and from autumn 1968 to mid-1969 the movie was all but left to rot. Sandy began to wonder if they really had made such an evil, corrupting film.

In spring 1969 Warners were bought out by Kinney National Services, whose revenue had come mainly from car parks. The new vice-president in charge of foreign production, George Ornstein, was about to inherit a film that most executives had privately washed their hands of. But Ornstein, who'd previously commissioned the Beatles début for United Artists, rather liked it, as did executives John Calley and Fred Weintraub, who had also persuaded Warners to back *Woodstock*, the user-friendly version of counterculture. Seasoned editor Anthony Gibbs re-edited the film, while Warners' Don Simpson touted it around *Easy Rider*'s core hippie audiences.

In July 1969 a preview was arranged for the public and for Warner–Kinney executives at a cinema in Santa Monica, California. Having been an agent himself, Sandy had some idea of what previews were like, 'usually fairly tame situations where people sat through a film and filled out cards, and that was the end of it. I was hoping it would be something similar to that. But it turned out to be something quite different.'

Unusually for a test screening, the selected cinema had been a neighbourhood one. Warners had wanted something low profile, something that wasn't going to attract too much industry attention. In those days cinemas showed the main movie – in this case *Midnight Cowboy* – followed by the unannounced preview. 'After the first couple of minutes you could tell something was wrong with the audience's reaction,' says Sandy. 'They were very surprised and disturbed, didn't know what the hell was going on. As the film unspooled, they just became incensed with it, yelling and shouting "Shut this off! This is obscene! This is crap!" '

Approximately a quarter of the way through the film, a studio executive's wife doubled over and threw up on her neighbour's shoes. The sight of James Fox being beaten by Joey Maddocks's boys had proved too much. 'You couldn't have a much better reaction than that,' thought Donald. Worse, Mick Jagger – Warner's golden ass – hadn't even shown up in the picture for the first forty minutes. Amid uproar, the screening was terminated and money refunded to those paying patrons who had been disgusted with Nic and Donald's effort. It was evil, they said. Morally void, and frankly un-American. Even the bath water was dirty. As Roeg told the BBC, 'Donald and I went to a party that evening and people walked away from us. We found ourselves in a room on our own, pariahs.'

Warners insisted that Donald now shorten and radically re-cut the picture, condensing the gangster elements and introducing Jagger as early as possible (in the event, they'd have to settle for a glimpse of the pop star spray-painting a wall). Roeg was now making *Walkabout*. So in a Los Angeles studio Donald worked with the editor Frank Mazzola to compress the first four reels of the picture. The result of their Burroughs cut-up style editing was to turn the movie into a fascinating montage of often ironic, poetically juxtaposed images, which, typically, the Warners executives also found completely incoherent.

Ornstein, *Performance*'s strongest internal supporter, resigned in 1970, and Warners' president Ted Ashley ordered further cuts. Revolted, Donald and Jagger sent a telegram: 'You seem to want to emasculate the most savage and most affectionate scenes in our movie. If *Performance* does not upset audiences, it's nothing. If this fact upsets you, the alternative is to sell it fast and no more bullshit.' No doubt partly motivated by the success of *Easy Rider*, Warners finally, grudgingly relented, releasing *Performance* in the US in the summer of 1970.

If *Performance* had crystallised the glorious burn-out of the 1960s, it was a very different decade that the film now entered. *Time* magazine's Richard Schickel thought it 'the most disgusting, the most worthless film I have seen since I began reviewing'. *New York* magazine's John Simon simply called it 'the most loathsome film of all'. The British premiere was held in a brand new Warners cinema in London's West End in January 1971 in aid of the charity RELEASE. When Stanley Meadows left the cinema with John Bindon that night, people literally cringed at the sight of them. '*Performance* is quite simply an exhibition,' wrote the *Standard*'s Alexander Walker, 'the farthest outcrop yet of screen violence and social sickness ... it is also hopefully the last'. For Walker, two identically talented artists had lost the plot on a wealth of imagery.

Donald left for Hollywood, later marrying China Kong, the daughter of one of Marlon Brando's girlfriends. In 1977 he made *Demon Seed*

(1977), starring Julie Christie. According to Donald, the post-production had twisted the movie beyond repair. 'The film may be shit, but I think [Christie's] work in it is extraordinary.' His underrated *White of the Eye* (1986), an uneven if highly original 'love story' involving a woman and her sociopathic husband, was critically acclaimed, but neglected at the box office, and he wouldn't make another film for eight years. He'd coast a living directing rock videos – notably for U2's *Pride (In the Name of Love)* – and came close to directing *Robocop 2*, *Bad Influence* and a dark little tale about a prostitute and a millionaire called *Pretty Woman*. He worked on a number of screenplays, including *The Beard* and an unrealised Brando vehicle called *Jericho*.

James Fox returned to 'Notting Hill' with Johnny Shannon in 1986 for Julien Temple's *Absolute Beginners*. Captain Plugge's daughter Gail fell foul of Powis Square's self-styled British Black Panther Michael X, who had her murdered in Jamaica in 1972, and was later hanged for the crime despite a plea for clemency from John Lennon. The irascible evergreen Leonard Plugge – inventor of 'Television Glasses' – died aged 91, in Hollywood, in 1981.

Since its British release in 1971, *Performance*'s cult following has grown like nightshade, following showings on the midnight movie circuit, endless mythologising surrounding the shoot and its aftermath, and its championing by artists, writers and film-makers, whose passionate reference-spotting is well served by the movie's Aquarian smorgasbord, as cluttered as a New Age Fayre's trestle tables. Oliver Stone paid close attention prior to filming *Natural Born Killers* (1994), while John Maybury, whose Francis Bacon biopic, *Love is the Devil* (1998), has much of the tone and feel of *Performance*, cites the film as a key influence.

Despite the heartache connected with his involvement, Sandy Lieberson still burns a candle for the film. 'I think the thing that classifies many cult films like *Performance*, like *Blade Runner*, is initial rejection, eventual acceptance, then some kind of adulation. And *Performance* is a superb film. It looks at so many different aspects of society, the establishment, the corruption within it, challenging all the traditional ways of looking at cinema.' For David Cammell, 'It's a very romantic story. It could well have been made as a costume piece, set in the Middle Ages, a knights of the round table sort of thing. Donald was rather steeped in the Arthurian legends as a child, and *Performance* is a sort of grail myth. In *Le Morte D'Arthur* you do have all the villains, the heroes and the beautiful women – and they are all there in the film. That's why it's such a rattling good story. Its cult aspect is almost a kind of cross it's had to bear, rather than being accepted absolutely on its own terms.'

Paul Buck, a noted authority on *Performance*, and who had originally been commissioned to pen the novelisation for Sphere Books before Warners 'screwed me too', offers a further interpretation: 'To me, the most interesting three people behind the film are all women, strong, intelligent women – Dixon, Pallenberg and Faithfull. In different ways, supplying the ideas. At that time, even the likes of Germaine Greer were being used and playing games like everyone else – and so the fact that women had any say whatsoever was very rare – and not acknowledged.'

Film-maker Chris Rodley first saw the film with a friend and their respective girlfriends on its initial British release (he was at art school at the time). On leaving the cinema he 'knew life was never going to be the same again. It was supposed to be a nice date, going out and seeing Mick Jagger, and it turned kind of sour. The girls really didn't like it, the boys really liked it – and we didn't quite know why. We went to the pub afterwards and it was a strange kind of drink and it wasn't a very good evening. I think that's a very good recommendation – this is not a movie you go and see and then chat about.' For Rodley, 'It feels, looks and smells absolutely accurate – the only movie that captures that precise moment in time. You really feel, probably because of Donald's insider situation, you've been given a privileged glimpse into a very private world.'

Michael Moorcock reckons the film's ambience actually has more in common with the 1950s Soho scene, which Bacon, Freud, Daniel Farson et al. helped to mythologise: 'To some extent *Performance* is cultural imperialism – it struck people as bizarre and wonderful, which it wasn't if you were just fucking about in it. As far as I was concerned you'd heard so many wankers going on about assassins and hashish that by the time you started hearing it again on the big screen you weren't interested. The "counter culture" got swiftly colonised by middle-class repressed undergraduates from Australia,

Oxbridge and, especially, Sussex. Having lived in Notting Hill since the Fifties, I got a distinct sense of being colonised. And then colonised some more. And then some more. And then I buggered off.'

The area itself has since become an immense Trustafarian theme park, teeming with 'Portobelles', colonials, Westminster gofers and dot.com merchants dreaming of Hugh Grant and Julia Roberts. The average price of a Powis Square flat in 2001 ranges from about £200,000 to £300,000. A *Notting Hill* locations tour has since started up, steering sightseers past the Westway and around the Ladbroke Grove area – where crack cocaine dealers fight it out – to the safety of the Portobello Road. Some sightseers are bemused when the tour takes a left-turn into Powis Square, as the amiable guide attempts to explain the attractions of the location for one particular film. Most have no idea what he's talking about and are keen to move on to Hugh Grant's travel bookshop off the Portobello Road.

Jonathan Raban's 'elderly children' of the Portobello Road 'smirking complacently under broad-brimmed hats' may still be with us, but a sense of genuine community spirit in Notting Hill is gradually dissolving, prompting local counter-culture chronicler and one-man publishing legend Tom Vague – a lone wolf howling at the revisionists – to publish his series of 'London Psychogeographies', an invaluable source of detailed memories, anniversaries, and atmospheres.

In 1995, the events surrounding the post-production of *Wildside*, starring Christopher Walken, would spirit Donald back to the boardroom struggles of *Performance*. Production Company Nu Image – the people behind *Cyborg Cop II* and *Hard Justice* – were about to market his soft-porn parody as hard-faced porn. Under fire and paranoid, Donald started bringing his gun to executive meetings. Finally he removed his name from the credits after Nu Image re-edited the picture and sold it to a cable TV network. At the time of writing, a Director's Cut of the film has been re-released, patched up and broadened for DVD by Frank Mazzola.

For manic-depressive Donald, who'd taken to wearing a T-shirt inscribed with the legend 'Murder is a Work of Art', there was no division between life, art and death. As China Cammell said later, 'He believed in experiencing death. I think his great horror was to die by accident.' His brother David says, 'He'd obviously thought about it for a long time. It had been a recurring theme for him for years. But he was certainly not in a down mood at that point.' Donald's Nietzschean, code-of-the-Samurai philosophy, combined with an artist's eye for the stage-managed performance, had infused his every move since his Chelsea days. He would now carry it to its logical conclusion.

At around 9.45 p.m. on 24 April 1996, he shot himself in the forehead with a handgun. China, who'd been taking a call, dropped the phone and ran to his side to find him slumped on the floor, smiling serenely, almost ecstatically. According to China, he'd been studying the best place to aim the bullet in order to achieve a painless, even pleasurable death. Coolly, Donald asked her to hold up a mirror to his face as his life slipped away. For the next forty-five minutes he spoke lucidly and apparently without pain, asking his wife at one point, 'Can you see the picture of Borges now?' In a jarring sequence of cuts, life and film collided and were one.

TODAY DAVID CAMMELL resides in a basement flat in Chelsea, tending the flame of his brother's legacy. 'Basically my instinct is to try and keep the record accurate,' he says. 'There have always been fantasies floating around, and so where they are inaccurate I try to put them straight.' Dotted around his home hang poignant examples of his brother's brilliant illustrations, from the days before the fall. In his bathroom, a painting signed 'DC' shows two young lovers: the girl sitting on a branch, offering the young man an apple, as he peacefully scratches a love heart on to the trunk of the spreading tree.

WHAT WOULD JESUS SAY?

It's a three-hour train ride from London's King's Cross to Newcastle's 'craphole', but local-boy-made-bad Jack Carter is 3,000 light years from home, on a mission to extract the bloody truth about his brother's demise. A latter-day Jacobean tragedy of dark discovery, mixed loyalties and revenge, *Get Carter* blasts through auditoriums like a one-man killing machine, one of the very best British crime films ever made, affording Michael Caine his 'greatest ever role'.

'You know what I think about violence. For me it is profoundly moral, more moral than compromises and transactions.' Benito Mussolini

Dominating the Newcastle skyline stands Gateshead's central car park, rising out of the earth like a tilting house of cards. Perched on top is a series of glass-fronted blocks, which back in the 1960s were the basis for a proposed 'futuristic' restaurant and nightclub. The idea was that it would offer magnificent panoramic views of the city, except nobody took up the offer. The restaurant was abandoned before one bar of music was heard or a set of cutlery laid. One summer's afternoon in 2000 about seventy-five men and women climbed to the car park's summit to re-enact scenes from a thirty-year-old film. This was the first time in years that anyone had been allowed access to the site and everyone was understandably very excited. One local told reporters, 'The car park was very important to the film. It is part of the scenery of the area, and although it has seen better times, something could be done to restore it.' Later, as the crowd left the building, several devotees stuffed bits of concrete from the restaurant's floor into their pockets, as souvenirs of their day out. It seems odd that a car park, this most functional and drab of buildings, could elicit such passion in anybody. But this is no ordinary car park. It is the movie star among car parks. As such, it has become something of a temple in the canon of British cult films, a testament to the devotion of cult film followers worldwide. The car park awaits destruction. The film is *Get Carter*.

IN OCTOBER 1944 American army deserter Karl Hulten and his 'Americanised' accomplice Elizabeth Jones shot their way into the public's imagination, after murdering a taxi-driver in cold blood. It later emerged that, in carrying out her crime, Jones had consciously modelled herself after the classic Hollywood 'moll'. At this stage, the British still preferred America's gangsters – and American crime movies – to their own. The Americans themselves held a special place in their hearts for the more successful variety of hoodlum, a legacy perhaps of that deep-rooted frontier spirit. As George Orwell noted in 'Raffles and Miss Blandish', his 1944 essay comparing the two crime cultures, 'Books have been written about Al Capone that are hardly different in tone from the books written about Henry Ford.' Britain's breed of gangster was lower key, drove less expensive cars, dressed smartly, not flashily. Firearms were certainly a last resort, with only four armed robberies reported in 1954.

The policeman Jack Warner had played in Basil Dearden's 1949 film *The Blue Lamp* (the character was later revived for the long running BBC series *Dixon of Dock Green*) had then been the popular face of British policing – always the hero, occasionally the victim, but never the villain – a throwback to coppers on bicycles stopping to tell the time and cuffing young whippersnappers who answered back. From the late 1930s through to the late 1960s the most recurrent cinematic felonies committed in the name of British crime were jewel thefts, smuggling and counterfeiting, all very glamorous and more often than not perpetrated by raffish, Robin Hood-like characters – Basil Dearden's *The League of Gentlemen* (1960) – or bumbling Ealing wideboys. Crossing the class divide, more straight-forward robbery, usually involving some small degree of physical violence to a soundtrack of moody oboes and lead pipes, was played out in the pubs and back streets of working-class England. Among those few films that dared to buck the formula was the Boulting brothers' *Brighton Rock* (1947), energising Graham Greene's novel into a Benzedrine-paced, seaside shocker.

In terms of honest grit, British crime drama still had some growing up to do over the next couple of decades. If the Great Train Robbery of 1963 was initially perceived as a cheeky unloading of cash, Peter Yates's *Robbery* (1967), loosely based on the incident, would also undermine the real viciousness of the crime, sporting bright colours and entertaining high-speed chases – a precursor to the director's *Bullitt* of the following year. If several violent sequences from Ken Loach's *Poor Cow* (1967) briefly brought some stark reality into auditoriums, Peter Collinson's *The Italian Job* (1969) served as a last-ditch bid to prolong the Swinging Sixties and attendant cultural icons, entertaining the masses with likely lad antics and bullish barrack-room sing-alongs. As artist/sculptor/musician Nick Reynolds, son of Great Train Robbery mastermind Bruce, says, 'Because crime wasn't then looked upon as favourable, making it seem humorous was one way of getting around that. You'd get to the point where you'd get these fantastic characters but you knew, at the end, they'd always get caught by the police – who were even more spectacular in their own way.'

'British crime films had a completely romantic, charming idea of criminals,' says *Get Carter*'s director Mike Hodges. 'Our criminals were quite nice in comparison to the horrible American ones – "Move over, Guv, it's a fair cop" – and they didn't carry guns. The British also thought their police were wonderful. I remember having violent arguments with my parents, saying that the British police were just as corrupt as any other police force.'

By the end of the 1960s, however, the dirty laundry was there for everyone to see. The Kray/Richardson trials in 1969 prised open a can of worms from which the reality of gritty gangland violence and corrupt policing would finally emerge, culminating in early retirements for several high-ranking officers a few years later. Far from cheeky folk heroes, the East End's 'Merrie Men', they were now labelled sadistic killers. Careful admiration was replaced by a kind of voyeuristic fascination. As Nick Reynolds acknowledges, the

Krays' real appeal and power lies in their *'Image*. Image is everything. It burns on the back of the retina.' The 'Affluent Society' had now become the 'Violent Society', the seedy decay of *Performance* all too widespread. If the 1960s had practically airbrushed violence from the media, news images – from Vietnam to Northern Ireland – now demanded that cinema follow suit and toughen up; a relaxing of the 'morality code' all round. Crime shows on TV had already started pushing back the boundaries of acceptability and good taste with *Big Breadwinner Hogg* (1969), starring Peter Egan as a lone-wolf gangster, with a penchant for snappy suits and snapping ribs.

In July 1970 producer Michael Klinger was hired to oversee a number of films for MGM, which had begun to wind up operations at Borehamwood. Co-financed by EMI, these films were intended to placate the British film unions, who were reeling from the closure of the studio. Klinger's credentials were impressive, if eclectic. He had started out running nightclubs in London's Soho (finding and hiring the likes of Rolf Harris and Lance Percival) before entering the film business in the early 1960s. After making a number of soft porn movies, he went on to produce Roman Polanski's British-based classics *Repulsion* (1965) and *Cul-De-Sac* (1966).

Klinger was looking for a vehicle to capitalise on the immense interest generated by the recent Kray trials and bought the rights to the crime thriller *Jack's Return Home* by cult author Ted Lewis. He now chose Mike Hodges to bring the novel to the screen. Hodges was born in Bristol on 29 July 1932, and spent his early life in what he calls 'the chocolate-box environs of Salisbury and Bath, cities with soft centres'. After qualifying as a chartered accountant, his career was put on ice when he was conscripted into the Royal Navy. He'd next spent two years aboard mine-sweepers as part of the official protection squadron, patrolling mainly in the Arctic. Two years spent fishing waterlogged corpses out of the ocean can't be everybody's idea of a good time, but Hodges regarded it as his salvation. 'The great thing about it,' Hodges recalls today, 'was that it transformed my view of life. My blinkers were ripped away. It was a great example of the class structure in this country. Even then the officers were called "pigs". All of my views of British society were transformed by being with these people.'

On the way to the Arctic, Hodges regularly put in at such northern ports as Hull, Grimsby and North Shields, where he witnessed a side of life he'd scarcely believed existed. Here was the armpit of England, its poverty and depression all too apparent, especially to a boy from a relatively prosperous background. He visited Newcastle for the first time in 1957. As Hodges recalls, 'The hinterland area by the jetty where we were docked was referred to as the "Jungle". There was a black guy called "Blackadder" who ran all the vice in the area – for a black man to be doing that in those days was unbelievable. So the whole place had an air about it, and the people, of course, were extraordinary.'

After National Service, Hodges embarked on a television career. Within a few years he was producing, writing and directing for the flagship current affairs programme, *World in Action*. In 1969 he directed *Suspect*, his first TV drama, about the disappearance of a child amid a family break-up. His next TV film, *Rumour*, concerned a corrupt political journalist. As Hodges told an audience at the NFT in 1997, 'I had seen a certain element of truth which Britain was trying to keep hidden. It was as corrupt as every other country, it was as bleak as every other country – and it was worse, in a sense, because it pretended it was something else.'

Klinger had seen Hodges's TV dramas, had been impressed, and correctly assumed that Hodges might bring an appropriately *noir*ish tension and gritty homegrown social realism to the film version of Lewis's novel. Lewis had offered to transfer the book to screen, but Hodges wanted full control and wrote the screenplay for the project, now called *Get Carter*.

London gangster Jack Carter returns to his Northern hometown to avenge those responsible for his clean-living brother Frank's death. While there he uncovers a nest of sleaze and corruption, involving old arch-enemy Eric Paice, now working for local Newcastle crimelord, Cyril Kinnear. Kinnear's mob, in cahoots with Frank's prostitute mistress Margaret, has cast Frank's pathetic daughter Doreen in a porn film. Doreen, it is implied, may well be Carter's own daughter, following a fling with Frank's first wife. In order to undermine Cyril's authority and get Kinnear's mob off his back, local fruit machine entrepreneur Cliff Brumby, attempting to branch out and set up a restaurant in a local car park, arranges for Frank to see the film. Understandably, Frank goes nuts, confronts the 'film-makers', and is murdered by Eric Paice. Ignoring his London boss Gerald Fletcher's warnings – Fletcher has a business relationship with Kinnear, and doesn't want to lose his major porn supplier – Carter arrives in town, closely followed by Fletcher's hitmen Con and Peter, and another signet-ringed assassin, who'll ultimately kill him, although not before he has left behind a trail of bloody vengeance.

Hodges jettisoned some of the novel's back story, but much of Lewis's memorable dialogue was to remain intact. 'Having agreed to do it, I really wanted to make it as truthful as I possibly could, to the way crime was now being perceived in Britain,' says Hodges. 'I don't like violent films myself, so it wasn't that sort of attraction. But having made the decision to direct, I had to go to the absolute with it, determined to make it as real as possible.'

This included scouting out some suitably gritty locations. Lewis's original novel plonks Carter down in Doncaster, changing trains bound for the steel town of Scunthorpe. Hodges had wanted to find a 'really hard place', somewhere that would provide some justification for Carter's nature. As the director told the *Independent* in 1999, *Get Carter* is 'not just about the villain, it's about observing the social structures and the deprivation of the country from which this character comes. You see the hardness of the environment he was brought up in.' While location hunting in Northern towns, Hodges was appalled to discover that the cafés, pubs and dilapidated boarding houses he had been familiar with from the 1950s were gone, the 1960s planners having replaced them with a dour functional modernity. 'Now, I'm coming by car to look at North Shields, which meant I had to go through Newcastle to get to North Castle. And as soon as I saw Newcastle, I realised that's where I wanted to shoot the film. Visually, it was absolutely extraordinary.'

Dryerdale Hall, near Hamsterly, would serve for Cyril Kinnear's sprawling residence (although the entrance to the Hall and surrounding grounds were actually filmed at Hardwick Hall Park). The parallels with the film were striking. Dryerdale was the former dwelling of Newcastle fruit machine entrepreneur Vincent Landa. During the early 1960s Landa had built up a substantial business empire in the North of England in classic rags-to-riches fashion.

By the time he was thirty, his business interests were coining in a cool million a year. He'd specialised in importing one-armed bandit machines from the States and within four years had built up a network of over 500 Northern clubs that housed his machines. Landa also immersed himself in the community, organising charity appeals and club concerts to raise money for local hospitals. In 1964, after selling a sizeable stake in his fruit machine company, Landa entered the night club business. The golden boy of the North now underwent a transformation. According to press reports of the time, Landa had become a 'shadowy figure, invariably wearing dark glasses'. Two years later his 'Piccadilly' club – an unwelcome target of protection racketeers, said Landa – spontaneously combusted in suspicious circumstances.

In 1967 Landa's younger brother Michael and an accomplice were found guilty of the vicious gangland-style murder of a fellow gaming machine collector. They claimed they were the victims of a set-up, but both were sentenced to life imprisonment. Vincent Landa was never called to give evidence and, when summoned before magistrates in an unrelated case a month later, failed to appear. The rumours were that he had holed up in Europe. By 1969 three of Landa's former associates were on fraud charges related to the 'milking' of fruit machines, but Landa himself was still nowhere to be found.

On coming across the now vacant Dryerdale Hall, and hearing of the Landa connection, Hodges inquired whether or not it had been sold. When he found out it hadn't, Hodges and his 200-strong crew hired it for filming for four days to add an eerie touch of credibility. 'Much to Michael Klinger's chagrin, because it was about an hour's drive outside Newcastle, but I hung on and insisted that we used it, and I'm really glad because it was such a strange location – and a very unpleasant house. When we went there, Assheton Gorton [*Get Carter*'s art director] kept bringing me all these incredible things he'd found, including two children's drawing books. In the process of going through these books we found they were all filled with prayers. In particular, there were two pages in which an adult had written, "Cain and Abel, Cain and Abel, Cain and Abel" . . . It must have been written over twenty times in big letters and the implication, I would have thought, was to do with Landa's brother.'

Hodges next began the casting process. Michael Caine was offered the part of Carter. By this time, after having appeared in *Zulu* (1963), *The Ipcress File* (1965) and *Alfie* (1966), he had become one of the big stars of the 1960s. 'I was never told that he was going to be in it,' says Hodges. 'I suspect neither he nor his agent would give the go-ahead until he'd read the script. When I'd finished the script it was given to him and Klinger came in and said, "Caine would like to play it," and frankly, Carter was such a shit, I was astonished. I hadn't thought of a star.' With hindsight, Caine's casting as Jack Carter made perfect sense, a logical progression from the quietly insolent Harry Palmer with a licence to kill and the bitter-sweet Cockney chappie of *Alfie*.

'I researched [the role] very thoroughly,' Caine noted in *Get Carter*'s press book. 'I know a few gangsters and I talked to them about the sort of man he is. You find actors often know gangsters – maybe they have a lot in common, when you think about it. Jack Carter is based on someone I know – dress, attitude, frame of mind, talk – even the walk.' To Hodges's immense irritation, as soon as Caine agreed to star in the film, the studio then attempted to flesh out the picture with as many sexy names as possible. 'They started to try and get me to have all sorts of people in the film,' says Hodges, 'which I found completely ridiculous. Caine did jack the film up, away from reality in some ways, because you had a star and the star brings a lot of baggage with him. My next fight was to surround him with unknowns, to help ground the character in the film itself. And I had a real hard fight to get all these pretty well unknown actors at the time to play all the subsidiary roles.'

But Hodges, who'd muttered dark threats of resignation, had to compromise at least once. Britt Ekland, at that point a massive pull in British cinema, was enlisted for a small cameo as Anna Fletcher, Gerald Fletcher's wife. Billed as second lead, her scene would amount to a mere couple of minutes of screen time – perhaps the briefest co-starring appearance in cinema history. 'Her name came up,' says Hodges, 'and that was my card, that I would accept Britt for the role, to get all my other actors. She was very good in it, but it's a very small role.' As Caine recalled for William Hall's biography, *Raising Caine*, 'It's difficult to talk about Britt. She's a beautiful girl, and was very good in the movie. I didn't have many scenes with her. It was mainly love over the telephone. But I don't think she's terribly interested in a movie career. She wants to be in films to be famous and rich. She never took it seriously.' Ekland later remarked, 'I don't like tall blonde men and I don't like men who wear glasses. That picture was not the happiest of experiences for me.' (Ekland would go on to have a similarly miserable time baring all for Robin Hardy's *The Wicker Man* two years later.)

Playwright John Osborne was cast as Cyril Kinnear, the suave, smooth-talking kingpin of local crime. If cold sperm could talk, it would probably sound much like John Osborne in *Get Carter*. Lewis had originally envisaged Kinnear as 'very, very fat . . . the kind of man that fat men like to stand next to . . . no hair and a handlebar moustache that made his face look a foot long on each side'. As Caine recalled in his memoir *What's It All About?*, '[Osborne] seemed to be someone who didn't like many other people so I kept out of his way in case I was one of them. The only contact that I ever had with him was of his own volition. Every afternoon he would come into my dressing-room and borrow my newspaper and, in the evening, just before we'd finish work, he would drop by with his own glass for a shot of my vodka.' Osborne, whose acting credits were sporadic at best, said of Kinnear: 'He's a villain – and villains are always fun to play. He's a big-time provincial crook, a big fish in a small pond. Kinnear has pretensions too. He's the type of man who's been a warrant officer in the army and then wears a brigade of guards regimental tie in later years.'

Ian Hendry was cast as Kinnear's sleazy henchman Eric Paice. Appearing alongside Patrick Macnee as an Avenger in the series' first incarnation in 1961, Hendry would later establish a reputation for playing weaselly characters in film and TV. 'Ian had been a quite major film star in this country, some quite big feature films,' says Hodges. 'That had evaporated for him because of his alcoholism. I suggested that the night before we shot that we went to Michael's suite in the hotel in Newcastle and we'd just read through the scenes for the following day. It's not something I normally do, but it was my first feature film and I was nervous. So Ian turned up drunk and just started abusing Michael.' As Klinger recalled for Elaine Gallagher's and Ian MacDonald's *Candidly*

Caine, 'It became apparent that [Ian] really hated Michael because he was such a big success. It was a smouldering situation and I thought, "How am I going to handle this? We hadn't even begun shooting yet." Michael said to me, "Don't worry, he hates me and that's good, I'm going to make this work for the film." He really did, that edge between them comes over very well.'

Leeds-born Bryan Mosley, the nation's favourite cornershop owner, played local amusement arcade entrepreneur Cliff Brumby. He'd go on to star in *The Avengers*, *Doctor Who* (under a stage name 'Buddy Windrush') and, in his best-known role, as Alf Roberts in Granada TV's *Coronation Street*, a role he maintained until his death in 1999 from a heart attack. Glynn Edwards, forever associated with his subsequent role as Dave, the Winchester Club steward in *Minder*, had known Hodges since childhood, when they'd appeared together in amateur dramatic productions in Wiltshire, was cast as Albert Swift. Finally, many of Tyneside's hard-looking locals were rounded up to pepper the picture with authenticity.

The film begins in Gerald Fletcher's penthouse apartment in London. In defiance of his boss's warnings Carter decides to go to his hometown of Newcastle to attempt to divine the reason behind his brother Frank's untimely and suspicious death. While taking a train bound for the North, Carter is seen sharing a carriage with his own nemesis – a hired hitman, who's accompanying him up for the journey. But blink and you'll miss him. As Hodges told the NFT, 'I don't think anything should be stated obviously . . . I've always been obsessed by the detail in pictures. Y'know, Carter's reading *Farewell My Lovely*, which was basically saying, "You're going to die." The titles are going to run over you at the end of the film, and the killer is sitting there in the corner. If you see, the newspaper story he is reading is about the Mafia or something.'

Arriving at Newcastle's Central Station, Carter's first port of call is the Long Bar pub. Recalling Caine's performance, for Tom Dewe Mathews of the *Evening Standard* in 1999, Hodges noted, 'In the script, Carter was softer and sleazier than he was in the final film. But Michael gave him an edge – he really knew Carter and made him more ruthless. Remember when he's in that Newcastle bar and he asks for his drink – "In a thin glass"? Nobody forgets that moment. And you know why? In the script, Carter says, "Please."

But Michael left it out, and that little choice just makes Carter even more terrifying.'

Jack Carter's odyssey of rediscovery takes him through the sleazy environs of his old stomping grounds. And for Caine, the Newcastle upon Tyne of 1970 was an eye-opener, 'Charles Dickens meets Emily Brontë, written by Edgar Wallace,' the weather dark and foreboding. To the south of the Tyne lies Gateshead (in which many key scenes of the film were shot). Newcastle itself slopes into the Tyne, carrying with it 2000 years of recorded architectural history, a frontier of Roman England and perennial pioneer of industrial fortitude, regardless of its aesthetic shortcomings.

Brother Frank's house was found in the aptly named Frank Street, in Benwell. Frank's funeral procession makes its way from Benwell to a local crematorium, locally known as the 'Crem', situated off the busy West Road, about two miles out of town. 'Michael was on the location but stayed a little apart, wanting to be very quiet,' Hodges recalled for William Hall's biography. 'I told everyone to keep everything at a low key, and the atmosphere became quite taut. When he was ready we began rolling the cameras – and he cried of his own volition, real tears, he induced them himself. It's no easy thing to do, especially in front of other people. But Michael had this enormous intensity that can be switched on when he has to, and that was one time when we needed it.'

As the funeral cortège makes its dismal way from the busy West Road and into the crematorium, it passes a fleet of hearses heading for the exit – a symbolic indication of the future number of culls that will take place before the credits roll? Hodges claims not: 'I never really counted them. I just wanted to emphasise that the funeral before was considerably bigger and this was just a meagre miserable little one.'

Carter next meets his old foe Eric Paice at the Newcastle racecourse. Smelling a rat, he follows Paice to his boss, Cyril Kinnear. Of Osborne's performance in this scene, Hodges says, 'He was very clever because he did it very quietly. The sound man was going mad and saying, "Can you ask him if he could lift his voice," and I said, "No, under no circumstances, you've just got to get him." And if you look at the scenes with John, I go tighter and tighter, so that the sound man can actually get his boom in apart from anything else.'

Kinnear's not the only one who wants to get Carter. Local hood cum entrepreneur Cliff Brumby sends his messenger, 'Thorpey' (played by Bernard Hepton), to warn him off. The ensuing chase leads Carter to the dance floor of the Oxford Galleries nightclub. Caine recalled this particular shoot for William Hall's biography. 'A huge bouncer – he was from Glasgow and he had a scar down his face – said to me, "You'll be out of here by seven o'clock won't you?" So I said, "Why, what's happening at seven o'clock?" He said, "We open for the dance then." I said, "What's it like?" He said, "Vietnam!" and added, "The kids are between fourteen and eighteen, and they are the most vicious people I've ever met in my life. You know why it is, don't you? Because there's never any blood when anyone hits anybody on television. So what happens is that directly they start here I give them one straight in the face, so that for once in their life they know what it feels like to be on the other end of it – and it's not like John Wayne or Clint Eastwood."'

Shooting such scenes would make a lasting impact on one impressionable fifteen-year-old. 'Jimmy Nail, who I worked with much later on, said he'd been standing outside the Mecca when we were shooting,' recalls Hodges. 'He saw Caine walk up and walk in, and saw me go up and say, "Can you do that again?" He thought, "Fuck me, I can do that!"'

The appearance of a full-scale film crew in Newcastle created considerable interest among the locals, obviously flattered that their hometown had been chosen over Hollywood. But on at least one occasion the crew may have been in danger of outstaying their welcome. Hodges recalls, 'I wanted some wild lines from George Sewell [who plays villain Con McCarty] when a car door gets torn off. Something like, "Why don't you fuck off." We were going back in two cars from North Shields into Newcastle. The soundman gets out in the middle of what looked like a bombsite between North Shields and Newcastle, and George Sewell leans out of the car and says, "Why don't you fuck off." We did that about three or four times and the soundman gets in and we drive off. Now, during the course of this, lots of people had lifted their windows, they had no idea who we were, and suddenly there were these guys shouting abuse at each other in the middle of nowhere and they really looked terrified.'

Caine momentarily let his supercool exterior slip during the sequence in which Carter discovers his niece's appearance in a pornographic home movie. As Hodges recalled in *Raising Caine*, 'He had to come up the stairs, adjusting his cufflinks, walk into the bathroom, take the girl by the hair and duck her in the water again and again. We had the camera poised above them so she would be going up and down, in and out, with the camera zooming after her. It was a focus-puller's nightmare to follow them. Michael did that scene with such anger and passion that it was totally real. And at the end, the focus-puller had to say to him, "I'm sorry, Mike, I blew it. I think I lost the focus." Christ, I thought Mike was going to strangle him. I swear to God, he was living Jack Carter at that moment. It's the only time I've ever seen him blow his cool.'

For the penultimate sequence, in which Kinnear is arrested at Dryerdale Hall following a tip-off from Carter, Hodges employed a neat touch of ultra-realism. 'We got a lot of the extras who had been going to Vincent Landa's parties,' says Hodges. 'The shot at the end with all those faces suddenly came to me because I kept looking and thinking, "All these amazing people and I'm not using them." So I just did these tracking shots along their faces and involved them in that way.'

The film's dénouement pits Carter against arch-enemy Eric Paice, Carter having finally learned it was Eric who killed his brother Frank. Having filmed Caine pursuing Hendry along Dunston Staithes, Hodges shot the final harrowing sequence at Blackhall Beach, near Peterlee, then boasting the last working example of a coal removal chute. In the film this conveys Paice's body to its final resting-place in the sea. Ian Hendry's preparation for the scene was typically unconventional, as Hodges recalls. 'I'm down on the beach with Ian and Michael, and there were two policemen down there making sure that no one came into shot. I said, "Ian, I'm going to shoot the end part where you go up there, can you muddy up your suit?" He's standing there in this perfectly good suit, and he drops on his knees and rolls over in the disgusting coal sand. I suddenly look at the two policemen who've just freaked out, they've no idea what's going on – there's this guy rolling around on the deck, covering his suit in shit. They never said anything, but they pointedly thought we were all demented.'

One of the last tasks left was to score the picture. Michael Klinger suggested jazz pianist Roy Budd (nicknamed 'Sparky, the magic pianist') for the job. Budd's hypnotic score has latterly contributed to *Get Carter*'s cult appeal, its main theme later covered by the Human League for their best-selling *Dare* album. 'I'd seen him at Ronnie Scott's,' says Hodges, 'and so I knew his music, but I must confess he didn't cross my mind to do the score. [But] when they suggested him, I thought it was a terrific idea. I left out quite a bit of his music, I'm really a passionate believer in its careful use. What was interesting was that in Roy's "train" music, there was this wonderfully catchy theme. The more I listened to it, the more I wanted it extracted, put on to vibes, and put in certain places. It works so incredibly effectively.'

In September 1970, Klinger took the film to the States to drum up support. Hodges recalls, 'I was getting all these phone calls because he was just terribly excited. He was ringing up and saying Don Siegel, who was one of my heroes, had seen it and loved it – and was astonished at how quickly we'd shot it.' True to form, studio bigwigs at MGM demanded the initial section of the dialogue track be re-recorded to make it more palatable for American ears. The scene in question, in which Carter's boss Fletcher and his cronies discuss Northern sexual practices, now featured different accents and fewer British colloquialisms, with 'bare-assed naked' replacing Fletcher's 'bollock-naked'. As Hodges says, 'When I heard what the two actors they had hired to redo the lines had done, it was just dire – just excruciating – with all this brash laughter and the lines rewritten. I just went absolutely crazy. I told Michael, "I can't believe you've done that." And I've practically spent all my life since then making sure that the original voices were put back.' During the redubbing process, the negatives were lost and as a result the released video version was the inferior Stateside copy. Years later, when the British Film Institute re-released the film, Hodges insisted that the missing sections were reinstated after he'd discovered an untouched print in a cupboard (as all good things are).

When the film was about to be released in South Africa, the censors demanded that Britt Ekland's phone sex scene be completely excised, leaving only a fleeting appearance at the beginning of the film as her sole contribution to the picture. 'I think a lot of South

Africans thought she was playing the landlady,' laughs Hodges. But, with hindsight, he admits he got away with murder. As he later told the *Independent*, 'I'd written the script, cast it, found the locations, shot the film, edited it, put the music and sound effects on . . . all in 36 weeks. You wouldn't even get a phone call returned in 36 weeks these days, let alone make the film. That's how hot it was. And I thought it was going to be like that for the rest of my career. Was I wrong!'

Of Ted Lewis's own Carter sequels/prequels (*Jack Carter's Law*, *Jack Carter and The Mafia Pigeon*) Hodges states they were written after he made the film. 'At the end of Ted Lewis's book we are never quite sure whether Carter's died or not. But I insisted that he died. They tried to convince me otherwise, needless to say, but I'm afraid I refused. I was determined to have him die at the end. There was quite a bit of pressure on me to let him live because they would have loved a sequel. But I felt, because I went as far as I did with the violence, that he had to be disposed of as casually as he disposed of other people. That was the morality of the piece.' He had in fact come up with his own possible cinematic sequel concerning 'the genetics of violence', in which Anna Fletcher's and Carter's violent offspring finds himself in jail and questions the behaviour that landed him there. 'But Warner Brothers, who owned the rights, weren't interested.'

In Britain the film was released on 11 March 1971 to mostly bad reviews. 'What's that strange smell in my nostrils?' sniffed Felix Barker of the London *Evening News*. 'What is this garbage clinging round my ankles? It's a film called *Get Carter* . . . At any time this would be a revolting, bestial, horribly violent piece of cinema . . . Caine (who really should know better than to stoop to this sort of thing) is a horribly effective smiling killer.' George Melly wrote in the *Observer*: 'If *Love Story* is like a loaf of sliced bread, this is a bottle of neat gin swallowed before breakfast. It's intoxicating all right, but it will do you no good.'

'I think that people who were upset by *Get Carter* were upset by the fact that he is so cold and unremitting,' Hodges told *Cinema Rising* magazine in 1972. 'They were sociologists who don't like the idea that some people are irredeemable, there's no way you can touch them. I am personally terrified of meeting some guy I couldn't talk to, to stop him killing me or doing me over. I can run reasonably well, I could duck, I'm small and could weave in and out, but I couldn't win. I'd have to rely on convincing the guy that he shouldn't hit me. And I've met people you just wouldn't be able to do that to.'

One spectator was left particularly dumbstruck. Vincent Landa took his girlfriend to see the film on its release in Paris. As it progressed, he sensed an unnerving familiarity about the subject matter: dodgy fruit machines, dodgy clubs, dodgy geezers wielding shooters and knives. Then suddenly, the picture switched from the coal-spattered hues of Newcastle to Kinnear's house in the lush Durham countryside. Vincent felt a heavy cloud of déjà vu descend. Now, as Caine breezed around the building, Landa began to notice familiar shades of wallpaper and furniture, doors and staircases. 'That's my home!' he murmured to his girlfriend in disbelief. But he was in for a greater shock at the film's dénouement. As Kinnear was arrested and driven away by police, a succession of Landa's real-life associates began to fill the screen in a nightmarish procession . . .

'When you sit with an audience and see how they react, it's quite frightening,' Hodges told the NFT. 'I was terrified. I ran. And I made a comedy next, I tell you.' That comedy was *Pulp* (1972), again starring Michael Caine – a satirical comment on crowd manipulation and the glamorisation of violence.

The release of the film in America was delayed by MGM's re-dubbing. It was then rushed on to the drive-in circuit. 'The pace is relentless and picks up momentum like a freight train,' wrote the *LA Times*. The indomitable Pauline Kael, writing in the *New Yorker*, found 'nobody to root for but the smartly dressed sexual athlete and professional killer in this English gangland picture, which is so calculatedly cool and soulless and nastily erotic, that it seems to belong to a new genre of virtuoso viciousness.'

In 1973 MGM commissioned George Armitage to turn *Carter* into the blaxploitation flick *Hit Man*, relocating Jack Carter (now called Tyrone and played by Bernie Casey) to the urban ghettos of America ('He aims to please,' ran the tag line). 'It was like running the negative,' Hodges said later.

Carter's southern cell-mate, *Villain*, written by Dick Clement and

Ian La Frenais, was released five months later in August 1971. Richard Burton starred as the homosexual psychopath Vic Dakin in a film that drew heavily on the world of the Krays. British TV then took up the cudgels of ultra-realism. Thames TV's *The Sweeney*, which ran from 1974 to 1978, featured the Carter-like John Thaw as Regan, a bullshit-free flying squad officer, whose propensity for bending the rules makes Uri Geller look positively arthritic. As Regan informs one scumbag, 'When you murder one of us there are no rules at all.' His sidekick Dennis Waterman was named George Carter in another probable homage to the film.

The Sweeney, which must have caused more than a few sherries to tumble on Middle England's lap, spawned two spin-off films, the imaginatively titled *Sweeney!* (1977) and *Sweeney 2* (1978), commendable attempts to broaden the original premise. Stacey Keach's performance as the alcoholic ex-cop Jim Naboth in Michael Apted's superb, vastly underrated *The Squeeze* (1977) also owes much to *Carter* in terms of gritty onscreen realism, the film going further than most of its genre by completely eviscerating its anti-hero.

Perhaps the most ground-breaking Britcrime movie after *Get Carter* was 1981's *The Long Good Friday*, writer Barrie Keeffe's and director John MacKenzie's own take on the nation state. *Friday* remains one of the most prescient takes on Thatcherite economics at grass-roots level. For Bob Hoskins's Harold Shand – British bulldog in attitude and physiognomy – ideology takes second place to his need for profit, and the movie succeeds best in its depiction of embryonic gentrification – witness proto-Thatcherite Shand's Docklands eulogy from a champagne-swilling pleasure yacht. 'I hate Docklands,' says Keeffe. 'Maybe because I remember what a spunky and vibrant village it used to be before the men in striped suits and flash Porsches moved in. I wrote the film in a passion of outrage at what was happening. If it were a tribe of Brazilian Indians being kicked out of the jungle, the United Nations would be involved. When it's Cockneys being moved out of East London, it's a kind of Cockney genocide.' Ironically, rather than a rapacious gangster-turned-entrepreneur, it would take a government-appointed quango, the London Docklands Development Corporation, to act as midwife to this stillborn ghost town.

In 1980 Hodges brought out *Flash Gordon*. The original director Nic Roeg had bailed out of the movie a month into shooting after producer Dino de Laurentiis objected to his attempts to 'make Shakespeare out of a comic strip'. With a soundtrack by Queen at their best, *Flash* is a much-loved and deliberately cornball classic, about as far removed from *Carter* as one could possibly imagine. Hodges's other films include *A Prayer for the Dying* (1987) and *Morons from Outer Space* (1985), perhaps one film Hodges aficionados would love to forget. 'Die before you see this film,' one critic said. More recently, *Croupier* (1999), a casino-based *noir* film, starring Clive Owen, was hailed by many critics over here and across the Atlantic as a masterpiece, the director's finest film since *Get Carter*. Hodges, it seems, is entering something of a second renaissance.

Carter's recent cult resurrection undoubtedly owes much to the mid to late 1990s phenomenon of 'gangster chic', and the rise of those incestuous bedfellows Britpop and lad culture – the latter, an ironic (mostly middle-class) take on received notions of (mostly working-class) masculinity. The 'Lads' of the mid-1990s embraced Caine's classic blokey icon unquestionably, like wide-eyed, impressionable first years cosying up to an expelled sixth-former in the hope that some residual hardness might rub off. 'I knew it was on its way back when they turned it into a strip cartoon in *Loaded*,' says Hodges. The recent spate of British gangster flicks may be directly attributable to the film's cult afterlife: *Carter*'s welcome and successful re-release in 1999 serving to highlight the gulf between intelligent, nuanced film-making/acting and generally poor imitation.

'*Carter* tries to break the rules,' says Nick Reynolds. 'There's no glamour, it's so fucking bleak and stark – and the dialogue is great.' Along with *Withnail & I*, few British cult movies from the past thirty years can ever have been quite so mass (and mis-) quoted. To paraphrase the Good Book, whenever two or three are gathered together in one pub they shall perform the Brumby scene ('You're a big man, but you're in bad shape. With me, it's a full-time job. Now behave yourself'), while student union barstaff are no doubt still grimacing through interminable demands for cider and black 'in a thin glass'.

Roy Budd's soundtrack album, recorded with bassist Jeff Cline and drummer Chris Karan, and made for just £450, is now more popular than ever. Prior to release it was one of the most obscure records on the market, initially only available in Japan (it was reported that when a copy did surface in the UK it was sold at auction for £1,500). In 1998 it was re-released for UK buyers on the Castle Cinephile label, padded out with choice snatches of dialogue from the film. Such was the interest in the vinyl version that in some shops it was outselling the Manic Street Preachers' latest offering by ten to one. Following the tradition established by the re-release of classic 1960s soundtracks and cult TV theme tunes, such as Herbie Hancock's *Blow-Up* and the Cult Fiction franchise, *Carter*'s trance-like grooves found immediate favour among the clubbing community, neatly dove-tailing into the retro/house revival. Sadly, Budd didn't live to receive the plaudits from *Carter*'s re-release, dying of a brain haemorrhage in 1993 at the age of only forty-six.

At the turn of the century Gateshead Council, in a millennial clean sweep of anything resembling the grey and distant past, decided to demolish the central car park. More concerned with the city's joint bid to be European City of Culture in 2008, Gateshead's councillors now have little regard for a rotting car park's place in film history. 'In the 1960s my buildings such as Gateshead were applauded and given medals and commendations,' says architect Owen Luder. 'In the 1970s they were questioned; in the 80s they were doubted; in the 90s they were ridiculed; in 2001 they're in danger of being listed. If they take the car park down Gateshead is going to be like somebody who's lost their front tooth.'

Leading the battle to save the car park is Chris Riley, the amiable forty-two-year-old co-ordinator of the *Get Carter* Appreciation Society – a group of Newcastle residents wishing to highlight the film's cultural importance and relevance to Newcastle's heritage. 'Gateshead is not York, so it's no good councillors pretending other-wise,' says Riley. 'In our view the car park should not be demolished and we have written to the council to tell them so. It is a Sixties icon and, I believe, the first multi-storey car park built on Tyneside. Obviously it's an ugly building, but it has its own form of beauty. I think it is to Gateshead as the Eiffel Tower is to Paris, and it's the real focal point of *Get Carter*, a bit like the Monolith in *2001: A Space Odyssey*.' For Riley, *Carter*'s greatest strength isn't just that the film deliberately expands gangster culture beyond London's borders, but also that it 'doesn't try and portray both towns as having great beauty like York or Edinburgh. It puts certain sections of Newcastle and its people across exactly as they are. Down to earth, with not a great deal of money, but with lots of hospitality. Here in Newcastle, Mike Hodges is more of a hero than Michael Caine.'

In July 2000, Riley organised a two-hour-long tour of *Carter*'s Newcastle-based locations to launch the Appreciation Society. Like some celluloid pied piper, he led about seventy-five devotees of the picture, armed with cameras and filming equipment, around those *Carter* landmarks still clinging on to life. They visited the High Level Bridge (where Carter confronts Margaret), its sister Swing Bridge (the site of Carter's heroin deal) and Carter's lodging house at 25 Coburg Street. But, for the most, the literal highlight of the tour was a rare glimpse of the derelict restaurant teetering atop Gateshead's central car park. 'Everyone seemed to look forward to the car park and wanted to get to that spot,' says Riley. This was the first time *Carter* fans had been granted access to the upper floors of the building and the atmosphere was highly charged. As security unlocked a huge steel door to usher the faithful through its portals a few attendees attempted a re-enactment of the Carter/ Brumby scene (although no one actually went so far as to hurl 'Cliff Brumby' over the edge). 'I think the society will blossom,' says Riley. 'The press interest has been phenomenal, we've even been interviewed by a blind person's talking magazine. We hope to have an annual event and a regular publication and we hope, with the approval and help of the tourist board, it will increase tourism to Newcastle and Gateshead.'

And despite the demolition plans, certain quarters of the City's civic hierarchy, keen to regenerate tourism in the area, have latched on to the film's heritage to draw punters into town. Following *Carter*'s re-release in 1999, Local MP Fraser Kemp, a member of the All-Party Film Group, was enthusiastic about the possibilities of a *Carter* revival, similarly demanding an official locations tour. 'I am raising it with the Northumberland Tourist Board' he told *The Times*. '*Get Carter* had a dramatic impact on people like me when I was growing up in the North East and we should be encouraging people to visit the locations.'

However, wander into Newcastle's tourist information office in the Central Station today and mention *Get Carter* and you're likely to get a somewhat weary smile. They're used to troublemakers around here: keeping up with the trail of demolition *Carter* left in its wake is a full-time job. The staff are much happier handing out miniguides to the area, depicting pastoral city scenes bearing scant or no resemblance to the 'craphole' Carter once ploughed through. Opposite the train station, the Long Bar Public House, which in 1971 claimed to have the longest bar in the world, has long ceased serving pints in thin or any other kind of glasses, the entire premises having been gutted and transformed into one of a chain of Baker's Oven's. Today, staff are completely nonplussed by any cinematic connection, although they will happily point out that they have an exceptionally long cafeteria counter.

Frank Street, Benwell, has since been levelled and transformed into a modern housing estate. Benwell has the dubious distinction of being one of the country's most undesirable districts. Where house prices for the rest of the UK have rocketed, Benwell's have reached rock-bottom. A crime-ridden paradise for vandals, Benwell's estate agents have since had to resort to offering enticements to potential homeowners, such as two-for-one deals on houses worth little more than the average monthly wage, and the promise of household goods thrown in for good measure. For its part, the West Road remains unchanged after thirty years, a constant thoroughfare for the living and the dead.

IN THE YEAR 2000 a Hollywood remake of *Get Carter*, with Sylvester Stallone in the lead role and Michael Caine in a cameo as Cliff Brumby, was released in America. It flopped at the box office and fared no better with the critics. The *Washington Post* wrote: 'Stallone is so artificial, tanned and leathery you could replace his mouth with a zipper and sell him as a pocketbook.' The film has yet to receive a British release. Says Hodges: 'It's of very little interest to me I must be honest,' though he does find Caine's involvement 'sad. It seems to me such a completely different film. I gather Carter's married in it and it's a redemptive film now. He lives, of course . . .'

SUBWAY NUMBER ONE

**In this small quirky canon of British cult movies, *A Clockwork
Orange* is regarded, almost by default, as among the 'cultiest' –
certainly the one film we couldn't have afforded to omit from this
book: to do so would have been like writing the New Testament
without mentioning Christ. Aside from the fact that most Kubrick
films instantly became 'events' on their release, this is a film whose
British cult credentials have been largely based on the fact that
nobody was actually allowed to screen it in Britain for nearly three
decades. But what happens when a film, made infamous by absence,
is finally granted the oxygen of release?**

'I thought we'd made a comedy.'

Malcolm McDowell

On the evening of 4 April 1973 sixty-year-old David McManus, a
well-known local vagrant, tottered into the Swan Hotel, in Fenny
Stratford, Buckinghamshire. In a corner of the bar fifteen-year-old
ex-grammar schoolboy Richard Palmer – 'Dopey' to his mates –
huddled with friends discussing the sex and violence in a film he
was not yet legally entitled to see. Hassling the patrons for fags,
McManus reached the boys' table, where Palmer offered him a
cigarette.

After buying a take-away pasty and chips, McManus left the Swan
and shambled across to the nearby St Martin's church, a favourite
dossing-down venue, where he slumped in a porchway to eat his
last supper. From nowhere, a blow sent him reeling, his blood
splashing the walls and porch door. Frenziedly, Palmer attacked

114

him again and again with slabs of crazy paving and empty glass lemonade bottles until they broke. The battered tramp managed to crawl as far as a local garage forecourt, where Palmer finished him off with a stick. Before he left the murder scene, the teenager coolly emptied McManus's pockets of one and a half pence, which he threw away in disgust as he made his way home on a pushbike.

Palmer was picked up by police on a building site seventeen hours later, still wearing his blood-spattered clothes from the previous night, and showing no sign of remorse. In his statement the teenager mentioned Stanley Kubrick's latest hit, *A Clockwork Orange*, saying 'it was about the beating up of an old boy like this one'. During the trial, in July 1973, Prosecuting Counsel John Owen said, 'If this was robbery, it was all for one and a half pence. Or it may have been carried out for excitement, the attack being carried out as a result of the film. If so, the producers of that film have much to answer for.' Palmer's defence lawyer Roger Gray quickly drew parallels between *A Clockwork Orange* and the crime, despite the fact that Palmer hadn't actually seen the film. By this time, however, *A Clockwork Orange* had become the nation's favourite bogeyman. Such was the hype and vilification surrounding the release of Kubrick's movie in Britain that it was now being blamed for all society's ills. Gray referred to a recent police report in which it was stated that televisual and cinematic violence was acted out by the 'impressionable young'. 'The link between this crime and sensational literature, particularly *A Clockwork Orange*, is established beyond any reasonable doubt,' said Gray. 'What possible explanation can there be for this savagery other than this film?' Palmer pleaded guilty to murder and was detained for an indefinite period at Her Majesty's Pleasure.

A CLOCKWORK ORANGE's 'cult' history really begins to take off after its withdrawal from British screens. But *Clockwork*'s true genesis begins with the birth of its creator, the writer Anthony Burgess. Burgess had been born in dire poverty in a Manchester slum on 25 February 1917. In the first part of his autobiographical trilogy,

Little Wilson and Big God, he describes 'lying chuckling in my cot while my mother and sister lay dead on a bed in the same room', victims of Spanish flu. After graduating from Manchester University, he served in the armed forces until 1960, when he became a full-time writer.

In January 1960 Burgess was incorrectly diagnosed with a terminal brain tumour and told he had just twelve months to live. In a drugs-driven literary frenzy he wrote a brace of novels so that his family might gain from his publishing advances. Of all the novels Burgess was to write during those 'end days', *A Clockwork Orange* would – much to the writer's chagrin – attract the most attention for the rest of his life. 'It was the most painful thing I've ever written, that damn book,' he said later. 'After that, I had to learn to start loving again.'

Inspiration came from three violent sources. In 1944, while stationed in Gibraltar, Burgess received a letter from family friend Sonia Brownwell (later Sonia Orwell), informing him that his pregnant wife Lynne had been attacked. Late one night, while leaving the War Office in London, she had been set upon by four GI deserters who had beaten and robbed her and, reacting to the helpless woman's cries, kicked her into unconsciousness. As a result of the attack, she miscarried and was never able to have children. In the following months she sank into a deep depression and attempted suicide. To compound Burgess's misery, he was refused compassionate leave and his letters to Lynne, expressing his horror at what had happened, were censored. 'The work of deleting "fuck" with a razor blade must have been laborious,' he wrote.

In the early 1960s, Britain's youth, emancipated by the end of National Service, were regrouping into tribes with almost military precision. Burgess had observed one such battle in Hastings between Mods and Rockers 'knocking hell out of each other ... These young people seemed to love aggression for its own sake.' A trip to Leningrad in 1961 confirmed, for Burgess, that this sort of adolescent violence was not simply confined to capitalist nations, but a universal phenomenon, common to the second half of the twentieth century. In Leningrad Burgess had come across the 'Stilyagi', or 'Style Boys', young disaffected Russians who indulged in 'smashing faces and windows. The police, apparently obsessed with ideological and fiscal crimes, seemed powerless to keep them under. It struck me that it might be a good idea to create a kind of young hooligan who bestrode the Iron Curtain and spoke an argot compounded of the two most powerful political languages in the world – Anglo-American and Russian.'

The story would be set in 1970, in a violent post-war society coming apart at the seams. So as not to render the book hopelessly outdated, the noted linguist avoided using period teenage slang, figuring 'it might have a lavender smell by the time the manuscript got to the printers'. Instead, he invented his own slang, 'Nadsat', which meant 'teen' in Russian, a hybrid of English, Latin and Russian. Breasts were now 'Groodies', eyes 'Glazzies', head 'Gulliver', and good was 'Horrorshow', from the Russian *horosho*.

The title itself was appropriated from a Cockney phrase he'd overheard on the bus – 'As queer as a clockwork orange'. To Burgess, speaking through *Clockwork*'s liberal writer character Frank Alexander, the phrase suggested 'the attempt to impose upon man – a creature of growth and capable of sweetness – laws and conditions appropriate to a mechanical creation'. For Burgess, the ideal of free choice was paramount. 'Moral choice cannot exist without a moral polarity.' The concept of conditioning a human soul, however wayward, to the 'greater good' by using Pavlovian techniques – such as those then being proposed for criminals and homosexuals – was abhorrent, spiritually and ethically.

A Clockwork Orange was published in May 1962, and received almost universally poor reviews. 'English is being slowly killed off by her practitioners,' said *The Times Literary Supplement*. The book did miserable business in the UK, shifting just 3,872 copies, fewer than any other work Burgess had written up to that point. In an attempt to secure an American deal he agreed to jettison the final chapter that chronicled his anti-hero's burgeoning 'respectability'. Alex's demonic resurrection was left intact, and the book became a huge critical success in the States.

The poisoned orange now rolled towards celluloid, coming to rest at the feet of screenwriter Terry Southern in 1966. With his off-beat style, Southern was something of a maverick in the film industry, having built up a sizeable list of screen credits, including Kubrick's *Dr Strangelove* (1964). Having been 'turned on' to Burgess's book by Michael Cooper, the photographer of the *Sgt Pepper* album, and thinking it would make a great movie, Southern sent Kubrick a copy of the novel, along with a screenplay he had written with Cooper. Kubrick didn't even bother to read it. 'Nobody can understand that language,' he told Southern.

Southern continued to hawk the screenplay around the British film industry. Distributors London International Studios, representing Paramount, showed some interest in the project, but dropped it after seeking the reaction of the British Board of Film Censors and its secretary John Trevelyan to the script. 'An unrelieved diet of vicious violence and hooliganism by teenagers is not fit for other teenagers to see,' commented the Board. 'The visuals, however restrained, could not possibly get to even the "X" category unless we are willing to turn our existing standards upside down for the sake of this one film.'

With Paramount in retreat, and with more pressing film projects piling up, Southern handed the *Clockwork* project over to his lawyer Si Litvinoff and Litvinoff's business partner Max Raab. In 1967 Sandy Lieberson approached Litvinoff with a view to casting Jagger, a reported fan of the novel, as *Clockwork*'s teenage gang leader Alex, and his fellow Stones as Alex's fellow thugs, or 'Droogs', Dim, Georgie and Pete. The film would be shot almost entirely in London's Soho. Lieberson had already picked out a Chinese restaurant that might double for the Droogs' favourite hang-out, the Korova Milkbar, and Michael Cooper would direct. But although a new screenplay was commissioned from Burgess himself, the project was dropped when the Stones couldn't find time to make the picture, and Lieberson went on to cast Jagger in *Performance* instead.

Around the summer of 1969 Kubrick eventually got round to looking at Burgess's book again. This time, he read it in one sitting. And having finished it, he wanted in. 'It's the kind of book that you have to look hard to find a reason not to do,' he told *Rolling Stone* magazine at the time. Kubrick had seen Dennis Hopper's *Easy Rider*, which had grossed over $50m, and wanted a cut of the burgeoning New Wave pop culture market. His *2001: A Space Odyssey* (1968) for MGM had inadvertently attracted a youth cult following as tripping hippies turned up in great caravans for the closing Star

Gate sequence, and now he made a conscious effort to appeal to this important new audience.

Kubrick rang Terry Southern, who told him that he had passed the movie rights to Litvinoff. Kubrick asked him to find out Litvinoff's asking price, 'but don't tell him I'm interested.' According to Southern, however, his agent's wife learned of Kubrick's inquiry and informed Litvinoff, who charged Kubrick a then whopping $75,000 for the movie rights. A deal was struck with Warners, giving Kubrick 40 per cent of the profits and the final cut. In spite of the huge commercial success of Kubrick's last movie and the director's elevated status, Warners anticipated that a probable X certificate would limit the audience and set the budget at a modest $2 million. Costs would have to be kept low, which influenced Kubrick's choice of locations and actors – very few studio sets, and no international stars.

In 1970 Kubrick wrote his own screenplay from his US edition of the novel, significantly the version that excluded the final, more reflective chapter. He knew of the final chapter, but felt that to use it would skew the movie. Kubrick wanted Malcolm McDowell to play Alex. He'd seen the adolescent-looking twenty-seven-year-old in Lindsay Anderson's *If* . . . five times and, like Anderson, had been utterly besotted. In January 1970 Kubrick sent Malcolm a copy of the novel and arranged to meet him at Malcolm's house. As McDowell later recalled, Kubrick went to the toilet and got stuck there for twenty minutes. 'I heard this muffled banging, he was beginning to panic. Stanley is a brilliant man, but he is a peculiar fellow in many ways.' Having been given few clues about how to play Alex ('Ah, gee, Malcolm, I'm not RADA.'), McDowell conferred with his old 'headmaster' Lindsay Anderson, who advised him to keep in mind a pivotal scene from *If* . . ., in which Travis throws open the doors of the college gymnasium to receive his caning with the utmost insouciance, like an unrepentant fop flouncing towards the guillotine.

In the event, McDowell would play it for laughs. It was supposed to be a black comedy, wasn't it? Alex De Large was a bloody hoot, and playing him was 'like being on drugs'. As Malcolm told David Peet of the *Face* in 1990, 'I always felt the style of the film was high, it was real but not realistic. There was no blood and all that, so to me it was extremely funny. It was hard not to laugh and I went to play for the comedy. There's one scene in there I know which is purely my interpretation of Eric Morecambe.' And Kubrick thought Malcolm was a riot: this funny little man, tipping over bookshelves like some sort of unhinged painter and decorator. Ah, gee, it was all too much, and he'd ram his handkerchief into his mouth between snorts of laughter.

McDowell's supporting players were mostly stage actors well respected within the industry for their versatility – Warren Clarke, Steven Berkoff, Michael Bates and Patrick Magee. Former body-building champ Dave Prowse (the future muscle behind Darth Vader and the Green Cross Code Man) became Julian, Frank Alexander's bodyguard, while Phillip Stone (a stalwart of British comedies including a couple of *Carry On*s) was chosen to play Alex's father. He'd reappear in Kubrick's *Barry Lyndon* and, notably, *The Shining*, as O'Grady, the Overlook Hotel's deceased caretaker.

For locations, Kubrick pored through back copies of various architectural magazines, looking for unusual buildings that would fit his vision for the film. Because of the number of 'genuine' locations that were found just four sets had to be constructed in an empty warehouse in Borehamwood: the Korova Milk Bar, Frank Alexander's bathroom and entrance hall, and the prison reception hall.

If *A Clockwork Orange* looks bleak, chilly and grey throughout, this is no trick of the light. Filming took place over the autumn and winter of 1970/71. We first encounter Alex and his Droogs in the Korova Milk Bar, getting wired up for a night of 'Ultraviolence'. Kubrick's production designer John Barry had envisaged the Korova as a kind of debauched Dionysian cathouse decorated with life-size statues of full-breasted nudes. Obsessed with detail, Kubrick demanded that real milk should squirt from their fibreglass teats. Given the ferocity of the studio lighting the milk quickly went off and had to be replaced every hour.

The Droogs set off from the Korova Milk Bar for a night of violence. They soon come upon a drunken down-and-out whom they batter senseless. For this sequence the production crew bussed over to the Wandsworth Roundabout, South West London. Here Kubrick filmed in one of the underpasses – Subway Number One, Structure 17 (easily located by its inaugural plaque) – shooting with a wide-angled lens to give the impression that the walkway was both wider and longer than it was in reality. The only change that has occurred to these ghastly concrete subways since filming has been the addition of a new set of strip-lights, the sockets for the old ones having been plastered over.

After their attack on the tramp, Alex and his Droogs encounter a rival gang about to rape a woman in what appears to be a disused theatre. In reality, this was a derelict hotel called the Karsino on Tagg's Island in the Thames near Richmond, South-West London. The hotel has long gone, and there remains only a garden, along which are moored sixty houseboats. Having dealt with the gang in a gloriously operatic set-piece, the Droogs take to the road, driving fellow motorists into the bushes and, pulling up outside Frank Alexander's house, don face masks and force their way in. The location for this was the wonderfully named Skybreak in the Warren in Radlett, Hertfordshire, owned by Tony and Shirley Jaffe. Much to the annoyance of both cast and crew, Kubrick erected a marquee in the grounds for those not immediately connected with the sequence. Here they shivered while Kubrick made his headquarters in the comfortable and warm house. Braver souls would occasionally creep back to the house, but the director, unmoved, would always order them back.

McDowell's rendition of Gene Kelly's 'Singin' in the Rain' while crippling Alexander (Patrick Magee) and raping his wife was a happy accident. Kubrick had spent a week trying to figure out the scene, but it wasn't working. The invading Droogs looked like badly choreographed pantomime dames, he thought. On the third day of filming, Kubrick had an idea. Could Malcolm sing? Jokingly, McDowell began a soft-shoe shuffle and started singing the only song he knew all the lyrics to, 'the most euphoric song ever to come out of Hollywood'. Oh, my. They nearly died laughing. And Kubrick, dabbing his streaming eyes with a hankie, immediately snapped up the rights to 'Singin' in the Rain' for $10,000. When the director of *Singin' in the Rain*, Stanley Donen, heard that the song was in the film, he asked for a private screening. Kubrick paced nervously up and down outside the viewing-room waiting for Donen to emerge. The two Stanleys looked at each other. 'That was very mischievous,' said Donen. 'But very good.'

Returning to his parents' flat – the interiors were filmed in Bore-hamwood on the top floor of a tenement overlooking Elstree Studios – Alex tenderly removes his pet snake from his bedside drawer and settles back in bed to enjoy his favourite composer Ludwig 'Van' Beethoven's Ninth Symphony. 'The snake was a squeezer,' McDow-ell recalled for the *Daily Telegraph* in 2000. 'Basil the Boa. Stanley said, "Action." I got off the bed, opened the [drawer] and the snake had disappeared. The whole room cleared so fast. They had to get the handler to come out and find it.'

The next morning Alex's probation officer, the lascivious P. R. Deltoid (Aubrey Morris), calls round and warns Alex to stay out of trouble. Ignoring his suggestion, Alex bunks off school and visits an emporium, where he picks up two teenage girls – they were ten-year-olds in the original novel – seducing them to the sound of a comically speeded-up William Tell overture. For the emporium sequence, Kubrick and crew took over the Chelsea Drug Store at 49 King's Road, SW3. A 1960s shopping legend, the Drug Store was held together by sheets and poles of shimmering aluminium. The December 1968 edition of the *Aluminium Courier* reported that nearly six and a half thousand square feet of brightly polished aluminium had been used in its construction. Alex is seen in the lower-ground-floor record kiosk inquiring about an order he's placed. Clearly visible in shot is the *2001* soundtrack album, not placed, but actually on sale there at the time. Today, the heady days of the Drug Store, immortalised in the Rolling Stones's classic 1969 track, 'You Can't Always Get What You Want', are long gone. The building is now a McDonald's.

For the following scenes, in which Alex neatly quashes a leader-ship rebellion by his fellow Droogs by hurling them in a marina beside a modernist housing estate, the director chose Thamesmead in South East London. Kubrick must have clapped his hands with glee when he first came across it: his proposed visual scheme had beautifully coincided with a British modern architectural revival. Vast tracts of London's pre-war streets and houses were being torn down to be replaced with experiments passing for homes. This was the result of a blueprint produced in 1970 by the Greater London Council to relocate families from ageing terraced streets. 'The chimera of an unobtainable balanced community,' trumpeted the

Architectural Review magazine. 'Thamesmead's most significant architectural contribution has probably been its linear housing which really does articulate the individual dwelling while still managing to keep it within a strong, unified framework.'

Thamesmead's name was chosen by readers of the London *Evening News*, but this was one of only a few concessions those 60,000 new home-owners would get. In reality, Thamesmead (current population 30,000) is little more than a glorified car park surrounding a vast man-made puddle. As such it continues to combine a kind of crazed modernity with an absence of any inherent humanity whatsoever. GLC architects and planners were bemused when occupants complained that there was nowhere for their kids to play, that their flats leaked and the smell of the nearby sewage works was, as one local put it, 'strong enough to peel paint at fifty paces'. When we visited the place to retrace the steps of Alex and his Droogs along the marina, we feared for our lives. The crime rate here is daunting, and the marina, filled with spent condoms and discarded beer cans, does little to raise the spirits. Painted signs quite unnecessarily forbid either swimming or fishing in its dank, dismal waters. In need of a friendly face we made our way through the lashing rain to the area's sole pub, Dexter's, boasting a cast-signed Albert Square street sign. Clearly far from home, when asked what our business was we told the barmaid we were currently engaged on a 'day tour of Thamesmead'. And with that remark, a regular missed her shot on the pool table and, staring up at us with amazement, uttered: 'You what?!' Which summed it all up really.

Having forcibly patched up their differences, Alex and the Droogs break into the house of a cat-loving health-farm owner, Miss Weathers. Alex murders her with a phallic sculpture and is hauled off for questioning by the cops. The police station was actually an old part of Brunel University, in Uxbridge, West London. Kubrick required McDowell to endure twenty-five takes of being spat in the face by Aubrey Morris before he was satisfied that the actor's phlegm had hit Malcolm squarely on the lips. To add insult, as McDowell told the *Telegraph*, 'Stanley shouted out to the crew, "Does anyone want to spit at Malcolm?" They all came over and took turns.'

Alex is sent down for murder. Aerial shots of the hexagonal prison where Alex is incarcerated were obtained from stock library footage, while the cell and prison yard scenes were shot at the Royal Artillery Barracks (since demolished) in Woolwich, South East London. In prison Alex learns about a controversial scientific treatment – the Ludovico Technique – that the new Minister of the Interior, who has been elected on a law and order platform, has initiated in order to restrain criminal impulses. Despite the prison chaplain's forebodings ('When a man cannot choose he ceases to be a man.'), Alex signs up for a course of brainwashing.

The exterior of Brunel University served as the Ludovico Research Centre, while the college's viewing theatre was used for one of the most iconographic sequences in modern cinema. McDowell is straitjacketed to an auditorium seat, has his unblinking eyelids clamped open and is forced to watch violent films while being fed 'Serum No. 114'. One unforeseen side effect of this will be his inability in future to enjoy Beethoven's Ninth Symphony, the 'Ode to Joy', which accompanies a film showing the horrors of the Third Reich. Kubrick employed a real optician to administer saline solution to McDowell's 'lidlocked' eyes during the shoot. 'I go home, the anaesthetic wears off and I feel that I've been cut open by razor blades,' McDowell recalled. 'I'm in so much pain I have to be given morphine. Both corneas were scratched. I see Stanley just before I go home and I've got a huge patch over one eye. He goes, "Oh my God. Can we shoot on the other eye?"'

Having had every violent impulse drained out of him (including his libido), Alex is publicly paraded to government officials and, for demonstration purposes, brutalised by the campest of stooges – a ten-take job, which was filmed in South Norwood Library. As McDowell told *Uncut* magazine in 2000, 'Stanley was going, "That doesn't look right! Stamp on him! And of course [the actor] put his boot through my chest. It didn't show up on an X-ray but a couple of days later I passed out, because I had a blood clot under the rib. I went straight in to see a specialist and he literally put a needle right through my ribcage to dissolve it.'

On Alex's release into society, a lonely walk brings him to a small underpass beneath the Albert Bridge on the Chelsea Embankment, where local vagrants led by the tramp at the movie's opening, exact their revenge. As in the film, the underpass provided a temporary home for vagrants and latterly featured an elongated graffiti slogan stretching the length of the tunnel: 'We live in a system, you say that it's just ... but there ain't no justice ... just us,' now been painted over. Hauled away from the scrum by his former Droogs, who have now become fascist policemen, Alex is dragged off to Joyden's Wood, near Bexley in Kent, to be half drowned in a trough. 'There was an oxygen tank with a mouthpiece, but to go down and find it in a trough of Bovril water was not easy,' McDowell told *Uncut*. 'It took many tries to find it and it's horribly claustrophobic to be under there, hearing muffled sounds and being whacked on the back with rubber truncheons. Stanley hated the shot because it was self-conscious, it took you out of the film to think: how did they do that? Did he really hold his breath that long?'

Seeking refuge, Alex is rescued by Frank Alexander, whose wife Alex previously raped, and who doesn't recognise the boy. The liberal writer plans to publicly embarrass the government by parading Alex as a victim, a hapless guinea pig of the new conservative regime. However, when Alexander learns of Alex's true identity (he overhears him crooning 'Singin' in the Rain' in the bath), he tortures him by locking him in his spare bedroom and blasting him with Beethoven's Ninth (actor Patrick Magee is wickedly framed to look exactly like Beethoven in one shot). Unable to bear it any longer, Alex leaps from the bedroom window in a suicide attempt. To achieve Alex's point of view as he plunges to the ground, Kubrick dropped, in all, six £1,000 cameras out of the window until at last one hit the ground full on.

Alex survives the fall. In hospital he is visited by the Minister of the Interior who has come under attack for his Ludovico treatment. Wishing to quell the public outcry in the midst of a new election, the Minister now condemns the technique, blaming the troubles with Alex on Frank Alexander. After being 'cured' of his non-violent impulses, Alex agrees to become a tool of the government, as it campaigns for re-election on a law and order ticket. To film Alex's final recuperation, an entire ward of Harlow Hospital was taken over. Dave Prowse recalled arriving on set at 11 a.m. while Kubrick was on take 37. He'd wrap on take 76. 'I got off lightly.' By March 1971 the film was in the can.

Kubrick personally supervised all aspects of the movie's post-production. For the soundtrack he hired Walter Carlos (now Wendy Carlos, following a sex change) to perform 'transformed' versions of the classics. He had come to prominence with his 1968 best-selling synthesiser album *Switched on Bach*. On first inspection, the director discovered a hairline shadow on part of the negative. Most directors would simply have told the lab to sort it out. Kubrick turned up in a twelve-seater Land Rover, dressed in anorak, faded trousers and army boots and personally transported the sixteen reels of precious negative to another lab. Such precautions required one of his editors to drive in front to absorb the impact in case there was a crash.

The premiere was held on 1 December 1971 at the Cinema One in New York. The screen was composed entirely of white cement, so Kubrick asked the manager to provide a black border for the screening. But in a mix-up caused by the title of the picture, the lines were painted in a vivid orange. The film was nominated for four Oscars – best picture, screenplay, director and editing – but won nothing. It did, however, win the New York Film Critics' Best Film Award, although there were many dissenters. 'I am tired of the cult of violence,' wrote Andrew Sarris in the *Village Voice*. 'I am tired of people smashing other people and things in the name of freedom of self-expression ... what we have here is simply a pretentious fake.' Beverly Walker, writing in *Woman & Film*, decried it as 'an intellectual's pornographic film', a view shared by Pauline Kael, who charged it with 'catering to the thugs in the audience'.

Kubrick had in fact attempted to do just the opposite. Through overtly stylising the violence, by turning it into a 'performance', the director hoped, as Burgess had done through the use of slang, to distance the viewer from its reality – to engage an aesthetic response. 'There has always been violence in art,' Kubrick told critic Michel Ciment in a later interview. 'There is violence in the Bible, violence in Homer, violence in Shakespeare, and many psychiatrists believe that it serves as a catharsis rather than a model.'

Believing an inherently violent impulse to be the cause of much great art, Kubrick had transformed Burgess's novel into a sumptuous theatrical production for the screen. Just as Burgess had structured his novel into three sections of seven chapters each (adding up to twenty-one, the age of maturity), so Kubrick had constructed his movie like a three-act play: the first segment was in the style of grand opera, the second was like a traditional stage play, with its smaller sets and stilted deliveries resembling 'first reading' sessions, and, finally, the third returned to opera.

Practically every frame of the picture contained theatre references. The Droogs' fight with the rival gang takes place in a dilapidated theatre and is staged like a ballet. The ground floor of Alex's estate looked like the backstage area of a theatre, classical wall hangings resembling stage scenery. Alex's bedroom mirror could have come straight out of a theatre dressing-room and, with his fake eyelash and bowler hat, Alex makes himself up like an actor. (During the same scene, Alex's mum knocks on his door like a stage hand alerting him to a curtain call.) After his successful rehabilitation, which takes place in an auditorium, Alex is even paraded before an audience on a real stage. He is introduced as though he were a stage hypnotist and ushered in to the strains of a Shakespearian madrigal. Carrying the conceit to its logical conclusion, the hospitalised Alex is presented with a post-performance bouquet at the end of the picture.

A Clockwork Orange opened in the UK on 13 January 1972 at London's Warner West End. At the time of its release, violent and sexually explicit films like *Soldier Blue* (1970) and *The Devils* (1971) were causing considerable controversy. Most notorious was Sam Peckinpah's *Straw Dogs* (1971), a grisly account of rural in-breeding, rape and revenge that successfully transferred the gory realism of the director's native America to the Wild West of England. One sequence depicted Susan George being raped by an ex-boyfriend – an assault which she appears, at times, to enjoy. The British Board of Film Censors to this day continues to deny it a video release until cuts to the rape scene have been made – which the film's distributors refuse to do. But because of its stylised and unrealistic nature, the BBFC passed *A Clockwork Orange* uncut and without hesitation.

The timing could not have been better – or worse: *Clockwork*'s dowdy ambience eerily echoed the depressed mood of the country. The 1960s Technicolor hues had faded, replaced with sunny oranges and shit browns. Britain's entry into the Common Market seemed to many to threaten the country's national identity; the Troubles had recently erupted in Northern Ireland; and the might of the unions had led to power cuts and a three-day week. In this land gone to seed the equivalent of Alex's Droogs might be found lurking around every street corner and in the marriage of two prominent youth fashions: Glam in which men dressed like transsexuals and chased women. And the Skinhead movement, which had begun in the late 1960s as a celebration of proletarian machismo and gradually became infected by extreme nationalist elements. If Alex's false eyelash looked like a nod to Glam, his uniform was out and out Skins. Former Skin Tony Parsons recalled for *Empire* magazine, 'It was all there . . . you could see the ghost of the Skins in the uniform of the Droogs – the thin braces, the white strides, the rakish use of hats, the combat boots as combined fashion accessory and blunt instrument. Someone had been paying attention. And we were flattered beyond belief.'

As Alexander Walker noted in his book *National Heroes*, 'For the first time in a Kubrick film the native accents and urban landscapes [were] recognisably British . . . sections of public opinion were "waiting for it", ready and indeed willing to be outraged . . . it was the rage of Caliban seeing his own face in the mirror.' Or, as *Clockwork*'s Alex says, 'It was old age having a go at youth.'

Two weeks after the film's British premiere, Labour MP Maurice Edelman wrote in the London *Evening News*, 'When *A Clockwork Orange* is generally released it will lead to a *Clockwork* cult which will magnify teenage violence.' Cecil Wilson of the *Daily Mail* was horrified: 'What on earth induced our censors to pass those startling scenes of rape and violence?'

Well, actually, they'd rather liked it – respected it even. BBFC censor Stephen Murphy told one local authority, 'Censorship of this film would undoubtedly be seen, publicly, as a censorship of ideas. The film is, in its stylised way, simply a vehicle for all kinds of speculation about the human spirit . . . we were satisfied by the end of the film that it could not be accused of exploitation: quite the contrary, it is a valuable contribution to the whole debate about violence.'

In an effort to assuage the anger of a sizeable group of MPs, Home

Secretary Reginald Maudling asked the BBFC to explain why it had not made any cuts. Thirty MPs then demanded a screening, but Kubrick and Warner Brothers refused to supply a print.

Warners hoped that if they waited long enough the furore would die down, but when they released the film in the provinces a year later, there was an even greater outcry. In April 1973 the Borough Councils of Accrington and Louth banned the film from their theatres.

Kubrick was exasperated: having taken great pains to undermine his movie's violent themes with 'Art', he'd somehow overlooked the appeal it held for less culturally-minded, non-theatre-goers. Real-life Droogies were, instead, about to hone in on one very attractive facet of the film: the uniformed gang mentality. On 7 May the *Daily Mail* reported that a '*Clockwork Orange* Gang' – dressed like Droogs – were wanted for the murder of a fifty-year-old firewood seller in the North of England. More such copycat crimes followed and defence lawyers began to cite the movie as the motivating influence for their clients' crimes. 'Does This Film Breed Killers?' asked the *News of the World*.

'I don't believe the general public didn't understand [the film],' Kubrick's daughter Anya reflected for *Sight and Sound*'s Nick James in 1999. 'But there was a concentrated group of journalists who spotted a way to spin a story. Instead of "Thug Beats Up Old Lady" it was "Clockwork Thug Beats Up Old Lady". Thug was going to beat up old lady anyway, and you're going to report it anyway, but now you get to call him a Clockwork Thug.' As Kubrick told Michel Ciment, 'The simplistic notion that films and TV can transform an otherwise innocent and good person into a criminal has strong overtones of the Salem witch trials. This notion is further encouraged by the criminals and their lawyers who hope for mitigation through this excuse.'

Meanwhile, Anthony Burgess, who had liked the film visually but had been disappointed with the ending, and was very disturbed by the reaction to the film, was having a very unhappy year. On 9 May he took out a lawsuit against Si Litvinoff and Warners (though not Kubrick) 'for conspiracy to defraud' him, claiming that Litvinoff's misrepresentation had led him to relinquish valuable rights to his novel. Uncertain whether he'd win the case or not (he did), Burgess agreed to go on *Clockwork*'s promotional tour alongside McDowell. The respected polyglot now took on the role of sacrificial lamb, paraded on one dismal talk show after another as 'the man who wrote *A Clockwork Orange*'. 'If a couple of nuns were raped in Berwick-on-Tweed I would always get a telephone call ... It was clear that I would never be awarded the OBE.'

On 4 July 1973, Mary Whitehouse of the National Viewers' and Listeners' Association called on the Home Secretary to ban the film, branding it as a chief contributor to British juvenile crime. The following October, Terence Collins murdered Fernande Brydon and made the now familiar claim that he had been inspired by Kubrick's movie. Meanwhile, Kubrick had begun to receive death threats. As his wife Christiane later told interviewer Paul Joyce for *The Last Movie*, a 1999 Channel Four documentary, 'We got so many threats that the police said we must do something ... he was both artistically hurt and also scared.'

In early 1974, Kubrick's patience finally snapped. Appalled at the way his meditation on social conditioning had been misrepresented, the director made a decisive cut of his own. At great expense to themselves, Warners – who had a good relationship with Kubrick – complied with his wishes to withdraw it indefinitely. As the film had already reached the end of its theatrical run, at first no one noticed.

Meanwhile *Clockwork* was having a growing influence on wider culture. Throughout that pre-video decade *A Clockwork Orange* – film and novel – had begun picking up serious admirers, particularly among the New Wave/Punk scene, attracted by its 'No Future' outlook, its stylish iconography, its anarchic tribalism (if that's not a contradiction in terms) and Alex's wicked anti-authoritarianism. The Sex Pistols' John Lydon claimed Alex as one of his on-stage role models, while Pistols drummer Paul Cook famously boasted of having read just two books in his life – John Pearson's *The Profession of Violence*, about the Krays, and Burgess's novel. Malcolm McLaren recalled for *Uncut*, 'During the course of managing the Sex Pistols, I did ask Stanley Kubrick to direct a movie about the band, but he told me he had already made that movie and it was called *A Clockwork Orange*.'

In 1979 the National Film Theatre sought to screen the film as part of a Kubrick retrospective and were refused a print: the ban became public. From this point onwards *A Clockwork Orange* entered the realms of cult exile. Prior to its British re-release in 2000, the forbidden fruit of British cinema had naturally proved rich pickings among the bootleg circuit. For many years, the only way British audiences were going to see this movie was via a ferry to France or on a fifth-generation, appropriately orange-hued VHS passed under the counter, or notably over a stall in Camden Market. By the mid-1980s Camden Market had become *the* bootleg centre of London ('*Straw Dogs*? Yeah, we've got one round the back.'). For years one such trader sold nothing but *Clockwork* pirates, alongside copies of Walter Carlos's soundtrack album. Despite many purges by the copyright police it always reappeared a few weeks later.

Groups Sparks and Heaven 17 would both take their names from bands billboarded in the Chelsea Drug Store, while fellow Brit band Campag Velocet carried the homage even further by writing their lyrics in Nadsat. In 1990 the RSC staged a production of the novel called *A Clockwork Orange 2004*, starring Phil Daniels as Alex, while dance-friendly Moloko christened themselves after a motif in the Korova Milk Bar, and Blur paid tribute to the movie in their video for the 1995 single 'The Universal'.

One of the biggest myths associated with the movie concerns the one-time flagship of independent fringe cinema, the Scala, in London's King's Cross. Contrary to popular belief, *A Clockwork Orange* didn't close the cinema down: it just helped it on its way. Throughout the 1980s the cinema (a real labour of love for owner Stephen Woolley and his staff) had attracted scores of cult devotees (among them Francis Bacon and Nic Roeg), undeterred by the freezing auditorium, dilapidated seating, bad ventilation and the intermittent rumblings of underground trains shaking the foundations. The Scala's speed- and booze-filled all-nighters have since become the stuff of legend for film buffs of a certain vintage, these authors included.

Towards the end of the decade, as Woolley became more involved with Palace Pictures and his own Company of Wolves Productions he had less and less to do with the running of the cinema. Audiences had begun to dwindle too in the face of the area's rising crime wave and burgeoning Ecstasy culture which offered alternatively intoxicating nights out. Competition with Channel Four, plus the video and satellite boom, forced the programmers into tracking down ever more obscure and rare films. One of the biggest attractions was Kubrick's forbidden film. As Woolley recalls, 'Someone had approached the Scala with a print of *A Clockwork Orange*, and it was shown a couple of times without any advertising. We'd just put it with a film that said "Plus support", and people would be pleasantly surprised. That happened a couple of times. Then they got a little bit pushy with the programme, and sort of put stupid clues on – like "A Fruit Clock" – they'd sort of give it away. One of the things that happened when word got out we were showing it was that we had people turn up dressed in the white sta-prest, the white shirts, the big boots, the bowler hats and the eye make-up. We had about thirty of them turn up once, with a little dog. They were National Front supporters. And at one point this horrible little bulldog ran across the screen and people started screaming because they thought it was a giant rat.'

But *Clockwork* was sneaked into the programme one too many times. On 9 April 1992, the picture was billed at a matinée showing as a 'surprise film' accompanying Lindsay Anderson's *If...* This time word leaked out. According to Woolley, 'There was some animosity between the Scala projectionist and the manager, something had happened. He walked from the cinema, got a job at Warners, and he told someone there that the Scala had shown it.'

As a result of the screening programme, manager Jane Giles was found guilty on 23 March 1993 of breaching copyright laws. In her defence she claimed she knew nothing of copyright control and hadn't thought about the implications when she was offered the print by a private collector. Giles was fined £1,000 and Warners refused the cinema permission to screen any of its productions. 'It was the nail in the coffin,' says Woolley. 'Palace had gone down by this stage, and we ended up owing people money. The people who owned the building had been yearly hiking up the rent and wanted to take control. I had just made *The Crying Game*, and I just felt so sick about the whole affair. We'd never been in debt, but now owed £10,000 – exactly the same amount of money I'd been given to start it off.'

An appeal for funds was launched during April 1993. Charity

oranges and 'Droog in the Dock' T-shirts were sold in the Scala's cafeteria, alongside public reminders of films which would never have made it to the major circuits had it not been for the Scala's diligent efforts. Sympathetic parties, like bookshops Forbidden Planet and Murder One, sponsored programme bills in those final days, while a charity *Orange* Ball was organised at the West End's Café de Paris, with cheques and messages of support coming from Scala stalwart John Waters. But to no avail. The unprecedented success of Palace's *The Crying Game* had come too late in the day to save it. Woolley paid the money and closed the cinema on 7 June 1993. Having retained its name, it has since become a venue for club nights. In an industry now dominated by impersonal multiplexes, the Scala Cinema is sorely missed.

Stanley Kubrick died from a heart attack in the early hours of Sunday, 7 March 1999, just days after taking delivery of the final print of *Eyes Wide Shut*. He was seventy. Following the director's death, one of the first questions to be raised was how soon it would be before *A Clockwork Orange* was re-released in the UK. Alexander Walker, for one, did his best to persuade Kubrick's family that *Clockwork*'s debt to cinematic history couldn't be denied, it had to be seen, and re-evaluated. Any pre-publicity would have to be very low-key, the Kubricks having come to an agreement with Warner Brothers that the film shouldn't, as Walker has it, 'rekindle the controversial embers'.

A Clockwork Orange finally reappeared in March 2000. It received a positive press, twenty-first-century critics lavishing the picture with belated praise. The BBFC made its position clear: 'Despite the notoriety, the Board does not consider that concerns expressed at the time of the film's original release, about its possible influence on young people, are a serious issue now. The Board is satisfied that the scenes of violence depicted in the film are acceptable under the Board's guidelines.' Seen today, the violence of *A Clockwork Orange* is considerably less in-yer-face than that of countless other films that have been made in the thirty years since its original release. Tabloid journalists were no doubt frustrated when repeat occurrences of copycat violence failed to materialise.

Once it had been reappropriated by market forces, any 'dark power' *Clockwork* may have accumulated over the years was largely

diluted. *The Exorcist*, another highly anticipated re-release, suffered much the same fate. Woolworth's, the epitome of high street
probity, welcomed *Clockwork*'s video and DVD release, including it
in their advertising campaign as Santa's perfect Christmas gift.
Thousands of once highly coveted pirate videos with jaundiced
photocopied sleeves must have been taped over or tossed away.
Fans who'd previously had to endure muffled bootlegs were dazzled
by the clarity of the digitally enhanced cinema prints, and the
powerful Dolby surround-sound. Newcomers probably left cinemas
wondering what all the fuss had been about. Where was that
infamous aura they'd heard so much about? Where was the 'evil'
that had reportedly inspired some to murder? It was notably absent.

Since the re-release the boil of controversy would appear to have
been lanced. 'Cured, alright'. 'I would say it's not a cult now,'
says Alexander Walker. 'It's bigger than a cult. It now has a more
historical status.' Jane Giles concurs: 'If you tell people they can't
see something, they'll want to know why. But if you're talking about
the film in those terms, you have to completely reassess it in terms
of other countries, like America and the rest of Europe, where the
film has never been unavailable. Is the film a cult in those countries?
Well, probably not. Is the film a cult in the UK now, when it's freely
available in the cinema and on video? Well, probably not.'

Now that *Clockwork*'s brief revival is over, the film must be seen
on its own terms. It remains a superbly shot movie. No one frames
a picture quite like Stanley: so absorbed in the aesthetic, he'd kept
a top-range Porsche in his garage, purely to marvel at its contours.
It is an effective political satire made stronger, cinematically, by the
exclusion of Burgess's final chapter, and McDowell's performance
remains as fresh as ever (while his Droogs' obviously advanced ages
just makes the whole thing more crazily perverse). It does run out
of puff toward the final reel. But, for Alexander Walker, at least,
the movie's strengths remain undiminished. 'Successive Home
Secretarys have got ever more like the one in *A Clockwork Orange*.
Willie Whitelaw even talked like him. And you can easily see
Michael Howard or Jack Straw applying the Ludovico technique,
can't you? Tough on crime, tough on the causes of crime – let's
apply the electrodes, put on the lidlocks!'

Stephen Woolley remembers 'queuing up in the snow round the

Warner West End, aged fourteen, with three of my taller friends from school so I could get in to see *A Clockwork Orange*. In those days, there was only one cinema at the Warner, and it was huge. We sat in the back row, and I actually recall being quite disappointed by the film. Its excesses of violence were simply that – excessive. It wasn't an enjoyable film for me. But there was something about the visuals, and about the original novel, about the dialogue – and also the portrayal of the bleakness, and the barrenness and the brutality of the sex, that was alien to most movies – and it drew me in. I don't think it was simply about the banning. From the moment it was released, *A Clockwork Orange* was a cult film.'

AT THE END of 2000 the release of a new Japanese film called *Battle Royale* caused a commotion throughout Japan. Described as a cross between *A Clockwork Orange* and *Lord of the Flies*, it depicts a teenage crime-wave of the near future, in which young school-uniformed offenders are sent to a jungle penal colony and ordered to kill each other off. This they proceed to do very effectively. The sole survivor is allowed to go home. The movie was blamed by the Japanese media and politicians for a series of copycat crimes. Within hours of the film's opening, a seventeen-year-old boy went on the rampage in Tokyo, lashing out at bystanders with a baseball bat and hospitalising a pensioner. As the *Guardian* reported in February 2001, 'it is not certain whether he had seen the film, but its critics pointed to the incident as proof that the general atmosphere in which violence is glorified leads to more violence'. Due for release in Britain in autumn 2001, the film was at the time of writing (spring 2001) to be submitted to the BBFC, which in the course of 2000 had refused a certificate only once. 'We have been told by the public that they do not think that the Board should prevent adults from seeing material they want to watch. They want to be able to make up their own minds.'

THE TRUE NATURE OF
SACRIFICE

**Set against the backdrop of the eponymous sacrificial structure,
which offers a new life for both hunter and the hunted, *The Wicker
Man* passes through a labyrinth of twists and turns to end with one
of the most dramatic and unexpected climaxes ever experienced in a
movie. As the flames of the majestic dénouement recede to ash, you
are offered a conundrum. Has anyone really lost or won?**

'The most remarkable and unique screenplay ever written. There will
never be another one like it.'
                                              Christopher Lee, actor

'No pictures are that important.'
                                              Michael Deeley, producer

Late one Friday in September 1993 a small party of holiday-makers,
having enjoyed a peaceful week in a remote part of Scotland, prepared an end-of-vacation barbecue. Their caravan site was situated
high on a secluded peninsula known as Burrow Head, some thirty
miles down the coast from Stranraer. Entertainment was limited
to a small social club in a village three miles away – its proximity to
the cliffs making it a perilous walk for those intoxicated by anything
heavier than Scotch mist. The holiday-makers looked for a suitable
position to light their fire. A towering wooden superstructure set
on a naturally raised dais, the last remaining relic of a film shot
there years before, made for a perfect windbreak. The party set up
their barbecue, and while the children helped their mothers unpack
the food from the ice-boxes, the men began to get the fire going.
From nowhere, a strong gust of wind whipped some embers from

the grill and hurled them at the structure. Tinder-like after twenty summers, it burst into flames, sending the families scattering for cover. A crowd watched from a safe distance as the campsite owner arrived with a tiny fire extinguisher, managing only to save the structure's right leg. The beefburgers and kebabs, needless to say, were ruined.

IF EVER THERE was a story to rival the complex plot of *The Wicker Man*, it is the tale of the troubled post-production and afterlife of the film. Like two other gothic blockbusters from 1973 – *The Exorcist* and *Don't Look Now* – *The Wicker Man* would mark a transition in cinema from gritty realism to fantasy – fantastic in the truest sense: a retreat, perhaps, from contemporary woes, or an indictment of the previous decade's occult dabblings. But while those two movies would go on to achieve worldwide critical acclaim and sales, director Robin Hardy's film, starring Christopher Lee, Edward Woodward and Britt Ekland, would be woefully mishandled and overlooked, only to be belatedly recognised as a brilliantly original, audacious début. Grudges, rampant paranoia, fractious egos, heartaches, heart attacks and bad timing have all contributed to the movie's martyrdom. And, like many cult films, *The Wicker Man* has been kept alive only by the eternal diligence of its fans. Although it's tempting to ascribe some sort of evil spell to its initial failure, the reality is far more banal.

So what went wrong? 'The film business – or what's left of it in England – likes to play safe,' the late playwright Anthony Shaffer, who wrote the film's screenplay, told the US film magazine *Cinefantastique* in 1977. 'Originals are difficult to get done, and I think it's the fault of those who sell the films and advertise them.'

Anthony Joshua Shaffer, born 15 May 1926 in Liverpool, had originally intended to embark on a legal career after graduating from Cambridge in 1950. Having practised as a solicitor between 1951 and 1955, he next worked for advertising giants Pearl & Dean before finding his niche penning scripts for TV documentaries and screenplays.

By the early 1970s, Shaffer's scriptwriting talents had brought him worldwide acclaim; notably with Hitchcock's *Frenzy*, and with the screen adaptation of his own play, *Sleuth*. Shaffer, who had collaborated with his twin brother Peter on a trio of gothic novels, was a horror nut and had become friendly with Hammer actor Christopher Lee. Born in 1922, Lee had appeared in numerous pictures, but was always felt to be too conspicuous as a lead, due to his 6ft 4 inch frame. Exploiting his size, Terence Fisher cast him as the monster in *The Curse of Frankenstein* (1957). Though no Karloff, his success brought him title roles in Hammer's *Dracula* (1958) and *The Mummy* (1959). Hammer would go on to become the watchword for British horror, winning the Queen's Award for Industry at the end of the 1960s. Peter Cushing and Christopher Lee rivalled Morecambe and Wise as the most popular double-act of the era. Following the Lord Chancellor's relaxing of censorship in 1967, such films helped to push back the boundaries of good taste, becoming increasingly gore-soaked and cleavage-heavy.

Hammer's example inspired others to stain the celluloid red: Amicus's series of portmanteau films were immensely popular, usually sticking to a template of four horror shorts of varying shock-value, plus a comedy thrown in for light relief throughout the 1960s and early 1970s. These included Freddie Francis's *Torture Garden* (1967), Roy Ward Baker's *Asylum* (1972) and Kevin Connor's *From Beyond the Grave* (1973), perhaps the most effective. A trio of comedy-horrors, starring Vincent Price – Robert Fuest's crazily effective *The Abominable Dr Phibes* (1971), its anaemic sequel *Dr Phibes Rises Again* (1972) and Douglas Hickox's wonderful *Theatre of Blood* (1973) – would follow similar formulas.

By the early 1970s Lee had become tired of running around cardboard sets, sporting oversized plastic fangs, and was looking for more intelligent vehicles (horror or otherwise) to get his teeth into. In 1971, Lee, along with Shaffer and Shaffer's acquaintance Peter Snell (an anglicised Canadian independent producer), bought the film rights to David Pinner's 1967 novel *The Ritual* for £15,000. The novel – a cross between Dennis Wheatley and Agatha Christie – told of the mysterious disappearance of a teenage girl in Cornwall, perhaps through ritual murder. But Shaffer cited serious flaws in the novel's construction. Although Pinner would claim that there were similarities between his novel and Shaffer's future screenplay (notably, an infamous seduction sequence), he would later request the removal of all reference to himself or his book from the credits of *The Wicker Man*.

However, Shaffer persevered with the theme. Later, while researching the subject of sacrifice, he came across a picture of the Druids' legendary wicker man, which inspired him to write a screenplay. Its story would owe much to J. G. Frazer's account in *The Golden Bough* of pre-Christian Celtic customs that had survived in some parts of Northern Europe into the nineteenth century. Such rites had involved animals being burnt alive within basket-work effigies of men, and Frazer believed that the animals were substitutes for humans who had once been sacrificed in this way. Many historians now believe these reports of human sacrifice to have been anti-Celtic propaganda, initiated many centuries earlier by the invading Romans.

Shaffer already had an idea about who might direct such a story. Robin Hardy had made documentaries for the Canadian National Film Board before moving to England, where he joined the BBC. In the early 1960s he formed a commercials agency with Shaffer called Hardy Shaffer Associates (HSA), and like his partner had a pronounced fascination for the esoteric.

Despite being a member of the consortium that purchased the Pinner novel, today Lee admits little knowledge of what Shaffer and Hardy were concocting. He recalls being rung by Tony Shaffer in 1971. 'He had an idea for a story, and he wanted to see how I looked and moved, to see if I had a sense of humour.' Hardy and Shaffer told the actor they'd decided to write a script 'but weren't prepared to say what it was about'. As soon as they'd finished it, and received the financial backing, they promised to send it to him, because they wanted him to star in it – not quite Lee's contention that the film was actually written specifically for him.

During the early part of 1972, Hardy and Shaffer retreated with their respective partners for a weekend away in the country. It was during this brief sojourn that the two thrashed out an idea that would eventually see life as *The Wicker Man*. 'We agreed it would be fun to do a film which didn't depend on a phoney series of rituals drawn from the post-medieval period,' Hardy recalls, 'but to go back to the roots of the whole thing, the old religion, which in effect had been suppressed by the church and re-appeared as a kind of witchcraft – and to make it accessible to twentieth-century filmgoers.'

Hardy and Shaffer also drew on an experience they'd had some years previously, while making commercials in Cornwall. Hardy recalls, 'One May Day we went to see the Padstow Mystery. A lot of what goes on in the film happens there. They keep it fairly secret, and they were pretty shy about it. We were decidedly not welcome. But we observed from a distance and there was a Hobbyhorse and a Teaser and things like that – and there it was in twentieth-century Devon. It was very unpleasant being a stranger there that day.'

The concept for *The Wicker Man* was unique – a film mining the rich undercurrent of pagan tradition in Britain from a modern perspective. Few mainstream screenwriters and directors had attempted an intelligent exploration of paganism in itself before (the subject being banned from British cinemas for many years in any case). Jacques Tourneur's scholarly 1957 classic, *Night of the Demon*, was one of the exceptions, along with Michael Reeves' 1968 *Witchfinder General*, the latter exploring the motivations behind Matthew Hopkins's witch purges. While Piers Haggard's genuinely creepy *Blood on Satan's Claw* (1970) presented a more literal account of demonic possession, high praise must be given to its sense of place and atmosphere, and powerful, if slightly ramshackle, evocation of seventeenth-century small-town paganism. As in *The Wicker Man*, the film's British location is imaginatively seen as a place where anything might happen in the broadest of daylight. Hardy told *Cinefantastique*, 'We wanted an island setting, to bring in microcosmic aspects; that there would be a character who would be the subject of an island's plot, with the endpoint a sacrifice. And there would be a lure to get him to come there.'

In Shaffer's story, a repressed, virginal lay-preaching policeman, Sergeant Neil Howie, is summoned to Summerisle to investigate the disappearance of a young girl, Rowan Morrison. There he encounters a pantheistic clan, led by the manipulative Lord Summerisle, who venerate ancient pagan gods and rituals. For an isolated island, surrounded by barren islets, Summerisle's abundance of fruit and vegetables seems curious – even miraculous – and is taken by the islanders as a blessing by the gods for the sacrifices they offer to them. Howie uncovers the scientific explanation for the harvests – methods initiated by Summerisle's free-thinking, agronomist grandfather. Too late the policeman discovers that Rowan Morrison was simply the bait and that it is he who is to be sacrificed – burned alive – in an immense wicker man to ensure a bountiful harvest.

The script may be read on a number of levels: not least about the conflict between two types of (superficially redundant) faith, the younger having its roots in the older, with Howie's hilltop sacrifice an ironic martyrdom echoing Christ's crucifixion. Much of the power of the film lies in the audience's identification with Howie: he is the outsider, a butt of jokes, and the community in the film knows what he does not – that he is doomed. Yet as Howie approaches ever closer to his martyrdom, his intolerant, unerring faith never wavers. A real stickler for tradition, this one. As Lee told *Cinefantastique*: 'The film is not an attack on contemporary religion but a comment on it, its strengths as well as its weaknesses, its fallibility. It can be puritanical and not always come out on top.' Ultimately, Howie, 'the perfect sacrifice' (a virgin, and a man who has come to the island of his own free will), will become the Wicker Man of the title – a once upright, brittle, though tangled knot of appropriated rituals and prejudices, rendered all too fallible before the cleansing flames of faith.

Throughout, Howie's religion is pitted against the islanders' older, pantheistic variation, highlighting Frazer's opinion that 'Christianity develops through incorporating pagan primitive myths, deities and rituals'. Here, too, Christianity is portrayed as having absorbed, among other things, the concept of parthenogenesis and reincarnation. For the island's schoolchildren, raised in a loving, nature-worshipping environment, the idea of reincarnation after bodily death makes perfect sense; resurrection simply does not. As Lord Summerisle tells the uncomprehending sergeant: '[God] had his chance and, in modern parlance, blew it.'

Hardy and Shaffer's vision would offer a hugely detailed catalogue of pagan rituals – from the ritual slaying and replacing of priest kings to nail-bound beetles (to bring back runaway slaves) and the carrying of dolls (to drive death and decay from villages). Other references included the seasonal shedding of stag antlers, the collecting of foreskins to induce rain, fire leaping and pregnant women stroking apple buds (to infuse themselves with growth).

In 1972, Christopher Lee rang Shaffer back, to see what was happening with the script. 'He said, "Well it's finished and it's called *The Wicker Man*," and I said, "Is it something about the sacrificial rights of the Druids?" I remember him saying "I hate you! You're the first person who's been able to make the connection!"'

Shaffer had another useful contact with which to get back in touch: Peter Snell. Snell was now the managing director of British Lion, having been rapidly promoted from Head of Production in 1972. The company was struggling to keep afloat. It was symptomatic of the times: by the early 1970s US investment in the UK film industry had dwindled from £100 million to £30 million. The most financially rewarding films now lay in versions of successful British TV dramas and sitcoms. Such 'End of the Pier' films came with ready-made audiences and existing sets and storylines, sure to convince wary backers of sound returns. *Dad's Army* (1971), *The Lovers* (1972), along with the numerous *Carry On*s and *Confessions Of . . .* movies, attempted to enliven an increasingly moribund industry.

In May 1972 young millionaire businessman John Bentley took control of British Lion and its studio arm, Shepperton, with the underlying intention of capitalising on the studio's sale. In order to allay the suspicions of the powerful screen unions that he was out to asset-strip the company, Bentley needed to get a film into production fast, and was pleased to accept Peter Snell's suggestion that British Lion should make *The Wicker Man*, modestly budgeted at £420,000. Snell had read Shaffer's script and liked it so much that he offered to become the film's producer.

Such was their faith in the project that Snell and Lee agreed to defer their salaries and pre-production began in summer 1972. Employed as an editor was Eric Boyd-Perkins. He had worked on many Hammer films and notably on *Fall Out*, the chaotic finale to Patrick McGoohan's series, *The Prisoner*. Robin and Eric struck up an immediate rapport, to the extent that Hardy invited the hugely experienced Boyd-Perkins to go location-spotting with him around south-west Scotland. As Boyd-Perkins was about to take charge of British Lion's new mobile editing bus, he was keen to see at first hand the sort of terrain Hardy was planning to film. The first location they spotted was Skye's mountainous region, known as the Storr, lying just off the A855, whose 'Old Man' obelisk juts vertically from the range.

As filming was scheduled to start in late autumn for a story that led up to May Day, Hardy used some aerial library stock footage shot in South Africa of rich and fertile orchards to make the deception believable. Snell, meanwhile, frantically divided his time between Scotland and Venice, overseeing production on British Lion's other venture, Nic Roeg's *Don't Look Now* (1973).

Edward Woodward was chosen to play Sergeant Howie. By this time, Woodward had become one of the industry's most prolific actors (more than 2,000 television appearances in his career to date). At the time of casting he was best known for his role as David Callan, the Secret Service dog's body-cum-assassin. Woodward, then forty-two, would carry his role as a middle-aged virgin with utter believability. 'I was looking for something that was entirely different,' Woodward told *Movie Collector*'s Trevor Willsmer in 1994. 'And the Shaffer brothers are probably the best writers in the world.'

Shaffer's future wife Diane Cilento would play the part of Miss Rose, the island's schoolmistress, while Lindsay Kemp (then David Bowie's mime-teacher) was selected to play the island's peculiar landlord, Alder MacGregor. Self-styled 'Queen of Horror' Ingrid Pitt was cast last as the island's nymphomaniac librarian. Pitt would retain her Eastern European accent throughout. As Hardy says, 'Ingrid was thought to be an important ingredient of a horror film as far as the distributors were concerned. Suffice to say she wasn't Scottish . . . but then neither was Britt.' Ekland's casting had been another decision imposed by the needs of the distributors. 'I felt she was fine providing she would agree to be revoiced,' says Hardy. 'She was a very pretty and believable Goddess for us. I thought she did a perfectly creditable job.'

The American Italian Paul Giovanni, a close friend of Shaffer's brother Peter, was hired to compose the film's distinctive score. A multi-talented performer, Giovanni had been introduced to Tony Shaffer after a production of *Twelfth Night*, for which he had performed an experimental folk-rock arrangement. Impressed, Shaffer commissioned him to produce the film's musical interludes.

Giovanni immersed himself in the roots of Celtic folk lyrics, ploughing through anthologies of antiquated verses and period music.

With casting and budget secured, filming began towards the end of autumn 1972. Loch Carron, the lake that Sgt Howie lands on prior to exploring Summerisle (in reality Plockton, 'the jewel of the Highlands') is bordered by some very out of place palm trees, although the village really does have some due to the above-average temperatures in a Gulf Stream cove, which gives life to many exotic plants. Hardy recruited some of the locals to throng the harbour for the policeman's arrival, the villagers adding an unnerving realism to the initial meeting. The red and blue rowing boat that ferries Howie to the mainland is, remarkably, still moored at Plockton, with its trademark evil eye intact.

With the commencement of filming in October, Newton Stewart, in the heart of Dumfries and Galloway, served as the production base for most of the shoot. From here, cast and crew embarked on a whistle-stop tour of some fifteen locations that included Kirkcudbright, where many of the Summerisle's shops and houses are situated in reality, the Logan Botanical Gardens, Culzean Castle on the West Coast, and finally the Stranraer coastline, where the closing sequence was shot.

Seven miles east of Newton Stewart, in the small village of Creetown, lay the Ellengowan Hotel that would provide interiors for the Green Man pub, Summerisle's local watering hole. 'Good God,' one of the locals remarked, as one day during filming Kemp strolled into the hotel bar in yellow kaftan and hooded Moroccan robe, 'Is that a man or a woman?' Exterior shots of the pub were filmed outside an estate agent's (Cally Estates) in a neighbouring village, Gatehouse of Fleet. 'The Landlord's Daughter,' the song Howie hears when he first enters the pub, was based on an eighteenth-century song which, as Giovanni told *Cinefantastique*, 'was a bit weirder . . . our song is a bit more incisive in its specific kind of filth'. The rear of the building was used for a scene in which Lord Summerisle offers a boy up to Willow MacGregor, the landlord's daughter, to be ritually initiated into manhood. Lord Summerisle reads from Walt Whitman's poem, 'Leaves of Grass', as the initiation takes place. 'I was handed the poem about ten minutes before we shot,' Lee recalls, 'because the light was fading. I had to memorise it very quickly.' Over Lee's soliloquy Paul Giovanni would take the lead vocal on the soundtrack's 'Gently Johnny' – a reworking of a traditional English folk-song, dealing with a Jingolo – or gigolo, in today's parlance.

Shooting proceeded throughout October and into November without a hitch, despite mysterious visits by the 'money men' in limousines, and the freezing weather. According to Hardy, 'There were days when we had to put ice cubes in the artists' mouths for long shots so they wouldn't breathe steam. We had electric heaters held up for close-ups at chest level so it would disperse the air.' The crew were continually called upon to fake springtime, dressing bare trees with artificial blossoms and pointing the cameras away from the snow-tipped mountains in the background. The scene in which Sergeant Howie arrives in a horse-drawn carriage at Lord Summerisle's residence was filmed in the grounds of Culzean Castle. To establish the springtime setting, members of the crew had to recycle their limited number of potted trees, using them in shot after shot, as the carriage made its way to the castle.

Britt Ekland's role as saucy barmaid Willow called for a raunchy, hip-grinding scene in which she attempts unsuccessfully to seduce the frigid Sergeant Howie into sexual submission. As Ekland was a few months' pregnant at the time and not too happy about baring her all, a body-double was required. A local twenty-four-year-old, Jane Jackson, had been helping her friend out in the Calley Hotel, a stone's throw away from the house they were using for the shoot. 'We were standing watching the filming,' she recalls, 'when Robin Hardy came over to me and said, "Has anyone ever told you that you look like Britt Ekland?" We were a similar height, with similar hair. They asked me to do some stand-ins but I had no idea what was to be involved. At first I thought I was there to dub her voice ... It was almost like an Ealing farce! It was unreal! And I was paid cash in hand. My daughter saw the film for the first time last year – she thought it was the most hysterical thing. The next day at her school it was all, "Your mum's a *stripper*!" All good fun.'

According to Jackson, Ekland 'had an attitude. She was very unpopular with the locals. It's a close-knit community and she didn't go down too well, she wouldn't mix at all.' According to the former proprietor of the Ellengowan Hotel, Jim Gordon, not only had she considered the part beneath her, but also she took to passing judgement on the town's illegitimacy level and the locals' love of booze. In an interview with the *Sunday Express* on 17 December 1972, Ekland named Newton Stewart 'the worst place in creation . . . the bleakest place I have ever seen'. To smooth feathers Snell issued a statement to the local newspaper, the *Galloway Gazette*: 'Any goosepimples which our Sassenach skins suffered during our stay with you were quickly smoothed away by the warmth of our personal relationships with you all. On behalf of the entire British Lion Film Company I would like to disassociate all of us from the comments made by Miss Ekland.'

On Saturday 23 December the *Galloway Gazette* printed an open letter to the star. Under the heading, 'You May Have Been Around A Bit But You Haven't Learned Much . . .', Ekland was castigated for comments she had made during the shoot. 'If you don't believe in marriage, how come you're so superior about unmarried girls who have children? You know the trouble, of course, Britt? You don't think at all. You don't think that in November it can be damned cold without the protection of a comfortable sable . . .' This last snipe, a reference to an incident witnessed by Ingrid Pitt: 'Britt used to fling her sable coat in the bushes before she was on. Once, she came off, and found the extras huddling under her coat. She went berserk, and I said, "You can't blame them – you slung it in the thistles!"'

Having been duped and led a merry dance by the islanders, Howie is finally rounded on and offered up for sacrifice to Nuada, the sun god. This finale was actually shot in the middle of the shooting schedule, on 25 October. Though blessed with a beautifully blue sky, cast and crew shivered in the late autumn chill. As Lee recalls, 'It was freezingly cold, the girls weren't having much fun either, even with Long Johns on, presumably. I had Long Johns on, and I was cold. And poor Edward Woodward, bare to the waist, being anointed and lifted up!' Pitt's cameo required her to spend a lot of the day on the clifftop, hanging around nattering with Ekland – and fending off Woodward's feet. 'He'd come up and stick his ice-cold plates under my frock and I'd say, "Do you mind?" He'd say, "My feet are falling off with the cold!" I'd say, "Don't worry, you'll burn in a minute – you'll be hot then."'

Woodward's sacrifice took place at Burrow Head, an imposing peninsula on the south-west coast, situated near St Ninian's Cave, a site of Christian pilgrimage since AD 397. A sixty-foot Wicker Man was erected on a hillock overlooking the sea, perilously close to the cliff edge. If Woodward fell, there was no guarantee that he wouldn't roll right over the cliff. 'I was lifted up by this giant and carried up those steps into the Wicker Man,' Woodward recalled. 'That was the most frightening thing I've ever done. I kept saying to him, "You drop me and you're dead." He said "No lad, I drop you, *yer dedd.*"'

As an imminent gale had been forecast, the order was given to shoot the scenes of Woodward inside the burning effigy as soon as possible lest the structure topple over in the ensuing storm. But Woodward hadn't yet learned his lines. 'I was 50 to 60 feet up, so the only thing they could do was to hang vast sheets on an opposite cliff, about 60 feet away ... It was the biggest crib card in the history of movies. They had to keep pulling it up as I was going through it and screaming, "The Lord's hand is upon you! God help you!" In the event, Woodward broke his little toe, only discovering this the next morning.

Filming was completed on 24 November. The budget was £30,000 over. Hardy returned to Shepperton to edit the picture in late February 1973. Given that every line of the 120-page script was shot, there was to be some serious pruning to bring the film in under two hours. Hardy now sat side by side with Eric Boyd-Perkins, meticulously poring over the virgin threads of film. As Boyd-Perkins recalls, 'Robin was really ebullient in his way. He obviously wanted to make the thing a success – so keen all the time – to excess. He must have had an amazing constitution.'

During editing, Hardy's stamina and willingness to burn the candle at both ends temporarily deserted him as he collapsed with a heart attack. Eric had to rush him to hospital. Nonetheless, he soon returned to the Moviola to finish supervising the cutting. It is important to note at this point that huge swathes of a sequence in which Christopher Lee confusingly informs Edward Woodward about the joy of apples were excised, on Hardy's instructions, to help the story flow midway through the film, as were several vignettes of the Summerisle locals as they prepared for the May Day celebrations.

After much heartache and trimming, a 99-minute cut was ready to go. All looked well. And then the ailing British Lion was taken over again in March 1973 by a banker named Vavasseur. Ousting Snell, the Dickensian-sounding partnership of Michael Deeley and Barry Spikings was put in charge. A former *Farmers' Weekly* journalist, the affable Spikings had got into the film business through his friend Deeley, who had started his career in 1952 as an editor, splicing the likes of *The Adventures of Robin Hood*. In 1969 he produced *The Italian Job* and in 1976 *The Man Who Fell To Earth*. He received an Academy Award for his 1978 production of *The Deerhunter*, and in 1982 produced *Blade Runner*. He was a formidable presence in the British film industry, with a reputation for toughness, and he got people into cinemas.

At about this time Peter Snell informed Christopher Lee that a print of *The Wicker Man* was ready to be viewed. Still high from his tenure as Lord Summerisle, the actor requested a private showing in a basement viewing theatre in West London's Broadwick House. As he had recently received some of his most damning notices with the release of *Dracula AD 1972* (aka *Dracula Chases the Mini-Girls*), he was hoping that this latest project would redeem his reputation. The screening only served to confirm his conviction that the film contained his most magnificent role – a sure-fire Oscar-winning triumph. He was already beaming as he settled into his seat alongside his wife and agent. The lights dimmed as the roar of a seaplane's accelerating propellers gave way to the traditional Celtic pipes. Ninety-nine minutes later Lee bounded up the stairs to the offices of British Lion to thank them personally for arranging the preview.

According to Lee, Deeley, now ensconced behind British Lion's managerial desk, asked him what he thought of the picture. 'It's an extraordinary movie,' Lee enthused. According to the actor, Deeley just looked at him and said, 'I think it's one of the ten worst films I've ever seen.' Lee was gobsmacked. 'Well,' he murmured, 'you're entitled to your opinion. But I think you're totally wrong.' Lee lurched out into the cold streets of Soho, completely flummoxed and convinced that there was 'quite obviously something going on'.

'The problem was, British Lion wasn't performing at the time,' Deeley recalls today. 'I understood about films. I understood that the reason films were made was to encourage people to walk through turnstiles and pay money. I'd made some films for the Americans and I had begun to know something about the business. England was still very short of producers because they believed that there were films that "ought to be made" because they were good, good in the literal sense, meaning virtuous. Now, you can't go spending vast amounts of money on a film unless you get an awful lot of people to see it. *The Wicker Man* was a very intriguing idea. It was also very difficult to place. In those days we had to pre-sell films, something we did very successfully later at EMI. This film had gone way over budget, made with no regard to the fact that British Lion were a piss-pot little company that didn't have any money. When we took it over it had probably £40,000 in the bank, if that, and a huge debt.'

Lee's recollection of Deeley telling him it was one of the ten worst films he'd ever seen is not how Deeley remembers it. 'I wouldn't have said that to him. Why would you say it? It would have been a very nasty thing to say. I might have said it in my cuffs – to somebody else. It was certainly one of the ten most *unsaleable* films I'd ever seen. And probably the worst film I'd seen from British Lion, because it was the *first* film I'd seen at British Lion (laughs). My alleged statement to Lee would never have occurred because it wouldn't make any sense at all. You're running a movie company, a difficult movie company at that, and the last thing you are going to do is blow up at someone who is in one of your films, whatever you think of it. What I also never made public at the time, because it wouldn't have been a nice thing to say either, was that I'd shown the picture in its rough cut to the circuits. The circuits said, "No fucking *way*! We will *not* play this picture" – and no one's ever discussed this with me before.'

The circuits Deeley referred to decide whether a film has a market value and will translate into bums on seats. They literally control the eventual fate of the finished product. Without their support a film is dead in the can. The makers of *The Wicker Man*, intoxicated by their scholarship and originality, had blissfully ignored the fact they would still have to sell the thing to the masses.

According to Peter Snell, 'Deeley and Spikings looked at [the first cut] and said, "Not only is it awful, but it's so long, and those moments when Christopher has his soliloquy, what's all that about?"' The scene in question called for Lee to whisk Woodward around his sub-tropical gardens to confuse the policeman's investigations. Originally, five pages of Shaffer's script had required Lee to go into immense detail when describing the various strains of fruit that were grown by the islanders. 'When I first read the script,' says Lee, 'I remember saying to my wife at the time, "My God, as an actor I really can't complain if on my very first appearance I have something like twelve pages of dialogue." Summerisle literally never stops talking. It was wonderful for me as an actor to have all these marvellous and witty things for me to say.'

But this lengthy scene, around five minutes of screen time, never even made it to the first cut. Hardy, with all the material at his disposal, decided to cut it back to the length it is to this day, rightly assuming that even the most die-hard viewer would have fled to the lobby for a revitalising cup of Kia-Ora. 'Chris lost huge chunks of waffle about apple trees and buds bursting,' says Ingrid Pitt, 'frustrating after learning all those lines, no doubt, but ultimately to the benefit of the audience, I'm sure.' As Deeley says, 'It was supposed to be a film – not a nature programme.'

At that year's Cannes film festival, visitors were bemused to see a huge replica of the Wicker Man towering over the seafront. Snell recalls, 'We took a Wicker Man structure to Cannes in May 1973 to try and sell off the foreign rights. We erected this bloody great Wicker Man. We got past all the Cannes bureaucracy and they let us put this thing up, 60 foot high ... They've never let that happen since. The single largest exhibit.' In the event, lack of interest back home meant that the print never turned up at Cannes. Hardy recalls the film was seen as 'wildly esoteric by British film standards. British Lion distribution hadn't the faintest idea what the film was about. Here was something which was actually more like the French Film Fantastique genre, which they were completely unused to and didn't know how to sell. They just hated it. Management said, "Our sales people don't know what to do with this thing. It's a disaster and we'd better get rid of it."'

Wishing to salvage something to sit alongside a main feature, Deeley sent the 99-minute version to the powerful American distributors for feedback. A copy also found its way to Horrormeister

Roger Corman at New World. According to legend, the veteran B-movie-maker felt the picture was overlong and made some suggestions on cuts and how best to pitch the film to the US market. Despite Corman's recorded claims to the contrary, Deeley says he had no such dealings with Corman. 'Why would I send a copy of the picture to Roger? He made the cheapest nastiest pictures there were. His may have been one of the companies we offered it to for screening, because it was certainly sent to America to get it released, get it sold there. It was sent everywhere.'

What is known for certain is that Deeley, with his experience as a former editor, and Boyd-Perkins cut the film to 84 minutes – the version currently available on video – without consulting the film-makers. Hardy further alleges that he and other members of the crew were locked out of the studio while the pair reassembled the picture. 'You can't lock anyone out of Shepperton,' grins Deeley, 'there's no gates. Mild-mannered Eric was there, practically having to fight them off.' Joking aside, he explains, 'The director has the absolute right to deliver his cut, and then he's got a review period and then another right to cut. If the studio don't like a film in terms of length or whatever, they can then take the film over. At that point they can hire another cutter, in this case probably me, and they wouldn't be invited to watch the cutting. You're going to invite a scriptwriter to an editing session?!'

Deeley's editing had filleted the film dramatically, all but disjointing the storyline. One whole day and night had been lost along with the entire mainland footage. Most cruelly, the 'Gently Johnny' sequence was jettisoned. The hastily re-edited film would now mystifyingly credit cast members who had been cut out of the finished picture.

Christopher Lee was first to voice his disapproval with the latest version of the film. 'I was horrified. It was butchered.' He immediately contacted Hardy, Shaffer and Snell. 'I went through a list. "What about the Fishmonger, the Baker and the Doctor's scenes? They've all gone. What about all that wonderful dialogue? The Greenhouse has gone, most of what we shot at Logan Botanical Gardens has gone, there's nothing about apples, it's all gone. Where is it? You should put it back, not just because of me, but because a lot of it is important to the story." "We'll have a look at the negative and out-takes to see what we can do," they said. And that was it for the next 25 years, never to be seen again.'

As Snell remarks of Deeley and Spikings, 'These two guys took over the company and moved straight on to *The Man Who Fell to Earth*. *The Wicker Man* was history to them.' By the end of December 1973 (and some would say, to his lasting credit) Deeley had negotiated a release. *The Wicker Man* crept out as the lower half of a double bill with *Don't Look Now*, a film that Deeley had no trouble in championing. '*Don't Look Now* was a wonderful piece of work,' says Deeley, 'and in those days you had to have a B-feature supporting feature – no matter what it was like. To get some revenue we stuck *The Wicker Man* out with that and they agreed to take it.' According to Lee, there had been no announcements, and no publicity (there was in fact a test screening, held at the Metropole Cinema in Victoria, in London). 'I did something I've never done before or since,' says Lee. 'I rang up all the critics I could think of and said, "Look, I'll pay for your seats if that's what it takes, but just please go and see this film as a favour to me."'

And so they did. The *Daily Telegraph*'s Patrick Gibbs thought it 'an interesting failure', the *Sunday Telegraph*'s Margaret Hinxman considered it something 'a little higher than the norm', while *Monthly Film Bulletin* described the film as an 'encouraging achievement for those who had begun to despair of the British Cinema'.

Claims that British Lion refused to promote the film stand at odds with the fact that a trailer, press book, posters and publicity shots were compiled for the release. Admittedly, the trailer is one of the worst in the history of motion pictures, giving away the surprise shock ending. On 21 January 1974 *The Wicker Man* was granted a stand-alone release at the Odeon Haymarket in London's West End and the following month it had a regional run. In Newton Stewart the locals weren't too impressed as they crowded into the cinema. Britt's body-double Jane Jackson recalls: 'When it first came out it was such a dreadful flop that everyone thought it would reflect badly on Gatehouse of Fleet.'

In early 1974, having turned down a $50,000 bid for the film from Roger Corman, British Lion found an American buyer in National General, which promptly went bankrupt. The American rights then passed to a tax-shelter company called Beachhead Properties and Warner Brothers distributed the film at several drive-ins.

In order to avert possible controversy (and presumably to try and ignite some much-needed publicity) Hardy and Lee arranged some very particular Stateside screenings. Lee recalls, 'We showed it in Jackson, Mississippi – now that's in the Bible Belt – and we also showed it to ministers from all different faiths. We asked, "Do you find this blasphemous?" They said, "No, not in the least, because the things you are saying, although they could be construed as blasphemy, are totally logical according to the kind of person you are. Also you don't say them offensively. We shall tell our congregations – go and see this film!"' After showings around San Diego and Atlanta in order to satisfy its tax shelter requirements, Warner pulled the plug on it as a tax loss. However, it did win first prize in the 1974 Festival of Fantastic Films in Paris.

In 1976 Abraxas Films, an independent US distribution company, bought a substantial share in the movie's distribution from Beachhead Properties. Having learned of the existence of a 99-minute print, Abraxas, along with Robin Hardy, tried to locate the missing out-takes and negatives, with Hardy allegedly 'writing God knows how many letters to Deeley and Spikings, none of which were answered'.

Eventually he was told that the missing footage had been destroyed. Christopher Lee recalls that 'Snell was taken to a road-work beside the studio where there were lots of film cans at the bottom of the hole. Someone said to him, "*The Wicker Man*'s down there."' 'Down there' was the M3, running alongside Shepperton Studios. While looking for roadfill, builders had emptied British Lion's vaults of positive trims. 'They were all chucked in,' Snell laments. 'I suspect the negative was, quite innocently, taken away with the positive trims and dumped.' Christopher Lee was outraged: 'Wouldn't you have climbed down and got them out?'

Editor Boyd-Perkins was shattered. 'I knew the vault-keeper, and I went down when I heard these stories about it being missing and he said, "It was a genuine mistake, I assure you, I was horrified when it happened."' Nugatory trims and spares were always collected about a year after films had been shot, but, somehow, during one van-loading session *The Wicker Man* negative had been wheeled away as well. 'It's unusual for the negative to have got mixed up with positive,' says Snell, 'but it seems to have happened. I do not believe for one minute that two guys would quite maliciously have said, "Oh, Christ, why don't we destroy the negative."'

In desperation, Hardy called Roger Corman, remembering that a 16mm preview print of the full version had been sent to his company for suggestions prior to release. Corman let Hardy take delivery of the print. The director cut portions of the print back into the picture, producing a composite version that ran to some 95 minutes. Hardy took the opportunity to excise the mainland footage from the new version, a portion of the film he'd never been happy with. (This version was later screened by the BBC for the Alex Cox-fronted 'Moviedrome'.)

Stateside, *The Wicker Man*'s renaissance was about to begin in earnest. The film collected a sizeable art-house audience and an enthusiastic reception – mainly on the West Coast – which directly inspired the influential *Cinefantastique* feature in 1977.

By the late 1970s, fingers were beginning to point. An interview that the composer Paul Giovanni gave the magazine led to Eric Boyd-Perkins being accused of deliberately cutting out scenes he deemed immoral in defiance of the film-maker's original intentions. 'I think the editor undermined it,' Giovanni commented. 'He seemed to keep losing things, saying that they hadn't been shot, but we knew that they damn well *had*. There were things in there that Boyd-Perkins *hated* – I mean, he used to get red in the face and say, that's *disgusting*!'

Today, Boyd-Perkins balks at the suggestion: 'I didn't object to any of it. They probably thought I was a bit like Sergeant Howie, but when you've been at sea for twelve years you don't have any feelings about those sort of things. All I can think is Giovanni must have repeated things he heard me say in the cutting-room, which were taken out of context. He didn't understand how one talks in a cutting-room. I mean, you say all sorts of things.' At any rate, the scene in which Ekland dances seductively nude survived the allegedly uptight editor's attentions. 'When we ran through those dailies, we had Britt dancing around with her bare boobs. While it was running I happened to look around and the projectionist was so taken with these scenes that he hadn't noticed the bottom spool had lost the friction and there was a huge pile of film on the floor.'

As Hardy says, 'They were incredibly different personalities. Paul was a most attractive, young cosmopolitan Italian American, and the whole film was absolutely up his street. The whole film wasn't absolutely up Eric's street. But Eric, being the good editor that he was, took the material and made it work. But I would have said of those people that they were absolutely not calculated to be in sympathy with each other.'

As Boyd-Perkins points out, his chief responsibility was in any case to Michael Deeley, under whose instructions he was recutting the film. 'As an editor you have to side with the producer who's employing you,' says Boyd-Perkins. 'You'd have to be in a very strong position to upset anybody deliberately. You have to go along to a certain extent. You can't say, "I think that's awful, I'm not going to do that," because in nine cases out of ten they'd say, "All right, we'll get someone who will."'

Whatever Paul Giovanni may have thought, at the time Boyd-Perkins was aware only of satisfaction with the work he had done. 'After running my version for Deeley, the next morning in the cutting-room was a crate of whisky and a note that said, "We need more editors that can do this type of thing". So Deeley was evidently very happy with what I was doing and so was Peter Snell.' Boyd-Perkins had not been consulted for the *Cinefantastique* feature, and had been advised to take legal action on its publication. He'd have to wait a further twenty-two years before presenting his own version of events. 'Eric is a fabulous man,' says Michael Deeley. 'I've always had great admiration for his ability. He wouldn't have had the authority, power or wish to get rid of anything.' Boyd-Perkins professes to actually liking the film, with just one or two minor caveats: 'There were a couple of scenes I didn't like ... one was a panning shot along a group of these callow youths with spotty faces ·[the 'Gently Johnny' sequence], but there is some of it left in there. I can remember my wife didn't like looking at Edward Woodward being burnt. The only real qualms I had at the time were about the animals.' But they too were spared the licking flames, lifted out by cherry picker.

Today, only Lee has any hope that the original negative might be salvaged and the film reconstructed in a form true to the original script: 'From the time Peter Snell, Robin Hardy and Tony Shaffer started to look for the negatives and out-takes in 1976, they have disappeared, and to this day have not been found. I have my own theories on this. Every studio keeps the negatives and trims of every film it makes, good, bad or indifferent. How do you destroy cans of film "by mistake"? That's in the realms of fantasy. Something very strange is going on here. I firmly believe those negatives do exist, either in cans bearing the label of another film or with no label at all. But somebody, I think, still knows where those cans are. If that person or persons know where it is, they should hand it over to us to re-cut, and we could really make a work of genius.'

Snell shrugs bemusedly at the notion: 'I guess they could have moved the negative out of Shepperton's vaults and put it in other cans ... Talk about the proverbial "needle in a haystack". But Christopher and Shaffer have held on to this story that it was a deliberate mistake.'

Looking back on *The Wicker Man* today, Barry Spikings, who now lives in Malibu, comments that it was 'a very well made, quirky movie that was going to be hellishly difficult to market. And whether that was a self-fulfilling prophecy I don't know, but that's the way it turned out. We'd bought movies that were not appropriate for the market, and we were all under a lot of pressure. People here in the US still talk about it. In the middle of a conversation they'll suddenly ask, "Were you involved with *The Wicker Man*?" And I say, "Well, I can't really take any credit ... but I was involved in some way!"'

The Wicker Man's notoriety continues to be felt. In 1991 the film was pulled off the air by the BBC, following allegations of ritualised sexual abuse. The Corporation's switchboard was jammed by over two hundred callers. The allegations were later discredited and the film was broadcast six months later.

Over the years, rumours concerning the re-release of the full 102-minute version have constantly excited the *Wicker* community. In 1998, one fan went some way to satisfy the demand that had built up for something – anything: Jonathan Benton-Hughes, the director of Trunk Records, announced that he had discovered a treasure-trove of previously unreleased soundtrack material after a painstaking two-year search. 'It was hell, a nightmare,' he told the *Daily Telegraph*. 'It was a case of non-stop detective work. Nobody knew anything about it all. Then we discovered these twelve reels of music and effects . . . Where exactly? About an hour's drive outside of London. I'd rather not say who owns the rights. That's a weird one. They're over in . . . in . . . another country. I don't mean to be cagey but there were a lot of people after this – I heard that one company hired a private detective – and I don't want to reveal too much.'

Jonathan's cloak-and-dagger act guaranteed a healthy response from both the media and *Wicker* fans for the soundtrack version that Trunk Records released, and its first pressing sold out in three weeks. But something was amiss. The record did not contain 'Gently Johnny', and the versions of the movie's most familiar tunes ('The Landlord's Daughter', 'Willow's Song') were the crudely cut ones on the 84-minute print. There was also the unwelcome inclusion of the various random sound effects that had accompanied the film. For the film's aficionados this wasn't to be the discovery they'd hoped and prayed for. Nonetheless, Benton-Hughes became a beacon of light for the family of *Wicker* fans and folklorists, including one 'Lord Summerisle'. 'Christopher Lee rang me and started singing a folk song down the phone,' recalled Jonathan after the album's release. 'The worst thing now, is that it's getting more mad. People are sending me bits of wood through the post from "the man" himself – you know, the charred remains.'

True *Wicker Man* aficionados are a warm, friendly and dedicated bunch. Dave Lally, an irrepressible Irish film buff, had been initially intrigued by the film while attending a rare screening of the 16mm 99-minute version that surfaced in the mid-1970s. Already caught up in the burgeoning *Prisoner* revival, Lally decided to start his own *Wicker Man* appreciation group. He soon began to receive mail from a small band of devotees and compiled a magazine of *Wicker*-related gossip and trivia called *Summerisle News*. Lally was possibly the first *Wicker* fan to visit the original locations in 1981. On discovering the Wicker Man itself, Dave collected several pieces of bark from the original superstructure, going on to obtain one of the last remaining 'bread props' from the bakery used in the film. He later spent the evening at the Ellengowan Hotel entertaining barflies with a copy of the film.

Although *The Wicker Man* Appreciation Society has long since folded, Lally, whose enthusiasm for Hardy's film remains unabated, still happily assists authors and researchers. 'The *Wicker Man* has a number of different elements of interest for me,' he says. 'First of all it is about a clash of religion, and we Irish find this fascinating for obvious reasons. And of course the ultimate aspect of the film is the fact that the master negative appears to have been lost, perhaps destroyed – it's certainly missing – while subsequent editions of the film keep coming out with added sections. All these things merge together to make it an unusual cult event.'

Another lifelong *Wicker Man* fan, Gail Ashurst, produces an irregularly published, beautifully designed and researched journal called *Nuada*, which is devoted to the film. Gail prefers to concentrate on the film's deeper thematic issues, which she feels that the controversy over the film's post-production has caused to be overlooked. For Gail, *The Wicker Man* 'casts its spell over the viewer, seducing us with its quirky charm. But it also utters truths, about religion, about the insidious nature of western institutions at large. The real horror of it is that it very nearly contradicts everything we've grown to believe in: the fairy tale, the happy-ever-after of the here and now, and the man in the sky. Yet it gives us something back in their place – the courage to face up to what we've probably known all along.'

ANTHONY SHAFFER AND his wife Diane Cilento settled in Queensland, Australia, running their own theatre, the Karnak Playhouse, until Shaffer's death in November 2001, aged 75. Peter Snell regained control of British Lion, and maintains a desk at Pinewood Studios. Director Robin Hardy continued to make documentaries, directing only one more feature film, the obscure *The Fantasist*, in 1986. He is planning a return to the Scottish Highlands to make a film called *The Riding of the Laddie*, but is tight-lipped about its theme. His main occupation these days is setting up multimedia theme parks around the world. The Lee–Hardy connection jumped a generation when in 1995 Christopher Lee starred in the film *A Feast at Mid-*

night, directed and co-written by Robin's son Justin. Lee continues to maintain that the film contains his greatest role and that 'if released today for the first time, would collect Oscars for best film, direction, photography . . . the most remarkable screenplay'.

Celebrated fans include Brian De Palma, Martin Scorsese and Francis Coppola. The *League of Gentlemen* comedy team has cited the movie as a chief influence ('you did it beautifully'), while websites jostle for cyberspace, connecting fans so obsessive they'll willingly pay small fortunes for fragments of the original Wicker Man superstructure. Edward Woodward says that 'practically four out of every five letters' he receives mention the movie.

As this book's second edition goes to press in 2002, there are plans for a Hollywood remake with a contemporary America setting, to be written and directed by Neil 'In the Company of Men' LaBute and star Nicolas Cage. Meanwhile on a windy outpost of south-west Scotland, the last few remaining fragments of the Wicker Man superstructure have nearly disappeared, as legions of the film's followers make their way up to the Burrow Head caravan site to pay homage and to take home their own little piece of cinema history.

'I don't suppose it shows a profitable position today, even for the little it cost,' says Peter Snell. 'None of us have ever seen a dime from *The Wicker Man*. We have a lot of kudos from the picture now, but that's all we've got out of it.'

Would Michael Deeley have financed the film today? 'No, I wouldn't and I wouldn't have done then. Unfortunately, it's not like wine, when you stick it in a bottle and wait ten years. This picture sort of exemplifies the conflict between financiers and creators of movies. Robin Hardy was a very skilled camera-user; he came from commercials, a very specific art, but by the time he came to this picture he'd gone a little bit beyond doing what the advertisers wanted. In the end there was some degree of conflict between what we thought *could* be sold and what he thought *should* be sold. "Could and should" are the big conflicts in the movie business. Hardy had not made any pictures at that point, and I don't think he knew as much as he should have known about how to release a picture. The fact is that the picture didn't do well on release.'

Deeley – *Blade Runner*'s producer, and a *South Park* fan – professes not to know what a 'cult standing' is. 'It's a thing that slightly worries me, this deification of movies. Film-making is simply an attempt by people to make some money, to have some fun, to make a living, to do whatever you want to call it, but films are not visitations from Heaven, they are not tablets on the Mount.' Referring to protestations from the *Wicker* followers, he says: 'They can all scream their heads off now, but they're very lucky, because it could have just gone into oblivion. You don't get two cracks at it. It was a complicated piece, a film ahead of its time, and it makes total sense to me that it could be interesting to audiences now – they are far more sophisticated. I'm glad its time has finally come.'

'JIMMY DID IT HERE'

Graffiti on the wall of Little East Street, 'Jimmy's Alley', Brighton

Quadrophenia **is an album, a film, a lifestyle: its sole currency is adolescent abandon mixed with nostalgia. Ostensibly the tale of a young Mod battling to preserve his identity within the narrow constraints of his chosen peer group, the movie serves as a wider allegory for the frustrations and struggles of youth in general. As Jimmy tells his friend, without a shred of irony, 'I don't want to be the same as everyone else. That's why I'm a Mod, see?' After skirmishes in London and Brighton, Jimmy is pitched into a whirlwind of discovery and disappointment, as the foundations that support his hopes and dreams begin to crumble.**

'You were under the impression, that when you were walking forward, you'd end up further onward, but things ain't quite that simple.'

From 'I've Had Enough', Pete Townshend

'I thought it was awful.'

Paul Weller

As dawn broke over the Brighton coastline on the morning of Monday 18 May 1964, the retreating tide revealed a secret. Lying on the shingle was the body of seventeen-year-old Mod, Barry Prior. A hundred feet up, an empty sleeping bag was the first clue something was amiss. Tent-mate Fred Butler, of Leyton, told the *Brighton Evening Argus*: 'I don't know what could have happened. There was no trouble or fighting. We came out here to get out of the way. Perhaps he got up in the night and went for a walk. No one saw anything and there were no screams.' Colin Goulden, recovering from the comedown to end all comedowns, recounted Barry's last stand. 'One of the boys said he was missing and we started looking for him. Someone looked over the cliff and saw him lying there. He shouted out but at first we thought he was mucking about, trying to get us all up.'

A huddle of Mods formed a protective circle around Barry's Lambretta SX175 as ambulances arrived. Police and emergency services worked side by side with Mods, making the half-mile trek to the foot of the Saltdean cliffs to collect the body. One Mod went to pieces at the sight of the bloodied parka, red running on green: 'It was horrible. He was lying there, wearing a green anorak and socks but no shoes. He was horribly bashed up.' As several Mods accompanied the police back into town to give statements, the rest of the party packed their tents and headed back to London.

Twenty-four hours earlier the story had been very different. Not since the Second World War had the townsfolk of Brighton witnessed such an invasion. By 1964 Mod, originally a dandyish, narcissistic movement that had grown out of the 1950s Modernist ethos, had emerged overground, infiltrated by coarser, loutish packs. As Nik Cohn wrote in his classic article on 1960s fashions, 'Today There Are No Gentlemen', this second wave 'had none of that generic Mod self-absorption . . . instead, they hung out in dance halls and got into fights and had sex, and they screamed into Carnaby Street, buying everything that was gaudy and cheap, while the original Mods looked on in disgust'.

On that Sunday, 17 May 1964, traffic had poured into Brighton at a peak of 2,000 vehicles an hour, with hordes of tourists filling the beaches and basking in temperatures of 70 degrees. The heat was rising. The tunes wafting from the Palace Pier's dodgems and amusement arcades told stories of Cadillacs, T-Birds, and sweaty sex under splintering boardwalks. The Rockers, ton-up boys in black studded leather, had become the unofficial guardians of this little piece of Americana and they didn't want it interfered with, especially by a load of pilled-up small faces. But this was May, traditionally the period for pagan festivals of rebirth, and Elvis was about to be dragged kicking and karate-chopping towards a custom-built, wing-mirrored Wicker Man of his own.

Three thousand Mods, astride Vespas and Lambrettas, swept on to the promenade. As trouble had been expected, 150 policemen (and one twelve-year-old horse called Kim) were waiting. But, more used to ferrying away the odd heart-attack victim on the bowling green or a boisterous young Tory relieving himself during the annual conference, they struggled to maintain order. Deckchair attendant and local poet Tony Mandeville stood by helplessly as a troop of Mods commandeered his stand and handed out chairs as ammunition to waiting footsoldiers. The action moved south, spilling under and around the Palace Pier, as holidaymakers ran screaming to the relative safety of the promenade. A thirteen-year-old boy broke ranks and was chased by a gang of 200 Rockers, the lucky lad escaping with just a leg injury.

As police broke up the lynch mob, several hundred Mods broke free from the cordon to attack a dozen Rockers, who had escaped a savage beating by scrambling down the terrace on to the beach. Passing cars were pelted with stones and traffic was brought to a standstill. A lone Rocker in the wrong place at the wrong time was dragged off his motorcycle as a crowd screamed, 'Down with the Rockers', and hurled rocks at arriving police vans and the adjacent ABC cinema. As Rockers admitted defeat and slunk back to the suburbs, a group of Mods christened Brighton 'NewModTown'. That evening the heavens ripped open, bathing the blistering streets with rain.

Fifteen months later, on a warm August night, the Who's Pete Townshend stepped out of the Brighton Florida rooms. The last dregs of the audience had finally left the ballroom. Gazing around at the serene vista before him, Pete was mesmerised by the sound of the sea stroking the pebbles. From behind him a speaker began to blare the sweet sounds of Tamla Motown, as he watched Mods board their scooters and rev off. He later recalled it had been the 'most perfect moment of my life'. And if *Quadrophenia* has any sort of dawning, it was here.

QUADROPHENIA IS YOUTH, fucked up, fragmented, and searching for an identity. Although most would class it as a film about Mods,

'Mod' is really just a backdrop for more universal themes. The original Who album was partly inspired by the story of Barry Prior's untimely demise, but ask a dozen people who really conceived *Quadrophenia* the movie and you're liable to get five dozen answers.

What is known for certain is that in the mid-1970s Townshend received a request from first-generation Mod, Alan Fletcher, a neophyte writer absorbed in Mod culture, to turn 1973's best-selling *Quadrophenia* album into a film. A follow-up to *Who's Next*, the album had initially been conceived as a mini-opera about the band members, with the working title 'Rock Is Dead – Long Live Rock'. Ultimately, like *Tommy*, it was to focus on a single character, who would embody both the Mod-era Who fan and respective members of the group. The title emerged from Pete's misunderstanding of the schizophrenic condition and the band's desire to make the record in Quadrophonic sound – a proposal that their record company would eventually reject, as it was a costly new process.

Amazingly, given the influential nature of the Mod movement during the early 1960s, no 'Mod' film as such had been produced up to this point. Their sworn enemies, the Rockers, had had their own lifestyle enshrined in Sidney J. Furie's excellent production *The Leather Boys* (1963), but no one seemed bold enough to do the same for the Mods. The film that came closest was Barney Platts-Mills's *Bronco Bullfrog* (1970). It covers much the same ground as *Quadrophenia*, but with a greater degree of realism. Set in London's East End in the late 1960s, it focuses on the activities of three petty teenage criminals. Like *Quadrophenia*, it only begins to breathe when the main character Del Quant (Del Walker) escapes with his underage girlfriend to the country. Although it is not strictly a 'Mod' film, its ambience echoes the grittiness of the photobook that accompanied the original *Quadrophenia* album. For on-street reality and attention to the colloquialisms of the time, *Bronco Bullfrog* is as close to pure Mod poetry as you're going to get and it's a crying shame that this masterpiece has only been seen by a handful of those in the know.

Ken Russell's *Tommy* (1975) had been enormously successful, and it was felt that *Quadrophenia* could translate just as easily into moving pictures. Pete Townshend had in fact originally planned the album as a soundtrack to an imaginary film, using narrative, photos and sound effects to imbue the record with a cinematic scope. In 1977, as part of the Who's renegotiated recording contract, their record company agreed to pay for a screenplay adaptation.

Like the vast majority of movies being made in Britain at the time, *Tommy* had been produced with an eye to the international market (hence the presence of Jack Nicholson and Tina Turner). The band, who had never been that happy with the finished picture, were now concerned that their next cinematic foray should remain as British as possible, with no concessions made to the overseas market. Furthermore, the finished film would carry a roster of mostly unknown performers and, at the director's insistence, eschew much of the album's soundtrack.

Townshend's original story concerned Jimmy, a young Mod, who battles against the status quo represented by his parents, his employers and, ultimately, his own peer group. Alienating himself from all structures that gave his life cohesion, he returns after a rebuff from the girl he fancies to Brighton, where he had his first true experience of freedom. But his Mod dreams are shattered when he discovers that his idol, Ace Face, is just a hotel bell-boy, and he begins to live life on his own terms. *Quadrophenia* the movie would throw Townshend's original prose poem into sharp relief and would be, as co-producer Roy Baird had it, 'England's first street film'.

At 8.30 p.m. on 9 November 1977 Pete Townshend was leafing through the TV guide. His eye was drawn to a feature about a documentary drama called *Dummy*, in which the director commented that he had wanted to 'expand the margins of your tolerance'. Directed and produced for ATV by thirty-year-old Franc Roddam, *Dummy* told the harrowing story of a young deaf girl, Sandra X, who had been forced into back-street prostitution after being rejected by an uncaring community. Ninety minutes later, a shocked Townshend reeled away from the television set. He was not alone. The whole country would be talking about it the next day and questions were raised in Parliament. Townshend had found the director for *Quadrophenia*, which was then in the early stages of pre-production. The Who's manager Bill Curbishley made a deal with Polydor's film wing, Polytel. Roddam was contracted on 16

June 1978 and was filming by 21 September. Less than two months later the film was in the can.

Having secured their man, Townshend and the rest of the group stepped back from the film and allowed Roddam complete directorial freedom. Though a beatnik at heart, Roddam was no stranger to Mod. He had grown up in the North of England, where the movement had thrived, and had witnessed the Mod scene first-hand.

Newspaper libraries were pillaged for Mod-related stories and photographs, while Charles Hamblett's and Jane Deverson's 1964 cult classic book, *Generation X* – a platform for teenage voices – was picked clean for moods and atmospheres. TV writer Dave Humphries wrote a script, and playwright Martin Stellman was drafted in to roughen up the dialogue. Alan Fletcher's seaside resort adventures would be woven directly into the film. 'That bit where Chalky and Dave bed down with the Rockers in Brighton was one of my contributions – it happened to a friend of mine in Skegness.' 'Irish Jack' Lyons, the Who's original and now legendary superfan, added his memories of Goldhawk Road Social Club, the group's early power base.

Roddam pulled these 'massive amounts of input and inspiration' together, and began the casting process, auditioning thousands of kids. At Townshend's request, the *Sun* ran an ad in July 1978, calling for young Jimmys to step forward. 'My mum saw the story and sent me a copy of the *Sun*,' a young Phil Daniels told the newspaper. A King's Cross caretaker's son, Daniels got into acting after collecting a friend's sister from the famous Anna Scher Acting School in Islington, North London. Scher had gained a reputation as someone who could identify talented youngsters from the streets and foster their acting potential by encouraging them to draw on their own, sometimes gritty, experiences.

'When I first saw Phil he'd been ill and he looked incredibly scrawny,' says Roddam. 'His tongue was coated yellow and he looked very sick.' While filming *Zulu Dawn* in South Africa, Daniels had pitched camp in a native village, as a protest against his indigenous co-stars' conditions – and gone down with something nasty. 'I was a bit anxious about it, and then I met Johnny Rotten [John Lydon] who really wanted to play Jimmy.' Roddam considered Johnny Rotten so seriously that he screen-tested him for the part. 'He'd even cut his hair,' says Roddam, 'but the insurance company wouldn't go with it.' According to Trevor Laird, who played the drug-dealing Ferdy, Daniels and Lydon didn't get on. 'There's history there. We all grew up in the same manor; Lydon would say on seeing Daniels: "Oh, there's that wanker who can't act and supports Chelsea." Daniels would retort: "Oh, there's that wanker who can't sing and supports Arsenal ..."' Following an improvisation, Daniels was reinstated as Roddam realised 'he was a brilliant actor'.

As Roddam acknowledged, Jimmy's character 'had to be an amalgam of youth, ambition and fear – something we all have. There were also parts of Townshend in there and, in fact, Daniels does look a bit like Townshend with that long nose. The shot we did in his bedroom, where we panned off the photograph of Pete on to Phil, was deliberate, and for a moment you see the similarity.' Unlike Townshend's original protagonist, Roddam's Jimmy isn't seeing a psychiatrist, although his parents in the film allude to a hereditary mental illness. 'I felt there was no point making a film about someone with extreme mental illness,' says Roddam. But someone who was average, mismanaging a trauma. The picture built up in the film is of a young Mod, suffering from an identity crisis.

For Alan Fletcher, 'the casting of Phil Daniels as Jimmy was inspired. Peer pressure drove the Mod machine and Daniels didn't look quite Mod, just missing it. This is the fulcrum of *Quadrophenia* and a basic analysis of someone trying to keep up with his peers and just failing. The ironic thing is, although Jimmy never quite looks like the actual Mods in the mid-60s, he eclipses most of the cast.'

The part of Steph, the film's *femme fatale*, called for an equally confident performer who could inject some femininity into this most laddish of films, but still retain a certain working-class spunkiness. Alan Fletcher, who dreamt up the character, originally conceived her as 'a cool Mod crop princess'. 'In the town I came from, every now and then, you'd get a very pretty little girl who everybody fancied,' says Roddam. 'Leslie Ash is like that – and very South London. So even though she didn't have much experience as an actress, she was the real McCoy. She'd left home at fifteen, got herself a flat, earned her own money, she was quite hard in some ways.'

Jimmy's mate Dave was played by Mark Wingett, at that time 'a sixteen-year-old Punk with tight trousers and a dog collar', says Roddam. 'He got a bit carried away when we were on location, turning up one day with a huge love bite on his neck that we had difficulty hiding. One of the assistants told him off rather harshly, and he got a bit upset. "Fuck it!" he said. "I'm leaving the movie. I can't stand the way people are talking to me."' Roddam had a unique peace offering. 'I'd become mates with Johnny Rotten, and he'd given me a present – Sid Vicious's shirt – which he'd puked on and drawn all over. I bribed Mark with it. I gave him Sid Vicious's shirt. "I want you to know how important you are to me," I said, and he went, "Oh, man!" and stayed.'

Gary Shail, who would play Spider, a key member of Jimmy's crowd, nearly didn't get the part. Roddam recalls, 'Shail came into the room and he was really coming full-on, saying, "I want to be in your film." I said, "Look, you're great, but I just don't think you've got the strength, you're a bit too young-looking." "Go on," he howled. "Attack me! Attack me! Kick me!" "For fuck's sake," I muttered, and took a big fucking kick at him. He did a backward somersault, and landed about ten feet away.' Shail was in.

No less charismatic was a twenty-seven-year-old schoolteacher turned model/actor/musician, Gordon Sumner, then on the verge of going stellar with pop Reggae band, the Police. Sting, as he was now known, initially charmed the director by drawing beatnik Roddam into a discussion about Hermann Hesse. 'I had originally cast Garry Cooper as Ace Face, but I hadn't been certain about him,' says Roddam. 'Then I met Sting.' The Police cadet told the *NME* in September 1979: 'It transpired that I was going to appear in a £2m movie and I'd never even been in a school play.'

Roddam wanted to test Sting's mettle during the casting process: 'I set these two big actors on him, telling them, "I want you to intimidate him." Then I said to Sting, "I want you not to be intimidated." And these two big lads, improvisational actors from Anna Scher's, really had a go at him, screaming at him. But he remained very, very cool, and started intimidating them back. I thought, "Great, now I've got my Ace Face." He was slightly older and he had that self-possession thing and it just worked. He also had a very different look and he stood out from everybody else.' He'd still have to shoulder the indignity of the rest of the cast chanting 'Gordon is a moron' at him – the titular refrain from the 1978 Jilted John Punk novelty hit.

Trevor Laird had attended Anna Scher's with Daniels. They were best mates, even forming a band, Renoir, together just before Punk took off. Laird played sax, while Spandau Ballet's Gary Kemp had taught Daniels to play guitar, in the days when Spandau were called the Cut and supported Renoir at gigs. Daniels had taken Laird along to the audition for support. While there, Townshend pulled Roddam aside and asked him who the black kid was, as he really reminded him of Winston, an old dealing friend of the Who's. Roddam then wrote in the part of Ferdy, the Mods' resident 'pharmacist', specially. 'I had slight problems with that role at first,' Laird recalls. 'I was a young kid, twenty years old, just beginning to tiptoe through the whole black identity thing. Stellman told me he'd really wanted to make my character Caribbean. In 1964 I probably would have had a West Indian accent, but at the time, being a Londoner, I wanted to be one of the lads.'

In order to imbue his actors with a proper understanding of their characters, Roddam and Who bassist John Entwistle introduced the cast to some original Mods, encouraging them to ape the life-style. They were soon rifling their dressing-up boxes and burning the candle at both ends. 'We took them to meet some old Mods in Fulham, who used to do a lot of speed,' says Roddam. For Mods, drugs were employed purely as tools for staying awake. Weekends were sacrosanct. *Ready Steady Go*'s familiar opening logo, 'The Weekend Starts Here', was the clarion call for most working-class youth to down tools and to start living for real. But they only had forty-eight hours.

'Dexys' extended the boundaries of the two-day break. Amphetamine derivatives, they were originally prescribed for slimmers, although their energising qualities had also been championed by the armed services. Soon they leaked out of the clinics and on to the dance floors. This wasn't mind expansion – it was time expansion. As stronger black-market products like Leapers and Bombers hit the streets and clubs, horror stories circulated about the horrific come-downs and advanced states of paranoia that would hospitalise many a confused Mod. 'I'll never forget,' laughs Trevor Laird, 'at one of these parties, in the house of an old Mod called

Mickey, Sting suddenly appeared at the top of the stairs, swimming. "I've got to get there, I've got to get there," he was murmuring. That broke the ice. What was he on? French Blues? I dunno.'

Roddam gave the cast motorbikes, 'letting them go out in the street, so they could learn to handle the scooters really well. I said, "Drive to work, drive around and get really good on the road; get really cool."' Jimmy's Lambretta is a Series Three Li-150 Standard, not exactly a class scooter among the scooter fraternity but more of a reliable workhorse – an average scooter for an average Mod. Today, Jimmy's scooter can be seen at various Mod rallies around the country. For Roddam, the Mods' mode of transport was an important facet in the development of working-class independence: 'Just before the First World War the working class got bicycles and it gave them a means of transportation. It made people nervous because it meant they could start meeting with each other and communicating. When you got to this period it was the first time the working class had spending power. The Mod movement not only represented an expression of violence and energy but also one of political mobility. "We've got a voice mate, you'd better fucking listen to us."'

For many of the London-based locations, Roddam steered the cast and crew around the Who's old stomping ground of Shepherd's Bush, West London. One harrowing scene, written by Alan Fletcher, in which Jimmy's old friend turned Rocker, Kevin Herriot (played by Ray Winstone), is attacked by a baying herd of Mods took place in Shepherd's Bush Market. Roddam let Winstone perform the motorbike stunt himself, no doubt driving the film's insurers into a frenzy. 'That was the first time I'd ever been on a bike,' says Winstone today. 'I was a bit apprehensive about it. It was a good bike an' all, a cross between an old BSA and a Triumph. I was about seventeen or eighteen and a bit foolish back then!'

Interiors for a house party scene in Kitchener Road were shot at Lea Studios in Wembley, an educational day's filming for the young Trevor Laird. 'A girl I grew up with called Linda was always shadowing me at the party, to suggest we might get off with each other. Just prior to the scene where everybody ends up in bed with each other, someone came up to me and said: "Here, take this bottle of champagne and go back to your dressing-room. You're not in the scene." Phil Davis and I sat there drinking it, while I wondered, "What the fuck's going on here?" I started probing, getting a bit lively with people, until John Peverall [associate producer] told me: "The way things are we can't have you in the scene. This movie's going to be released in South Africa and we can't have you as a black guy seen getting off with a white girl."'

While it was deemed acceptable to portray a black guy pushing drugs to young impressionable whites, the sight of Laird engaging in a bit of slap and tickle was not. 'Roddam found out about this later, got very upset, and fought for the scene's inclusion. In the end, he was overruled. You live and you learn.' Roddam recalls nearly coming to blows with Peverall during that day's shoot, though he cannot remember whether it was sparked by this particular incident. 'I was fighting these guys all day and every day, but that's the time it came to a punch-up level. If push came to shove, he would have won the fight, but he would have got fired.'

Roddam was determined to preserve some soon to be condemned British working-class establishments on camera. That's why you'll see one of the last examples of a public baths on film, shot in Porchester, West London, a pie and mash shop in Dalston, a traditional barbers' shop in Islington, a chemist's in King Street, Hammersmith. Alfredo's Café in the Essex Road, Islington, replete with original advertising boardings, provided the perfect meeting point for the young Mods. The *Quadrophenia* crew took over the small café for three nights. Proprietor Vincent De Ritas, whose family had, up until recently, owned the premises for over seventy years, recalls, 'They filled the place with charcoal and incense to make a smoky atmosphere. Consequently, when they left, my shop stank. We washed the ceilings, the walls, and thought, "That's the end of that. We won't see them no more." Two weeks later they returned. My poor old dad was alive. He lived upstairs, keeping an eye on the place. About five in the morning a customer came in and asked him for a packet of fags. He paid for them, took his change and left. Those cigarettes were dummies, props for the film. And he never came back.'

For Jimmy's encounter with boxing promoter cum drug-dealer Harry North, John Bindon was brought in to add an extra frisson of realism. Just prior to filming, he'd stood trial at the Old

Bailey for murder, in what was described as a gangland stabbing, although he was later acquitted. Bindon brought some of his gangland fraternity to the shoot. 'It got a bit heavy,' says Roddam. 'At one point they suddenly decided, "This is a good gig, we can make something out of this," and it got a little bit East End matey for a while, it got a bit mean. "We don't want to fucking do this scene again, we've done it three times already." And Bindon was a tad dangerous. He got a bit unmanageable for an hour or so that evening. But I thought he looked great.' After a succession of court appearances in the early 1980s, Bindon found himself at odds with a new politically correct film industry: now, of course, with the likes of Dave Courtney and Frankie Fraser reincarnated as media dahlings, he would have fitted right in. He died from an AIDs related illness in 1993.

Leaving London behind, Jimmy and crew ride to Brighton for a bit of aggro. One of the most memorable scenes occurs when the Mods gaze on Brighton from a winding road leading down to the coast. Roddam cheated here. There is no such vista overlooking Brighton. The crew travelled an extra twenty miles or so to the outskirts of Eastbourne for the required shot. But it was clear that the film's riot scenes should be shot in Brighton. The ghosts of '64 still haunt the beaches and stalk the alleyways. Walking around the streets on a hot summer's day, with the constant crash of wave and sea salt spray acting as a soundtrack, you cannot help but feel the film coming to life around you; the locations are so cemented in the mind that you are instantly transported back into the film. The natives have embraced *Quadrophenia* and Mod culture to such a degree that the only thing missing is a memorial statue to the Unknown Mod.

George Wells, owner of the Beach Café, lower prom, Madeira Drive – open 'Eight Till Late' – fondly recalls the time the cast and crew paid a visit to his eatery – and stayed for three weeks. 'They had a mobile food unit but preferred to come here and we eventually took over their catering for the Brighton shoot.' The waitress who told Daniels to take his feet off the table was George's mum Betty. Wells, a former Teddy Boy, swears the riot scenes were an accurate representation of the 1964 flare-ups, but is keen to point out that he personally 'never had any trouble from the Mods. They was all well behaved.' A few years ago, George wanted to refurbish the Café in green and white. There was an outcry from the locals. Leave it exactly as it is, they cried, don't change it for the world. He hasn't. It still looks exactly the same as it does in the film, and fans come here from all over the world to have their photos taken at Jimmy's table. Daniels still occasionally pops in for a fry-up, often sitting alone at the same table, gazing out of the window. Recently, Mark Wingett paid his first trip back there. 'This place ain't changed much!' he said.

A derelict ballroom in Southgate, North London, doubled as the Brighton ballroom in which Daniels, in an attempt to impress Ash as she dances with Sting, leaps from the balcony. 'I have a very, very strong ego,' commented Sting, 'and scenes like the one in the Brighton dance hall, where Jimmy attempts to steal my limelight by dancing on the balcony, well, that look on my face, were that to have been a real situation, would have been exactly the same. Ace is very, very close to my personality when I'm on stage . . . I will not be upstaged.' The ballroom is now the LA Fitness Centre, a health club. Most staff are unaware of the *Quadrophenia* connection but are happy to show you around, join you up, and keep you fit. As heaving punters gyrate and stretch to Happy Hardcore, little do they know that one night in 1979 the building rocked to the sounds of the Orlons, Kingsmen and Booker T. 'We did three weeks of dance lessons every day,' Laird recalls. 'I'm sure he won't mind me saying this, but Sting could never get into the swing of the 60s dancing.'

For the riot scenes (the first to be filmed) three square miles of Brighton were fenced off for two weeks and filled with period cars. An outer ring of stuntmen was employed to shield the principal actors from physical trauma. In the event, an ambulance knocked down an extra, while Toyah Wilcox, who played Monkey, broke her arm. About 5,000 real Mods and Rockers had also shown up for the shoot (according to the director, most of them got on extremely well). Roddam recalls, 'The cameraman told me some of the extras playing policemen were larking about and a couple even had their helmets on back to front. Just before we were ready to re-shoot I ran across the beach toward a group of Mods and said, "Those policemen over there are fucking this up. Go for them for real." The policemen, who'd put their helmets on straight came running over, looking not too serious about it and the Mods laid into them full-on.'

For many cast members, reality and fantasy were practically indivisible. Wilcox recalled for *Film Review* in 1997, 'I was with at least two hundred kids running down the street and a policeman grabbed me. I can remember hitting and kicking the shit out of this policeman – it seemed about as real as you can get without damaging someone.' As Philip Davis (Chalky) recalled for *Empire*'s Dick Sweeney in 1997, 'We all kept getting mixed up. You'd arrange to push one in the back and he'd just turn around and growl, "Er, not me, son."' For Roddam, 'If you set a film up in a naturalistic way, and you get your cast in the mood, you get them into the reality of the situation. I was always concerned about English stunts because they always looked as if people were simply bouncing off trampolines. So with the fight on the beach, I disturbed the perfect action by giving it some imperfection. And we did it all in one take.'

Sting's involvement with the Police was taking up more and more of his beat. He specially requested an afternoon off for the band's début appearance on the BBC's flagship alternative music show, *The Old Grey Whistle Test*. Sting had to borrow a pair of women's sunglasses for the gig because he sustained an eye injury during the morning's filming – not, as was commonly assumed, because of his participation in the riot scenes, but because he had got liquid in his eyes while dyeing his hair.

In the midst of battle, Jimmy and Steph duck into a narrow alleyway. Jimmy's alleyway shag was filmed down Little East Street, in the backyard of Choy's Chinese Restaurant. During the scene Roddam was suspended in a sling for an impressive overhead shot. It's a moving moment as Steph, the cynical instigator, draws the lovesick Mod one step closer to ultimate disillusionment. Jimmy's climactic cry of 'Ug!' might be seen as his first and only achievement, but it will be undermined by his arrest seconds later. The shoot itself was no less fraught. 'Leslie's older boyfriend was a bit anxious about it,' says Roddam. 'He'd called her up the night before, asking her not to do it. On the day, she felt she wasn't ready for it, and we lost half a day's filming.' That day a police dog attacked a cameraman, who, in turn, accidentally bashed Roddam over the head with his equipment.

For the brief but poignant scene in which a huddle of Mods

lick their wounds and count their losses (just outside the little Volks Railway on the promenade), Roddam deliberately panned across his actors for a few seconds without their knowledge. Laird remembers, 'We were all standing around on Brighton beach, and I heard Franc tell the camera operator to switch the camera on. He didn't know I knew this, and I thought, "I know what I'll do here. I'll just sneak one in – something that I really feel, with no words. My motivation was "I like hanging out with these kids, plus they buy my pills, but I'm not part of this territorial thing". To me, that shot summed up my character. A few days later Franc came up to me, having just seen the rushes, and praised the scene as the pivotal moment during the Brighton shoot.' As Roddam says, 'Trevor shrugs them off. He's thinking, because he's the dealer and the only black person, as far as he's concerned, they're just a bunch of cunts.'

The Mods are called back to Brighton to face charges. Bizarrely, for a scene recalled by all as an off-the-cuff bit of improvisation, Sting's cocky comeback (filmed in Lewes Magistrates Court) when being fined by the judge for his part in the riot, has its basis in fact. As reported in the London *Evening Standard* in May 1964, 'The boy who said "I'll pay by cheque" when fined £75 at Margate yesterday admitted last night: "I don't have a bank account." Seventeen-year-old bricklayer James Brunton said: "I was just being sarcastic. I thought I could make a little joke. It didn't work. I have been given two weeks to pay."'

Like fellow director Alan Clarke, Roddam wasn't averse to playing a few mind games with his cast. For the scene (shot in a housing estate in Wembley) in which a despondent Jimmy, having returned from his first trip to Brighton, loses his prized scooter under the wheels of a post office van, Roddam told Daniels to lose his rag for real, to 'really go for it', having sussed that the actor playing the driver was a sensitive, 'very low-key kind of guy. The guy got involved and started apologising saying "I'm sorry, I'm sorry", apologising for real, because Daniels had engaged him so strongly.'

Having been spurned by both Steph and his peer group, Jimmy returns to Brighton in an attempt to recapture the magic. For the final scenes, in which Daniels is filmed hurtling along Beachy Head, the suicidal capital of Europe, a converted Citroen 2CV was used as a crude camera platform. A helicopter was commandeered for overhead shots which, for Roddam, 'was quite hairy. While we were waiting to take off, the pilot, who was quite a character, balanced the 'copter on the edge of the cliff, so we were rocking backward and forward. He'd let us freefall and then take us up again, testing our nerve, seeing if we were cool enough to fly with him.' In the event, the camera crew, hovering 150 feet from the cliff edge, were nearly knocked out of the sky by the flying scooter. The director had been much more disturbed by the tyre tracks on the cliff, picked up by the unforgiving lens, because it was take two. 'Had it been today, it would have cost you about $500 for a bit of CGI to paint that out. But you couldn't do that then.'

Daniels recalled for *Empire*, 'I got a lot closer to the edge than I was meant to. The first assistant director, Ray Corbett, said to me, "Listen, it's the third day of the film. If you fell off that cliff, d'you know what would have happened? They would have recast you tomorrow."' Much was made, and continues to be made, of the ambiguous ending: does Jimmy follow his Vespa over the edge? 'Originally, I wanted him to die,' says Roddam. 'I thought it was the death of his old life on one level or a true physical death if you wanted to take it that way.' Jimmy doesn't follow his motor over the edge – as evinced by his appearance in the opening sequence, significantly shot against the setting sun. As Roddam told *Empire*, 'When I met all these guys and they were so optimistic, I realised that the idea of death was only some kind of morbid thing that Townshend and I had because we were over thirty. In the end I was glad to have him cast off his job, his parents, his girlfriend and end up free of it all.' The trappings and trimmings of the herd culture are jettisoned as Jimmy stumbles back to an uncertain future – alone.

Quadrophenia was released in September 1979, to very mixed reactions. While the *Sunday Express* considered it 'a chastening experience, a powerful antidote to the sloppy sentimental movies about the 60s', the *Daily Mirror* harrumphed, '*Quadrophenia* takes a long time to say very little about the Mods and Rockers of 1964 ... it will mainly appeal to past and present members of those rival youth gangs.' Felix Barker of the *Evening News* loathed its 'mindless violence ... it is a terrible picture, and we see its manifestation in a middle-class suburban party wrecked by surly gatecrashers'. The *Financial Times* – given a plug in the film by a couple of commuting city gents – offered perhaps the best review of all: 'It's fairly squalid . . . but it's also funny and unpredictable and insidiously intoxicating.'

Fittingly, the movie found its core audience among another youth cult: retro culture was creeping back. As Mark Perry, former editor of Punk 'zine *Sniffin Glue*, acknowledges, 'The Punks had more in common with the Mods than any other movement of those times.' (Roddam disagrees: 'The Punks were much more anarchic. Mod was a rebellion, not a revolution.') Townshend must have felt vindicated: as far as he was concerned, he'd 'invented Punk' in the first place. *Quadrophenia* would also owe a lot of its initial success to the burgeoning Mod revival of the late 1970s and early 1980s: this latest (perhaps third) wave comprising those who hadn't fitted that clique's strict parameters.

The Punks themselves, jeering in the face of Callaghan's government, had been left with the ironic legacy of a Conservative government pledging 'harmony'. For Mrs Thatcher, this entailed a war against trade-unionism, reduction of public expenditure, mass-privatisation and, affecting the nation's youth most, the abandonment of a commitment to full employment. If the original Mods had been the original C1, 2 and 3s (Thatcher's core voters), Britain's political climate in 1979 was so confused that this new wave of Mods might conceivably have been called left-wing.

Mod clubs resurfaced after fifteen years, and many neophytes took their inspiration directly from *Quadrophenia*. Riding uneasily on the crest of this new wave flailed the Jam, led by Paul Weller, who had found his niche after being ostracised by the Punk élite. The twenty-one-year-old's songwriting fused the fury of Punk with the Mod sensibilities of the Who, the Kinks and the Small Faces. A slew of pre-fab Mods followed in his wake, eager to catch the magic bus. Some were good (Chords, Purple Hearts), some were blatant cash-ins (Secret Affair, Lambrettas), and some were just plain awful (Merton Parkas). Carnaby Street, London's own seaside pier, underwent a resurgence as shops like Sherrys, Carnaby Cavern, Melandi and Merc cashed in, flogging parkas that resembled abattoir suits and Union Jack coats that looked like they'd been fashioned from duvet covers.

If the Tories had reintroduced the Union Jack as an object of pride, the National Front were also employing it as a weapon against what they saw as a tide of immigrants swamping the Motherland. 'People are really rather afraid that this country might be swamped by people of a different culture,' mused Thatcher, granting virtual legitimacy to the far right's excesses. The Ska revival had been partly kick-started by the Clash's forays into Dub and echoed the Mods' love of Blue Beat culture. In accordance with the times it was also partly wedded to a political, anti-racist agenda, though this was by no means all-embracing: the hapless Clash roadie from the 1980s' film *Rude Boy* is a potential NF recruit, to boot. Rock Against Racism, an anti-racist musical movement founded at the time, was set up as a reaction against one of Townshend's home counties peers, Eric Clapton, who had suggested in September 1976, at a Birmingham concert, that Enoch Powell was right and that Britain was 'overcrowded'. On pop's front line, crowning the 2 Tone roster, the Specials welded Ska and Mod perfectly: 'Too Much, Too Young' could have come straight out of *Quadrophenia*, while in 1981 the single and video of 'Ghost Town' brilliantly caught the contemporary come-down.

Dispensing with *Rude Boy*'s arty, often contrived agitpop, Franco Rosso's superb study of young black Britain under siege, *Babylon* (1980), drew a fundamentally honest, unsentimental portrait of the late 1970s – none of *Quadrophenia*'s mythologising here. Filmed around Deptford, Lewisham and Brixton, and financed on a dreadlock by the National Film Finance Corporation, *Babylon* employs an unsubtitled patois so rich you could crumble and smoke it. The flawed but exhilarating *Dance Craze* (1981), in which a stable of Ska bands pogo awkwardly before a backdrop of Pathé news footage, offered a snapshot of the movement at its peak, with strong performances from the Specials, the Selector, the Beat and Madness. A year later, amid confusion and lack of direction, most neo-Mod bands folded, leaving the Jam, Madness, and the Specials to chart an uneasy passage through New Romanticism, Burundi drums and the Soul Boy revival, all wedge cuts and pink Pringle sweaters.

The Jam reached number 4 in the UK charts with 'Funeral Pyre' in the summer of 1981. Phil Daniels was starring with Hazel

O'Connor in *Breaking Glass*. On August Bank Holiday it happened all over again. Rioting began when a fight erupted between Mods and rival Skinheads. Frix, 'the Southern Skin', told the *Brighton Evening Argus*: 'Word is out that a load of Mods from Scarborough are coming down here. The only reason they come here is because of that film *Quadrophenia*. All these young kids just copied it to follow the trend. They go around with their scooters and tonic trousers like something out of *Quadrophenia* and they have the nerve to take the rise out of us. We hate everyone of course, but we hate the Mods and Soul Boys the most, 'cos they're flash. I reckon there's going to be a lot of trouble down here in the summer 'cos that's what Skins are all about. Skinheads never really went out of fashion. Sham '69 started them up again and they've just come back.'

Where the rioters of 1964, liberated from National Service, strutted their new-found affluence in the face of bemused, harried authority, the contingent that made their way to Brighton over a decade and a half later met with a very different sort of policing. While the constables of 1964 had more or less herded the masses from pillar to post, Thatcher's troops employed a radical new method of control. Following a petrol bombing, police rounded on 300 Mods, driving them towards a grassy area along the promenade. After making them remove their shoes, jackets and crash helmets, police forced them to lie face down for six hours, as a senior officer bellowed through a megaphone: 'No one is to move or talk. You might as well go to sleep.'

At Sussex Police HQ in Lewes media spokesmen fielded an avalanche of press inquiries, as police downplayed comparisons with the glorious summer of '64. Professor Stanley Cohen, author of the classic Mods and Rockers case study, *Folk Devils and Moral Panics*, told the *Brighton Evening Argus*, 'The issue is a massively deep one, stretching into unemployment and urban tension of the kind that helped cause the Toxteth and Brixton riots. It would appear the police are taking on the role of the courts, deciding on punitive action before anyone has even been before a magistrate or a sentence has been passed.'

A more traditional response came from Kemp Town's Tory MP Andrew Bowden: 'It's a total misrepresentation to make out these problems have anything in common with Toxteth. I think the police handled the situation superbly, although of course the public of Sussex have every right to be cross at having to pick up the bill for extra policing.' Magistrate Ray Long, imposing exceptionally stringent fines, said of the rioters: 'When a gang of 300 youths come to this town and act like animals they must be expected to be treated as such.'

Today, 'Irish' Jack despairs that 'a lot of kids came away from *Quadrophenia* thinking the Mod movement was all about fighting. It wasn't.' Alan Fletcher thinks *Quadrophenia* is 'definitely not a Mod film. It's a film about Mods. There's a subtle difference.' It's also worth pointing out that the Who were not Mods themselves. Early photos show them dressed like any other Beat group of the time. They were simply a band the Mods liked. Arguably, there's yet to be a film made that really tells the true story of Mod, but if anyone ever gets around to making an unexpurgated, unadulterated biopic of the Small Faces, they'll be doing the movement a big favour.

As Fletcher says, 'The look of *Quadrophenia* wasn't 60s Mod, and the kids in the film just don't look Mod. It had a look of 70s revival Mod in it.' Paul Weller thinks its 'awful – there's no attention to detail. They had a chance to do it with *Absolute Beginners*, but totally blew that as well. *Absolute Beginners* is the ultimate Mod book, though!' A noted authority on Mods and Modernism, Paolo Hewitt has recently penned a definitive tome on Mod history with Paul Weller. 'The problem with the film is that a Mod-like attitude to detail is not expanded upon,' he says.

There are so many historical gaffes in *Quadrophenia* that you run out of fingers and toes trying to catch up, and after a while they even begin to look like deliberate insertions. Seventies Cortinas cruise up and down the Goldhawk Road, the principal cast's clothes and haircuts are wrong, rioting Rockers wear Motorhead T-shirts, the Who's 'My Generation', which features on the soundtrack, wasn't released until November 1965, over a year after the events of the film were supposed to have taken place – Mods were always keen to get their hands on the newest releases, but surely they would never have got this lucky. The blue and yellow train that speeds past Jimmy's bedroom window wouldn't see service for another fourteen years, while a copy of the Who's special edition

LP *The Who Sell Out* and *A Quick One* (which wouldn't see daylight until 1974) crept into the Kitchener Road party scene.

Paolo Hewitt questions whether there were even any genuine Mods in *Quadrophenia*. 'Mod was finished by 1963,' he says. '*Ready Steady Go* nationalised Mod, and that signalled the end of it. The Mod thing went overground and was taken up by idiots really, just beer boys and thugs – no self-respecting Mod would have been down at Brighton. Everybody who was there at the beginning of the scene had the same attitude – as soon as the media knows about it, it's finished. Who wants to be part of something the *Daily Mirror* knows about?'

A curious state of affairs, this: a case of contemporary audiences dressed like Mods, watching actors playing Mods, in turn acting out a received version of the real thing. In other words, a bunch of unruly wannabes sticking their heads through Brighton Pier's 'Your Face Here' boardings, alongside the Diver and the Bather, for a cheeky souvenir snapshot. For purists like Paul Weller, this is frankly insulting. For cult aficionados, it's a large part of the appeal: democracy in action – one big happy family of Mods, past and present. The movie's re-release in 1997 only served to elongate this hall of mirrors: a legend replicating itself, growing ever more mythical. For Roddam, *Quadrophenia*'s Mods pulling balletically away on their scooters during Townshend's 'Love Reign O'er Me' instrumental represents 'the mythology of Mod, sort of a dream, and something bigger than the individual'.

It might be argued that *Quadrophenia* avails itself of the myth-maker's prerogative to mix anachronisms in order to achieve a sense of timelessness. In the riot scenes, Jimmy's war cry outside a ransacked Brighton café is 'On my life, I was there! I was there!'. For a brief moment, you can see through Daniels' character to the real nineteen-year-old boy who is, with a genuine exhilaration, drawing strength from his peers; in his mind, maybe, he has tripped back to 1964. He's living it for real. Roddam's own comments suggest such an interpretation. There's a shot in the film of a Brighton cinema advertising Warren Beatty in the 1970s version of *Heaven Can Wait*. 'It was such a quick shot,' commented Roddam. 'It looked so good with the characters in the foreground I let that go deliberately. I always joke that there are ten deliberate mistakes in the film. I once did a lecture at the Lincoln Centre in New York and they showed the film with an audience of 600 people asking questions. The first question that came up was: "There's a double yellow line. Double yellow lines didn't come out till 1967." I said, "What are you – a Traffic Warden?" Never let the facts get in the way of the truth – that's what I say.' Roddam's sometime-mentor Michael Powell, and Tony Richardson adored *Quadrophenia* for that very reason. 'They both admired the emotional truth in the work,' comments Roddam.

Even Paolo Hewitt gives credit to *Quadrophenia* as a great youth film. 'If you forget about the whole Mod thing, then it actually works.' As Roddam acknowledges, '*Quadrophenia* has an enduring quality because it looks at all those problems and passions and then says, "It's OK to be no good, it's OK to be useless, it's OK not to be good at sex, not to be good at fighting, not to like your parents, to be fired at work. I was always interested how passionate you feel when you are young. Those passions don't last very long, but they're very powerful. And in that sense I think it's an instructive film, in that it says, "I embrace what you're thinking and what you're feeling, and I understand what you feel 'cos I felt the same. It's great to fight, it's great to fuck, it's great to take drugs." But it also has a bit of objectivity too.' For Trevor Laird, 'It's so quintessentially London, and beautifully British. At the moment we're trying to keep track with the Yanks. *Quadrophenia* succeeds because it's not trying to sell to America – it's about Britain. It's where we all come from.'

Such was *Quadrophenia*'s popularity that plans for a sequel were often discussed, and Roddam fended off many advances to revive Jimmy (one such proposal was 'Jimmy goes to India' on the Hippie trail). 'It was talked about quite a lot – Roy Baird wanted him to become an advertising executive. What they were thinking was "What is the next movement? Can he get into it?" He would probably have ended up supporting Margaret Thatcher.' Townshend did briefly employ another 'Jimmy' character for his 1985 short, *White City*. Partly autobiographical, Townshend again used the backdrop of his native White City, West London, to present a crisis-ridden thirty-something eking out his days in a council flat.

Brighton's still a Mod town, always will be. *Quadrophenia*'s landmarks are regularly visited by devotees from all over the world. Staff at Choy's Chinese Restaurant continue to fight a losing battle to protect Jimmy's Alleyway against graffiti artists who have turned the tiny passageway into a shrine to *Quadrophenia*. Things turned nasty some years back when visiting pilgrims and their girlfriends stormed the fortress of barbed wire, broken glass and heavy padlocks to recreate the movie's most intimate scene. Police were called. To this day, the owners remain bemused that the back entrance, usually used for dumping kitchen scraps and garbage, could be treated with such reverence. 'I always have a quick look in the alleyway, whenever I'm up there,' says Roddam. 'I know Mods from Holland go there, and it's a shrine for so many fans, but it makes me laugh. What do these Chinese guys think is going on in there?'

Back in London – in Wells Home Road, Acton, to be precise – Jimmy Cooper's terraced family home remained derelict for many years. *Quadrophenia* devotees would walk out with various items, the fireplace included. The scrapyard in which Peter Fenton (Garry Cooper) worked as a car breaker is still there, lying just across the road from the Bramley Arms pub, off Latimer Road, West London. The 'Beware of the Dog' sign still dangles threateningly over the wreckage of the scrapped motors. But these days, Colin and Marco, along with 'Mao' the cat, maintain security.

'The 1990s are the 1960s standing on their head!' cried MC Wavy Gravy from the stage of Woodstock 2 in 1994. *Quadrophenia* and its iconography fitted the decade like a bespoke three-button suit: the hankering for labels, pills and dance records, a virtual retread of the mid-1960s. London-based Baggy band Flowered Up employed soundbites from *Quadrophenia* for their 1992 'Weekender' single and accompanying film – an astute marriage of Mod and Ecstasy culture. While UK Garage – a black-driven music scene, with its own labels and fashions, and beloved by the working class – must be Mod's latest incarnation. The film is still very much with us; you might find it doing the rounds on the Stella Artois-sponsored outdoor cinema screenings with Mods conspicuously in attendance, joining in Jimmy's orgasmic cry of 'Ug!' with collective gusto. Daniels would reprise his role for the Who's 1996 *Quadrophenia* tour. In a strange twist of cross-cult appreciation, some three weeks before the Midsummer's Solstice celebrations at Stonehenge, a group of sun worshippers and New Age travellers begin their annual pilgrimage across Beachy Head along what they call the 'Quadrophenia Route' while Brighton tour guide and *Quadrophenia* devotee Glenda Clarke is currently running an exhaustively researched guided walk of the film's Brighton locations (see Bibliography). One of her favourite tours, it regularly attracts sightseers and fans – including original Sixties Mods – from all over Britain. 'Academics will say *Brighton Rock* is the definitive Brighton film', she says. 'Oh no it isn't! I have come across people who have seen it two hundred times,' says Roddam. 'There was even a Mod club in San Diego with Mexican Mods. They called *Quadrophenia* the Bible.'

Another invasion of Brighton occurred on 29 January 1997, as the film was relaunched during the tail-end of the Britpop revival. Original cast members and the press boarded the 'Quadrophenia Express' at Victoria to be met at the other end by a phalanx of Mods and minders. This time round, the establishment joined in, with the Mayor of Brighton introducing the screening. As Franc Roddam left the party at the Grand Hotel afterwards, a large, anonymous-looking man in his thirties tapped him on the shoulder. 'Your film saved my life,' he said. Then he walked away into the night.

Barry Prior, whose finale may well have started all this, rests peacefully in a North London cemetery. And it is to you, Barry, that we dedicate this chapter. May the Lord Mod rest your soul.

ALL RIGHT HERE?

Two 'resting' actors eke out a chemically assisted lifestyle in their festering flat in Camden, London. They are linked together by chaos, failure and hopelessness, from which only one will escape. Fresh air is required and they embark on a jaunt to the country, followed by the inevitable come-down back in town. *Withnail & I* has crossed generations and oceans to become one of the best-loved comedies of all time; the ending is also one of the saddest and most moving in cinema's history.

'*Withnail*'s almost spiritual in a way. I actually judge whether or not I am going to get on with people by asking them if they like the film.'

Seamus Smith, fan

Like some slow-burning 'Camberwell Carrot', *Withnail & I* (novel, script and film) has been passed around intoxicated fans for well over thirty years now. And, like a good joke and a fine wine, the story improves with age. The movie's belated resurrection through university halls, student union bars and on video, gathering legions of dialogue-quoting admirers, copycat drinkers, and trivia fiends in its wake, has seen it become a true British classic, surpassing even its original cult status. Of all the films in the second half of this book, *Withnail* probably inspires the most love, protection and, above all, sense of ownership and bonding among fans, hence statements like the one above. 'It obviously touches a chord in people,' says actor Ralph Brown, who plays Danny the Dealer. 'It makes them feel sad while making them laugh.'

Much of this sense of sadness undoubtedly springs from *Withnail*'s

troubled creator, Bruce Robinson, now something of a very reluctant, so-called 'bad boy' cult figure himself. Despite his critical reception as one of the greatest writers working in any medium today,
he actually considers his career a failure. *Withnail* may well be one
of the most brilliantly original comedies, but peel off the celluloid
scab and you'll find a deep wound. Until its cult revival, this most
personal of films had been abused, meddled with, fleeced, hounded
and dogged with as much ill-fortune as its makers.

Robinson was born in 1945. Six years later his family moved to
Broadstairs, in Kent, summer home to Charles Dickens. Out of
season Broadstairs had a spumey desolation, sporting clapped-out
arcades, empty chocolate machines, and yellowing 'Miss Kent Coast'
posters along the promenade. And Robinson's formative years were
hell on earth. Brought up 'like vomit' in an abusive, dysfunctional
family, he'd regularly shit himself until the age of ten and used to
pile saucepans behind his bedroom door to provide an alarm in case
his father, who kept a Luger automatic pistol by his bed, came in
the middle of the night to murder him. As Robinson told film writer
Alistair Owen, 'The only time [he] ever touched me was when he
was hitting me . . . I never saw him kiss [my mother] once . . . his
whole personality was like a fucking knuckle.' For comfort Bruce
turned to his beloved, 'incredibly weird' grandfather, who was dying
of cancer. Later, when Robinson was thirty, he discovered his mother
had had an affair during the war with a GI and got pregnant. To this
day, he's never known who his real father was.

As chronicled in his heavily autobiographical *Thomas Penman*
novel, Bruce hated his crummy secondary modern, except on those
occasions when he acted in school plays. In 1964 he won a place
at London's Central School of Speech and Drama, 'a singularly
unpleasant experience'. By his second year he knew he didn't want
to be an actor, but had become exhilarated by the company he was
keeping. His friends included Michael Feast, Lord David Dundas and
a drop-dead gorgeous, upper-class rake called Vivian MacKerrell.
The four ended up sharing a squalid, teeming flat in Camden Town.
They were broke, but they were happy, and they were obviously all
destined for greatness. Life at Albert Street followed a predictable
pattern of daily rituals, punctuated by the odd audition. At 11
o'clock they'd all troop down to the Spread Eagle pub across the

road, boozing till 3 in the afternoon, then totter back home to start on the red. Girlfriends – *chicks* – were a barely heard of luxury. The one time someone did manage to score, he'd have to smear underarm deodorant over his reeking bedsheets just to get her into position. Bruce's own waterlogged bathroom mattress had long since passed caring.

Eventually Dundas and Feast moved out, leaving Bruce and Vivian to stay on in the flat together. For Robinson, Viv, for ever subsisting on family wills, was a ranting, boozing, highly intelligent star-in-waiting. He said so himself. Oh, how he said so. As Robinson told Adrian Sibley for his 1999 Channel Four documentary on *Withnail*, 'He had this pomposity of the thespian, very smart guy, very bright, but he was sad too, because he was a jack of all and master of none. He always used to say to me, "If I wrote, I'd write a fuck sight better than you would, or if I painted I'd paint a fuck sight better than you ever would, or if I was a photographer I'd be a better photographer than Bailey" . . . But the fact is he never did anything. All he ever did was booze and rant.' Meanwhile Bruce, the admiring lost boy, expanded his classical repertoire to include Viv's own love of Keats, Gerard Manley Hopkins, Baudelaire, fine wine and Scotch before breakfast.

In 1968 Bruce found himself pursued by Franco Zeffirelli to play the part of Benvolio for the director's *Romeo and Juliet*. Ruby Wax pressed him for details on her late-night BBC chat show *Ruby* in 1998. Unaware he was being recorded throughout, a tired and emotional Robinson revealed the connection between the Italian rapscallion and the future Uncle Montague Withnail. 'I arrive in this apartment, downtown Rome, and it's filled with little Gucci guys with these Gucci shoes and Gucci bags, and Franco says to me, "Oh, you must be tired. Long flight? Why don't you have a shower?" Next thing, he comes in with this blue silk caftan and dries my hair . . . and now I'm back in the room and all of these faggots . . . disappear. Now I'm on the bloody couch with Franco and there's a line I used in *Withnail & I*, it's the only rip-off line: "Are you a sponge or a stone?" Then he's suddenly fishing in my tonsils with his tongue.'

Back in London, according to Bruce's diary, on 30 April 1968 he and Viv attempted to blag their way into a wine-tasting event at

Sotheby's before being turned away by 'a bloke with ears and a green hat', who refused them entry with the immortal line, 'You two cunts can hop it.' The pair retired to watch the wolves in Regent's Park, an event Robinson would incorporate in his future script. On 16 November Robinson lay in bed for two days after a gruelling session with MacKerrell, listening to the man mewling and puking for England. Then, in the winter of 1969, Vivian left. Remarkably, he'd got a job. Bruce was left penniless and starving, with just a gas oven and a box of matches for company. One snowy day, alone in his room, he began to weep and scream at the floorboards, 'begging the God of Equity, or any fucking God, to help me'. It was such a ludicrous, clichéd situation that Bruce began to laugh. Hysterically. Manically. And, grabbing the old Olivetti typewriter he'd used to try and write poetry on, he sat down and poured it all out – the story of his friend, their adventures, his friend's leave-taking, his own predicament, everything. He called the novel *Withnail and I*. It was the first time he'd truly found his voice. Bruce borrowed the name 'Withnail' from an acquaintance called Jonathan Withnall, but he never made a secret of the fact that Withnail was based on Viv, and after Viv's death from throat cancer in 1995 he dedicated the published screenplay to his memory. At the film's finale, Paul McGann can be seen placing a copy of Baudelaire's *A Rebours* – one of Viv's favourite books – into his suitcase, along with Bruce's novel.

While Bruce began to get some acting work, the unpublished novel circulated among friends, friends of friends and acquaintances, lovingly photocopied and passed on. In 1970 Bruce's old screenwriting friend Andrew Birkin handed a copy of the novel to David Puttnam. On the strength of the writing, Puttnam commissioned Robinson to write a thirteen-part TV show, the first of a series of Puttnam screenwriting commissions, which would include Roland Joffe's *The Killing Fields* (1984). Around 1980 *Withnail & I* made its way, via an actor friend of Robinson's called Don Hawkins, into the hands of Moderick (Mody) Schreiber, the son of an oil businessman. Schreiber liked the book, and gave Bruce a few thousand pounds to convert it into a screenplay.

In Bruce's story, perennially resting actors Withnail and Marwood escape from their self-imposed hellish Camden lifestyle for a jaunt to the country, holing up in a Lake District cottage that belongs to Withnail's Uncle Monty. It was very much based on fact: back in the late 1960s Robinson and Camden flatmate Michael Feast had found an ad in *The Times* for an 'idyllic cottage' in the Lake District for a tenner a week. Having driven up there in actress Lesley Anne Down's dilapidated old Jaguar (Bruce was dating her at the time), all they discovered was a freezing barn with a leaky roof. They'd had to burn the furniture just to keep warm, and tramp around with polythene bags on their feet because they'd neglected to bring wellingtons. For food, they'd half-brained a chicken with an axe. The decapitated bird had strutted around without a head, so they'd had to whack it again until it stayed down. After they had driven Lesley's Jag into a ditch, a passing farmer hoisted it to the back of his tractor and pulled the entire front off. The pair couldn't wait to leave. The incidents would later find their way into the finished screenplay. Having narrowly avoided a buggering from Uncle Monty, and secured himself an acting job, Marwood drags Withnail back to London, where the two part company: Marwood for the boards, Withnail for an uncertain future alone.

Around 1981, Bruce commissioned a poster from cartoonist Ralph Steadman. 'Bruce came to me, early one morning,' Steadman recalls. 'He was pissed out of his brain on whisky. His stepfather had just died, he was really quite upset. It was the first time in his life he'd really felt close to him. I'd never heard of Bruce, but he knew of me through my *Fear and Loathing* stuff for Hunter S. Thompson.' Though penned some two years after Robinson's novel, and a more political than personal work, Hunter's *Fear and Loathing in Las Vegas* might be seen as *Withnail*'s Stateside equivalent, with its story of the druggy, boozy camaraderie between a bombed-out duo of Uneasy Riders searching for the American dream. Steadman's accompanying ink-splat artwork was as deranged and extreme as Hunter's prose, winning him hordes of admirers, Robinson among them.

'Bruce asked me if I'd do a drawing for the film,' says Steadman. '"The only way we can sell it," he said, "is to get something up front, like an image." Which is where the poster came from. As my mother used to say, "Never turn down work." At this time, I'd never met or heard of Richard E. Grant or Paul McGann, but drew it on the basis of what I was reading in the script. I got paid £200 from Bruce himself. That day I'd shown him the big old horse chestnut in our garden, about five hundred years old. I'd said, "Here, do you like my tree?" He'd said, "It's not your tree Ralph – it's everybody's tree." And therein lies his wisdom.'

By 1985 Bruce was the talk of BAFTA, having won a best screenplay award for *The Killing Fields*. But although he would be taken a bit more seriously around the industry, his success wouldn't automatically guarantee *Withnail & I* an easier ride. Bruce recalled a conversation at about this time with Jake Eberts, the Goldcrest founder, who completely rubbished this 'most goddawful unfunny' screenplay he'd been recommended about two out-of-work actors, unaware he was talking to the man who'd actually written it. However, veteran US producer Paul Heller, the man who had financed *Enter the Dragon* and who was a long-standing friend of Bruce, had also read the screenplay and loved it. He encouraged Bruce to direct it himself and secured half the budget from his good friend, Lawrence Kirstein, a Washington-based property developer. Another one of Bruce's friends, the producer David Wimbury, presented the package (including Steadman's gloriously sleazy poster) to Ray Cooper at HandMade Films, which was headed by American producer Denis O'Brien and ex-Beatle George Harrison.

O'Brien had walked into George Harrison's life after he'd dumped manager Alan Klein in 1973. O'Brien seemed to have the right credentials: a former merchant banker, he'd managed Peter Sellers during the 1970s, and had encouraged George to invest in films. HandMade had originally been formed to bankroll *Monty Python's Life of Brian* (1979) after EMI pulled the plug on the production. Harrison stepped in, throwing everything he could at it, and was handsomely rewarded, as the film proceeded to take more than £40 million worldwide. The pair soon discovered a niche for homegrown, low-budget movies, relying on a wealth of British talent, most often to be found among the nest of Pythons themselves.

When Harrison read Bruce's script, he loved it. 'I could relate to *Withnail*,' said Harrison. 'The Beatles were at the other end of the scale in 1969, but it was us in '61 with things growing in the sink.' Bruce was paid £1 for his script, and a one-off director's fee of

£80,000. The total budget was £1.1 million. Within weeks Bruce was ready to begin casting.

Richard E. Grant, who was to play Bruce's eponymous rogue, was born in 1957 in Swaziland. When Richard was eleven his mother walked out on the palatial family home for an affair with a mining engineer. Richard was left to 'parent his own parent'. He went on to study drama at the University of Cape Town, and tour Africa with his own avant-garde theatre company. Aged twenty-five, he left for London, taking parts on the fringe circuit, waiting on tables to make ends meet. An acclaimed appearance in the 1985 advertising satire, *Honest, Decent and True*, for the BBC brought him to the attention of *Withnail*'s casting director, Mary Selway.

Grant was invited to read for the part of Withnail (others up for the part included Daniel Day Lewis and Eddie Tudor Pole). The readings took place in Peel Cottage, Peel Street Notting Hill Gate, during the first rainy week of July 1986. Grant, thought Robinson, looked like a pudgy Dirk Bogarde. He'd have to lose some weight. To the director's immense irritation, Grant launched into an ill-advised Noël Cowardesque reading of the script. When he came to the immortal line '*Fork it!*' he lunged at Bruce and sent his script flying out of his hands. As Grant got down on all fours and hastily tried to piece the script together again, Bruce asked the panicking actor whether he'd ever 'attacked' a director before. 'Not to my knowledge,' Grant lied. He'd half strangled another director while auditioning for the role of Frankenstein's monster the previous winter.

Grant's act of near-lunacy won Bruce over. Above all, it had really reminded him of Viv. He asked Grant to come back the next day and read another scene with actor Paul McGann, who was to play Withnail's foil, Marwood. Marwood was Bruce, circa 1969: a naïve, lower-middle-class drama student, constantly striving to save the day. McGann, one fifth of the celebrated McGann clan, had been born in 1959 in Liverpool. Raised in a strict Catholic household, he attended a Jesuit Grammar school, where his acting abilities were spotted and he was encouraged to audition for RADA. The introverted McGann would suffer the worst fate ever to befall an acting student – stage fright. Nevertheless, he went on to distinguish himself in a series of Victorian period dramas. By the time Withnail rolled around, he was best known for his performance in Alan Bleasdale's controversial BBC series, *The Monocled Mutineer* (1985).

Richard Griffiths was chosen to play benevolent homosexual Uncle Monty. Born in Stockton-on-Tees in 1948 to deaf-mute parents, Griffiths's exuberant body language was partly a result of the fact that up until the age of five he hadn't spoken to anyone beside the baby-sitter who lived next door. Following radiation therapy to stimulate an under-active thyroid, his body ballooned. He was marked down as a trouble-maker at school, which he left at the age of fifteen, hoping to become a painter and eventually drifted into theatre, TV and film. 'Bruce told me he'd seen me playing Mr Allardyce in *A Private Function*,' says Griffiths. 'He'd turned to his gorgeous wife and said "That's Monty." I wanted to have fun with Monty and camp him up even more than I did. Bruce said, "Don't do that. Play it as straight as you can bear. Just keep up the fruitiness."'

In Bruce's script Withnail and Marwood are completely friendless apart from occasional unwelcome intrusions from the working-class hippie, Danny the Dealer – one of the most accurate characters Robinson has yet devised. The role was originally earmarked for Michael Feast, who turned it down, as he felt the part was too close to his own boozy, drug-addicted past. 'There was a type of Lewes person in the early Seventies and late Sixties who used to get terribly stoned and pontificate endlessly about things,' says Sussex-based actor Ralph Brown, who finally secured the part. 'Being young teenagers we were slightly impressed by these slightly scary people. But then, after cornering you for a while, they'd become slightly boring.' Danny's modulated cockney accent had come from a ridiculously stupid make-up woman at Pinewood Studios. The real Danny, according to Brown, was a hairdresser from Chelsea, who made a fortune in the City and now lives in Surrey.

Prior to the first rehearsals, Ralph Steadman arrived to take photos of the actors. 'I think they thought it was supposed to be "Gonzo". They were standing inside the toilet, getting into the bath, and sucking on the pipes. They were desperate to get on. Grant was ever so polite and enthusiastic. He has a pompous image for his part, but he's really incredibly shy and very kind.' An initiation ceremony was required for the strictly teetotal actor who was allergic to alcohol. Bruce was determined to get him steaming drunk, just once, so that he could appreciate what it was like to attempt to 'act sober' while pissed out of his mind. As Bruce insisted, he had to have a 'chemical memory'. A bar was set up, stacked with gallon-sized jars of vodka, champagne and Pepsi. Grant did his duty and then some, retching like a broken hydrant, while Paul and Bruce cheered him on, pleading with him to remember how it felt. As Grant recalled for *Premiere* magazine in 1996, 'I just remember them laughing because I was falling around and crying and laughing, completely out of my head . . . a huge Persian carpet came out of my mouth.' As Bruce told *Neon* magazine, 'The next morning we dragged him to rehearsals, pissed as a fart.'

The Lake District scenes were filmed first and the night before shooting began on 3 August 1986, Bruce holed up in the bar of the crew's Penrith hotel until the early hours. He couldn't sleep. He was absolutely petrified. It was his first shot at directing, he didn't know what the hell he was doing, and he was going to get shit-faced on vodka at 2 in the morning. At 5 a.m., he wearily emerged from the hotel. Gathering his cast and hand-picked crew around him, he climbed on top of a chair to offer an apologetic rallying call. Grant also had good cause to be anxious. It was his first feature, too, and thirteen days earlier his baby daughter had died, just a few hours after childbirth. As Ralph Brown says, 'I found out later about the terrible grief that he was going through at that time, which accounts for a lot of the intensity of the performance.'

Nevertheless, the on-set atmosphere was mostly, by all accounts, pure joy. 'We were all fused with excitement,' says Richard Griffiths. 'There was something about Bruce and the way he worked that was more special than any other film I've ever worked on. We knew we really had something.' For his part, cinematographer Peter Hannan recalls, 'I couldn't get to work quickly enough.' But Bruce was superstitious as hell. 'For God's sake, stop laughing,' he'd groan, if anyone, particularly Griffiths, a notorious giggler, corpsed on set. On these occasions, he'd stop the shoot and rethink the scene. As Steadman says, 'If anyone says anything is brilliant, it's not brilliant to Bruce. He doesn't feel the brilliance. Why should you? "What's the matter with you, you fucking idiot," sort of thing. He doesn't know he's being funny. Or if he does, he's pretending he's not. With Bruce it's a self-immolation, a denial of his own brilliance.' The one time Bruce had spontaneously burst out laughing during filming was when Grant accidentally got a bit of pork-pie pastry stuck in his teeth during a take in the Old Mother Black Cap pub. It was just too good to lose.

The film begins in London, with Withnail and Marwood festering in their Camden flat. Over the legend 'Camden, 1969' play the bittersweet tones of Procol Harum's 'A Whiter Shade of Pale', as interpreted by King Curtis on 'Live from Fillmore West', whose association with George Harrison went back to the days when Curtis supported the Beatles on their 1965 US tour. The track's made even more moving when you discover that Curtis was murdered just hours later, following a row in the concert hall's car park. Aside from the strains of Al Bowlly that accompany Monty and the boys en route to Penrith, incidental music was composed by Robinson's old flatmate, David Dundas (with noodlings from Rick Wakeman).

Withnail & I's hangover of a house was a suitably condemned building (since demolished) in Chepstow Villas, off Kensington Church Street, W8. Given the state of the place, all the art department had to do was further distress the rooms. Miles from Camden, the Old Mother Black Cap, to which the duo repair for sustenance, remains a very real pub situated in Notting Hill's Tavistock Crescent by the Westway flyover. To the right is a narrow wire-arboured bridge, familiar from many urban 1970s films and documentaries, evoking the spirit of the Clash and other punk icons. The monstrous carbuncle of Trellick Tower still looms in the background.

Determined to flee their squalid Camden flat, Withnail asks his Uncle Monty if they can stay in his cottage for a holiday. When they visit Uncle Monty in Chelsea to sound him out, Withnail informs him that the blissfully unaware Marwood is a 'Toilet Trader', pricking his uncle's interest and thereby securing the residency. Monty's Chelsea house, too ornate to be wholly convincing, is in fact a real location, 35 Glebe Place, SW3, sandwiched between the King's Road and the Albert Embankment. Then, as now, it's the home of fabric designer Bernard Neville, a big mover for Liberty (the shop, that is) during the 1960s. Its distinctive wooden door with brass knocker remains intact and the velveteen 1870 Howard sofa that Monty collapses into – to his cat's chagrin – still takes pride of place in the living-room.

'I remember being very pissed off with the cat,' says Griffiths. 'They'd brought this wimpy, tiny Blue Persian. And the thing was inert with fear. I could have brought one from home, we used to have a lilac pointed Siamese, and it would have been much funnier and more beautiful. This one just kept collapsing. It was very hard not to make it look like a dishcloth. The cat's owners were in despair, because they'd assured Bruce that this thing would do what was required. It did fuck all. There's a shot of me flopped on a couch, and what's supposed to happen in the script is that the cat leaps on to the back of this couch and Monty chases it off. Well, of course, there was no way the cat was going to move. Eventually its owner was throwing it from behind the couch and hoping it would land on top of it. Occasionally it would miss and crash down beside me. It would go everywhere other than the top of the couch. It took for ever. And then of course it went missing and we had to get this search party to find out where this terrorised little infant thing was. I think it never recovered and, as far as I was concerned, that wouldn't have been a bad thing particularly, because I was quite happy to pull it inside out.'

Today, Bernard Neville is nonplussed at the interest taken in his property, but none the less makes a point of charging anyone who wishes to photograph its splendiferous interior ('free to those who can afford it; very expensive to those who can't'). A self-confessed eccentric and *bon viveur*, he fits perfectly into the crusty Chelsea artists' community. Like Montague Withnail, Bernard is convinced that he belongs to another time, perhaps the period in which the house was first erected.

There are few obvious icons in *Withnail* to suggest a time period. Aside from Danny the Dealer and the legend 'Camden 1969' at the film's beginning, there's nothing to suggest that the picture is set in the 1960s. *Withnail & I* is a deliberately crusted-over paint-pot; in place of the psychedelic colours of the decade are autumnal browns, lethargic greys and dismal blacks, which were stippled into the frame on Bruce's insistence. Elsewhere, Robinson's tight thirty-day shooting schedule meant a few bloopers would find their way into the finished picture – signs for the M25 and EEC hedgerows that didn't appear until the 1980s.

The scene of Withnail and Marwood setting off for the Lake District in their rickety old Jag was shot in Barlby Road, Notting Hill. During filming, Grant and McGann were chased at sixty miles per hour down Kensal Rise by a police car. As McGann recalled for *Empire* magazine in 1996, 'We hadn't really got permission to film, and on the fourth take, just as we get to where the crew are, the traffic lights go red . . . I thought "Bollocks" and I *stood* on it and we took off through this red light.' A terrified Grant, convinced he was about to be deported back to Swaziland, had bailed out of the speeding vehicle and hared off down the road. 'They found him in someone's garden,' recalled McGann.

The use of Hendrix's version of 'All Along the Watchtower' during this scene, and 'Voodoo Child' during the drive back to London, was a particularly expensive investment: £50,000 per second of music, which, according to McGann, Robinson paid for out of his own pocket. According to Ralph Steadman, since *Withnail*, Hendrix's estate has now disallowed the tracks to be used in any film about drugs or drink, as Terry Gilliam discovered twelve years later when he tried to use them for his own take on *Fear and Loathing in Las Vegas*. The inclusion of Harrison's 'While My Guitar Gently Weeps', in the scene where the pair arrive back home, would have been quite impossible to include under normal circumstances, as the Beatles rarely licensed their recordings for films.

If most 1980s movies portrayed the English countryside as a pastoral retreat, *Withnail*'s boys find only horror here. Bulls run amok, locals greet their overtures with suspicion, the rain is constant, the darkness blinding. Stephen Poliakoff's *Close My Eyes* (1991) similarly subverts any notion of a peaceful world beyond the wood – where even a glide down sun-dappled provincial rivers is fraught with potential danger. The pair's holiday retreat, 'Crow Crag', is in fact an eighteenth-century cottage called Sleddale Hall, that nestles in the Vale of Eden area of the Lake District National Park, a few miles outside the hamlet of Shap. The night-time interior shots, when the pair first arrive, were achieved by draping enormous black curtains over the windows. 'It was a horrible shambles of a place,' Griffiths recalls. 'Cold, damp, unoccupied, abandoned. We were all a bit like refugees coming across a place in the middle of a war-torn countryside.'

Sleddale's roofless barn was converted into a green room; the art department placed a fibreglass cover across the roof to prevent the cast and crew from getting rained on between takes. 'It was pure arse,' recalls Peter Hannan. But otherwise 'perfect conditions for us. When McGann meets the farmer's wife we ran rain machines, but everything else was virtually natural. We were incredibly lucky all the way through.' When Monty arrives the place is transformed, the cottage interior mysteriously enlarging to accommodate his generous girth (Robinson deliberately switched to using a wider-angle lens). Monty brings colour with him, red meat, root crops and claret, as welcome as the sunlight streaming over the lakes.

'George Harrison came down a couple of times,' says Griffiths. 'He was always good news. It always boosted our morale, because he is so bloody famous. Whenever Dennis O'Brien came around people looked a bit hunted.' Three days into the shoot, HandMade's larger-than-life executive producer and guardian of Beatle George's purse, arrived to check on the progress of HandMade's 'Swinging London comedy'. O'Brien was incandescent. A scene in which McGann charges at a bull was ripped right out of the call sheet before their eyes. They were all behind schedule, he glowered. Furthermore, to judge by the rushes, Bruce had shot the scene in which the pair first arrive at the cottage in pitch darkness. *Pitch darkness!* What the fuck did Robinson think he was making here? A nature pro-gramme about bats? 'HandMade,' said Bruce, 'were just being a gang of cunts.'

In fact, they'd expected Monty Python. This line about 'coming on holiday by mistake' – was that supposed to be some sort of punchline? And what was so funny about sitting around trying to figure out how to kill a chicken? Grant, thought O'Brien, should be playing Withnail like Kenneth Williams. Swinging his arms about, flaring his nostrils, and shrieking. As for this Uncle Monty character, what was he, some kind of a faggot? In which case, why wasn't he mincing around with his arse in the air, like all those other old British queens? Now that was *comedy*. That was *funny*.

Principal cast and crew were ushered away. Bruce faced off. *Withnail*, he told O'Brien, was a comedy without jokes or punchlines. The comedy would come from the desperation of the characters' situation. They were going to have to trust him on this one. Otherwise, he'd take the first bus out of there. As Griffiths recalls, 'The script was so burnished and polished that the film had been cut like some great Amsterdam jeweller cutting a diamond. The whole thing was so beautifully edited in Bruce's mind that he'd look at most of the shots and say, "Yeah, that's OK," and then apparently be quite carefree about it. The fact is, he knew almost frame by frame how it was going to work.' Ray Cooper persuaded O'Brien to leave them alone. And, anyway, HandMade figured the picture was so cheap it wouldn't really matter that much if it flunked. They'd simply sling it out for a couple of weeks around town, and bury their losses. By the end of the day *Withnail* was back on course. That night Griffiths arrived, bearing wine and cigars, cheering everybody up no end.

Bruce's fellow Central School of Speech and Drama graduate Michael Elphick was drafted in during the filming to play Jake the Poacher, who the duo come across in a country pub. For his scene, Elphick would be accompanied by several live eels, housed in plastic bags strapped to his legs. As the actor told *Neon* magazine in 1996, 'I can't remember whether I was so pissed that I had to lean on the bar to stand up. That shows how pissed I was.' Jake's 'Here Hare Here' notice had been the only thing Bruce had dreamt up on the spot. As Griffiths recalls, 'It had to say something, but the Poacher is pretty inarticulate and not very literate, so it had to be something very simple. Here Hare Here. All the rest of it was organised down to within an inch of its life.'

The boys' Monty-funded trip to town to buy some wellies takes them into Penrith, a beautiful little market town at the northernmost end of the Lake District, harbouring deep Celtic origins. Despite being the central hub of Eden Valley, in reality not one frame of *Withnail & I* was shot there. The 'Tea Rooms', 'Pub' and 'Market Square' that feature in the film are nowhere to be found, however hard you look. The Tourist Information Office is daily plagued by legions of *Withnail* fans, often arguing heatedly with staff as they seek the whereabouts of these locations. As office head

Sandie Johnson confirms, 'It's the number one question in people's mind: "Where are the tea rooms?" Everybody comes here thinking they are going to find them in Penrith. But they don't exist here. Where? Who knows?'

We are happy to confirm that the 'Penrith Tea Rooms', the 'Pub' and 'Market Square' were all found some two hundred miles away in a little village outside Milton Keynes called Stony Stratford. It was the briefest of shoots; cast and crew spent just two days in the small market town. Today, the square retains the air of gentility that ushered in Monty's Rolls. 'I remember thinking that Monty must have been quite extraordinary to give them each a couple of fivers to get some rubber boots,' says Griffiths. 'A pair of wellies would have cost them about ten-bob each – a lot of money – and they could still have had four quid to go and get pissed on. But no, they wouldn't even do that. That's what Bruce has got right, they're that ruthless – they couldn't give a shit. Especially in Withnail's case. He is so out of control. As far as I was concerned, their student days, for all its shittiness, were far more glamorous than mine.'

The King William pub, to which the duo repair, is actually the Crown, at 9 Market Square. Across the road, at 1 Market Square, is Cox & Robinson, the local chemist's. In 1986 the building was derelict, its vacant shop front doubling as the tea rooms where the pair cause havoc. Robinson had recruited elderly locals to sit in for the scene, but hadn't told them what was about to happen. To add further to the silliness two asthmatic pug dogs were placed behind Grant's chair, wheezing away throughout the shot. In the event, Grant ruined take after take by laughing so much, so Bruce thought 'what the hell' and left it in.

After their weekend away, the pair return to the relative safety of their squalid flat. HandMade refused to pay for what they considered to be unnecessary shots of the Jag returning to London. Bruce was forced to shell out £30,000 for the day's filming. The crew closed off the roads and hired period cars to stream down the M25, prior to its official opening, while the dilapidated Jag itself had to be taken to the shoot on the back of a trailer as its engine had failed to start. Robert Oates, who played the non-screeching policeman, recalls being genuinely taken aback by his fellow actor's outburst. 'I was in such shock. I hadn't know he was going to say the line. ("*Geddinthebackofthevan*") like that.'

In the flat Withnail and Marwood discover that they have visitors – Danny the drug dealer and his side-kick Presuming Ed, laden with drugs. Untypical of the times this film is awash with alcohol, with only the occasional interruption of a spliff or two (most notably, Danny's Camberwell Carrot), and ranging the upper-class propensity for expensive vintage wines against the emancipation of synthetic or natural highs for all. Withnail, now at the mercy of the grass grown 2,000 feet above sea level, is still blissfully ignorant of his friend's imminent *volte-face*; Marwood, having refused the joint, and having finally secured a stage role, chooses another path. For the original finale, Robinson had planned that Marwood would pack his belongings and depart for the station. Withnail remains back at the flat. He later takes a shotgun he'd brought back from Monty's cottage, filling both barrels with 1953 Margot, toasting himself 'Chin chin' and drinking from the shotgun. The film was to have ended with a freeze frame of him pulling the trigger. But Bruce had second thoughts, thinking it 'a little too morbid'. Instead, the director had Withnail accompany his friend to Regent's Park en route to the train station (presumably Euston), and the film closes with Withnail howling Hamlet's soliloquy in the rain to a couple of disinterested old wolves.

'Towards the end of *Fear and Loathing*, Hunter returns to Las Vegas in a fury,' says Ralph Steadman. 'But there's a poignancy in Bruce that Hunter would never succumb to. With *Withnail*, that wonderful Shakespearean ending was so poignant it made me cry. You know the poor bugger's lost. He's finished. He's had it. He obviously had the promise to be a great actor, but he got in the way of himself. Viv may well have said something so derogatory to Bruce that he felt he had to try and play the system. But the film finishes so wonderfully because Bruce still cares about paying his dues to Viv.'

Stephen Woolley recalls thinking, 'For a film about a time gone by, it seemed very close.' In Monty's post-prandial diatribe and Danny's stoned soliloquy there's much that resonates (however unintentionally) with the era's malaise. As Robinson told *Empire*, 'The symbolism of the very short haircut of the "I" character, at the end, was based on the horror of Thatcherism coming along.' Danny's portentous musing was precipitous indeed: the stock market crash and inevitable recession was just around the corner.

Exterior scenes for Monty's house were among the last to be shot. McGann and Robinson had attended the wrap celebrations prematurely and McGann, slightly the worse for wear, drove the old Jag into the side of a skip. 'I'm not being in this scene with a fucking drunk!' Grant had cried, leaping out of the car and slamming the door behind him. Once filming was completed, champagne and caricatures of cast and crew were distributed for an impromptu street party. Grant, who had started this project cloaked in grief, later recalled driving home in 'shocked silence'.

Such was the script's tight economy – a testament to Robinson's extraordinary writing talent and directorial control – that very little of the finished product hit the cutting-room floor. Snipped sequences included a fencing, Shakespeare-spouting Withnail smoking a cigarette under his fencing mask, and a scene in which the boys buy up enough booze to see them through their rural retreat.

With the film in the can, Bruce looked forward to an imminent release, but the timing couldn't have been worse. By 1986 the British film industry had hit rock-bottom. The rise of home video and the government's abolition of a long-standing agreement to fund British film-makers from box office receipts had seen to that. In the decade of Thatcherism, British cinema had, in the aftermath of the hugely successful *Chariots of Fire* (less of a movie than a cultural task-force), been largely reduced to churning out polished heritage films – a picture postcard of the Tory ideal and an escape from its bitter reality.

'HandMade was very nervous about *Withnail* and they were trying to sell it,' recalls Stephen Woolley. 'I saw it on my own in a preview theatre, and I remember just laughing so hard I fell to my knees.' The picture was previewed to 150 youngsters from a nearby hostel, specially invited by HandMade to garner some feedback. Thirty minutes into the screening Robinson began to feel the heat. No one was laughing. Not one titter. Quite reasonably, Bruce fired his publicists: the entire audience had been made up of non-English-speaking German students.

'There's no great intrigue to why the film took so long to come out in England,' Paul Heller told *Neon*. 'One of the realities in England is that the theatre chains are controlled by very few people. It's very hard to get a decent booking unless you're a major studio. You wait till you can get decent screen time.' *Withnail* was finally picked up by Recorded Releasing, an independent British distribution company (now no longer in operation) who'd previously handled Spike Lee's *She's Gotta Have It*, and the film was released in February 1988.

Critical reaction was quietly encouraging on both sides of the pond and, initially, *Withnail* did better business in the States, where it picked up a small but dedicated cult following. As an English take on Hunter's *Fear and Loathing*, it couldn't be beaten. Vincent Canby of the *New York Times* thought the film 'genuinely funny [but] *Withnail & I* is not the whole story of the Sixties, it's a small, wise, breezy footnote'. In the UK, the *Guardian*'s Derek Malcolm called it 'one of the most original and certainly the most personal of the current British revival', while Scarth Flett of the *Sunday Express* was suitably moved to write 'Bruce Robinson calls it a comedy, but I was left with a sense of sadness'.

The film's run in British cinemas quickly came to an end before it could benefit from any word of mouth. As George Harrison told *Neon*, 'Everybody who hadn't seen it was trying to find out where it was on, but it had already been whipped off. That's the problem. If you don't pack out the cinemas in the first week, that's it.' Griffiths recalls: 'The picture came out to nothing ... and I cannot tell you how gutted I felt. I thought, God, Bruce will never recover from this. This should be a fucking Oscar in anybody's money. Can they not feel what he's done with the fantastical script?'

If *Withnail*'s initial publicity, what little there was of it, had missed its mark, the film was about to reap a huge following over the next decade through video and one-night stands in rep cinemas. As Mary Selway told Channel Four, 'A few years ago, a boy of twenty started quoting me huge passages from it and I said, "What on earth are you doing? That's *Withnail & I*, how do you know that?" And I didn't realise till about five years ago it had become this huge cult movie.'

The media hadn't cottoned on at first. But in May 1994 an article headed 'Withnail, You Terrible Cult', in the first issue of a highly influential magazine, changed all that. 'If *Loaded* hadn't come along, I always thought that *Withnail* was what my life would have been like,' says *Loaded*'s original editor James Brown. A former *NME* writer and legendary hell-raiser, Brown lived it like he wrote it. *Loaded*, the first and best of the New Lad mags, would be fashioned in his image. Now the dust has settled it's easy to overlook just how good, and how pioneering much of its initial journalism had been. 'From a journalistic perspective, I'd wanted to write about stuff that I knew was going on but nobody else was covering,' says Brown. That included cult movies. '*Withnail* had been my favourite film for quite a few years at that time, and the film had infiltrated the language so much.' And Brown understood the market: the article confirmed the fact that the *Withnail* cult had become firmly established.

As Brown has written, 'In every bar in the land stands a drunken youth shouting "What fucker said that?" Every street has a car full of druggies screaming, "Scrubbers!" Or so it seems.' Says Brown: 'I'm sure the article won hearts. I'm sure a lot of people said, "Yeah! We love that film as well!" It was a deliberate ploy to use that article.' Brown's piece also introduced one of *Withnail*'s more notorious offshoots to a larger public. 'Somebody at *Loaded* said they'd known someone who had played the Drinking Game.' Tucked away at the bottom of the *Loaded* article ran the instructions: 'Stick in the video, and as the film unwinds, tuck into a "here's some I prepared earlier" bounty of intoxicants . . . And no pausing the video either. Or rewinding.'

Guardian TV critic Julia Raeside first saw *Withnail* in her late teens. 'I instantly fell in love with the debauchery of it all,' she says. As Raeside tells it, one inspired night in 1994 in a student house in Coventry, she'd planned a viewing, complete with appropriate Game tools. 'Two of us had an end-of-year exam the next day but everyone else was determined to finish term with a bang. We had the requisite bottles of scotch, cider, red wine and pork pies. Ignoring countless maternal warnings about mixing drinks, we stuck the video on and matched Withnail and Marwood, drink for drink. It was ugly to say the least. One *Withnail* virgin, Craig the Economics student, had bent down to the gas fire in order to relight his half-smoked Carrot. Unfortunately, he was rather taken unawares by the noise of the gun going off in the cottage scene. Narrowly avoiding a scorching, he stood up too quickly and nutted himself on the big Victorian mantelpiece, taking a small chunk out of his forehead. Later, in casualty, he lay there with five stitches in his head, smiling. He hadn't felt a thing.'

In 1996 *Withnail* was re-released to great acclaim, while the movie received its biggest exposure in the summer of 1999, when Stella Screen organised an enormous outdoor screening of the film on Brighton beach for 20,000 revellers. A bewigged Ralph Brown introduced the film, as a flotilla from Brighton Marina sailed coastwards to watch *Withnail* from the comfort of their decks. In 2000, Grant organised a charity screening and auction to raise money for his old Waterford school. Ultimate 'kidult' Chris Evans bought Withnail's Edwardian-style tweed coat for £5,000, while *Withnail*'s costume designer Andrea Galer is now offering bespoke copies of the other costumes from the movie.

'I'm very pleased for *Withnail*,' says Griffiths. 'I really am, but I just wish to God I had a penny for everybody who asks what it was like to work on the film. The thing is set to make millions from now to the end of time, but it's other people who are benefiting from it. I've turned down endless opportunities to talk about it on TV because it seems to me that there is always somebody out there making money out of *Withnail* except the people who were in it.'

Withnail's wider fan base is now as strong as ever, crossing age, gender and nations. In Bruce's words, 'everybody's tree'. 'I'd definitely term *Withnail* a cult film,' says Raeside, 'because you get this sense of ownership over the characters, these lovable drunkards who are getting away with stuff every self-respecting youngster would love to do.' For those people who were directly involved with *Withnail*, the film's cult status remains pretty perplexing. Says Griffiths: 'I find it very confusing that people, especially young people, are very moved by it in a surprisingly big way.' Moved enough to shout, 'Monty, you terrible cunt?' at him? 'It's a constant,' Griffiths confirms. 'There's this endless recognition on the street. I remember this guy said to me, "You've done two things that are quite amazing for your reputation. For people who are at school you were in *The Naked Gun*, which is a big deal. For people who have left school and are at university you're in *Withnail & I* and that's major, and that will always be with you. Isn't that great?" And I said, "Well, up to a point it is, but I promise you, it butters no parsnips."'

Withnail fan Mike Hall runs the Internet's *Withnail & I* Multi Media Archive website. It's his favourite movie. 'How many films can you name where the very real threat of anal rape is the primary motivation behind a classically funny scene?' he says. 'The film is also uniquely British. An American Withnail wouldn't be the pathetic alcoholic we know – he'd be a wisecracking funny guy with designer stubble and beefcake build.' Since landing on the Net in 1999, Hall's website has attracted hordes of devotees, many of whom were only toddlers when the movie was first released. As they jostle to leave their mark in his guest book, the words 'brilliant' and 'authentic' crop up regularly. 'Quite simply the best film I have seen,' writes one contributor. 'This is the only film that justifies the invention of film,' comments another.

Fans still regularly visit *Withnail*'s locations. Referring to the scene in which McGann surveys the morning sun breaking over the lakes, Griffiths says, 'I'm sure legions of drunken students have trudged all over the Lake District, killing themselves trying to find a view of the lakes. They're about five miles away from the cottage.' A few minutes' walk away from Uncle Monty's cottage, at the base of the valley, lies the small waterfall where Withnail goes fishing with a shotgun. The phone box, in which Withnail rings 'Squat Betty', is still there, in the nearby village of Bampton.

Finding Crow Crag itself, lost amid a labyrinth of footpaths, horse tracks and private properties requires tenacity and a broad compass needle. Not that this has deterred the hardy: Sleddale Hall has paid dearly for its association with the movie. From a distance it's how one would remember it from *Withnail*, quaint and picturesque against the skyline, but on closer inspection the boarded-up windows and doorways tell their own story. And once inside, the sheer extremity of what some people will do to collect a piece of their favourite film is all too apparent.

Sleddale Hall has been devastated. The elegant fireplace that a bedraggled Grant snuggled up to has been ripped out. 'Maybe it's in Noel Gallagher's front room,' Eden District conservation officer

Elizabeth Murphy told the *Daily Express* in 1998. The kitchen sink has also disappeared, along with the ornate wall-fittings. A stench of stale fags, mould and sheep shit permeates throughout, while the floor is littered with old beer cans and rubbish. In 1998 the owners of the cottage, North West Water, put it on the market *au naturel* after local planners opposed their plans to renovate the property on the grounds that it would alter the valley's character. Three years on, no one has taken up the offer – not even a well-heeled celebrity or young dot.com entrepreneur looking for an off-beat retreat. At the time of writing, the future of Crow Crag is uncertain. The place is in desperate need of repair and the depredations of *Withnail* obsessives have forced North West Water to put up an enormous fence around the property.

As for that other memorable setting, Notting Hill's Old Mother Black Cap pub, today it languishes under the name of Babushka's Wine Bar. But whatever romantic Zhivago visions the name might conjure up, inside it's familiar *Withnail* territory. The coffin-coloured wooden benches are still there, and in the toilets the urinals are exactly where they were in the film. The graffiti that caused McGann such consternation, however, has long since gone.

Following *Withnail*, HandMade sunk more than £5 million into a series of box office turkeys – *Shanghai Surprise*, *The Raggedy Rawney*, *Checking Out* – and was sold in 1994 to a Canadian company called Paragon for a mere £5.6 million. An innocent like Marwood where business was concerned, George Harrison dragged his once trusted right-hand man through the courts on a $25 million lawsuit, claiming that O'Brien had duped him out of a fortune for over twelve years. According to Harrison's defence team, the 'faithless and fraudulent' O'Brien had supported a lavish lifestyle 'while subjecting his trusted client to massive economic risks and losses'. Particularly upsetting for Harrison was the fact that he'd created something entirely original outside the Beatles strata. Finally he opted for a £7 million settlement, but none the less he had been left so out of pocket that he acquiesced to a contrived Beatles reunion in 1995, something he had vowed never to do 'as long as John Lennon remained dead'. For the most part, this reluctant star kept his head down. Richard Lester recalls meeting Harrison a few years ago at a party. 'Hullo George!' he said. 'Oh dear,' said George. 'You recognised me.' Harrison died from cancer, aged 58, in November 2001.

Bruce Robinson still hasn't made a penny out of *Withnail*, and is still owed £30,000. Meanwhile, *Withnail* continues to command huge affection. Ralph Brown, for one, finds it very difficult to pin it down. 'It's strange. I think the dialogue is very funny, although there are people who don't find it funny, and there is a certain kind of educated adolescent thing going on with it; a kind of intensity of despair.' Richard Griffiths thinks, 'It's because the writing is absolutely truthful and recognisable – but only to people passing through a certain period in their lives. People my age now looking at it would think it's a bit unpleasant, don't like the language, they're nasty odious characters, all the stereotypical things that are wrong with youth are there for people in their fifties to dislike. But people forget just how scallywaggish and idiotic they were, and the film gets that.'

'*Withnail*'s been grafted onto my life,' says Ralph Steadman. 'It's part of me. I think it has a wonderful, essential innocence. It didn't just become a cult by accident. It somehow got picked up by people who said, "I felt like that! I've been a piss artist! It's me!" People have identified with it so strongly. There's not a pretension in it.' Ralph's old friend and collaborator Hunter S. Thompson caught pneumonia in 2000 and was placed in an oxygen tent. He insisted on smoking. 'But Bruce is a far more sensitive being,' says Ralph. He called Bruce recently, while Robinson was working on another quite possibly doomed screenplay. 'He said, "Ralph, quite frankly, at this moment I'd rather have cancer." He kind of meant it.'

ROBINSON'S VOICE IS a notable absentee from this chapter. He's decided he's had enough of *Withnail*. He finds it strange that it excites so much interest. We did get to meet him, however, just once. In 1999, he was invited to give a reading from his novel *Thomas Penman* at Putney Library. We kept an eye out for him on the steps. A dark car approached and three men got out; we recognised Robinson immediately. He was the one whose legs weren't working.

We followed him to the bar across the road, where we found him slumped over his sausages and mash. He was several bottles the worse for wear, eyeballs cartwheeling behind a pair of rock star shades, the Colonel Kurtz of the British film industry.

We approached with caution. Suddenly stirring, he cocked a tremulous finger toward Ali Catterall's sling (consequence of a broken arm sustained during an immense piss-up to celebrate this book's commission). 'Did you do that wanking?' he cackled. He then clutched at his publisher. 'I don't want to do this, I don't want to do this!' he keened in a high-pitched voice. Barely ten minutes later, to our utter astonishment, he practically bounded up the road like Captain Kangaroo, a vision of health and sobriety, a Polaroid negative of his previous state, a miraculous, Lazarus-like transformation. With a nod to the writers, he burst through the door of Putney Library to greet his waiting public.

MEAN TIMES

Johnny makes his way down to London from Manchester in a stolen car to escape from himself. On a sleepless odyssey through the capital's nightspots, cafés, office blocks and bedroom floors, Johnny (something between a slice of John Lydon, and a dose of Mark E. Smith) vents a spleenful of bile on whomever he encounters. An intellectual who has all the answers, but no one asks him any questions. His parallel, city psycho Jeremy, shadows his every move, with only his upwardly mobile accoutrements to distinguish him. Chuck in a hotchpotch of truly dysfunctional characters and *Naked* presents a portrait of a land and a people that have given up on themselves.

> 'When I put my key in the door
> And I sat in my bed
> And looked for lumps on my skin
> And thinking about the end of the world,
> I waited for the world to begin.'   From the poem 'Another
>   Night' by David Thewlis (by kind permission)

On a chilly morning in April 1992 harried commuters shuffling past railway station newspaper stands were greeted with one of the most brazen headlines ever to grace a tabloid: 'If Kinnock Wins Today, Will the Last Person in Britain Please Turn Out the Lights.' In the run-up to the General Election the *Sun* newspaper had been running what can only be described as an open hate campaign against the Labour leader. Now it was going in for the kill, resurrecting the clanking phantoms of the 1980s 'Loony Left' – a faction that the

Opposition leader himself had attempted to purge during Labour's mission to redefine the Party image.

There was a change in the air. The previous decade's boom and bust had seen many come away with their fingers burnt. The 'community care' fiasco had polarised popular opinion: with the selling-off of the nation's psychiatric institutions to private developers, the patients found themselves released into communities which either didn't exist, or didn't care about them. The Falklands, the miners' strike, the asset-stripping of the NHS, the Public Order Act, Clause 28, Wapping, Greenham Common . . . there was a long list of issues that had, over more than a decade of Tory government, helped to fracture the post-war consensus. But the single strongest factor in Labour's favour was the mishandling of the poll tax, a universally hated levy, fleecing the poorest communities while propping up the richest. With Labour now slightly ahead in the polls for the first time in years it appeared that the stranglehold of Thatcherism was coming to an end. Among those anticipating its imminent demise was director Mike Leigh, then rehearsing his latest film, *Naked*, taking time out one weekend to attend the first of two anticipatory Labour victory bashes. 'I was one of a load of media wankers at Millbank down on the South Bank the previous Sunday, and you just thought, "This is going to happen."'

Mike Leigh has lived in London for the last forty years. For an Oscar-nominated director with an OBE he remains pretty much a face in the crowd, travelling by tube most mornings, taking the Piccadilly Line from his Wood Green residence down to Leicester Square. From here it's just a few minutes' walk to his modest office in Soho's Greek Street, which shares a stairwell with three French prostitutes. He is very happy in London these days, but once, he confessed, he had a love–hate relationship with the capital. It reached a pitch shortly before that unexpected Tory victory of 1992. Returning to the West End to carry out post-production on his film *Life is Sweet*, he came across more people – especially youngsters

– huddled in doorways and wandering the streets than ever before. It appalled him and got him thinking, among other things, about tackling the subject of homelessness.

Naked was one result of this disturbing stroll through the capital. Along with *Abigail's Party* and *Meantime*, it's one of the director's cultiest works. A large part of this cult appeal stems from David Thewlis's performance as the scabrous, ranting, eminently quotable Johnny – an anti-hero for our times. Other factors include its use of gritty London settings, unflinching sex and violence, and the director's famously unconventional working methods. Unlike the anti-Thatcherite *Meantime* or *High Hopes*, *Naked* shouldn't be taken as chiefly a comment on the ravages of Maggie's administration; the film is working out of a broader European tradition of dark metaphor and existential malaise. For Leigh, it also incorporates such heavyweight themes as 'integrity, materialism, some tougher aspects of the relationship between men and women and, indeed, the impending apocalypse'. However, as Leigh told *Cineaste* in 1994, 'In so far as it *is* about England, the fabric of society is collapsing. People are insecure, there is a sense of disintegration which is, as much as anything else, a legacy of the Tories.'

Mike Leigh was born to Abe and Phyllis Leigh on Saturday, 20 February 1943, sharing his birthday, though not the year, with that other cinematic maverick, Robert Altman. To the east, Russian troops continued to resist the Nazi invasion, while back home in Blighty the nation huddled by the wireless listening to Percy Whitlock playing the organ on the Home Service. Abe (who'd changed his name from Lieberman in 1939 for obvious reasons) was a doctor and the family lived over his surgery. Growing up middle class in a working-class area of Salford, Leigh was instantly granted a simultaneous insider and outsider status. 'I have a completely genuine knowledge about working-class life,' he says.

Educated at Salford Grammar (Albert Finney's old alma mater), young Mike was a compulsive patron of Salford's Rialto cinema and the Cromwell – the oldest movie house in Britain. A highly creative kid, he'd immerse himself in the arts, drawing cartoons and caricatures, much to the annoyance of his mother, who accused him of making fun of people. Just scraping three 'O' levels, he hunkered down in the sixth form for a while but, at seventeen, desperate to

shrug off Manchester's provincial restraints, he relocated to London
– the Bejewelled City paved with unemployed scribes and thespians.
In his teens he was active within a Jewish socialist movement that
encouraged young Jews to take up residences in kibbutzim, and he
had also been involved with CND, attending the Aldermaston rally
of 1960. He won a scholarship to RADA that same year. During
stints in drama schools and arts labs he gradually developed his
trademark improvisational method.

Commenting on her work with Leigh, *Naked* actress Katrin
Cartlidge told Kenneth Turan of the *Los Angeles Times* in 1996,
'Not every actor can do it. You need a huge amount of patience and
the ability, if possible, to keep paranoia well and truly out the door
and under lock and key.' In place of a working script, Leigh demands
absolute, fanatical attention to detail and empathy from his cast.
The preparatory creative process, before shooting begins, can last
anything up to four months. Leigh, having had a loose idea of his
theme, begins by bringing in his actors, in streams. He then goes
tête à tête with individual actors, asking them to choose a character,
usually someone they know. Through a process of elimination a
character is found for which the actor can create a rich, solid history.

Like an alchemist mixing unknown elements, Leigh next brings
together his actors (who may not even have previously met) to
perform tightly structured improvised vignettes, in character. At
this point they still have no idea about the plot; they know only
how their character would react in certain situations. Leigh then
devises a series of scenes for the actors, which may be as basic
as 'X meets Y on a street corner'. Having remembered how their
characters interacted from previous improvisations, the actors then
improvise the new scenes within Leigh's guidelines and in selected
locations, while an assistant takes down their comments in short-
hand. Through this organic interplay, the story and the dramatic
tensions emerge. On the day of filming, the best passages having
been broken down into chunks, the actors fix exactly what will go
on screen – the most pertinent or funny lines – sometimes fifteen
or twenty minutes before the cameras are ready to roll. 'What we're
trying to do here,' Leigh told Sheridan Morley in 1977, 'is a form
of social documentary. I believe in improvisation within a structured
surrounding; this is not some kind of all-in anarchic democracy.'

NAKED

Leigh's first cinematic début, *Bleak Moments* (1971), grew from a seventy-five-minute theatre production he'd staged the previous year at Charles Marowitz's Tottenham Court Road Open Space fringe theatre, concerning the relationship between Sylvia (Anne Raitt), her retarded sibling, Hilda (Sarah Stephenson), and a visiting teacher friend, Peter (Eric Allan). 'That's the slowest film ever made with jokes in,' Leigh said in 1993. 'It's like watching paint dry.' Albert Finney, whose Memorial Films stumped up much of the cash, dubbed it 'Carry On Gloom'. But the critics loved it, lavishing praise on the young director, who had worked with a tiny budget of £18,000 and a cast of unknowns. Given the closed ranks state of the British film industry, Leigh wouldn't return to the big screen for seventeen years and, for now, he continued to direct his talents towards theatre and the BBC.

Leigh's second film for the Beeb (after 1973's semi-autobiographical *Hard Labour*) was 1976's *Nuts in May*, a tale of two rabid vegetarians Keith and Candice Marie Pratt (Alison Steadman and Roger Sloman) from Croydon, who embark on a ten-day camping holiday on the Isle of Purbeck in Dorset, with tragi-comic results. An early altercation with rugby-playing student Ray (Anthony O'Donnell) sets the mood for further fun and games; when Finger (Stephen Bill), an unemployed plasterer and motorcycling rocker from Birmingham, arrives with his girlfriend Honky (Sheila Kelley), confrontation with the Pratts is a foregone conclusion. Ultimately, it's the contrasting lifestyles of Keith and Finger and their total lack of communication skills that makes the film so delightful, but it's Leigh's acute eye for detail that leaves the most marked impression.

The 1977 stage production of Leigh's *Abigail's Party* at the Hampstead Theatre was successfully transferred to TV in the BBC's *Play for Today* season. A staggering sixteen million viewers (ITV were on strike) tuned in during a stormy night to revel in the suburban nightmare dished up with the olives and cheesy sticks by Beverly, Laurence, Tony, Angela and Sue. Here Leigh presented a gallery of grotesque, strutting bores, wading through imagined social niceties but ultimately unable to maintain the illusion.

What begins as an attack on lower middle-class pretensions gradually descends into a black farce that culminates with

Laurence's untimely death from a heart attack. The performances here are exemplary. A heavily pregnant Alison Steadman would win the *Evening Standard*'s Best Actress Award in 1977 for her portrayal of the slaggy, bullying Beverly – in Alan Bennett's memorable phrase, 'a brutal hostess, with shoulders like a lifeguard and a walk to match'. Leigh hated the televisation of the play with its technical shortcomings, but it was an enormous success with the public, making Leigh a household name. It remains an all-time classic, the most performed play by Am Dram societies, and itself a cult among devoted legions who regularly congregate to re-enact key scenes.

But not everyone was won over. Dennis Potter called the play 'a prolonged jeer, twitching with genuine hatred, about the dreadful suburban tastes of the dreadful lower classes'. The accusations stuck and would accompany the release of most of Leigh's output thereafter. Leigh admits to having become 'slightly worn down' by such criticism, but flatly defends his corner: 'So-called working-class people do not have a problem with my work,' he told Alan Riding of the *New York Times* in 1996. As Leigh stalwart Timothy Spall adds: 'Leigh is often accused of being patronising to the working classes, but he is only accused by the middle classes, which is interesting.'

If anyone thought Leigh's *œuvre* was forever entrenched in quirky suburbia, 1984's *Meantime* blasted those misplaced preconceptions into oblivion. Leigh had drawn inspiration from a news story concerning two unemployed kids from the North who had committed suicide. His finest piece of work, as far as these writers are concerned (and perversely the least seen of Leigh's filmed output post-1984), *Meantime* – set and filmed in a crumbling tower block in London's East End – painted a picture of a forgotten Britain. The Pollock family unit served as a microcosm for the state of England under the Tories: fractured, self-interested, and tearing itself apart. The film is predominantly shot through the eyes of brothers Mark and Colin, whose tenuous relationship is threatened when their upwardly aspiring Auntie Barbara – perhaps the most complex character – offers Colin a decorating job. Here Leigh skilfully tackles inverted working-class snobbery, pitching Mark as the guardian of proletarian ethics that would never stoop to anything as low as charity, especially within one's own family, however estranged.

The Pollocks' brow-beaten depression is further compounded by a catalogue of mounting disappointments: a broken pen short of a win in a Bingo Hall (even ordinary domestic appliances conspire against them); a visit from an ethereal, non-conformist estate manager (played by future *Naked* actor Peter Wight as a well-meaning but profoundly idiotic young idealist); and snide offhand remarks made by their Essex relatives. What ultimately shines through is the protective love Mark has for Colin and the oblique way he tries to protect him from those who would seek to use and abuse him. Superficially, Mark's often volatile behaviour to his brother could be seen as no more than adding to the insults he receives from everyone else. On closer inspection, it's Mark's over-riding love for his brother (even if it cannot easily be expressed) that redeems him. In contrast to the Thatcherite ethos, in which appearances and status are paramount, Mark's steadfast dedication to fundamental principles keep his head above water.

Leigh recruited *Quadrophenia* hero Phil Daniels to play Mark, a young man of great promise relegated to the sidelines of opportunity through enforced inactivity, and Tim Roth to play his retarded brother Colin. Anyone who doubted Daniels's ability to stretch his talents beyond a Borstal sneer was in for a shock, as he gave one of his most textured, complicated performances to date. Roth, meanwhile, who had previously appeared as a skinhead in Alan Clarke's *Made in Britain* (1982) and as John Hurt's henchman in Stephen Frears' *The Hit* (1984), was, as Colin, transformed into a walking failure, a lump of impressionable putty to be slapped and plied by everyone around him. The film's most outrageous character was Coxy, whom Gary Oldman played as a lager-driven skinhead. But for all his swagger, Coxy (the runt of the skinhead litter) is merely posing, and we know he probably couldn't punch his way out of a glue-bag.

Rarely, outside of Pinter or Beckett, has such an economical script spoken so many volumes. In this study of communication or, more precisely, the lack of it, certain words and phrases are so precise, so *right*, that they become instantly embedded in the memory after a single viewing. Everyone here struggles to assert themselves in the face of indifference and confusion. With almost every line being misinterpreted by another party, they have to fall back on the nuances of body language. As Colin wheezes his replies in the negative, and Mark in *non sequiturs*, Auntie Barbara's use of 'Eh?' at the end of her sentences, like a rhetorical full stop, deliberately invites no further response; and her software-driven husband John (a young Alfred Molina) regurgitates facts like tickertape. Meanwhile, mother Mavis simply plugs herself mute with a nicotine teat as an alternative to healthy discourse. The boys' parents anchor the piece through strong performances by Pam Ferris and Jeff Robert, as the past-his-sell-by-date father (expertly mirrored by Daniels's own visage and a future echo of his son's own certain resignation).

The early 1980s spawned a plethora of anti-Thatcherite dramas. With the print media mostly tied up by the Tories, TV drama was one of the few outlets left to send brickbats towards the Iron Lady. Clement's and La Frenais's *Auf Wiedersehen Pet* found a gang of unemployed dole-fugitives seeking work abroad. Alan Bleasdale's *tour de force*, *Boys from the Blackstuff* (1982) followed the ordeals of Chrissie, Dixie and Yosser, redundant thirty-somethings hugely ashamed of their predicament (since the 1930s, this was the first time a middle-aged generation had had to deal with mass unemployment). While their *Meantime* counterparts seem resigned to their fates – all but Mark, who talks of challenging the status quo – Bleasdale's Boys continually strive to fend off family pressures and growing debts. Bernard Hill's Yosser Hughes, the most memorable character to spawn a catchphrase ('Gissa Job') stood out among a cast of magnificent performances, the shambling embodiment of broken hopes and dreams. If the Boys were now Men (and once proud working men at that), *Meantime*'s boys are made even more pathetic for their lack of a P45.

After a preview at the London Film Festival in 1983 and its appearance on the newly launched Channel Four a year later, *Meantime* garnered a huge retinue of devotees. It thrived on the bootleg circuit until its video release in the early 1990s. Blur recruited Phil Daniels to narrate their sing-along *Parklife* on the strength of their love of the film (Daniels greeted the audience at an Alexandra Palace gig with a hearty 'Evening Muppets!' from the film).

Through unlucky timing the film was denied a British theatrical release, having been made in 16mm some months before Channel Four inaugurated their cinematic venture. 'It is the great tragedy,' says Leigh today. He had at the time inquired about the logistics of shooting in cinema-friendly 35mm, but the answer 'was kind of "not at the moment". But I know that if we'd made it six months later, or certainly a year later, it would absolutely have been given the go-ahead. For all we knew, at that stage, Channel Four was another television channel with a new outlet. We didn't know how different it was going to be from what we'd already experienced at the BBC. Over the years there has been talk of blowing it up to 35mm, which would be fun, but it's very complicated. For Central Television, who owns it, it's just some fucking ancient bloody television programme that somebody made and, "What's all the fuss about it?" Had it been made as a feature, as far as I and a lot of people are concerned, a lot of history would have been different.'

High Hopes (1988) focused on a likeable couple, beautifully played by Phil Davis and Ruth Sheen, coming to terms with Thatcher's Britain. Some people thought the film marred by David Bamber's and Leslie Manville's portrayals of the upper-class couple Rupert and Laetitia, which seemed to verge on caricature, but Leigh commented, 'The truth is, if you go to Harrods or the Henley Regatta, you will find behaviour that makes her seem really rather muted in comparison.'

Leigh's next film, *Life is Sweet* (1990), an ensemble portrait of suburban domestic blitz, was his most popular and accessible work to date. Certainly, it's deceptively lighter in look and feel, featuring loving, low-key performances from his then wife Alison Steadman and Jim Broadbent as Wendy and Andy, long-suffering parents of twins Nicola (Jane Horrocks) and Natalie (Claire Skinner). But there was a sad edge, with the family's happiness being undermined by Nicola's bulimia and related depression. Leigh was concerned to show that a condition usually associated by the media with middle-class girls knew no such class barriers. Light relief was provided by Timothy Spall as Aubrey, a hopeless, despotic restaurateur, and Stephen Rea as Broadbent's shady pal, Patsy. The story's moving ending, in which the distant siblings finally come together under blue skies to face the future, is the film's emotional high point, a rare note of optimism for a family seemingly heading nowhere.

Leigh's next project, *Naked*, was a kind of latter-day Pilgrim's Progress, in which young genius auto-didact Johnny drifts around London, upsetting almost everyone he meets, rejecting and being rejected in turn.

The boy who would be Johnny first saw light in 1963 in Blackpool, England. Born David Wheeler, Thewlis was the middle child of three, and brought up in a flat above the family store, which sold promenade novelties and kiss-me-quick hats during the summer months, wallpaper and paint out of season. Wheeler's father had previously been a miner and his mum used to assemble Monopoly boxes for Waddington's. During the summers the boy David was employed on Blackpool's Golden Mile as a test-your-strength machine operator. In his late teens he played in a punk band, then took an acting degree at London's Guildhall School of Music and Drama. At weekends he returned home and played gigs around Blackpool on the chicken-in-a-basket circuit, performing Simon and Garfunkel's 'The Boxer', among other covers. One gig found him at the headquarters of the British Limbless Ex-Servicemen's Association, where he sung 'You Need Hands' and 'I get a Kick out of You', which went down a treat. In 1985 he dropped out of Guildhall and took some parts in rep. When he got his Equity card, he adopted his mother's maiden name as there was another David Wheeler on the books, a ventriloquist working clubs in Halifax. Of French Huguenot stock, 'Thulis' means 'Ill mannered and lacking in virtue' – pretty apt when you consider the character he played in *Naked*.

In 1986 he made a cameo appearance in Dennis Potter's masterpiece, *The Singing Detective*. He appeared in Alan Clarke's lacerating version of Jim Cartwright's *Road* the following year, playing the wasted, tortured Joey (virtually a warm-up for his role as *Naked*'s Johnny). That same year he starred in Mike Leigh's eighteen-minute short film *Short and Curlies*, chatting up a chemist's assistant over the Durex counter. The performance convinced Leigh to carve out another role for him as Horrocks's anonymous boyfriend in *Life is Sweet*. But Thewlis came to feel 'disgruntled and paranoid' to find himself playing a small role after what had been an involved preparatory period. As he told Kenneth Turan of the *LA Times*, 'All I did was come in, cover Jane Horrocks with chocolate and lick it off. I'd done all this work, and they could have gotten anyone off the street to do that – no offence to Jane.' Says Leigh: 'David couldn't help but feel somewhat short-changed, but he understood. I said, "I guarantee you'll get a very big slice of the pie next time." And that was before we'd even embarked on what *Naked* was about.'

Leigh got together with Thewlis again in early 1992, to work on David's *Naked* character. As usual, Leigh required his leading man to perform a massive excavation of the character's roots. David was under strict instructions not to reveal Johnny's characteristics to anyone, not even his actress wife, in case his fellow cast members cottoned on to what he was all about. 'Mike asked me to tell him about everyone I'd ever met,' says Thewlis, 'the same gender, within 8 to 10 years of my age. No members of my family and no other actors. This went on for about three weeks; it was a big list. Eventually he's like, "Any more?" and I'm like, "Shouldn't think so." So he goes, "Just think," and I said, "Tell you what. There was this guy in a bar a few years ago I got chatting to for about five minutes," and he says, "What do you imagine he did for a living?" and I said, "Maybe he works in a Post Office." He says "What do you think his parents might have done?" and he made notes, and I'd go through this list over and over and do a lot of crossing out – it's like a beauty contest – until it got narrowed down to five people. Then he'd say, "Now compare them in terms of their appreciation of art; would they know who Jackson Pollock was?" He'd compare and cross-reference people, and about three weeks later he chose: "This is the guy we're going to do" – the Source Character. On *Naked*, when he named the name, I was like, "Oh, shit, not *him*. Fucking *hell*, I'm going to spend seven months being *him*!"'

Next, David shut himself in his poky bedsit in Soho's Old Compton Street, with books, pamphlets and magazines strewn across the floor, all open at relevant passages. He drew up giant character maps, covered with occult references, personality traits, psychic shrapnel and tortured inner dialogues. 'I got these marker pens and big sheets of paper from art shops and pinned them on the wall. I did a lot of cross-referencing, I wrote lines down – a lot are in the film – and wrote stuff all over the walls, cos I didn't want to write *on* the walls. Someone once told me a large percentage of graves are robbed for rings, money, anything that might be valuable. I thought, "That's good." Johnny had either known someone who'd done that or maybe done it himself. So on one of these sheets I wrote, "Rob graves for money", just to remember the idea. The woman from downstairs had problems with the plumbing and came up to ask if my pipes were working. She came into this room and she's like, "Oh, my God", and I'm going, "The pipes are fine, come and look at the pipes." She's looking around and she sees this huge sheet, and she says, "What does that mean, 'Rob graves for money?'" She hadn't known I was an actor making a film, so I just said, "Apparently, a large percentage of graves in Britain are robbed at some time. It's an option, isn't it?" She's like, "Well . . . I suppose so", and left very soon afterward.'

According to Thewlis, 'Mike wanted to compound my fear of death', both actor and director presumably having uncovered this trait in Johnny's character. Leigh arranged for him to visit King's Cross mortuary, where he saw an 'old bloke – which didn't bother me, and a young girl – which I wasn't happy about at all'. Says Leigh: 'I actually have a thing that everybody – and certainly actors – should go and see a dead body – at least once. Not everybody has. And David said, "Yeah, let's go for it." It's routine stuff . . .'

Leigh hadn't actually told the actor to lose weight, but for Thewlis, now bursting with words, images and ideas, food was the last thing on his mind. He'd now get by on endless cups of coffee and cigarettes, to the accompaniment of the Smiths, the Fall, Joy Division, New Order, Happy Mondays – Johnny's favourite Manchester bands. For some strange reason Frank Sinatra was also in the mix. As Francis Bacon wrote, 'Some books are to be tasted, others to be swallowed, and some few to be chewed and digested.' With the passion of a bulimic bibliophile, Thewlis, the better to convince as the ranting autodidact, now gorged himself on reams of philosophical and religious tracts, anything from the *Thoughts of Chairman Mao* to the Koran and the Bible, the works of Stephen Hawking and a treatise on the language of frogs. Once in character he'd venture outdoors, periodically stop passing strangers and inquire in that nasal monotone: 'Tell me what you believe.' Thewlis laughs, 'With one particular Hare Krishna, I really chewed his ear off.'

'The general assumption I make is that I will push each actor quite to the hilt and exploit them as much as I can,' says Leigh. 'I knew David could hack it with the reading and bring to it much brainpower.'

'My brain was on fire!' says Thewlis. 'It's massively creative and that's why I love Mike, because he gave me that. It's like I was flying. Sometimes I'd hear myself say things and think, "Where the fuck did that come from?" Sometimes I was spending more of my waking hours as Johnny than David – but it was always in character. It's important to define that, because I think that's got a bit muddled. There was some rumour that I went nuts and was just walking around out of control. I wasn't wandering around the set screaming at the crew.'

Leigh, too, is at pains to differentiate between preparatory periods, improvisations, tight rehearsals – in which actors will come in and out of character – and the actual shooting. As Thewlis maintains, 'All these incidents happened under my aegis. But even out of character, I'd still have this energy; my remit was to look at the world in a very negative, very dark fashion, just looking at the darkest, darkest, darkest, so I did because I was very committed to it. I was like, "Yeah, let's go right out there and get as deep and dark as you can." A beautiful sunset, a beautiful sky, would be shit. It was like, "What's the fucking point of that? Why is that beautiful? Why is a child in a pushchair beautiful? I'll kick its head in!"'

'Johnny's not cynical,' says Leigh. 'He's despondent, he's disappointed, he's frustrated, but in fact he's an idealist, who's simply pissed off with cynicism and materialism. That's the whole complexity of what he and the film is about.'

While Thewlis was haring around Soho, Leigh had been assembling the rest of his cast, typically ushering them in stream by stream, two at a time, for rehearsals lasting the next twelve weeks. These cast members included some Leigh loyalists, experienced unknowns and first-timers. Lesley Sharp would become Johnny's long suffering ex, Louise. She'd previously appeared in Alan Clarke's *Rita, Sue and Bob Too* (1986) and *Road* (1987) alongside Jane Horrocks and Thewlis. Katrin Cartlidge became Louise's flatmate, the 'wicky wacky' goth, Sophie. She had previously acted with the Royal Court Youth Theatre and with Steven Berkoff's travelling caravan, and had also starred in Channel Four's Liverpool-based soap, *Brookside*.

Claire Skinner – almost unrecognisable from her role as the tomboyish Natalie in *Life is Sweet* – became Sandra, the third flatmate, an absent-minded safari-going nurse, while Greg Cruttwell became Jeremy, the girls' nightmarish Yuppie landlord. 'The most depressing thing is that people, who are otherwise very pro, say Jeremy/Sebastian's a caricature – which he absolutely isn't,' says Leigh. 'Obviously there is an argument – which I don't accept – that there is no explanation as to why Jeremy/Sebastian is the way he is, but there isn't any explanation why anybody else is the way they are, either; people are presented as they are, from their background. The point is, there are these people around.'

Ewen Bremner became Archie, a homeless twitching Scots straggler Johnny meets, and Susan Vidler became Archie's girlfriend Maggie. They'd both later show up in Danny Boyle's *Trainspotting*. Leigh had stumbled across one such Archie in the pouring rain while on a hitch-hiking trip in France in 1961. 'I fell in with a guy called Wilson McDougal, wearing a kilt, who came from Paisley, outside of Glasgow. This guy, who was completely, totally thick, thicker than Archie, was trying to get to Paris. Eventually I had to ditch him in Paris because I was going to Marseilles to catch a boat to go work on a kibbutz. The guy just festered at the back of the cranium for thirty-odd years. I suddenly thought, I could include a bit of him in this lad Archie. There's a lot of Archies around.' On another occasion, Leigh recalls, he and Alison Steadman 'picked up a bloke in our Beetle driving up to Liverpool. We finally had to pretend to go and visit some people spontaneously, because of the pong. This guy had come from somewhere like Paisley and had gone down to King's Cross and hung around for about ten days and, literally, was completely inert. Y'know, it's frightening for these kids. He'd hardly eaten, certainly hadn't washed and had probably shat his pants, and he needed to be back at home with his mummy, albeit that they'd beat the shit out of him.'

Peter Wight became Brian, an 'insecurity' guard Johnny bumps into on his travels. According to Leigh, Wight is 'a complete magpie. The trouble is, he's also obsessive.' While working on *Meantime*, once Wight had finished all his scenes, 'he then rang up to ask if he could continue researching anyway'. Gina McKee became a lonely café waitress Johnny tries to befriend.

With cast assembled, production designer Alison Chitty interviewed the actors, compiling 'possession lists' for each. Thewlis, for instance, had half a page of possessions, including his trusty bag and apocalyptic literature. Lesley Sharp's list was minuscule, and Katrin Cartlidge simply had a big 'S' to carry around, the S in question having supposedly fallen off a storefront.

Following his individual sessions with the actors, Leigh began to introduce them to one another in character. 'Katrin and I did this six-hour improvisation where we went down the pub – Mike followed us – had a few beers, and went back to her place,' Thewlis recalls. 'Violence and sex are obviously unethical to improvise, although Mike does take it pretty close to the edge. Katrin and I got on the sofa and started snogging. I've got my hand down her knickers and she's got her hand on my bum, and Mike has to stop it because it's about to become unethical. All he ever says is, "Come out of character", very quietly, just, "Come out of character." You're supposed to take about five minutes to come down – like hypnosis. Afterwards, I was like, "Hi, I'm David. I've just had my hand down your arse."'

Thewlis was also sent to the steps of a Marylebone church to rehearse a scene in which Johnny meets Archie, the young homeless boy. 'In an early improvisation I'd stolen a screwdriver from Lesley Sharp, and put it in my bag,' says Thewlis. 'I thought, "I might need that." It was always a mystery what was in this bag. I'd not met Ewen Bremner's character before, and Mike said, "Turn up at seven o'clock, sit on the steps of this church and see what happens," which is quite a usual instruction, so I went, talking to myself, in character. I'm thinking, "Something's going to happen," and I noticed Mike; you're always aware that Mike's somewhere. A few people come along, a vicar comes along for a start and starts speaking to me, and I get into a bit of patter with him, thinking, "Excellent, great, an actor playing a vicar." So I get into all this stuff like, "So tell us about the Big Man and all that." Then I realise the vicar's got the keys to the church and I'm going, "Can I come in and have a word?" thinking this is what Mike wants . . . Then I realised he was a real vicar. Ewen appeared, and I didn't get it was him at first cos he was so fucking good, twitching his head and doing all the "Maggie!" business.

'I got this screwdriver out. Acting in character, my motivation was, "I'm going to fucking have him." It broke into a physical fight. Ewen stood on my wrist, we struggled around. I thought, "Shit, maybe I should just stop this cos we are going to get hurt here," so I made sure we got the screwdriver out of it and Ewen had a beer can that he threw and I think it hit a Mercedes and then it just went off. Mike was just letting it carry on because he supposed it was all great material – and then the police car turned up.'

The sight of the dishevelled cast going at it for real was not enough to convince Her Majesty's constabulary that this was a drama class in progress. As Thewlis recalls, 'Mike was watching from across the road and eventually he thought, "I'd better stop this." People saw this little bearded bloke come up to us, say two words, and the whole situation was dissolved. The onlookers must have thought, "What did the little guy with the beard say? He should work with the UN." Ewen and I separate, do this five-minute coming-down thing and go our separate ways. The police were like, "What's the deal?" and Mike says, "We're making a film," and they say, "Well, where's the cameras?" They were going to arrest us for breach of the peace and I was like, "You can't arrest me – I'm fictional. I was possessed."' Cast and crew were escorted back to the rehearsal rooms to clarify their credentials. 'In character, I would have probably hit one of the policemen,' Thewlis told Sheila Johnston of the *Independent* in 1993. 'And I'm not sure whether it would be sufficient defence in court to say, "It was Johnny – it wasn't really me."'

For *Naked*'s central pad, the director had wanted something 'heightened, epic, dynamic. We finally found it in Dalston,' says Leigh, 'and apart from anything else you could shoot it from every angle'. Sophie, Louise and Sandra's house – a location manager's dream – is situated off the Sandringham Road, at 33 St Mark's Rise, Stoke Newington, E8, a pub dart's throw from London Fields, and a notoriously crime-ridden area. It was then occupied by student doctors, who were temporarily rehoused for the duration of the shoot. Under the production designer's eye it became progressively filthier, a hive of mouldering food and dog-ends.

'It was in the middle of a serious crack-dealing triangle in Hackney,' recalls *Naked*'s location manager Neil Lee. 'It was practically a no-go area for the police. There was an average of a mugging a day, and we had a lot of security guards there looking after the equipment and the gear. The locals were really happy to see them.' By the time cast and crew had arrived, the police had set up a temporary cop shop inside a local take-away restaurant in Sandringham Road to deal with the situation. (Stoke Newington's own police station would find itself under the spotlight during the middle of the 1990s, accused of corruption.) By contrast, Jeremy's house was found in wealthy Belsize Park, NW3, a million miles from Hackney's front line. Johnny's 'Manchester' was actually West London, as Leigh belatedly realised the cost of coaching cast and crew up north would be prohibitive.

Filming commenced in late November 1992 and continued for the next fourteen weeks. By this time, the plot had naturally emerged, bit by bit, scene by scene, from the collaborative process. The film begins in Salford, where we discover Johnny effectively raping his lover. 'I remember watching that and actually feeling physically sick,' Neil Lee recalls. 'I had to walk away because I thought, "This is for real", he was a complete monster. It was quite horrendous.'

Johnny then flees to London, where he shores up at his former girlfriend Louise's flat, which she shares with slatternly goth, Sophie. Having 'seduced' Sophie with his splenetic machine-gun wit, Johnny becomes restless and sets off on a wander through London.

Johnny's odyssey takes him through one of the sleaziest arcades in Soho, a narrow pocket of porn linking Brewer and Rupert Streets, reeking of rotting fruit, disinfectant and bad sex. Johnny hunkers down outside Lina Stores at 18 Brewer Street, an Italian delica-tessen, where he encounters young Scottish runaways Maggie and Archie.

On that day's filming police had split Oxford Street down the middle, due to an IRA bomb scare. All film equipment had to be transported by hand across the demarcation line, back to the unit base. Luckily, Westminster Council granted permission for the crew to shoot in the middle of the night in Brewer Street. The director remembers a 'hassle-free shoot' for most of the evening, until the filming attracted some unwanted attention. Neil Lee recalls, 'A window opened up and one of the prostitutes shouted down, "You're scaring away my business! While you've got cameras pointing down here no one's going to come to work," and I said, "Well, I'm really sorry but there's not a lot we can do. We've actually got permission to be here. Have *you*?" And then all these other windows came shooting up and there were about fifty prostitutes saying, "If you don't pay us off we're going to stand naked in your shot." It was suggested they could be used as extras later on, which they never were, but they were all hanging around getting very drunk.'

Archie having wandered off, in an attempt to locate him, Johnny and Maggie wander through a nocturnal London that owes more to a Dickensian vision of poverty than an idealistic Thatcherite theme park. The sequence was shot under the arches of Shoreditch railway station at Pedley Street, off Brick Lane, E1. 'Everyone said to me you can't go from Soho to Shoreditch, but I think you can,' says Leigh. 'Where *Meantime* and *High Hopes* have a kind of London literalness about them, and a sense of documentary, *Naked*'s a metaphorical London, more poetic, more of a distillation of the emotional texture of the world it depicts. The reality, the only thing that matters, is what is on the screen.'

Close to the City, the area is today one of the most sought-after locations in Yuppiedom, and the arches are now being developed into an exclusive health club. An initially striking aspect of this scene – and the film overall – is the grainy atmosphere, imbuing proceedings with a Victorian smog, an ambient throwback to *Bleak Moments*. 'Once I'd got a whiff of the whole spirit of *Naked*, Alison Chitty, Dick Pope (the cinematographer) and I started to talk about the palette of the film, which is very controlled,' says Leigh. In order to imbue this night-time film with what Leigh calls 'the unacceptable side of urban life', the negative by-passed the bleaching process in the lab, which gave the film a saturated quality.

Johnny drifts back to the West End. An entrance of Leicester Square tube station was employed for shots of Thewlis smoking and gazing impassively at passing commuters. To minimise public involvement, a concealed camera, wrapped in a black bin liner, was placed on a facing pedestrian traffic island. 'No crowd control, very natural, very spontaneous,' says Leigh. 'The place was thronging with Christmas shoppers, and we'd all fucked off to different corners ready to dive out in case anyone saw it. We didn't use the bit when Helena Bonham-Carter came out of the tube station, doing her

Christmas shopping. She walked past me and said, "Hello, what are you doing?" and I said, "Well, you're in our film!" And then Kenneth Cranham, the actor, who knows David, came up and said, "Hello, David," and David said, *sotto voce*, "I'm filming."'

After his hike through hell, Johnny finds himself outside a sterile-looking office block – a 'post-modernist gas chamber', as Johnny puts it. 'Alison Chitty said, "Wouldn't it be great if it was completely unoccupied?"' Leigh recalls. 'I said "What a fucking great idea!"' A temporarily empty property at 76 Charlotte Street, W1, was found, complete with glass-fronted doors, huge reception area and a well-appointed reception desk. Here, Johnny discovers Brian, a paternal, superstitious security guard. According to Thewlis, on the day of the shoot Peter Wight had most likely been sitting there for hours in character, twiddling his thumbs, before he showed up.

Brian tries to take Johnny under his wing, and inveigle him into a discussion about Nostradamus. 'By this time, my mind was coming out with every fucking theory I'd ever thought about,' says David. Johnny bamboozles Brian with revelations about Chernobyl that Thewlis had learned from his wife, who was then rehearsing a Russian play. He also warns him of the Number of the Beast that lies hidden in every barcode – information that Thewlis picked up from a pamphlet handed to him on the way to rehearsals. As Thewlis explains, 'In barcodes, the first strip, the middle one, and the last one always represent the number six. 666. That's absolutely true.'

To the rear of the building is Charlotte Mews, the alley the Beatles once hared through during *A Hard Day's Night* on their way to the Scala Theatre (Leigh, then living at 12 Tottenham Street, recalls watching this very scene being shot). The block has since become a base for a host of mostly media companies that include Prince Edward's Ardent Productions and Virgin Interactive.

Across the road from the empty office block, some rather run-down tenements were used to house the lonely attic bedsit for Deborah Maclaren's ageing 'Isadora Duncan'. Having nipped over there, then spent the night fending off her lonely advances, a listless Johnny buttonholes Brian the next morning as the guard trundles out to grab a spot of breakfast at a local café. In one of the film's core scenes, Brian tells Johnny of his plans for retirement, proffering a dog-eared Polaroid of a run-down cottage on the Irish coast. 'Don't waste your life,' Brian tells him over breakfast.

A rare moment of intimacy occurs when Johnny connects with the café girl Gina McKee. This is the Jubilee Café they're sitting in – a real eaterie in the heart of Borough Market, South East London. The Market, a couple of minutes' walk from Shakespeare's Globe Theatre, still maintains a seventeenth-century ambience, having long been an established trading-point for fruit and veg. The pubs and cafés here tailor their opening hours around the market traders' schedules; it's not uncommon to find a pub or a café open at four in the morning. At one point, Thewlis asks McKee what time she closes. Four o'clock she answers correctly.

In reality, the distance between this café's location and Charlotte Street is as great as that between Soho and Shoreditch. Fittingly, for a film encompassing rootlessness and displacement, Leigh's London has collapsed in on itself, entering a black hole that has no respect for normal dimensions. For the construction of the scene establishing the whereabouts of McKee's errant flatmates, Chitty actually went so far as to send mail to the location, addressed to McKee's flatmates. After a depressive, self-loathing McKee first invites him in, then throws him out of her rented flat, Johnny embarks on the final leg of his turbulent odyssey, winding up in Twyford Street, off the Caledonian Road, N1, with a harassed bill-sticker. His subsequent beating at the hands of passing brigands sends him back to the only sanctuary he knows in this foreign town.

Meanwhile, back at the flat, Sandra has been raped by her Landlord from Hell, the UberYuppie Jeremy, who Louise sees off with a pair of shears. 'From a thematic point of view, I felt it important for there to be a manifestation of unacceptable male behaviour in a way that upstaged Johnny, in order to put Johnny into some sort of perspective,' says Leigh. 'I thought it was important that nobody should read Johnny as being raw, unadulterated negative male behaviour.'

The film's denouement pulls the strands of the picture together as Johnny and Jeremy finally confront each other in the kitchen of the St Mark's Road property. According to Thewlis, Johnny's near-death throes on the landing were 'more or less real, that's how I felt – raging. The origin of that breakdown is where we experimented with him going inside himself. What I come out with at that point is fairly incoherent and ambiguous, and that's based on this day we had which we used to refer to as the "Wobbly". When we were filming the scene it was like, "OK, let's go there now." I went to a bit of a strange place in my head.' Johnny, by now a quivering wreck, is attended to by Sandra, who has just returned from her holidays. Having sufficiently recovered from his ordeal, Johnny reaches an apparent rapprochement with Louise. The next morning, he limps away to an uncertain future.

It was a warm, sultry evening in May 1993 when Leigh and Thewlis went up to collect their prize at Cannes for Best Director and Best Actor. Tagging along was Katrin Cartlidge, wearing an antique lace dress she'd found in a dustbin. Thewlis had stayed on in Cannes after the screening of the film some days earlier, while Leigh's entourage had left town. Quite skint, he was forced to doss around until Sunday's award ceremony. 'We were counting out our centimes to try and buy some fish soup. It was like, "I was a star only a few days ago!"'

Naked was released in the UK on 5 November 1993. The *Sunday Telegraph*'s Anne Billson took the presumptuous move of informing British cinema-goers that they wouldn't enjoy it. 'It won't teach you anything, not unless your address is somewhere in cloud-cuckoo land . . . *Naked* is desperate stuff.' Writing in the *Mail on Sunday*, William Leith opined: 'This is a bleak film, where almost nothing nice happens, but at least the main rapist is witty.' Stateside, Georgia Brown, writing in the *Village Voice*, sweetly championed the picture: 'This is a brilliant, radical work from Leigh . . . it's also so abrasive that some viewers are likely to be revolted.'

The *Sunday Times*'s Julie Burchill devoted an entire page to an attack on the director and his new film. Under the heading 'Crass Struggle', she wrote: 'Leigh's characters talk like lobotomised Muppets . . . doesn't Leigh ever feel the need to tilt at the ruling class just for a change? He should try it, it might be fun – though, of course, not half as easy.' Burchill then launched into an ill-researched tirade on Leigh's own lineage. 'His films look a great deal more cruel and patronising if not made by One of Us.'

Leigh's hackles still rise when the subject of Burchill's review is broached. 'That's not a review, it just comes from somewhere else.

That was the only time I went down the road of suing them and got through a grand and a half with a lawyer. We reached a stage when they said, "Well, the next thing we have to do is to take advice from a barrister," and I suddenly thought, "If this did fuck up, it would be terrible. Is it worth it?" I would have gone the whole way with that sewage, but I got cold feet, because I thought if it does fuck up, it'll screw me up big time.'

Accusations of misogyny followed – notably from Claire Monk in *Sight and Sound* – which the film's poster, depicting a semi-clad Katrin Cartlidge straddling Greg Cruttwell geisha-style, could only have encouraged. A terrible error of judgement, thought Cartlidge: 'What shocked me about the poster was not what I looked like, but that I didn't have a say in it, nor did Mike either. It misrepresented the film terribly. It wasn't some porno job.' Following Monk's article, one Helen Birch wrote an open letter to the director in the *Independent* in November 1993: 'Don't let all the plaudits fool you, Mike. And next time you decide to stray so far into male fantasy why not take a tip from (Michael) Winner and give a woman a gun?' This last comment was a reference to Winner's 1992 sleazefest, *Dirty Weekend*.

'That criticism is outrageous and offensive, to say the least,' says Leigh. '*Naked* certainly isn't misogynistic, though, of course, Jeremy is not exactly a feminist. The film definitely and unashamedly deals with some unacceptable aspects of male heterosexual behaviour . . . There's no question that he [Johnny] has violence within him. I'm merely saying it's more complex than that. Frankly, I think it's very common male behaviour, and the way that a number of women respond to it in the film is not uncommon either.' As Thewlis confirms, 'I was playing a character with a history of violence towards women, so I had to maintain the integrity of that character . . . I had to trust Mike was not making a film that would go against my own principles. I know his politics, I know he is responsible for some of the most positive portrayals of women in British film.' This is a fact plainly borne out by Leigh's treatment of female characters and their relationships with each other from *Life is Sweet*'s Wendy and Nicola to *Secrets and Lies*' Cynthia and Hortense.

The film took nearly £2 million at the UK box office. After *Naked*,

Leigh's status as a class act was now firmly assured, and the director went on to make the Oscar-nominated winner of the Palme d'Or, *Secrets and Lies*, with Marianne Jean Baptiste, Brenda Blethyn and Timothy Spall. His position as the UK's premier director was now unassailable. Leigh's first big-screen period drama, *Topsy-Turvy* (1999), told the story of the fraught genesis of Gilbert and Sullivan's *The Mikado* – the director now used his organic techniques to explore the creative process itself.

Thewlis went off to do *Black Beauty* (1994) – the story of man's inhumanity to horse – then wrote and directed a BAFTA-nominated short, *Hello, Hello, Hello* (1995). Further cinematic ventures included parts in *The Island of Doctor Moreau* (1996), *Seven Years in Tibet* (1997) and the Coen brothers' wonderful *The Big Lebowski* (1998) in a bizarre cameo. When Thewlis attended an Oscar award ceremony in LA, Steven Spielberg requested an audience with the man, telling him that he, Martin Scorsese and Brian de Palma had spent the night arguing about *Naked*. His *Naked* set-piece, an impressive juggling act featuring himself and Wight ranting around an office complex in silhouette, was later sampled by dance act, the Orb, for their track 'S.A.L.T.', from 1997's 'Oblivion'. Thewlis has just completed his first novel about 'Bereavement Envy'. He still gets work on the back of *Naked* and receives intense missives by people affected by his portrayal of the despondent Johnny. 'I get this quite a lot. People either come up to me and say, "You changed my life", "That was me", or "You said everything that I've ever thought." A few religious nuts in America wrote to me saying, "Remember, God loves you" . . .'

LONDON HAS CHANGED dramatically since *Naked* was shot in 1992. Brick Lane and its surrounding streets are undergoing a mass transformation. For years the citadel to the Great British Curry, the street is rapidly being taken over by chic coffee houses, Internet cafés and artists' studios. The more traditional Indian eateries are now being elbowed aside by aluminium-framed curry 'studios', pandering to the tastes of the new Raj.

33 St Mark's Rise is still occupied by peripatetic tenants, surprised by the celebrity the film has awarded the property. Dalston, as they say, is coming up. Now estate agents, not crack dealers, work the pavements in search of new and richer killings. In a gentle act of defiance against a world going increasingly mad, a tiny wild flower has broken through the tarmac outside the house where Johnny once briefly rested his head.

CHOOSE DIY

Here they come! Renton, Spud, Sick Boy, Begbie, and Diane. No, these aren't the New Monkees, nor the little darlings from *Swallows and Amazons*: these latter-day Railway Children have left sherbet dab and summer picnics long behind for more exotic powders and highs. If Irvine Welsh's novel *Trainspotting* had been a word-of-mouth phenomenon, *Trainspotting* the movie was another animal entirely: a triumph of marketing sold as an 'instant' cult film for a new, media-savvy generation.

'The people who should be making films in this country are in Blur, Pulp and Oasis.'
                                Trainspotting producer, Andrew Macdonald

Before 1993 you'd be forgiven for thinking that to associate the term 'Trainspotting' with users of one of the world's most powerful narcotics was a trifle bizarre. As actor Peter Mullan, who plays *Trainspotting*'s drug-dealing 'Mother Superior', says, 'If somebody had said to you ten years ago, "I've got a script, it's based on an unknown book, by an unknown Edinburgh writer, and it's called *Trainspotting*", the first thing you'd say is, "Well, change the fucking title, for God's sake."' But in 1996, when the *Trainspotting* express pulled into Platform One in the world's cinemas, it all made perfect sense. *Trainspotting* had successfully put its finger on the thing that binds the chemical generation with the notepad brigades at Clapham Junction: detail and routine – in pursuit of a buzz, both tribes are ultra-obsessed with arrivals, departures, late arrivals, late departures, breakdowns, no-shows, go-slows, and oh nos.

A true classic youth movie, *Trainspotting* was a real shot in the arm not only for the British film industry but also the music and fashion industries. An amazingly influential film, to be sure, and a brilliantly conceived, superbly written, vastly entertaining one. But a 'cult' film? Hmmm. It certainly 'looks' like a cult film, having duly doffed its driver's cap to *A Hard Day's Night*, *A Clockwork Orange*, *Quadrophenia*, *Withnail* and *Pulp Fiction*, among others. And it sure sounds like one, having employed a hip, rather knowing soundtrack. If it *has* become a cult film, we suggest it really couldn't have been otherwise. *Trainspotting*'s promoters pushed all the right buttons. They colluded with its target audience in a way few British films had done before, utilising already homogenised cults – such as those surrounding Britpop, the burgeoning Retro craze, the Rave scene and Irvine Welsh's novel – to add a synthetic veneer of cultish credibility. As such, *Trainspotting* may well be among the first in a long line of 'DIY' British cult movies.

HISTORICALLY, THE CINEMA had usually steered well clear of heroin addiction, preferring instead to demonise cannabis through blatantly exploitative anti-drug 'B' features such as *Reefer Madness* (1936), dangling straitjackets over the audience's heads if they dared venture into the realms of drug experimentation. On those occasions when it did tackle the subject, addicts were mostly portrayed as shambling sleazeballs and criminals, rarely as victims of a chemical entrapment. In 1955 Hollywood briefly flirted with the subject in *The Man with the Golden Arm*, in which heart throb Frank Sinatra was cast as a heroin addict, but, over the course of the next decade, heroin all but vanished from the screens. Save for a few underground classics, such as Andy Warhol's *Chelsea Girls*, Hollywood now preferred to cash in on the controversy surrounding LSD (*The Trip*, *Psyche Out*, *Easy Rider*).

During the 1970s, as heroin use increased exponentially, stark documentaries like the BBC's *Gail is Dead* (1970), and ITV's *Johnny Go Home* (1975) relayed shocking real-life images of wasted lives. Occasionally the stark horror of heroin addiction would be woven into a mainstream movie to add an element of gritty reality (Al

Pacino's appearance as Bobby in 1971's *Panic in Needle Park*, or Gene Hackman as Popeye Doyle experiencing cold turkey in *French Connection 2* (1975).) But it wasn't until 1981 that a mainstream feature focused fully on the issue. *Christiane F* told the harrowing true story of a fourteen-year-old Berliner who becomes addicted to the drug through peer pressure. The movie is still shown today as part of Germany's anti-drugs campaign. But, perhaps inevitably, the film glossed over an important fact: that people who take heroin usually enjoy the experience.

After the 1970s, drugs became sexy again. If 1987's *Less Than Zero* – a timorous take on Brett Easton Ellis's cult novel of young Middle America under the influence of cocaine – had been chockful of moralising, Gus Van Sant's *Drugstore Cowboy* (1989) took a humorous look at junkie family values, featuring sexpots Matt Dillon and Kelly Lynch blasting their way across the States to support their habit. Quentin Tarantino's *Pulp Fiction* (1994) saw John Travolta and Uma Thurman bumping and grinding on the dance floor while peaking on the drug. The sequence opened up a debate on the moral merits of mixing hardcore narcotics with beautiful people, who patently didn't look like the received image of heroin users. And ironically, it was the drugs issue, rather than the film's overt (if intentionally cartoonish) violence that occupied review columns on its release. *Trainspotting*, too, would have to run the gauntlet of moral zealots and tabloid missionaries for daring to present an altogether different picture of life under the needle.

Trainspotting's original creator Irvine Welsh was born in 1958 in Leith, Scotland, a place best known to outsiders as the home of Hibernian Football Club. The Family Welsh soon moved a short distance along the coast to a poky maisonette in Muirhouse, a cluster of tenements some twenty minutes outside Edinburgh. Muirhouse and its sister estates had been notorious post-war dumping grounds for Edinburgh's underclass, who had been relocated there in their thousands by the City's elders in a social cleansing exercise while they tarted up the town.

Given the harrowing subject matter of his books, you might suppose Welsh was the classic victim of an unhappy childhood, but he seems to have enjoyed his early years, only occasionally falling foul of the law for playing football in the streets. 'You'd get covered in dog shit when you were playing football,' Welsh recalled for the *Independent* in 1996. 'But to me it was a happy place. We used to play some really imaginative and fantastical games, believing that there was this underground city under the scheme.' A stint as a TV repairman hadn't exactly turned him on, and so – like a good number of those disaffected kids caged in housing estates like Muirhouse – the teenage Welsh took up Punk's leather reins and headed to London in search of the lifestyle he'd read about in the *NME*. Once there, Welsh immersed himself in the mosh pit, spending heady nights pogoing, drug-abusing, and during the day catching a few winks on local park benches. He joined a band called Pubic Lice, moved into a squat and took on a few labouring jobs to keep the wolves at bay.

During the mid-1980s, his punk dreams behind him, Irvine moved to Croydon, the toast of Surrey suburbia. Welsh had fallen on his feet and had moved into property developing. 'What galvanised me after I became disillusioned with Punk was the Yuppie years,' Irvine told a rather surprised John Walsh of the *Independent* in 1995. 'I got into buying and selling flats and doing them up and making lots of money.' Strange move. Even so, these experiences would find space in his later work.

Towards the end of the decade Irvine returned to his native Leith, finding a very different picture from his halcyon childhood days. Muirhouse, already racked by unemployment, AIDS and crime, was now completely swamped with heroin. For depressed youngsters looking to escape the living hell of unemployment, Job Start schemes had nothing on heroin's enticing silvery package deal. As Welsh told the *Independent*, 'I saw a lot of people I used to know from the [housing] scheme I'd grown up on, who were all HIV plus from sharing needles, and everyone was banging up on Smack. You'd get guys who used to go for a pint – now they'd go and bang up.' Welsh, it transpired, had also dabbled with heroin but had been less than impressed. 'It was never a drug I really enjoyed,' Welsh candidly informed *Time* magazine in 1998. 'It got to that stage where you're not really social. You become a liar and a thief as well, which isn't very good.'

By the late 1980s Edinburgh's City elders were attempting to sweep Muirhouse (and the even more notorious Craigmillar estate) under the carpet, well out of sight from cash-flashing tourists. Journalists and film crews now proclaimed Edinburgh to be the heroin and AIDS capital of Europe (a report commissioned at the time found a staggering 60 per cent of intravenous drug users were HIV-positive). For the residents of Edinburgh this only added to the total breakdown in community values. 'I think about my parents' generation,' Welsh recalled for the Internet's *Feed* magazine in 1996. 'They married someone from the next street and all their family lived round about. Now everybody's pulled out of these communities and bombarded with all kinds of advertising stimulus and self-help books about how you should be, what kind of man, what kind of woman you should be looking for in a relationship, how you can make those relationships better, how you can do this, how you can do that. I think that obsession and addiction is just a way of short-circuiting all that.'

In 1988 (and somewhat ironically, given his later tussles with the district's civic authorities) Welsh took a respectable position in Edinburgh District Council as a training officer. He was, apparently, a model employee. 'He could have gone right to the top of local government,' a fellow staffer later recalled for the *Sunday Times*. 'If he was taking loads of drugs and carousing, he kept it well-hidden because he was always well-dressed and on time.' Welsh was encouraged to enrol for an MBA Diploma in Business Management at Edinburgh's Heriot-Watt University. During one interminable lecture in the summer of 1988, he overheard a conversation about Edinburgh between a fellow student from the Home Counties and a middle-class Glaswegian student. Welsh was appalled: the image of a middle-class festival city was a lie, at best, just one small part of the city's culture. As an Edinburgh down-and-out told one of these authors in 1993, 'This town's got an edge . . .' Irvine was determined to show that other realities – including a large, urban underclass – also existed.

With the same passion he'd once reserved for Punk, Welsh was propelled into literary action, frantically scribbling down words and images directly drawn from his environment. Welsh was revealing a truth that most of the city knew about, but few had dared to reveal. The gritty diary of a bunch of Leith rebels without a clue was taking shape, heroin providing a powerful ambient wash to the tales. In certain passages the drug-taking would be described as an almost religious affair (which it is to those concerned), at times bordering on becoming dangerously attractive (because it is), but for Welsh, this whole book was about dancing on the wire.

For narrative, Welsh eschewed all literary niceties, invoking the broadest brogue he could muster to relay vivid snatches of his native landscape, smeared in smack, blood and depression, balanced with occasional black humour. And, notwithstanding Scottish novelist James Kelman's canon of work, *Trainspotting* would house the hardest vernacular to hit the streets since Anthony Burgess's Nadsat-ridden *A Clockwork Orange*, penned some thirty years previously. As Welsh told *Feed*, 'I really like Standard English, but it is an administrative language, an imperialist language. It's not very funky.' At times the reader would be lost in the hypnotic texture of the language; at other times, accelerated into an amphetamine-like rush, only to be cooled down into a MDMA salve. Welsh, who has never hidden his passion for Ecstasy-driven music, was now writing the literary equivalent of a rave.

At the beginning of the 1990s his observations began finding page space in a clutch of small but highly influential magazines on Edinburgh's literary fringes – notably *Rebel Inc.*, who would ultimately promote *Trainspotting* as a worthy contender to the Good News. *Rebel*'s publisher, Kevin Williamson, introduced Welsh to Robin Robertson, then an editor at Secker & Warburg. Impressed, Robertson commissioned Irvine to knock the fragments into a novel, and Welsh duly produced forty-three chapters of the most outrageous commentary on Edinburgh's flip side ever written.

An excited air of expectancy circulated in Edinburgh prior to the novel's publication in July 1993. Although Welsh and Robertson were enthusiastic about the impending launch, they were cautious about cracking open the champagne just yet. Fully aware of the power of controversy, especially at the expense of Edinburgh's notoriously stuffy elders, Welsh, like Joe Orton and Malcolm McLaren before him, had seriously considered dashing off anonymous letters to Edinburgh newspapers, complaining that the book besmirched the good name of their beloved city. He needn't have worried: the novel flew out of bookshops, with stores easily shifting the initially cautious print run.

Timing was everything. By 1993, it was estimated that the British dance scene was now coining an annual £1.8 billion a year. MDMA (dubbed 'Ecstasy') had leaked from New York and Chicago's black gay discos to become the underground drug of choice for UK clubbers, gathering thousands of huggy initiates – former punks, hippies, New Age travellers, football fans and wide-eyed teens – during 1988's Summer of Love. Illegal Acid House gatherings and sound systems sprung up around the country in warehouses and fields. Outwitting the police became a game. They should chill out a bit, take some Es, was the refrain of the day. As drugs went, Ecstasy had been 'different', 'spiritual', more socially acceptable (no horrible hypodermics involved), particularly among middle-class ravers. The mood of the time might be best summed up in a skit by the late great Bill Hicks: 'I have taken drugs before and . . . I had a real good time. *Sorry*. Didn't *murder* anybody, didn't *rob* anybody, didn't *rape* anybody, didn't *beat* anybody, didn't lose *one* fucking job . . . laughed my *ass off*, and went about my day.' By 1994, the days when clubbers floated around on a strawberry-scented cloud of good will, faith and Disco Biscuits were pretty much over. Gangsters hijacked the scene, 'Madchester', as far as the press was concerned, becoming 'Gunchester', and pure MDMA was giving way to harder variations, some allegedly cut with rat poison, ground glass and horse tranquillisers. But, for now, everything looked smiley.

In the wake of Ecstasy culture, Welsh's book soon became an exceptionally culty item, an emblem of cool, enabling the purchaser to buy into a very knowing scene. Heroin may have been the drug in question, but the voice – unapologetic and *laissez-faire* – was pure Rave. A stage adaptation followed, débuting at the Glasgow 'Mayfest' theatre showcase in spring 1994. Ewen Bremner, who had just finished playing Archie in *Naked*, was cast as *Trainspotting*'s anti-hero Renton. The BBC wanted to broadcast a radio version of the play but backed off after seeing the script's integral profanities (140 cunts). As playwright Harry Gibson, who had adapted the novel for the stage, told *Spike* magazine, 'When they realised that landing on Planet Trainspotting means you can't walk for two lines without bumping into a cunt, they bottled.' The play began a hugely controversial sell-out tour that ended up at London's

Ambassadors Theatre in December 1994. Normally sedate theatre critics, faced with profanity, simulated drug-taking and violence, were flabbergasted: 'West End Gets Smack in the Face,' cried *The Times*. 'Dirt, degradation, coprophilia, brutishness – the lower depths of abusiveness,' bellowed the *Sunday Telegraph*.

While theatre was being galvanised during the winter of 1994, British cinema was on another false high. Certain sections of the industry thought that the enormous success of *Four Weddings and a Funeral* signalled a return to greater days. In reality, the industry was in a bad way. Homegrown movies (then accounting for about 5 per cent of British cinema's offerings) hadn't stood a chance against the might of Hollywood. At the start of the 1990s two styles of film-making dominated British cinema: plush Merchant/Ivory-style period dramas, which travelled well, and gritty social issue dramas, which found most favour on the European art-house circuit.

Rejecting both forms, a new wave of young British directors strove towards a hipper, more commercially driven cinema of a kind that Stephen Woolley had inaugurated during the 1980s, and which Film Four now encouraged. It was the same old song: an attempt to appease the Americans, with only a soulless, cursory nod to British culture. But most efforts – Danny Cannon's *Young Americans*, Paul Anderson's *Shopping* – flopped badly. Cannon and Anderson bailed out of the UK film-making scene as quickly as possible, going on to make Hollywood's *Judge Dredd* and *Mortal Kombat*, respectively.

Figment Films was fronted by producer Andrew Macdonald and writer John Hodge. The company had been formed by Macdonald and his brother Kevin to promote an undistinguished feature, *Dr Reizner's Fragment*, in 1991. Whatever the film's shortcomings, no one could doubt the Macdonalds' celebrated cinematic lineage. Their grandfather was Emeric Pressburger, who, with Michael Powell, wrote, directed and produced some of the British cinema's greatest films, including *A Matter of Life and Death* and *Black Narcissus* (both 1946).

Hodge first met Macdonald after attending *Dr Reizner*'s sole screening at that year's Edinburgh Film Festival. At that time he'd been working as a junior doctor at the Edinburgh Royal Infirmary, writing screenplays as a sideline. The pair struck up an instant rapport, with Hodge somewhat in awe of Macdonald's elevated production CV (in reality Macdonald was a location manager for *Taggart* at the time). Macdonald was intrigued by Hodge's first script, which sported the working title 'Cruel'. The story, based on his experiences of flat-sharing in Edinburgh as a student doctor, concerned three young professionals who take charge of a suitcase of money after another flatmate dies.

Both men knew the kind of movies they wanted to make, and they had nothing to do with the sort of earnest films perennially being made in Britain, nor with the Hollywood-style action movies that Cannon and Anderson had attempted to ape. For Hodge and Macdonald, the US Indie movie scene – as characterised by Hal Hartley, the Coen Brothers and (especially) Tarantino – was the way forward. Tight. Funny. Quirky. No boring bits. The pair studied *GoodFellas* and *Blood Simple* obsessively for inspiration and after rewrites and a title change to 'Shallow Grave', their enthusiasm was bolstered by a grant of £4,000 from the Scottish Film Production Fund.

In November 1992 they attended a screenwriting course in Inverness, where one of the guest participants happened to be David Aukin, head of films for Channel Four. Unable to collar Aukin in the hall, Macdonald strode into the car park and made a beeline for Aukin's chauffeur-driven car. A £5 note exchanged hands, and the chauffeur ensured a copy of their script was left on his boss's seat for Aukin to read on the long journey home. The gamble paid off. Seven days later the pair were called into Channel Four's offices in London to discuss the project. A few weeks afterwards, the deal was struck. Channel Four funded the movie, with a contribution of £150,000 from the Glasgow Film Fund towards the £1 million budget. All they needed now was a director.

Enter television director Danny Boyle, who'd just completed the quirky BBC drama series, *Mr Wroe's Virgins*. Their script, he said, was great, just like *Blood Simple*. Bingo. Boyle, thought Hodge, had a sort of animal cunning. But he was sensitive and patient too, the perfect guy to deal with actors and industry alike. Boyle was born into a working-class Manchester family in 1957. During his twenties and early thirties he had directed for provincial and national theatre, before moving into TV, directing several quality dramas during the 1980s and early 1990s. One Boyle-directed *Inspector Morse* episode from 1992 called 'Cherubim and Seraphim' had provoked controversy by pitching John Thaw's Oxford-based detective into the world of Rave culture at a time when the newspapers were full of stories about Ecstasy-related deaths. 'We knew the sort of person we wanted was someone who was about to make their name,' Macdonald recalled in 2001. 'We wanted someone who was hot, and, in some ways, our equivalent, but a more experienced film-maker.'

The trio began casting in the spring of 1993. First choice Robert Carlyle (raised in Glasgow's rough-and-ready Maryhill district) rejected the role of Alex Law on account of difficulties he'd had with the character's middle-class background. Ironically, his exit opened doors for his later co-star, a twenty-two-year-old Ewan McGregor. Within three years he'd be Scotland's hottest screen property since Sean Connery. Born in Crieff, Scotland, on 31 March 1971, McGregor was a born entertainer. As a six-year-old telly-addict, he'd imitate his hero Elvis at family gatherings, slicking back his hair and wiggling his hips, before being packed off to bed. His initial exposure to cinema came through his uncle, *Local Hero* actor Dennis Lawson. Ewan adored his Uncle Dennis, especially as he'd had a part in the original *Star Wars* movie, which Ewan and his brother loved, tumbling around the living-room with plastic light sabres.

After flirting with Christianity, he enrolled for a one-year drama course in Perth in 1988, and took a place at London's Guildhall College the following year. Shrugging off his teenage depression, he excelled in all departments. To supplement his grant he used to busk outside Bank underground station before trekking back to the YMCA to bed down for the night.

Open evenings at the Guildhall are highly charged affairs. Aside from cooing relatives, the audience usually contains a large crop of agents and casting directors. On this particular night in January 1992, Ewan chose his performances carefully. The first was a rendition of a Barbra Streisand song. Next, a scene from *Withnail & I*, in which the undynamic duo wrestle with the washing-up ('Fork it!'). Finally, a scene McGregor devised himself, in which he played a limbless oil rig worker. Post-performance, twelve agents beat a path to his door. Jonathan Altaras got there first, and immediately secured him the part of Mick Hopper in Dennis Potter's *Lipstick on your Collar* for Channel Four. Following an appearance in Bill Forsyth's *Being Human* (1994), McGregor attended auditions for *Shallow Grave* and clinched the role. They were filming by late September 1993. McGregor soon formed a close, loyal bond with the Figment trio. 'I just want to work with them,' McGregor recalled for *Empire* magazine. 'It'd be weird if I wasn't ever to do another film with them.'

Shallow Grave exploded across the screen in January 1994 with a breathtaking ferocity unseen in British cinema for years. Aside from superb performances by McGregor, Christopher Eccleston and Kerry Fox, it wickedly combined a near-hallucinogenic ambience with sexy Tarantino-style violence and dark laughter. It took strong notices and box office receipts, multiplying Channel Four's modest £1 million investment twenty times over. Stateside, it barely raised a murmur, the Americans singularly unflattered by imitation. But, as a spearhead for a new kind of British movie-making, they could not have timed it better.

The year 1994 would prove something of a landmark in the way much contemporary culture is processed and marketed today: a politer word for it might be necrophilia. The post-modern ethic, usually the preserve of hip European philosophising, was once again tapping the market that mattered most. That year, Tarantino, having previously commanded unprecedented attention with *Reservoir Dogs*, released *Pulp Fiction* on an entirely expectant public. This glorious marriage of shrewd pop culture references and genres cleaned up worldwide.

It was also the year that Oasis's 'Live Forever' entered the charts, with Grunge and its attendant Seattle sound elbowed aside in favour of an unrepentantly British Swinging Sixties vibe, a pop culture *cul de sac* christened Britpop. Arm in arm with Dance music, it suddenly made the charts very sexy again. If the Criminal Justice and Public Order Act, introduced that November, had made it illegal to hold unlicensed gatherings around sound systems playing 'a succession of repetitive beats', such repressive measures would ultimately only drive the Rave scene underground. By the time Figment's follow-up emerged, Dance culture had fractured into varying different styles such as Garage, Jungle and Happy

Hardcore (a softer, poppier strain for younger teens). Effectively it had been neutered and tapped by the market to flog soft drinks and jeans. But for an insecure nation, all but flogged off to America under Thatcher, such an unapologetic pride in one's own output (however appropriated and diluted) would prove tremendously galvanising. Over the next couple of years both media and rulers-in-waiting deliberately drew comparisons with the great innovative decade of the 1960s. The Figment trio's next movie would be marketed with this exact same calculation.

Macdonald had first picked up a copy of Welsh's novel while putting *Shallow Grave* to bed. For Macdonald, it was familiar, if unpleasant territory. While visiting Muirhouse as a location manager a few years back, addicts had threatened him and hurled shit at the camera crew. Following *Shallow Grave* there were a variety of other projects on the cards – Hodge's *A Life Less Ordinary* among them – but *Trainspotting*'s potential lifted it head and shoulders above the rest. 'When you come across something that special, you just know,' Macdonald would later enthuse. Fellow movie-maker David Puttnam wasn't so sure. It was commercial suicide, he told Macdonald, a step back into the sort of socially aware British cinema *Shallow Grave* had pointedly ignored.

John Hodge was first to voice serious misgivings about the *Trainspotting* project, citing the difficulty of converting the vast array of stories, characters and almost alien vernacular into some sort of linear script. But in late 1994, after much cajoling and a series of intense brainstorming sessions with Boyle and Macdonald, he wrote a screenplay that welded Welsh's storylines together, ultimately producing a script in which drug use wasn't really the focus at all, but merely (as in Welsh's novel) a convenient device on which to hang the story.

In Hodge's version – the tale being seen through the eyes of Renton – teenage junkies Renton, Sick Boy and Spud while away their time injecting heroin in Mother Superior's dingy squat, funding their habit with shoplifting sprees and petty burglary. 'Choose life,' sneers Renton, citing a catalogue of 'boring' conventions, like families, careers and 'spirit-crushing game shows'. Having witnessed a cot death in the squat, the death of his former 'clean-living' friend Tommy from heroin abuse, and following a near overdose himself,

Renton decides to go straight, to embrace the 'boring' life in London as an estate agent. But his past catches up with him, in the form of Sick Boy, Spud and the psychopathic Begbie, who plan to carry out a major drugs deal. After the deal, Begbie glasses a punter in a London pub and Renton realises he isn't cut out for this way of life. He steals the drug money and does a runner, embracing the humdrum life for good. His ranted catalogue now becomes an affirmation of freedom. But Hodge wasn't moralising here: Renton is seen throughout as a two-faced brat, eternally selling his friends out – up to and including his escape. In Hodge's darkly satirical script, the ultimate message would appear to be, if you want to get on in life, stitch people up.

Hodge had jettisoned some of the darker incidents of the novel, such as Renton screwing his brother's girlfriend at his funeral, Begbie's vicious assault on his pregnant girlfriend, and bizarre tales of 'mud masturbation' and Tampaxes dunked in soup. (Not that Hodge was a shrinking violet. He had first-hand experience of treating HIV and drug abuse victims at Edinburgh's Eastern General Hospital.) The film adaptation further departed from the novel by omitting any references to the sectarianism that pervades Scottish urban society to this day.

In order to lend as much verisimilitude to the film as possible, the Figment trio went next to Leith to meet members of Glasgow's Calton Athletic Recovery Group, a drug rehabilitation unit that used, Zen-style, the science of football as a replacement for the drug. Calton's treatment required strict adherence to its methadone-free programme, which filled the addicts' every waking hour with sport in order to free them from the pull of the fix. 'They sit around tables, working-class guys, pouring out what they've done as a result of their addiction,' Boyle told the *Independent* in 1996. 'They support each other. They say, "I did this terrible thing," then someone else says, "That's nothing. I did worse than that."' As a result of their meetings, some of the clinic's attendees would become *Trainspotting* extras in a five-a-side football match at the beginning of the film, and the clinic would be thanked for their 'inspiration and courage' in the credits. Proceeds from the premiere party and 5 per cent of the movie's profits would also go directly to the centre.

During March 1995 a copy of the first draft of the script was passed to McGregor. At this point the actor was unaware he'd been chosen to play the part of Renton, although the Figment team had earmarked him for the part from the word go. McGregor read the script and was more than pleasantly surprised when he was offered the part. 'Renton was like a Christmas present,' he recalled for the *Independent* in 1996. 'I'd been waiting for him to come along and when I read the script, I thought, "Well, here he is – here he comes." For months beforehand I thought of nothing else, and I threw myself into it 100 per cent.' McGregor began to feverishly research his part while he was filming on location in Luxembourg for Peter Greenaway's *The Pillow Book*. Visiting a well-known meeting-point for the city's junkies, he observed their behaviour and noted a characteristic stooped posture, which he would later imitate. Returning home he went on a crash diet, and shaved back his hair. Junkie Renton was born.

The start of 1995 brought the film-makers their first major hiccup. The paperback publishers, Minerva (*Trainspotting*'s paperback publisher), had sold the novel's film rights to mighty entertainment agents, the Noel Gay Organisation, who wanted a deal that allowed them to act as co-producers. Figment refused to accept such an arrangement and as a result of the contractual bickering Channel Four promptly stalled. After three months of furious negotiations an agreement was finally sorted out, the Noel Gay Organisation agreeing to forgo their wish to co-produce in return for a slice of the profits and a credit. Channel Four were now able to stump up the film's £1.7 million budget, their most expensive project to date.

With only McGregor secured, casting continued at a furious rate. Ewen Bremner was chosen to play the wonderfully hopeless Spud. He'd been reluctant to accept at first: having played Renton for an extended stretch on stage, he feared he'd be totally Trainspotted out. Susan Vidler, his *Naked* screen partner 'Maggie', was selected to play Alison, the only female addict in the picture. Kevin McKidd played Tommy, the film's conscience. Before *Trainspotting*, he had just one feature credit to his name as Malky Johnson in *Small Faces* (1995), Gillies MacKinnon's paean to 1960s Glasgow teen gangs. McKidd, thought Boyle, was 'the perfect picture of innocence'. Peter Mullan, who, at thirty-five, was the oldest of the Smack Pack, had previously played a role as a heavy in *Shallow Grave*. He'd now play Swanney, the shooting gallery's 'Mother Superior'.

Having turned down *Shallow Grave*, Robert Carlyle was now charged with bringing to life the Beast of Leith, Francis (Franco) Begbie. Carlyle, who'd been embroiled in some pretty heavy scenes as a young man, hadn't needed to do too much method research, as he recalled for *Hotdog* magazine in 2000: 'I've met plenty of Begbies in my time. Wander round Glasgow on a Saturday night and you've a good chance of running into Begbie. But he isn't meant to be real, he's meant to be a heightened vision of reality, your worst fucking nightmare.'

The main cast's sole Sassenach (from Kingston in Surrey), Jonny Lee Miller, was auditioned for the part of Sick Boy by Boyle after he'd seen him convincingly playing a Scot on television. Like Andrew Macdonald, Jonny had a famous movie relative: his grandfather Bernard Lee had played 'M' in the early James Bond movies – in the film his character, Sick Boy, would trade 007 imitations with Renton.

Kelly Macdonald played Renton's one-night stand, the sassy and vivacious Diane. To find the right girl to play the film's schoolgirl diva, Boyle had sent out printed fliers ('Are you the new Kate Moss or Patricia Arquette?') to Glasgow's schools, colleges and hairdressers and had arranged an open audition in Glasgow. Kelly Macdonald had been working in a Glasgow bar and plucked up the courage to enter the audition hall with only a photo booth snap to promote her waif-like beauty. She couldn't believe her luck when she won the part of the precocious and sassy Diane. (According to Boyle, he'd known she was 'the one' before she'd even sat down.) For Kelly, the *Trainspotting* gig came not a moment too soon. As she told the *Scottish Daily Record* in 1996, 'I looked around me at the people who were working in the pub for years. They had lost their ambition and I was really scared of ending up like that.' Lost on everyone at the time was that Welsh's novel had featured a young barmaid also called Kelly.

Irvine Welsh was recruited for an unspectacular cameo as drug dealer Mikey Forrester, while housewives' choice, Dale Winton, was hired as a TV game show host during a scene in which Renton goes cold turkey. Other jobs for the boys saw Andy Macdonald appearing as a prospective flat buyer in London, while John Hodge was enlisted as a security guard, pursuing McGregor and Bremner through the Edinburgh streets in the opening sequence of the film. Keith Allen, resurrected from *Shallow Grave*, was cast in another shady role, as a major narcotics dealer.

Contact with Calton Athletic was maintained: project leader Eamon Docherty became 'Special Project Advisor' for the duration of the shoot. A former user, Docherty guided the cast through everything from cooking up (with cocoa substitute) to heroin withdrawal, handing out hypodermics and other paraphernalia with military precision. Docherty wanted to see if they could play junkies convincingly. As Peter Mullan recalls, 'We all stood in a line along a table, it was like something out of the *Generation Game*. He would go along telling everybody "that's good" or "that's crap" or "that's excellent". I got singled out for being "quite good" so that was kind of bizarre. He was painfully honest. We asked him early on what he thought of the script and he said in front of Danny, "I think the script's fine. But you do understand it's a pile of bollocks. There is no way on this earth that junkies would hang around with each other for any length of time, it's very much an individual kind of activity." Which was a big shock for us and Danny.' McGregor later told *Neon* magazine in 1998 that he had considered taking heroin to fully research Renton's stoned demeanour. 'The more research I did, the less I wanted to do it. I didn't think it was necessary. I've had to die on screen before, and I don't know what that's like, either. To take heroin for the part would just be an excuse to take heroin. So I didn't.'

The seven-week shoot began in May 1995. It was decided to concentrate activity in Glasgow, a decision that had generated much goodwill and support from the Glasgow Film Fund when Figment had made *Shallow Grave* there. The film required over fifty locations, many of them interiors, and so the film-makers took full advantage of the derelict Wills cigarette factory at 368 Alexandra Parade on the outskirts of the city, using it as a makeshift film studio. Until its closure in the mid-1980s the factory had been one of Glasgow's major sources of employment. Numerous sets were constructed within the building's vast expanses for the squats, flats, suburban bedrooms, offices and doctor's surgeries that feature in the picture. As the film called for a number of bar scenes, the factory's rotting social club was utilised to good effect.

Although the story was set in Edinburgh, the crew would use the city for just a couple of shots. The opening shoplifting sequence, which mimicked the beginning of *A Hard Day's Night* (and a remarkably similar scene from *Reservoir Dogs*), was shot on Princes Street. (A branch of W. H. Smith's was to have provided the location for the raid, but they pulled out when they learned the film's subject matter.) So John Menzies, at 107–9 Princes Street, now a branch of Next outfitters, was used instead. McGregor and Bremner then ran along Princes Street and fled down a flight of steps into Carlton Road, heading towards one of Edinburgh's cavernous railway bridges.

The next scene was shot in Maryhill near Glasgow. The gang were filmed playing football with recovering addicts from Calton Athletic on an Astroturf pitch at Firhill health complex in Hopewell Road. Having decided to kick his habit, Renton, under the lively influence of some opium suppositories, shoots into a betting shop at 620 Maryhill Road to relieve his bowels (the toilet cubicle itself was mocked-up back at the factory). A stone's throw away at 570 Maryhill Road lies Café D'Jaconneli, where McGregor and Bremner would snack out on milkshakes prior to a sequence in which Spud attends a speed-assisted job interview. Rouken Glen Park, on the southern outskirts of the city, served as the park in which Sick Boy introduces Renton to the delights of taking pot-shots at dumb, defenceless creatures (and their dogs).

The Crosslands Bar, at 182 Queen Margaret Drive, was commandeered for a scene in which Begbie hurls his pint glass into a crowded hostelry. Today, the pub is often visited by students from the nearby university campus, who clamber to take photographs of themselves at the spot. The film's nightclub scenes, which took the production over to the other side of Glasgow, were filmed at the Volcano, 15 Benalder Street, since demolished and replaced by a car park.

For a scene in which Tommy decides to haul his mates to the Highlands for some fresh air, the cast travelled to Corrour Station, as remote an outpost as you'll find in Scotland, some two hours' train ride outside Glasgow on the way to Fort William. A thousand feet above sea level, the area is legendary for the ferocious winds whipping across the nearby Rancah Moor. Just three trains stop there daily. In yet another Beatles homage, the cast stand 'Sergeant Pepper' style on the platform as a train passes by. During breaks the crew shot some footage of McGregor tied to the railway tracks as his friends wandered off into the distance laughing. This footage ended up as an oblique trailer for the film, earning location manager Robert Howe a severe ticking off from Scotrail, who had only licensed filming on the station platform.

One of the more harrowing scenes of the film would feature the death of a baby in the Mother Superior's squat. The scene would be painful to shoot for all concerned, but its relevance to the story was paramount. Boyle had brought in twins for the scene so that neither had to spend too long on set. Both toddlers had become favourites with the cast and crew. As Peter Mullan recalls, 'Prior to the scene we were all playing with the twins, they were lovely beautiful little creatures. None of us were allowed to go on set and see what was in the cot. When they shouted "action", and we all went running in, what shocked us to the core was that the dead baby's dummy had been modelled on the real baby, which we weren't expecting. When they shouted "cut", all of us went into another room and cried for half an hour. We were genuinely shocked. It was a deeply unpleasant sequence to do.'

A two-day shoot in London took place to film the gang's trip to the capital to conduct a smack deal. In yet another nod to the Fabs the gang are seen crossing a road in Abbey Road style. The Royal Eagle Hotel, at 26 Craven Street, W2, doubled as the front of the building they conduct the deal in, while interiors were filmed back in Glasgow, in a circular room at the George Hotel, 235 Bucannon Street (since demolished). Carlyle's Begbie would characteristically find himself in the middle of a pub fracas after the gang's successful negotiation. In an original version of the screenplay, Renton was supposed to have leapt out of the pub's broken window with the foursome's drug money. The sequence itself, in which Begbie glasses a punter in the face, was shot in Glasgow at the Wills factory's old social club.

A number of extras had been recruited for the scene and, because of lighting restrictions, it was decided to shoot the bystanders' reaction before Carlyle actually performed the assault. At first the extras appeared totally emotionless. 'They were terrible,' Boyle told *Hotdog*. 'I couldn't frighten them enough. Bobby just said, "Let me do my bit first – and then film them." So we did. And they were absolutely terrified. It was perfect.' As Carlyle told the magazine, 'That was the first time in my whole career that I've been surprised with the final result . . . there's something in the eyes which I didn't know was there on the day. Fucking worrying really.'

The final shot in London was of McGregor running to freedom over Waterloo Bridge during rush hour. By July 1995 filming was complete. There were few out-takes, and most seem well-chosen edits. Gone was Renton's meeting with the employment agency after Spud's chaotic interview, as were scenes of Sick Boy and Renton sparring over James Bond trivia and a sequence in which Mother Superior is visited in hospital by Renton after a leg amputation. These edits would be included on the limited edition 'Green' (as opposed to 'Orange') video release, foreshadowing the DVD age which so actively exploits movie out-takes and director's cuts.

Many of the novel's original hip literary devotees had voiced serious misgivings about the forthcoming movie. But *Trainspotting* was about to be aimed at a slightly different sort of audience. Yet again, timing would play a crucial role.

The Rave scene had now been so tamed by the market that Jungle was cropping up in advertising jingles and mainstream pop, the Ministry of Sound was turning over £10 million a year, and Boddington's beer was sponsoring club nights at Manchester's Hacienda. Dance outfit Underworld's chant of 'lager, lager, lager!', from 'Born Slippy', now echoed throughout the nation's clubs and football terraces. In order to woo the all-important eighteen-to-twenty-four-year-old clubbers back to the pubs, the alcohol industry (worth £25 billion a year) began manufacturing 'short sharp fixes' like alcopops, aimed at the younger Happy Hardcore crowd. The anxiety was misplaced: for Britain's youth, drugs – including alcohol – had become casual, largely pick 'n' mix affairs. Released when it was – in February 1996 – *Trainspotting*, sporting drugs, drink, dance music and, most importantly, tribal bonding, fitted like a white glove.

Through a highly sophisticated marketing campaign, *Trainspot-*

ting's core audience was about to be sold a lifestyle. 'I know many people who had bought the book and had not got past page three,' says Peter Mullan. 'But they had to have the book. While I was making a film in Ireland, the people I was staying with had two copies – one for the teenager and one for the father. They had no intention whatsoever of actually reading it; it was just something to put on the mantelpiece.' If a cult depends on exclusivity, *Trainspotting* would offer cinema-goers – perhaps those Happy Hardcorers who'd missed out on Rave's early, underground years – instant membership.

Polygram had picked up the distribution. Says former Polygram head of UK theatrical distribution, Chris Bailey: 'Because of the subject matter, I thought it would struggle to gross what *Shallow Grave* had.' Nevertheless, Polygram had splashed out £800,000 on publicity, more than five times the amount a production of this sort could normally have expected. Most of this budget, in a radical departure from conventional practice, was spent not on TV and radio exposure but on billboard advertising. As Bailey says, 'It really got on to the street, know what I mean?' Tantalising teaser posters were displayed at rail terminuses, bus shelters and tube station escalator panels a few weeks before the now famous orange posters appeared.

'Come in Hollywood, your time is up,' trumpeted *Trainspotting*'s poster quote; 'The best British film of the decade.' *Empire* magazine's Ian Nathan, who penned the above blurb, comments, 'It sounds grossly overreaching now, and in fact it's a misquote: my sentence had originally read, "*If Shallow Grave* was the best British film of the year, then *Trainspotting* is the Best British film of the decade." I.e., it's ten times better. I wasn't trying to make a blanket statement, like, "There won't be a better film than *Trainspotting* in the whole of the decade". But of course they cut the beginning bit off and ran the statement straight.'

The images directly underneath Nathan's quote were no less vital. A sexy, trendy young cast was presented as a series of numbered collectable human trump cards, (who's your favourite?), gleefully evoking memories of the 1970s 'Top Trumps' trading cards among retro-obsessed cinema-goers. Having a few years earlier employed the same tactic with their tremendously culty *Reservoir Dogs* posters, which were similarly numbered, Polygram already had a taste of the impact such a campaign – with the right film – could have on box office receipts. Renton's shivering form (dripping with toilet water, though it could just as well have been clubbing-induced sweat) tapped into the dark allure of 'heroin chic', pioneered by fashion photographer David Sorrenti, who later died from an overdose, and taken on to the catwalks by such models as Kate Moss and alleged addict Amy Wesson. The overall effect made the cast look like a Britpop band on tour. This was no accident: Polygram had used a design company that did album sleeves.

As with Tarantino's movies, *Trainspotting*'s integral soundtrack provided an ironic counterpoint to the on-screen action. The heavy subject matter was glossed over by a K-Tel of trendy Britpop performers, like Elastica, Blur and Pulp. Sleeper's Blondie cover brilliantly tapped the retro-buzz, while bands such as Bedrock, Leftfield, New Order and Primal Scream were nods to the club scene. Brian Eno's 'Deep Blue Day' was representative of its Ambient wing, and Underworld's 'Born Slippy' became that summer's alternative national anthem. Former heroin users and proto-punks Iggy Pop and Lou Reed represented the heroin cognoscenti. The latter's song, 'Perfect Day', accompanying the scene in which Renton takes an overdose, was an example of just how far heroin chic had spread; it was used a little later to promote the BBC's Children in Need charity appeal, the original allusions and associations of the song being conveniently ignored. EMI further sugared the pill, bringing out a lavishly packaged soundtrack CD with cool, silver-edged photos and movie quotes. Inside the CD booklet, an audio version of Welsh's novel was advertised by a 'Stop!! Look & Listen' motif – a retro play on the title of an early 1970s children's programme. A second CD, *Trainspotting II*, released well after the film's release, carried the concept further, featuring tracks by the likes of Joy Division and Goldie – which hadn't even been on the soundtrack; it was ventured that this was the kind of music that *Trainspotting*'s cast of characters – and by extension the movie's audience – would be listening to.

'With the exception of Tarantino, films were not then perceived as cool,' says Ian Nathan. 'Your granny went to the movies, everybody went. Suddenly *Trainspotting* arrived and changed the way people saw movies. It was like, "Are you part of this *Trainspotting* generation?" You became a *Trainspotting* person, a style you'd hook up into – which was genius. Everyone felt, "I've got to get a bit of this, to become part of the whole movement." Students had the poster on their wall, they could buy the T-shirt, and buy the cool tunes.'

'It's definitely a cult movie,' says Chris Bailey today. And from his marketing point of view it's obvious why he thinks so. Welsh's novel had been a cult success, so it was logical that the film should be marketed as a cult movie. But the film's publicist Jonathan Rutter claims that it was more of an 'organic' process. 'We didn't deliberately market it as a cult movie,' he says today. 'We felt there was a lot of heat around it, but we didn't want to burst the bubble too soon. And we really had to fight the press off. We'd already limited the amount of press on set, and limited the interviews. But the combination of the director, the book and the cast meant that by the time we screened the film, the press was beating down the door.' This explanation would hold a lot more water if it were not for the fact that limiting media access often creates an aura of mystery surrounding the film, which inevitably generates more media interest.

On 18 August 1995, just as *Trainspotting* was receiving its final airbrushing, Irvine Welsh handed in his notice to Lothian District Council. His meteoric rise to literary lion was now complete. 'We are genuinely sorry to lose him,' Council representative Frank Murray told the *Sunday Times*. 'He was good at his job and well liked.' Throwing away any chance of being awarded the Freedom of the City, Welsh and old *Rebel Inc.* cohort Kevin Williamson knocked together an alternative guide to Edinburgh, pinpointing the best spots to take Ecstasy and LSD. 'What a cheek,' Lothian Councillor Moria Knox told the *Sunday Times*. 'He should be writing to the council to congratulate them on keeping this magnificent city clean.' On hearing of the writer's move to Amsterdam, Moria put out the flags. 'I am delighted for Edinburgh that he is no longer here.'

The movie was laid before the censors in November 1995, the month teenager Leah Betts died in a tragic Ecstasy-related incident. Although the moral guardians of Soho Square judged no cuts were needed, the film would understandably receive an 18 certificate. It still had to get past the critics. On 9 February 1996, the *Daily Mail* devoted a full page to the film, critic Edward Verity bellowing his disgust under the heading, 'The odious culture that killed Leah'. *Trainspotting*, he wrote, was 'thoroughly nasty, insidious and self-consciously irresponsible towards drugs'. James Delingpole of the *Daily Telegraph* wrote: 'Read Welsh and you are scarcely likely to be seduced with Smack. See the film and there's a possibility you might.' Alexander Walker, who had been so outspoken in his defence of another 'controversial' movie twenty-three years previously, loathed it. 'In style, structure and subversive imagination it recalls Stanley Kubrick's *A Clockwork Orange*. [But] Kubrick's film made you think. Boyle's film, overall a clever pastiche of the senior director's style, makes one puke.'

Says Walker today: 'The reservations I had about it was that it was a film that seemed to me to come out fairly clearly in favour of drugs. Though some of the trips may be bad, the overall effect for someone like myself (who doesn't abuse drugs) was to suggest that there was no great harm in it if you were prepared to put up with the occasional trips down the loo. Considering the way that drugs have a hold – particularly on the kind of teenager who'd be attracted to see Ewan McGregor and Robert Carlyle in this immensely publicised film – I thought it was verging on the undesirable.'

Conservative minister Virginia Bottomley, then National Heritage Secretary, attended a Cannes screening prior to its official release. Bottomley's daughter, a medical consultant, had urged her mother to view the film. 'She is keen to see it,' a spokesman for Polygram confirmed at the time, 'because it is a British film of some note and because one of her children has recommended it to her as a particularly vivid description of drug culture.' 'It's very powerful and was made with great technical skill,' Bottomley told a fevered gang of reporters post-screening. 'Nobody would think that heroin addiction was an easy option if they saw it. It is not soft on hard drugs.'

Bottomley's cinema trip was undoubtedly prompted by nothing less than the highest integrity, but it's worth noting that in the run up to the following year's General Election, politicians had been falling over themselves to grab the youth vote and prove their

hipper-than-thou credentials, with a passion unheard of since
Harold Wilson awarded the Beatles their MBEs in 1965. As John
Major's faves, Status Quo, were consigned to Radio One's Z-list,
opposition leaders and political also-rans jostled to name as many
Spice Girls as they could, or inserted Blur or Oasis lyrics into their
platform speeches. As both sides of the House implicitly understood,
in a period of British devolution such unifying distractions were
political necessities.

  US censors had no problem with the film's depiction of heroin
abuse or overt profanity, but they would object to Diane's bedroom
frolics with Renton. Although the film had already given the novel
a sizeable linguistic going-over, US distributors Miramax, who had
handled *Pulp Fiction*, demanded that the cast's voices be post-
dubbed into more comprehensible English, to which Figment
agreed. Andrew Macdonald told the *Independent*: 'We didn't want
them to reject it from the beginning. After that, they either get it
or they don't.' America 'got it', all right, with *Trainspotting* taking
$262,000 on its first weekend in July 1996, and netting over $16
million by the end of 1996. 'Perversely irresistible,' gushed the *New
York Times*. The *Los Angeles Times* raved: 'Exuberant and pitiless,
profane yet eloquent, flush with the ability to create laughter out
of unspeakable situations.' Amy Taubin of the *Village Voice* was
more cautious. 'I laughed a lot at its combination of Scottish lava-
torial humour with Richard Lester's kineticism; I wasn't quite so
taken with the art direction and cinematography, which looks as if
a commercial art student had overdosed on Francis Bacon.'

  Irvine Welsh, who had originally kept his distance from the theatrical production, told *Feed* magazine, 'With cinema it's always gonna
find its way into more impressionable crowds. I don't necessarily
think that anyone who takes drugs is a victim. You can show why
people do it, they enjoy it, it alleviates pain, that sort of thing –
but you've also got to show what the consequences are.' Boyle reiter-
ated the point for *Salon* magazine: 'Although their world is terribly
depressing, there is something very exhilarating there. The film
celebrates the spirits of these young people, rather than the thing
they do that will eventually destroy them. It's also about being
young and all the crazy things you do in your twenties. It's not
trying to celebrate heroin, it's celebrating a kind of spirit that exists

in all of us before something like age, or a job – or heroin – crushes it.'

'I don't know that *Trainspotting* can be really accused of glamour,' says 'Rose', a recovering heroin addict. 'The characters were not presented as that attractive, they were all pretty fucked up in some way and their lives were shown as being pretty crappy. The drug itself is not that frightening. We're fed all these demon stories, "this is what heroin does to your brain – *smash!*". But in reality heroin is non-toxic; people can take it for years with no ill effects. It's the lifestyle associated with the drug – a lifestyle dictated by prohibition – that kills people, makes them paupers, miserable and turns users into criminals.'

Author Daren King's début novel, *Boxy An Star*, came out in 1999. King's pill-popping, blissed-out lovers were younger than those from *Trainspotting* – aged fifteen and thirteen, much younger. '*Trainspotting* had led me to believe that there was a huge market for drug films, drug novels, drug T-shirts, whatever,' he says. 'I began *Boxy* thinking it would sell bucketloads. It didn't even sell pocketloads. By the time I finished writing, the world was sick of the so-called Chemical Generation.' At the turn of the new century it was estimated that 99 per cent of all British banknotes contained traces of cocaine. Clearly, we have become a nation of casual drug-users. No big deal. 'I told my publisher not to put the phrase "Chemical Generation" on the cover of the book, but they did,' says King. 'Although I began my novel as an attempt to cash in on that market, it developed into something more personal. It's only a Chemical Generation novel on the surface.'

King first saw *Trainspotting* in Germany, with English subtitles. 'When Renton stole the money, I was on the edge of my seat. The bit where he sinks into the ground to the tune of "Perfect Day" is beautiful. I cried. I loved it. But the second and third time I saw it, I hated it. Too tacky, too shallow, too pleased with itself. It had no atmosphere. The characters in *Human Traffic* are far more interesting and likeable than those in *Trainspotting*, and not just because those in *Trainspotting* were doing something less socially acceptable than Ecstasy.'

Matthew Collin, author of the definitive book on Ecstasy culture, *Altered State*, comments: 'Like most attempts at capturing clubbing on celluloid, *Trainspotting* rings somewhat false, as the experience of being high on a dark dancefloor, with the bass pulsing through your body, is physical and mental, not visual.'

However, Channel Four's £1.7 million investment was rewarded with receipts of over £60 million. Neither cast nor crew would suffer from their association with the film; quite the reverse. All main leads went on to successfully consolidate their careers in the UK and abroad. McGregor followed his Uncle Dennis into the *Star Wars* franchise, while Carlyle became a huge star after appearing in *The Full Monty*. Lee Miller turned in a superb performance for Gillies MacKinnon's *Regeneration*, as did Kelly Macdonald for *Stella Does Tricks*. Both Kevin McKidd and Ewen Bremner popped up in another movie based on Irvine Welsh material – *The Acid House* – and Bremner was last seen in *Pearl Harbor*. The Figment trio is still together, having tried their hand at another 'cult' bestseller, Alex Garland's *The Beach*, to a somewhat more tempered reaction.

'I still don't believe that you can buy an audience,' says Chris Bailey's former Polygram marketing colleague, Julia Short, today. 'People are far too astute, they can smell a turkey a mile off. With *Trainspotting* we were lucky enough that it all came together because we had enough support. We spent the right money in the right place with the right images. When we screened it to the media they all thought it was as good as we believed it was.' Short's being modest: Polygram's campaign had deliberately tapped into the kind of media-literacy now common among audiences. Renton's 'Choose Life' monologue was simultaneously mocking advertising, while selling anti-authority to the masses: a knowing move, calculated to appeal to armchair nihilists – the self-same Pepsi Generation who would, in all probability, go on to buy those 'fucking big televisions, washing machines and electrical tin openers'. And, to closely paraphrase Renton's opening tirade, whether *Trainspotting* will become 'nothing more than an embarrassment to the movie brats it spawned to replace itself", remains to be seen. Why not ask Guy Ritchie?

THE FOOTBALLER, THE GANGSTER, THE ICON & HER LOVER

The plot's as convoluted as the visuals are dizzying. Following a rigged card game, four wide boys find themselves half a million in debt to local porn baron Harry 'the Hatchet' Lonsdale. With the threat of digit amputation (and worse) looming, the lads turn their neighbours' scheme to rob a bunch of public school 'chemists' to their advantage, planning to fleece the robbers in turn. That's when the trouble really starts. *Lock, Stock and Two Smoking Barrels*: 'cult' movie or marketing dream?

'Pay no attention to that man behind the curtain.'

Frank Morgan, *The Wizard of Oz*

Mid-March 2001. On the porch of Camelot Castle – that's Camelot Castle, South-East London – celebrity darling, court-jester to the masses, retired Face and extremely charming gentleman Dave Courtney is making a movie. Apart from his Lex Luther-like crown Dave's eyes are his most striking features – electric blue and wide-awake. Today, they're darting all over the place, trying to keep an eye on the camera crew, the props (taken from his living-room), and his mates, future film stars to a man, and once known for a different kind of notability. Let's call them Tom, Dick and Harry. And another man, who may be known here only as Mr Crimewatch.

It's a sprat to catch a mackerel. Dave met Quentin Tarantino in New York in 2000 while taking part in an on-stage discussion about gangsters, British and Stateside. Following the talk, the pair spent the night at a party, where Quentin asked Dave if he could act. 'Yes,' said Dave. 'Gimme proof,' said Quentin, 'and I'll make a movie with you.' So Dave came up with *Hell to Pay*, which drew on his two autobiographies, *Stop the Ride, I Want To Get Off*, and *Raving Lunacy*, which chronicled his days as a club security organiser in the Rave scene. The plot's a modern-day Cain and Abel story, concerning two brothers who fall out when one, played by Billy Murray (the grass from *McVicar* and a bent copper in ITV's *The Bill*), tries to fit up the other, played by Dave.

It's shot on 'shirt buttons' on a small digital XL1 camera by a first-time director, and nobody's been paid except the crew. With no working script (*à la* Mike Leigh), and rehearsals confined to set, *Hell to Pay* is guerrilla film-making at its best – the logical extension of *Performance*, *Get Carter*, *Lock, Stock and Two Smoking Barrels*. But this sort of thing blows those films, with their smattering of real underworld faces, out of the water. All the movie's publicans are played by real publicans, taxi drivers by taxi drivers, the brasses by real lap dancers and porn stars. And the movie's many 'chaps' are played by the genuine articles, like Roy Shaw and Joey Pyle. 'And I play a really fucking good Dave Courtney,' says Dave.

Dave says it's a springboard for his mates, an opportunity for them to flex their theatrical muscles. 'But no Oscar nominations here, cos this is the real deal.' As *Hell to Pay*'s director Rob Gomez says, 'With *Hell to Pay*, what you see is what you get. We told the "actors" to be themselves.' One performer, Harry, likes *Lock, Stock and Two Smoking Barrels* very much. He's only seen about fifteen films in his life, but was so impressed with Ritchie's movie he saw it twice and bought the DVD. The reason he likes it so much is because one of the characters is actually based on him. 'But nobody plays me better than me,' he says affably. '*Lock, Stock* opened the door for what I want to do,' adds Dave, 'but any cunt with a camera can make a slapstick gangster film. Guy Ritchie couldn't tell me how to hold a fucking gun properly.'

THESE DAYS, IT seems movies are no longer afforded the posthumous luxury of being nurtured into cults by devoted fans. Rather, 'cultiness' is increasingly being implemented at the marketing stage before the film has even come out. And, in these cases, marketing would appear to be the most important part of the creative process. Originality, characterisation and social comment seem to be irrelevant in a world where brand supersedes artistic integrity. *Lock, Stock* is a good example of this process at work. Its inclusion here serves to illustrate just how sophisticated industry marketing techniques have become – a fitting close to this book.

Which is not to detract from the film itself. *Lock, Stock* is a clever piece of film-making and a pretty entertaining movie to boot. It does its job, as they say. And yet, for all the plaudits, Guy Ritchie has become something of a punchbag among certain sections of the media these days. For his detractors, he's a 'Mockney' wannabe hardman. The only kind of 'claret' this phenomenally successful director ever really came in contact with, they say, must have come from his old man's cellar. In all fairness, he's never claimed any ties to the East End or the underworld. He's just been a little, well, 'hazy' on occasions. 'Uhm, I've never been to prison,' he told *Time Out*'s Tom Charity in 1998. 'Let's keep me as a man of mystery, shall we?' Hence descriptions like this one from the Net 'zine *Urban Cinefile* just prior to *Lock, Stock*'s release in 1998: 'Guy Ritchie is your typical working-class Londoner . . .'

Ritchie was born into a resolutely middle-class family in Hatfield, Hertfordshire, in 1968. His father John Ritchie directed TV commercials (notably, for Hamlet cigars) and his mother Amber was a successful model. When Guy was five his parents divorced – John relocating to Chelsea, Amber remarrying Sir Michael Leighton, the eleventh holder of a 300-year-old baronetcy. Guy moved with Amber and Sir Michael into the palatial surroundings of seventeenth-century Loton Park, Shropshire, where he indulged in huntin', shootin' and fishin' for the next seven years, until his mother divorced again.

By the time he was fifteen, Guy had attended a dozen different public and private schools. Adam Buxton, co-creator of Channel Four's *Adam and Joe Show*, was one of his classmates at Windlesham House, a Sussex-based prep school. 'He sat next to me for about three years, and taught me how to play cards,' Buxton recalls. 'He gave off this detached air, and dressed like a kind of country gent, all tweeds and flat cap and boots. He knew the names of trees and birds and was a romantic nature boy figure for all the girls; an image he worked perhaps because of his dyslexia. I imagined him thinking, "I don't care for your ways, your books and your words. The trees and the birds, theirs is the only poetry I need". Little did I know he was actually thinking: "He was called Harry Staples. Staples wasn't his real name. It was given to 'im on account of his fondness for stapling his victim's eyes open so they'd 'ave to watch while he gutted them . . ."'

Guy was expelled from one private college for dyslexics, Stanbridge Earls, Hampshire, then charging £5,000 a term, after, as he claims, having been caught 'doing a line of sulphate on sports day'. His father says it was because he'd been found in a girl's room and was bunking off lessons. Aided by John Ritchie's industry mates, among them Alan Parker and David Puttnam, Guy managed to acquire a GCSE in film studies.

In 1993, following aborted stints at Island Records and on a building site, Guy got a job through his father as a runner with a Soho film company. During 1995 he directed videos and promos for obscure German rave bands and then began shooting commercials, which helped to subsidise his first short, *The Hard Case*. This hands-on experience now gave him the technical confidence to write and direct *Lock, Stock and Two Smoking Barrels*. The London Gangster film, thought Guy, was due for an airing. *Get Carter* and *The Long Good Friday* had created a precedent, but, he felt, the niche hadn't been properly exploited since then.

In 1995 Guy hooked up with young producer and friend Matthew Vaughn. Together they would tout Guy's phonetically spelled, sprawling corkscrew of a script around for the next two years. At first they had huge difficulty getting the project off the ground. Despite the staggering returns for *Four Weddings* and *Trainspotting*, the British film industry was still dogged by the same old problems – lack of funding and poor distribution. But eventually, in 1997, they received backing from HandMade Films and the Imperial Bank. By this time, Ritchie and Vaughn had slashed the budget down to £1 million. Nobody would get paid – in for a penny, in for a pound – literally, in Sting's case, who agreed to appear for a quid. Actors were on deferred payments, which put off some potential cast members like Anna Scher's old soldiers, who still believed in cash in hand for a long day's slog.

Guy began casting. Self-professed 'scrawny bastard' Nick Moran was chosen to play Eddy, the unofficial leader of *Lock, Stock*'s wide boy pack. Moran, who'd been raised on a Hertfordshire council estate and left home at sixteen, had previously played junkies, squatters and hippies on TV and in the West End, also emptying bins and sweeping the streets to make ends meet. 'I was never perceived as leading man material,' he told the *Sunday Times* in 1998. 'So when *Lock, Stock* came along, I said to Guy, "If you give me this part I'll put on half a stone, I'll get a posh haircut and go under a sunbed."'

Redhead Jason Flemyng would play Eddy's mate Tom. He'd been a member of the RSC and had once played a ball of Edam cheese for a Japanese TV commercial. 'My character had to be changed slightly, because they were all meant to be hard,' he'd tell *Neon* magazine in 1999. 'When I got there I realised that I couldn't out-hard anybody on the set. So I kind of went for the goofy, foolish element.'

Jason Statham was cast as dodgy street vendor Bacon, the third member of Eddy's entourage. Statham had been a top European highboard diver, and a French Connection poster boy. He had also been a street vendor in real life; Ritchie had discovered him flogging imitation gold and perfume outside Harrods. As Ritchie told Edward Champion of the Internet's 24 Frames per Second.com, 'I made a documentary on him selling stuff on the street. Jason sold me two hundred pounds worth of gold, which turned out to be a supposititious acquisition. And I went back to complain about the fact that my gold had gone from gold to stainless steel overnight. And Jason refused to return my money. But he did it so tactfully that I felt that this was the kind of character I'm interested in.'

Dexter Fletcher had been acting since he was knee-high, with parts in *Bugsy Malone*, TV's *Press Gang* and *The Rachel Papers*. He played Soap, the fourth 'sensible' member of Eddy's gang. Vas Blackwood, who had appeared in *Only Fools and Horses* and *The Lenny Henry Show*, played Rory Breaker, a psychopathic drugs baron. 'We based Rory on a couple of guys,' Blackwood told *Neon*. 'I'm not even going to mention any names. One's dead and one's in prison.' P. H. Moriarty (Hatchet Harry) was a familiar face from *The Long Good Friday* (as the quiet but lethal 'Razors'), *Quadrophenia* and *The Professionals*.

Before becoming an actor, Frank Harper had worked for ten years in Smithfield meat market. 'The best drama school in the world,' he says. 'My Great granddad, uncle and dad (Millwall, Ipswich and Leyton Orient player Dave Harper) all worked there.' Harper was cast as Dog, the vicious leader of a bunch Eddy's mob would rip off. 'Dog was based on a guy I used to work with at Smithfield's. He was pretty scary. He was one of those guys, so intense, that if you accidentally had eye contact with him, you'd look at the floor.'

Prima donnas were definitely not invited. As Moran told *Neon*, 'The soundman was a Tae Kwon Do instructor, the cameraman was a kickboxer, Guy's a two-dan karate double black belt – and they weren't even the hardmen.' Ritchie had peppered the movie with ex-cons to lend instant credibility. He wouldn't have to look too far.

Criminals and media people, be they actors, artists or publishers, have always attracted each other, the common denominator being glamour, both groups hanging out in the same Soho private drinking dens, where lines are snorted, favours swapped, and everyone comes away with a bit of extra credibility. 'A favour for a favour,' says *Hell to Pay* director Rob Gomez. 'That's the way London has been brought up for the past three hundred years, from market stalls to nightclubs.' For Great Train Robber Bruce Reynolds's son Nick, 'Acting's a form of lying, isn't it? You put a camera in front of criminals and they're normally pretty good: they should be. They've spent years standing in court, telling lies to prison officers.'

The late Lenny McLean played Barry the Baptist, Harry the Hatchet's strong-arm. He is said to have come in particularly useful during moments when motorists complained that filming was holding up traffic. An East End legend and mate of the Kray brothers, McLean had been a huge draw on South London's unlicensed boxing scene, the veteran of 3,000 bare knuckle-bouts, all of which he won. The Mafia once flew him to New York to take on their own man, one John McCormack, in a multi-million-dollar boxing contest – McCormack is said to have lasted less than three minutes – and he was reportedly once hired to put the frighteners on an IRA-backed money-laundering gang. In 1992, McLean was charged with – and acquitted of – the murder of a young man in a West End nightclub, where he was working as a bouncer, but he still served eighteen months for GBH. 'Gissa cuddle,' he'd invite his fellow *Lock, Stock* actors. 'Be a man, son, gissa cuddle. Good boy.'

Guy had specified a 'Vinnie Jones type' for the role of Harry the Hatchet's conscientious debt-collector Big Chris, a character partly based on Dave Courtney. 'Very cool,' read Ritchie's notes. 'If he loses, he loses it – similar to Vinnie Jones the footballer.' And the real thing was available. Jones's role had originally been a cameo until Guy, with Moran's prompting, grasped what an opportunity he had here. Vinnie was special: his reputation preceded him. The sort of audience Guy was about to attract could be sold the movie purely through Vinnie's involvement.

For those New Lads who had previously felt excluded from football's core working-class base, Vinnie had become a bit of an icon. James Brown's *Loaded*, along with Rave's 'all in it together' spirit and author Nick Hornby's *Fever Pitch* had, theoretically, done much to bridge the class gap. Daily, it seemed, broadsheet journalists of both sexes belatedly proclaimed their love for the beautiful game. A throwback to the likes of early 1970s players such as Chelsea's Ron 'Chopper' Harris, or Leeds' Norman 'Bites your Legs' Hunter, Vinnie was notorious for his aggressive conduct on field and off, which would be summed up by a famous photograph of him backing into Paul Gascoigne and grabbing his balls. In one match, as a player at Chelsea, he had been sent off just three seconds after stepping on to the pitch.

A contribution to a video called *Soccer's Hard Men* brought Jones a £20,000 fine and a suspended six-month ban, while an appearance on the TV show *Gladiators*, presented by his former Wimbledon team mate John Fashanu, led to a punch-up with another competitor. He lost a *News of the World* column in February 1995 after viciously biting *Mirror* journalist Ted Oliver's nose in a Dublin bar. Overcome with self-hatred, Vinnie went off to the woods to blow his brains out. Fortunately, his suicide attempt was scuppered at the last minute by the sight of his beloved pet dog. A seemingly rehabilitated Jones left the woods, bound for a life on the silver screen.

With cast and distributor secured all looked well. Then HandMade for reasons unknown, suddenly lost interest four days before shooting was due to begin. Once HandMade's commitment evaporated, Imperial Bank also withdrew, leaving Ritchie and Vaughn thousands of pounds in the red. 'Lock, Stock and Two Smoking Overdrafts,' read a sign in Vaughn's office. With Guy at his wits' end, Matthew holed up in his girlfriend's kitchen with a soon-to-be cut-off telephone, hustling up a storm to raise the remaining cash. Vaughn's connections – who stuck in about a hundred grand each – included his godfather Peter Morton (the Hard Rock Café founder), *Forrest Gump* producer Steve Tisch, French Connection boss Stephen Marks and the owners of the *Financial Times*, the Pearson family. Finishing funds came from Trudie Styler, who had seen *The Hard Case* and liked it, and whose husband Sting would be practically guaranteed a role in Guy's movie. SKA Films, Guy and Matthew's production company, was born.

Shooting began at 8 a.m. on 6 November 1997 and continued for the next thirty-six days, with Guy employing a gallery of state-of-the-art camera effects, overcranked and undercranked steadicam shots and slo-mos.

With the exception of the public school chemists' hangout, which was found in Stables Market, Camden, and JD's bar, which was actually Vic Naylor's in John Street, Smithfield, *Lock, Stock*'s few shooting locations were in Bethnal Green and Southwark. The cavernous passage Statham and Moran run through, pursued by cops, at the film's opening is Rochester Walk, off Borough Market. The stone staircase they then hare down is the same one used for sequences in *Naked* and *Gangster No. 1*. To locate it, take a side turning about halfway down Brick Lane into Pedley Street and follow the road round past the small railway station until you come to a car park near some arches. The steps are found through the tunnel on your left.

Climbing the steps and walking over the narrow, corrugated railway bridge leads you into Cheshire Street. Some yards down, on the facing pavement, a small side turning leads to Repton Boys' Club – over a hundred years old and once frequented by the Krays, who were raised in nearby Vallance Road. *Lock, Stock*'s location manager Eddie Standish secured use of the club's boxing gym for the card shark scene. He claims he hadn't been aware of the Kray connection prior to shooting, 'but everywhere you go in that area the Krays are there'.

Artist Michael Challenger's studio, tucked away in an elbow at 13 Park Street, Southwark, below the rattling Thameslink railway bridge, became Dog's hideaway cum minicab office. Southwark's a peculiar place, where Georgian terraces and medieval monuments stand incongruously next to blank, Thatcherite monstrosities. 'There's a huge diversity here,' says Challenger. 'It hasn't really even started on the gentrification process.' Challenger has become used to film crews knocking on his door in recent years: *Howards End*, *Blue Ice*, *The Young Americans*, *Jude*, *101 Dalmatians*, *Keep the Aspidistra Flying* and *Entrapment* have all incorporated his studio front or interior. 'It's a fantastic road,' says Standish. 'It really does look that seedy.'

'Very late one night while I was working, someone rattled the door,' Challenger recalls. 'I thought it was the head of security, but it was some guy wanting a minicab. Maybe he'd spent a bit too much time at the pub.' Meanwhile, Challenger's neighbour, furniture maker Estitxu Garcia, saw her first-floor studio, replete with its distinctive green shutters, transformed into the lads' hangout. Beneath these shutters Vinnie, playing Big Chris, would head-butt Frank Harper, for one of the film's most memorable sequences.

On 11 November 1997, the night before he was due to make his début appearance on set, Vinnie Jones paid his next-door neighbour Timothy Gear a visit. Gear, who was a riding instructor, had removed a stile and gate Jones had built on a public footpath at the edge of his land, claiming he'd taken it down in order to steer his horses through the fence. At around 11 p.m. Jones noticed a light on in Gear's caravan. According to the prosecution, Vinnie smashed Gear's windows, sunk his teeth into his scalp, and kicked and punched him to the floor. With the riding instructor wedged between his bed and a chest of drawers, Jones stamped on his head a few times with his wellington boots. Jones was arrested and detained until dawn.

A few hours later he stepped on to the chilly East End set. During the scene his character would bludgeon Frank Harper – who had held Big Chris's son to ransom – first with a car door, then with his fists. A piece of wood substituted for Harper's head. 'There was a comment that they couldn't tell the difference between my head and the wooden block,' says Harper. Following the scene Jones looked up to see cast and crew gaping at him slack-jawed. He'd assumed he'd done something wrong – until they began to cheer and clap. 'Of course, had it been for real,' Vinnie told the *Observer*'s Jay Rayner in 1998, 'I wouldn't have stopped.'

Jason Flemyng provided some of the lighter moments during the shoot. At one point, the sound crew handcuffed him to a hand-held dolly, then 'accidentally' mislaid the key. Then there was the time Frank Harper pushed fellow actor Steve Sweeney through a wall. The wrong wall, as it turned out. 'The other thing that sticks in my mind is when we shot the Bren-gun sequence,' says Harper. 'We had special cameras set up, they'd rigged the room, and Guy came up to me and Steve Sweeney and said, "No pressure, guys, but we can only afford to do this once."'

At the time of filming Lenny McLean was forty-nine and dying of cancer, but he kept his spirits up. His favourite song, after all, was Monty Python's 'Always Look on the Bright Side of Life'. Jason Statham recalled for *Neon*, 'When we was being interviewed down on the set, someone came up to Lenny and said, "Have you ever thought of going to drama school?" And he says, "Look, I've been stabbed three times, I've been shot in the leg ten times, I've had a thousand bar-room brawls. Ain't that enough drama for anyone's fucking life?"' McLean's Hoxton funeral on 5 August 1998 was attended by friends like Charlie Richardson and Frankie Fraser, and Guy dedicated *Lock, Stock* to Lenny's memory.

There were another couple of casualties following filming. Laura Bailey, who'd originally been cast as Daisy, Eddy's love interest, saw all of her scenes jettisoned. In *Lock, Stock*'s original ending, Moran would drive off with Bailey in a Cobra. By the end of the shoot Ritchie had ditched Bailey's 'wussy' scenes and opted for an *Italian Job*-style cliffhanger, filmed halfway across Battersea Bridge. 13 Park Street and the surrounding neighbourhood is now under threat. As we write, there are plans for a steel concrete bridge to be built through Southwark's dense mediaeval streets. Railtrack claims this will ease congestion but, according to the Cathedral Area Residents Association (CARA), thirty buildings, many of them listed, will be demolished in the process. Park Street residences (including Challenger's) will have their backs sheared off to make room for the new railway line, while two upper storeys of the Wheatsheaf Pub in Stoney Street, along with premises and residences on Borough High Street and Bedale Street, will be destroyed. Green Dragon Court (where parts of *The French Lieutenant's Woman* was filmed) will be torn down, while part of Borough Market's iron and glass roof will also go the way of rotten fruit and vegetables. Towards the end of filming, Vinnie added his name to CARA's petition.

With the film in the can, a rough-cut screening of *Lock, Stock* won little enthusiasm from UK distributors: ten turned the movie down. But Trudie Styler's connections saved the day. Having persuaded her husband's record label Polygram to take a look, Polygram's acquisitions head Sally Caplan touted the film around Hollywood. Tom Cruise arrived out of the blue at one crucial LA industry screening. The diminutive heart-throb was soon falling off his chair. 'This film rocks!' he announced, bearhugging director and cast. Following Cruise's endorsement, a bidding war ensued. Gramercy, a division of Polygram, beat off the competition picking up the UK rights. Guy was able to make a deal with Sony for his next film *Snatch* – then known as 'Diamonds' – before they'd even read the script.

The film was released in Britain on 28 August 1998 and hailed by the *Guardian* as 'film of the week'. The *Evening Standard*'s Neil Norman thought it was the funniest film he'd seen in years, contending that 'every character seems like the genuine article'. But many critics thought Ritchie's movie a hollow pastiche, a 'DIY' cult movie, borrowing, though not building on, the templates of godfathers Tarantino and Danny Boyle – the picture populated by a collection of tedious caricatures. For an actor-director like Tarantino, soul and versatility of character, is essential – a windbreak against the flying bullets – directorial traits Ritchie seemed to have overlooked for his début feature. The Tarantino comparisons weren't really justified. There was a very British breeziness at play here, closer to the spirit of Ealing than Hollywood (via Hong Kong). Nonetheless, Ritchie's reliance on flashy tricks picked up from his commercials days really did get the critics' backs up. As Robert Stevens wrote on the World Socialist web site: 'It's supposed to be visually exciting but the result is more like a corpse-strewn Gap khakis ad than a triumph of technique.' The 'Gap' dig was apposite: notwithstanding the film backers' fashion house ties (and spiv suits supplied by Savile Row's Ozwald Boateng), here was a genre film made with more regard for bespoke tailoring than ever before, commanding almost as much attention on the fashion pages as it did on the arts pages.

Evening Standard fashion journalist Claudia Croft wrote, 'The appeal of the film's gangster look is simple. They appear 'ard but are so well-dressed that no one in their right mind would want to mess up their suits.' *Lock, Stock*'s wideboys wore Crombies, silk ties from Austin Reed and knitted Gabicci polo shirts, 'a favourite with early Eighties casuals and back in style again'. The *Observer*'s *Life* magazine ran an interview with Nick Moran for River Island fashions, while *FHM* quizzed Jason Flemyng on his Rockabilly wardrobe. It was entirely apt. By this stage British gangsters, so beloved of the New Lads, had been transformed into shotgun-toting clothes horses: likeable, mythological pop culture icons, the stuff of celluloid, photo shoots, magazine columns and best-selling autobiographies. Gangster Chic was big business. Ritchie's core audience came ready-made.

Many of the 'genuine articles' were quizzed for their thoughts on *Lock, Stock*. 'A crock of shit,' thought Freddie Foreman. 'A bit shallow, a cartoon strip,' thought Bruce Reynolds. 'You might imagine real gangsters like gangster films, but they don't,' says Dave Courtney. 'They're looking at something being portrayed which they actually know the truth of. Ask George Best if he likes football films, or Mohammed Ali what he thought of *Rocky*.' If these were fairly unsurprising responses, the real surprise was that they'd been pestered for their views at all.

Nick Reynolds, for one, was intrigued. A year after *Lock, Stock*'s release, he held his *Cons to Icons* exhibition, which featured portraits and life-casts of well-known villains. 'I wanted people to stand back and ask themselves, "Why is it that somebody who, on the one hand would be vilified by the media, is all of a sudden being fêted on the celebrity circuit? I knew by doing the exhibition I'd be stirring the whole thing up anyway, and that was actually the whole point: about how publicity works. I used the media to prove my point.' If the aura of the underworld has been kept alive by mystique, Courtney, for one, had turned the process on its head. 'He actually spends his time plotting and planning how to get one over on the police, while getting press at the same time,' says Reynolds. 'Now that is not what gangsters do: he's become something else. And by becoming something else, he's perpetuating the whole gangster myth. He's like a post-modern gangster – a performance artist.'

Make that *performing artiste*. Gary Clail and Adrian Sherwood had sampled gangster Charles Richardson on their *End of the Century Party* album back in 1989. Ten years later, Tricky's Durban Poison label upped the ante with their *Product of the Environment* CD, on which the likes of Courtney, Richardson, Frankie Fraser and Tony Lambrianou reminisced over techno soundtracks. If Frankie Fraser's track sounded like a horror movie, Lambrianou's sounded, as Courtney says, 'gut-wrenchingly beautiful' – perfectly pitched, with real insight. 'Certain stories can be a bit gruesome,' *Product*'s producer Gareth Bowen told *Time Out*'s Lisa Mullen in 1999. 'I cut out a lot of what they said.' Edited for mass consumption, *Product* now nestles comfortably on the rack alongside Gangsta rappers, reassuring customers with the information that some of the CD's profits would go to 'providing musical equipment and boxing facilities for deprived kids'.

'It's all about marketing at the moment,' says Reynolds. 'The moral stance has been thrown out, and nobody seems to care as long as they're making money. I think that's fucking irresponsible, quite honestly. But inevitable.' Dave Courtney concurs: 'I know right now I'm marketable. I'm not treated the way I am because I'm the biggest, baddest, most violent fucking gangster there is, I'm nowhere near it. But I'm as good a baddy as you're going to get.'

During 1999 Guy paired off with Madonna, pop's biggest icon, who surpassed even her husband in her capacity for reinvention. 'I saw him at the Comedy Awards a few years back,' Adam Buxton recalls. 'I went up to him, thinking maybe he'd seen our show and we could have a little backslapping session, but he claimed that not only had he never seen me before, he didn't even recall going to the school we attended either. It was odd and from then on I enjoyed his work less.'

Lock, Stock's first TV spin-off drama, *Lock, Stock and Four Stolen Hooves*, emerged in 2000. *Hooves* . . . spun another convoluted story of four laddish East End pub owners getting in over their heads with local crimelord 'Miami Vice' (*Withnail & I*'s Ralph Brown). As Matthew Vaughn told Neil Norman shortly before transmission, 'You can't move for tits. And swearing. And violence.' Vaughn compared it favourably to *Minder*. The series was critically mauled on release. Three episodes in and the only pertinent question to ask was: Exactly who was being patronised here? Hoxton's increasingly ghettoised working-class residents? Or Ginger Productions, misled into thinking it had a sure-fire hit?

Guy Ritchie's chortlingly titled *Snatch* came out that same year. He'd auditioned his actors in Dave Courtney's back garden. *Snatch* was more of the same, but faster. Ritchie was fashioning a brand. As Jason Flemyng told Edward Champion back in 1998, 'Already, there's been scripts that have come to me which have very, very similar usage of character, introduction, down to the names of the characters.' The predictable slew of mostly atrocious British gangster film projects, that got the go-ahead following Ritchie's success, have, perhaps unfairly, done nothing to salvage the director's credibility for many.

The slightly hysterical *Gangster No. 1* and Jonathan Glazer's *Sexy Beast* are thought to be the best of the bunch so far, but in the latter's case we're not so sure. Just how involving can a movie really be in which an ex-con refuses, for an hour of screentime, to go back on the job? As an experiment in genre, *Sexy Beast*'s a bit of a failure. Glazer's best work is yet to come. But these days it looks like directors are simply trying to break the record for the number of 'Cunts' they can fill a screenplay with. As Danny Leigh, writing in *Sight and Sound* in June 2000, commented: 'The Mockney-accented gunplay of the *Lock, Stock* era begins to look like easy-on-the-eye bourgeois pornography.'

If Rob Gomez's *Hell to Pay* initially seems like gangster chic's crowning glory, ironically it really has nothing very much in common with the phenomenon. As *Hell to Pay*'s editor Brian Hovmand suggests, 'The fact that it doesn't look like the typical

British gangster movie might be because I'm Danish, and the director's half Spanish.' Eschewing sepia-tints and Mockney accents, this quite understated movie looks like the real deal, because it is. No romanticising or mythologising here. Wives, the real bedrocks of working-class culture, hen-peck their spouses, girlfriends go on girls' nights out, murder is clinical, brutal and short, and murder victims stay down. As do bare-knuckle boxers. 'When people pull guns on you, you don't say, "Give me your best shot,"' says Courtney.

Prior to making *Hell to Pay* Gomez – formerly a well-respected LWT cameraman who has never been to film school – played Crow, a patois-affecting hard case in Ian Diaz's quirky crime thriller, *The Killing Zone*. His background is about as far removed from Guy Ritchie's as is possible to imagine, having been raised on a variety of working-class Battersea council estates, where 'someone could punch you in the mouth for just fucking looking at them'. For Gomez, Ritchie's brand of gangster chic is best summed up with a gladiatorial analogy: 'The people in the pit are the working classes and the middle classes have become the spectators: they've paid their money and they want to see something they've never had. Guy Ritchie exemplifies the Jam's "Eton Rifles". But some of those people "who'll be back next week" he's putting in his movies.'

'I thought I was making a film that the man on the street would appreciate,' Ritchie told *Neon*. 'What I didn't anticipate was middle England getting it – and they sort of have. I think a lot of them steered clear of it because they thought it was going to be too laddish.' For pure brass-necked comments, that one's hard to beat. During the scene in which Moran's gang get shit-faced in JD's bar post-heist, the film appeared to descend into a gratuitous appeal to your average middle England boy with a love of *Loaded*, dodgy hijinks, and beer-guzzling. Says the *Guardian*'s Julia Raeside, 'It's like Ritchie forgot he was making a feature film and just ran off a quick beer commercial in his lunch hour.'

'Guy Ritchie tried to create a cult around his film,' says *Empire*'s Ian Nathan. 'It's soulless.' Stephen Woolley concurs. '*Lock, Stock* was manufactured as a cult film. With *Lock, Stock* it's the violence and the language. You're basically cutting off what is perceived to be a general audience – but there is an audience that will thrive on it, and that's what creates a cult.' *Lock, Stock*'s ultimate success came through tapping into three closely intertwined, highly lucrative veins: gangster chic, New Laddism and Britpop. Each vein stems and flows from a central heart – the creeping phenomenon that is retro culture.

'Almost every scene, every single moment of *Lock, Stock*, reminded you of something else,' says Woolley. *Lock, Stock* ushers in the distinct feeling that we've seen it all before. We have – right up there in 70mm, sandwiched between kaleidoscopic commercials for King Cone ice-creams and scratchy, missynched plugs for Indian restaurants – just five minutes' walk from this theatre. 'Unlike the muscle-bound, sweaty likes of Stallone or Schwarzenegger, Ritchie's gangsters look good, sound good – shit, they probably even smell good,' says Raeside. 'They come in such a stylish package, and that whole look comes from the 60s and 70s.'

Of course, by definition, 'retro' isn't new – at least in the context of cinema. The latter movies in this book have, in some ways, set a template. Since Punk, we have begun to look backward: *Quadrophenia* and *Withnail & I* are set in the 1960s, and *Trainspotting* (and possibly *Naked*) in the 1980s. *Lock, Stock*, set in an imaginary cinematic past, is simply the logical conclusion. As publicist Jonathan Rutter says, 'We now have a generation of writers whose idea of a classic is something made in the 1970s.' In philosopher Fredric Jameson's wonderful phrase, Ritchie's kind of pastiche-making – a by-product of post-modernism – occurs when 'energetic artists who now lack both forms and content, cannibalise the museum and wear the masks of extinct mannerisms'.

Lock, Stock's boys sit around discussing Brian De Palma's *Scarface*, while Eddie Constantine's 'Bad night in Vietnam', from *The Long Good Friday*, becomes *Lock, Stock*'s 'Bad day in Bosnia', and so on. In this respect, Ritchie's citing of *The Long Good Friday* as an influence is highly significant. Writer Barrie Keeffe, steeped in an East End milieu, drew directly on gangster culture for his work. Yet Ritchie and his thirty-something media peers, currently mired in the biggest nostalgia boom this nation has seen in years, are taking their cues directly from cinema's recent past – from *The Italian Job*, from *Get Carter*, from genre *per se*.

'We live in the flicker,' mused Marlow in Joseph Conrad's *Heart of Darkness*, referring to the speed of the burgeoning industrial age. A century later, a new generation, nurtured by the flicker of the TV set and the cinema screen, was ripe for the picking. 'Our history, or at least my generation's history, stems directly from the media,' says Raeside. 'We don't have any world wars in our living memory, but what we do have is a wealth of archive footage. Our formative years have been kept for posterity on miles and miles of videotape. Is it any wonder that countless nostalgia TV shows and films are plundering that footage and dissecting it within an inch of its life?'

For Matt Worley, whose short-lived, situationist-style A3 pamphlet 'CRASH' laid into the media's cynically packaged Britpop phenomenon during the summer of 1997, the repeddling of popular culture is a ruse by big business to make more money rather than come up with something new. 'Those in positions of power are looking back through rose-tinted glasses at their childhoods,' he says. 'They're thirty-year-old blokes looking back at what they were doing when they were fourteen. In fact, it's horrible growing up. But people hark back to a nostalgia that never was.'

With Cool Britannia revealed as a temporary fillip at best – a vote-grabbing exercise at worst – the emphasis at the time of writing has subtly shifted from macrocosm to microcosm, with juvenile comforts replacing national celebration. One compelling theory holds that, having grown up with twenty years of emotionally wrenching Conservatism and New Conservatism, this generation appears to have snuggled back, like *South Park*'s Kenny, into the comforting folds of their fluffy orange Parka hoods: one big cultural phenomenon reduced to the size of a *Bagpuss* pencil case. 'It seems all we do now is make lists of our favourite things from a by-gone era, like Julie bloody Andrews,' says Raeside. 'The next cultural phenomenon ought, logically, to be Geek Chic – the ultimate result of all this trivia compiling. Watch out for models sporting pocket-protectors on the cover of the *Face*.'

The belated commercial success of a number of British cult films from the 1960s and 1970s has been closely allied with this backwards-looking retro craze – something not lost on the market. 'I sometimes have waves of anxiety that we are just cultural parasites and just criticise because we don't have an original bone in our body,' says Adam Buxton, who, along with Joe Cornish, delights in taking this sort of cynicism to task. 'But then I rent another movie or turn on the TV and get distracted by the amazingly complex ways modern culture tries to conceal the cynical, lazy, bankrupt way it is created.' No surprise for post-modernist philosophers like Fredric Jameson: all cultural objects have now been transformed into commodities – 'a thing of whatever type has been reduced to a means for its own consumption'.

Previously, the term cult was applied objectively. As film critic (and *It Happened Here* cameo) Barrie Pattison comments, 'Critics who by nature didn't see films unless they came with press books and free liquor were faced with all these movies which didn't conform to the standards of what they were familiar with but mysteriously still had a following. The idea of marginalising them, calling them "cult movies", solved that problem.' But it's now gone way beyond that.

'Back in the late 1980s there were more British publications around interested in discovering genuine oddities, films like *Hellraiser* and *Heathers*,' says Jonathan Rutter. 'A lot of these sort of publications, like *City Limits* or *Blitz*, no longer exist and so getting a small, quirky, off-centre and well-made film off the ground these days is probably a lot harder. Distributors are now less prepared to take risks with off-beat films, because so few of them work.' As Guy Ritchie told Edward Champion in 1998, 'The trouble with the film industry is that there's more business involved than there is creating. From a distributor's point of view, the fact that they've got to deliver does cloud their vision without question.'

Predictably, it does all come down to money. With dwindling investments and fewer British films being produced on an annual basis, the industry has now swooped on 'cultiness' as a viable commodity, having seen a number of cult movies like *A Clockwork Orange* and *Get Carter* clean up. In other words, 'Why wait?' Having previously employed a rather scattershot, blunt approach – 'It's a horror film, the kids will love it' in the case of *The Wicker Man*, for example – the market now increasingly mines potential projects for lucrative 'culty', pop-cultural references – 'smart-bombing' their target core-demographic audience. 'They want to hit the widest audience as quickly as possible,' confirms film publicist Roz Kidd.

As Chris Bailey, who'd handled the publicity for *Lock, Stock*, says, 'The market will definitely use the term 'cult' as a selling point. One of the first things you do is realise what sort of ingredients you've got, what message you want to give out. You might play the iconic card, to make a film bigger or more confident than it actually is. Considering calling it a cult would be part of the discussion.'

'Cult has a sort of prestige attached to it,' says Alexander Walker. 'The American majors now set up subsidiary companies, occasionally to produce, more often to buy, films of limited minority appeal that will confer a status of cult distributor upon their subsidiary.' 'They tried to manufacture a cult around the film *Showgirls*,' says Stephen Woolley. 'While I was working in New York on the post-production of *Michael Collins*, I went to a late-night screening where they gave out a four- or five-page photocopied sheet of words to shout out at the screen. They were trying to reinvent it as a kind of *Rocky Horror Picture Show*.'

Roz Kidd has been in a prime position to observe the process first hand, having flogged Tarantino's *Reservoir Dogs* to British journalists back in 1991. 'We planned our attack,' she recalls, 'to create the buzz around a really cool, cult thriller and kept our fingers crossed it would cross over to the mainstream. We had our targets, our angry young men and film buffs. We set up magazine interviews, screenings, and paced it until the word of mouth was hot. Then I was asked simultaneously to do the publicity for *Man Bites Dog*, which was really, really good timing, because there was all this kind of negativity around violence in movies. We thought, great, let's jump on board.'

By the time *Today* and the *Daily Mail* had tried to have *Reservoir Dogs* banned from British screens, Polygram had managed to achieve so much publicity they barely needed to promote it. It had become 'an easy way for an advertising executive to show his coolness', says Kidd. 'It kind of cheapened the film. If the Lads mags had then been around it would have got really ugly.' And for Kidd, the majority of the media are 'lazy sheep. As soon as they read an article in the *Face* or the *Sunday Times*, they'll go, "Oh, fuck, we'd better cover this because if we don't we'll look stupid." And that's why you'll get this huge snowballing effect, especially with British films like *Trainspotting*, where, regardless of the subject matter, it became a huge British project to be proud of, people overwhelmed by the topicality of it all.'

As Bailey acknowledges, 'In the true sense of the word a cult is something you'll discover later, it becomes part of an inside crowd. But if you use it as a headline quote it gives the idea that you should be discovering it. It doesn't always work, at the end of the day.' 'Hollywood has tried to do this many times,' says director Alex Cox, 'spending vast sums on supposedly hip culty projects like *Howard the Duck* and *Ishtar*. But it doesn't work. Things become cults after the event. Cultiness arises, like Dracula, after the dust has settled. *Easy Rider*, *Plan 9 from Outer Space*, *The Wicker Man* – no one could have predicted their status. There are cases where mainstream films flop as such but still become cults, but it seems unplannable. The obvious exception is *The Rocky Horror Picture Show*, but the stage play was already a cult and the film was extremely faithful to it.' To that he could have added *Trainspotting* and *Fear and Loathing in Las Vegas*. Although it watered down the original source novel, Boyle's movie did sterling business, having tapped into genuine movements like the Rave scene and Britpop. Terry Gilliam's movie – also based on a cult book – took rather less over here, probably lacking any real context for younger British movie-goers.

'We attempted to market the film *Dead Babies* as a cult,' says Bailey, 'but it was still a huge flop. Because it was the cult hip novel of the 1970s, it was believable that you could call it a cult at the same time. It was only going to appeal to students, who'd probably react to the phrase in a positive fashion. It hadn't cut the mustard with the exhibitors or the critics, and through our research we discovered that today's students really aren't aware of Martin Amis: he wasn't going to get us anywhere. So we used the iconographic jelly baby poster. And the film would have really gone like a train, had it been as good as the poster. The film was a bit of a duffer, frankly. It tried hard to be a bit controversial, but actually wasn't. There's nothing worse than that, to be honest.'

Says Kidd: 'There's a lot of bad films out there made by lazy unimaginative people who, in their desperation to make a cult classic, will use an Iggy Pop track or give Harvey Keitel a part. It's very cynical, and I think the real film fans out there will latch on to this and stay away.'

'I have very little patience with these kind of movies that Troma make in America,' says elder statesman of cult film criticism, Kim Newman. 'They realise they haven't got a chance of making a good film on any level, so they'll put a couple of crappy jokes in it, in order to try and say, "We weren't trying to make a proper film, we were trying to make a cult movie." These are films which are impossible to take seriously but also films which are impossible to enjoy on any level.' Newman despairs of those films coming off the back of *Trainspotting*, like *Human Traffic*, dismissing them as 'remakes of *The Blackboard Jungle* with Rave music. You need some kind of sense that films are coming from the street rather than the studio, and I don't think we get that. I suspect that the music industry doesn't allow proper youth cult movies any more because that's not how films are developed.'

'I always thought pop culture and youth culture was in part, an expression of non-conformity and individuality,' says Buxton. 'Half the fun of pop culture is finding things, and now because God forbid anyone should have difficulty in parting with their wad, it's right in front of you at HMV or Virgin, probably in a rack marked "Hard To Find/Obscure". Film-makers are rapidly falling into the same trap. Indie film means pretty much what Indie music means now – something informed by, or nicked from, old school Indie that won't alienate a mass market.'

For Newman, 'It's partly to do with the fact that all of us, audiences, film-makers, critics, are more sophisticated. And the selling is more sophisticated. Nowadays, if a film flops in cinemas, it's on cable TV within twenty minutes, and in every video store. It becomes invisible as a film product. With the demise of second features, like *The Wicker Man*, that means that more than ever now, once a film's had its two weeks in the West End, it's over. Without the possibility of a film hanging around for a long time, you can't have the possibility of a cult film.'

Before we call the pall-bearers and inscribe the tombstone we'd better remind ourselves that we, as consumers, have been partly responsible for this. The market has duly rounded up anything that looks or smells of cult, keen to meet our need for instant gratification. Where the trims and negatives from just one film might once have filled the average living-room to the ceiling, they can now easily be accommodated on a few CD-ROMs. The director's cut, along with nine different endings and trailers in forty different languages, awaits your purchase on a DVD box set. Those of us who remember smuggling a tape recorder into our local Odeon to preserve a portion of our much-loved film have gone the way of the dodo. Says Buxton: 'I don't for a moment think that any of these things will stop new generations from reacting against it all entertainingly and coming up with their own weird bollocks which will resist incorporation, if only for a few years. However, I think the time has gone when you could say, "They may have used 'Perfect Day' on telly, but they'll have a hard time selling trainers with Metal Machine Music." I bet the fuckers are working on it as we speak.'

Ian Nathan remains cautiously optimistic: 'The *Blade Runner* style of movie might carry on – initially flopping, then going on to become a word-of-mouth hit. There's probably something out there, which will blow us all away. Then the director will become immensely rich and go and make dreadful movies in Hollywood.'

Since we began to write this book, *A Clockwork Orange*, *Get Carter* and *A Hard Day's Night* have all been re-released, the industry counting on the fact that many of these movies have a timeless quality. But regardless of hype, a cult movie's successful revival is still dependent on the mood of the next generation, which may have little or no idea what all the fuss was about. There's no accounting for time. With modern culture having completely excavated its own bowel movements, it seems we're currently suffering from a bout of PMT (Post-Modern Tension), and have completely overdosed on nostalgia. 'People are going to have to start thinking for themselves,' says perennial social commentator Paul Morley. 'Which is going to be interesting, isn't it?' The consolation for those of us who lament the way in which the term cult has been misappropriated is that never has it been so easy to track down the genuine article. The Stella Screen approach has become one of the success stories of recent years, gathering young audiences together around a vast screen for free showings in the open air, where they can puff away and imbibe Stella lager to their hearts' content. Stella screenings have become great platforms for cult films, like *The Italian Job*, *Withnail & I* and *Quadrophenia*. One Sunday night in Battersea

Park, 16,000 people turned up for a showing of *Quadrophenia*. 'I think so many things worked well with the choice of *Quadrophenia*,' says Stella's Jeremy Wilton. 'It's a great movie, with a great soundtrack, it hadn't been shown on TV for a long time, and it was a good location. We got all the Mod clubs down with their scooters; we promoted that.'

The Internet has further challenged the notion that cult movies are hard to come by. If tracking them down once required an encyclopaedic knowledge of specialist magazines and contacts, most can now be acquired at the click of a mouse. Now modem speeds, thanks to Broadband, have increased sufficiently, downloading a film has become as easy as filing an MP3. *The Blair Witch Project* famously and successfully used the Internet to promote itself, teasing its potential audience with a whole history of the story months before it was released. The industry was quick to leap on the bandwagon. POP.com, designed to showcase story ideas before a film was made, was put together by two industry stalwarts, Steven Spielberg and Ron Howard, to gauge the feedback from fans. Trailers from forthcoming features are now regularly showcased on the net, while some companies even offer live webcams from film sets.

Ironically, the real future for cult movie-making might now lie with the Internet. As *Net* magazine editor Paul Douglas says, 'The advantage of the Internet is that it will provide a platform for a lot of independent film-makers, who can't afford the traditional channels, to stick their movies on their own website, so they can bypass the big film studios.' Stephen Woolley agrees: 'It's going to be kids on the Internet – that's where cults are going to begin. It's not going to be the Scala cinema any more, it's not going to be late night at the Paris Pullman – people are going to make weird films on the Internet and bypass the censor, the red tape and the cost of putting it out theatrically and on video.'

On this side of the pond, Jane Bussman and David Quantick have seen their Internet sitcom, *The Junkies*, completed on a budget of £3,500, without a commissioning editor or broadcaster, become a cult word-of-mouth success. Meanwhile, fed up with the industry's indifference to his work, British *enfant terrible* Ken Russell has now loaded examples from his extensive canon of films on to pay-per-view websites. Russell, who recently declared himself 'unbankable', has now shot his latest film, *The Fall of the Louse of Usher*, a 'horror-comedy musical' take on Edgar Allan Poe, with the express purpose of screening it on the Internet, via a series of ten-minute episodes.

He had explored more conventional avenues, but potential backers cried off when they heard his choice of leads (Roger Daltrey and Twiggy). 'I had a producer cost it on the cheap, cheap, cheap budget with everyone doing favours and it came to £200,000 – which I simply don't have,' Russell told Iain Fisher for the Savage Messiah Ken Russell website in October 2000. Undeterred, Ken finally pulled out his trusty camcorder and began filming, retaining total control over the camerawork, casting and budget – the price of the average Vauxhall – roping in family members as his crew. 'I have converted my garage and stable into a little studio and I am going to shoot it out of the cottage at Gorsewood as I call it,' he told Fisher. 'It's my answer to Hollywood. We are surrounded by gorse, so this is Gorsewood.'

BACK AT CAMELOT CASTLE, a few hitches. Mark Morrison was supposed to turn up at the *Hell to Pay* set, but has been stuck at the dentist. Luke, Britain's top Ali G impersonator, is depressed. He's forgotten to bring his Ali G wraparound shades with him and, sitting there, in his Tommy Gear, without the shades, he looks nothing like him. Courtney decides he'll play a rifle-toting bodyguard instead. Meanwhile, it begins to rain. The performers start protesting, particularly as Dave wants to do more takes. 'But this is great!' says Dave. 'The Americans love rain! They can't get it over there, so this'll look really great, really *British*!'

FILMOGRAPHY

A HARD DAY'S NIGHT

CAST

John Lennon:	John
Paul McCartney:	Paul
George Harrison:	George
Ringo Starr:	Ringo
Wilfred Brambell:	Grandfather
Norman Rossington:	Norm
Victor Spinetti:	Television director
John Junkin:	Shake
Deryck Guyler:	Police Inspector
Anna Quayle:	Millie
Kenneth Haigh:	Simon
Richard Vernon:	Man on train
Michael Trubshawe:	Club manager
Eddie Malin:	Hotel waiter
Robin Ray:	Television floor manager
Lionel Blair:	Television choreographer
Anna Seebohm:	Secretary
David Jaxon:	Young boy
Marianne Satone:	Society reporter
David Langton:	Actor
Clare Kelly:	Barmaid
Director:	Richard Lester
Producer:	Walter Shenson
Screenplay:	Alun Owen
Music director:	George Martin

Cinematography:	Gilbert Taylor
Editor:	John Jympson and Pamela Tomlin
Art director:	Ray Simm
Costumer designer:	Julie Harris

BLOW-UP

CAST

Vanessa Redgrave:	Jane
Sarah Miles:	Patricia
David Hemmings:	Thomas
John Castle:	Bill
Jane Birkin:	The blonde
Gillian Hills:	The brunette
Peter Bowles:	Ron
Veruschka von Lehndorff:	Herself (as Veruschka)
Julian Chagrin:	Mime
Claude Chagrin:	Mime
Susan Broderick:	Antique shop owner
Tsai Chin:	Thomas's receptionist
Harry Hutchinson:	Shopkeeper
Mary Khal:	Fashion editor
Chas Lawther:	Waiter
Ronan O'Casey:	Jane's lover in park
Reg Wilkins:	Thomas's assistant
Director:	Michelangelo Antonioni
Producers:	Carlo Ponti, Pierre Rouve (executive)
Story:	Julio Cortázar
Screenplay:	Michelangelo Antonioni and Tonino Guerra; English dialogue by Edward Bond
Music:	Herbie Hancock
Cinematography:	Carlo Di Palma
Editor:	Frank Clarke
Art director:	Assheton Gorton
Costume designer:	Jocelyn Rickards

IF . . .

CAST

Crusaders

Malcolm McDowell:	Mick
David Wood:	Johnny
Richard Warwick:	Wallace
Christine Noonan:	The Girl
Rupert Webster:	Bobby Phillips

Whips

Robert Swann:	Rowntree
Hugh Thomas:	Denson
Michael Cadman:	Fontinbras
Peter Sproule:	Barnes

Staff

Peter Jeffrey:	Headmaster
Arthur Lowe:	Mr Kemp
Mona Washbourne:	Matron
Mary MacLeod:	Mrs Kemp
Geoffrey Chater:	Chaplain
Ben Aris:	John Thomas
Graham Crowden:	History master
Charles Lloyd Pack:	Classics master
Anthony Nicholls:	General Denson
Tommy Godfrey:	Finchley
Guy Ross:	Stephans
Robin Askwith:	Keating
Richard Everett:	Pussy Graves
Phillip Bagnell:	Peanuts
Nicholas Page:	Cox
Robert Yatzes:	Fisher
David Griffen:	Willens
Graham Sharman:	Van Essen
Richard Tombleson:	Baird

Juniors

Richard (Robin) Davies:	Machin

Brian Pettifer:	Biles
Michael Newport:	Brunning
Charles Sturridge:	Markland
Sean Bury:	Jute
Martin Beaumont:	Hunter

Director:	Lindsay Anderson
Producers:	Roy Baird with Michael Medwin and Lindsay Anderson
Screenplay:	David Sherwin, from the original script 'Crusaders' by David Sherwin and John Howlett
Cinematography:	Miroslav Ondricek
Editor:	David Gladwell
Assistant editors:	Ian Rakoff and Michael Ellis
Sound recordist:	Christian Wangler
Production designer:	Jocelyn Herbert
Art director:	Brian Eatwell
Music:	Marc Williamson; 'Sanctus' from *Missa Luba* (Philips)
Costume designer:	Shura Cohen
Production:	Memorial Enterprises

Colour with tinted black and white sequences

PERFORMANCE

CAST

James Fox:	Chas Devlin
Mick Jagger:	Turner
Anita Pallenberg:	Pherber
Michelle Breton:	Lucy
Johnny Shannon:	Harry Flowers
John Bindon:	Moody
Stanley Meadows:	Rosebloom
Ann Sidney:	Dana
Anthony Valentine:	Joey Maddocks
Allan Cuthbertson:	Harley-Brown
Anthony Morton:	Dennis
Ken Colley:	Tony Farell
John Sterland:	Chauffeur

Lorraine Wickens:	Laraine
Directors:	Donald Cammell and Nicolas Roeg
Producer:	Sanford Lieberson
Associate producer:	David Cammell
Production manager:	Robert Lyon
Unit manager:	Kevin Kavanagh
Assistant director:	Richard Burge
Screenplay:	Donald Cammell
Cinematography:	Nicolas Roeg
Camera operator:	Mike Molloy
Editor:	Anthony Gibbs
Editors:	Brian Smedley-Aston and Frank Mazzola
Art director:	John P. Clark
Music:	Jack Nitzsche
Set dresser:	Peter Young
Design consultant (Turner's house):	Christopher Gibbs
Costume consultant:	Deborah Dixon
Wardrobe:	Emma Porteous and Billy Jay
Director of authenticity:	David Litvinoff

GET CARTER

CAST

Michael Caine:	Jack Carter
Ian Hendry:	Eric Paice
Britt Ekland:	Anna Fletcher
John Osborne:	Cyril Kinnear
Tony Beckley:	Peter
George Sewell:	Con McCarty
Geraldine Moffat:	Glenda
Dorothy White:	Margaret
Rosemarie Dunham:	Edna
Petra Markham:	Doreen
Alun Armstrong:	Keith
Bryan Mosley:	Cliff Brumby

Glynn Edwards:	Albert Swift
Bernard Hepton:	Thorpe
Terence Rigby:	Gerald Fletcher
John Bindon:	Sid Fletcher
Godfrey Quigley:	Eddie
Kevin Brennan:	Harry
Maxwell Dees:	Vicar
Liz McKenzie:	Mrs Brumby
John Hussey:	Architect
Ben Aris:	Architect
Kitty Atwood:	Old woman
Denea Wilde:	Pub singer
Geraldine Sherman:	Girl in café
Joy Merlin:	Woman in post office
Yvonne Michaels:	Woman in post office
Alan Hockey:	Scrapyard dealer
Carl Howard:	'J'

Director:	Mike Hodges
Producer:	Michael Klinger
Screenplay:	Mike Hodges; based on the novel *Jack's Return Home* by Ted Lewis
Music:	Roy Budd
Cinematography:	Wolfgang Suschitzky
Editor:	John Trumper
Casting:	Irene Lamb
Production designer:	Assheton Gorton
Art director:	Roger King

A CLOCKWORK ORANGE

CAST

Malcolm McDowell:	Alex DeLarge
Patrick Magee:	Mr Frank Alexander
Michael Bates:	Chief Guard Barnes
Warren Clarke:	Dim
John Clive:	Stage actor
Adrienne Corri:	Mrs Alexander
Carl Duering:	Dr Brodsky

Paul Farrell:	Tramp
Clive Francis:	Lodger
Michael Gover:	Prison governor
Miriam Karlin:	Cat lady
James Marcus:	Georgie
Aubrey Morris:	P. R. Deltoid
Godfrey Quigley:	Prison chaplain
Sheila Raynor:	Mrs DeLarge ('Em')
Madge Ryan:	Dr Branum
John Savident:	Conspirator Dolin
Anthony Sharp:	Minister
Philip Stone:	Mr DeLarge ('Pee')
Pauline Taylor:	Dr Taylor
Margaret Tyzack:	Conspirator Rubinstein
Steven Berkoff:	Constable
Lindsay Campbell:	Detective
Michael Tarn:	Pete
David Prowse:	Julian (Mr Alexander's body-guard/therapist)
Jan Adair:	Handmaiden
Vivienne Chandler:	Handmaiden
Prudence Drage:	Handmaiden
Richard Connaught:	Billy-Boy
Carol Drinkwater:	Sister Feeley
Cheryl Grunwald:	Rape victim in film
Gillian Hills:	Sonietta
Craig Hunter:	Doctor
Virginia Wetherell:	Stage actress
Katya Wyeth:	Girl
Director and producer:	Stanley Kubrick
Executive producers:	Si Litvinoff and Max L. Raab
Associate producer:	Bernard Williams
Music:	Walter Carlos

THE WICKER MAN

CAST	Edward Woodward:	Sergeant Howie
	Christopher Lee:	Lord Summerisle

Diane Cilento:	Miss Rose
Britt Ekland:	Willow
Ingrid Pitt:	Librarian
Lindsay Kemp:	Alder MacGregor
Russell Waters:	Harbour master
Aubrey Morris:	Old Gardener/Grave-digger
Irene Sunters:	May Morrison
Walter Carr:	School master
Ian Campbell:	Oak
Leslie Blackater:	Hairdresser
Roy Boyd:	Broome
Peter Brewis:	Musician
Barbara Ann Brown:	Woman with baby
Juliet Cadzow:	Villager on Summerisle
Ross Campbell:	Communicant
Penny Cluer:	Callie
Michael Coles:	Musician
Kevin Collins:	Old fisherman
Geraldine Cowper:	Rowan Morrison
Ian Cutler:	Musician
Donald Eccles:	T. H. Lennox
Myra Forsyth:	Mrs Grimmond
John Hallam:	PC McTaggert
Alison Hughes:	Fiancée to Howie
Charles Kearney:	Butcher
Fiona Kennedy:	Holly
John MacGregor:	Baker
Jimmy MacKenzie:	Briar
Lesley MacKie:	Daisey
Jennifer Martin:	Myrtle Morrison
Bernard Murray:	Musician
Helen Norman:	Villager on Summerisle
Lorraine Peters:	Girl on grave
Tony Roper:	Postman
John Sharp:	Dr Ewan
Elizabeth Sinclair:	Villager on Summerisle
Andrew Tompkins:	Musician
Ian Wilson:	Communicant

Richard Wren:	Ash Buchanan
John Young:	Fishmonger
Director:	Robin Hardy
Producer:	Peter Snell
Screenplay:	Anthony Shaffer
Music:	Paul Giovanni
Cinematography:	Harry Waxman
Editor:	Eric Boyd-Perkins
Art Director:	Seamus Flannery
Costume designer:	Sue Yelland
Make-up artist:	W. T. Parleton
Production manager:	Ted Morley
Associate musical director:	Gary Carpenter
Production secretary:	Beryl Harvey
Choreographer:	Stewart Hopps

QUADROPHENIA

CAST

Phil Daniels:	Jimmy
Leslie Ash:	Steph
Philip Davis:	Chalky
Mark Wingett:	Dave
Sting:	Ace
Ray Winstone:	Kevin
Garry Cooper:	Pete
Gary Shail:	Spider
Toyah Wilcox:	Monkey
Trevor Laird:	Ferdy
Kate Williams:	Jimmy's mother
Michael Elphick:	Jimmy's father
Kim Neve:	Yvonne
Benjamin Whitrow:	Mr Fulford
Daniel Peacock:	Danny
Jeremy Child:	Aganey Man
John Phillips:	Magistrate
Timothy Spall:	Projectionist
Olivier Pierre:	Tailor

George Innes:	Café owner
John Bindon:	Harry
P. H. Moriarty:	Barman at Villain Club
Hugh Lloyd:	Mr Cale

Director:	Franc Roddam
Producers:	Roy Baird and Bill Curbishley
Executive producers:	Roger Daltrey, John Entwistle, Keith Moon, David Gideon Thomson and Pete Townshend
Associate producer:	John Peverall
Screenplay:	Dave Humphries, Franc Roddam and Martin Stellman; original story by Pete Townshend
Music:	John Entwistle and Pete Townshend
Cinematography:	Brian Tufano

WITHNAIL & I

CAST

Richard E. Grant:	Withnail
Paul McGann:	Marwood
Richard Griffiths:	Monty
Ralph Brown:	Danny
Michael Elphick:	Jake
Daragh O'Malley:	Irishman
Michael Wardle:	Isaac Parkin
Una Brandon-Jones:	Mrs Parkin
Noel Johnson:	General
Irene Sutcliffe:	Waitress
Llewellyn Rees:	Tea-shop proprietor
Robert Oates:	Policeman 1
Anthony Wise:	Policeman 2
Eddie Tagoe:	Presuming Ed

| Director and writer: | Bruce Robinson |
| Producers: | George Harrison, Paul M. Heller, Denis O'Brien and David Wimbury |

Music:	David Dundas and Rick Wentworth
Cinematography:	Peter Hannan
Editor:	Alan Strachan
Casting:	Mary Selway
Production designer:	Michael Pickwoad
Art director:	Henry Harris
Costume design:	Andrea Galer
Make-up:	Peter Frampton

NAKED

CAST

David Thewlis:	Johnny
Lesley Sharp:	Louise
Katrin Cartlidge:	Sophie
Greg Cruttwell:	Jeremy
Claire Skinner:	Sandra
Peter Wight:	Brian
Ewen Bremner:	Archie
Susan Vidler:	Maggie
Deborah MacLaren:	Woman in window
Gina McKee:	Café girl
Carolina Giammetta:	Masseuse
Elizabeth Berrington:	Giselle
Darren Tunstall:	Poster man
Robert Putt:	Chauffeur
Lynda Rooke:	Victim
Angela Curran:	Car owner
Peter Whitman:	Mr Halpern
Jo Abercrombie:	Woman in street
Elaine Britten:	Girl in Porsche
David Foxe:	Tea bar owner
Mike Avenall:	Man at tea bar
Toby Jones:	Man at tea bar
Sandra Voe:	Bag lady

Director and writer:	Mike Leigh
Producer:	Simon Channing-Williams
Music:	Andrew Dickson

Cinematography:	Dick Pope
Editor:	Jon Gregory
Casting:	Susie Parriss and Paddy Stern
Production designer:	Alison Chitty
Art director:	Eve Stewart
Costume designer:	Lindy Hemming
Make-up artist:	Christine Blundell
Production manager:	Georgina Lowe

TRAINSPOTTING

CAST

Ewan McGregor:	Mark 'Rent-boy' Renton
Ewen Bremner:	Daniel 'Spud' Murphy
Jonny Lee Miller:	Simon David 'Sick Boy' Williamson
Kevin McKidd:	Tommy MacKenzie
Robert Carlyle:	Francis Begbie
Kelly Macdonald:	Diane
Peter Mullan:	Swanney
James Cosmo:	Mr Renton
Eileen Nicholas:	Mrs Renton
Susan Vidler:	Alison
Pauline Lynch:	Lizzy
Shirley Henderson:	Gail
Stuart McQuarrie:	Gavin/US tourist
Irvine Welsh:	Mikey Forrester
Dale Winton:	Game-show Host
Keith Allen:	Dealer
Kevin Allen:	Andreas
Annie Louise Ross:	Gail's mother
Billy Riddoch:	Gail's father
Fiona Bell:	Diane's mother
Vincent Friell:	Diane's father
Hugh Ross:	Man
Victor Eadie:	Man
Kate Donnelly:	Woman
Finlay Welsh:	Sheriff
Eddie Nestor:	Estate agent
Tom Delmar:	Pub heavy

Rachael Fleming:	Renton's nurse
John Hodge:	Store security officer
Andrew Macdonald:	Flat buyer
Director:	Danny Boyle
Producers:	Andrew Macdonald and Christopher Figg
Screenplay:	John Hodge; adapted from the novel by Irvine Welsh

LOCK, STOCK AND TWO SMOKING BARRELS

CAST

Jason Flemyng:	Tom
Dexter Fletcher:	Soap
Nick Moran:	Eddie
Jason Statham:	Bacon
Steven Mackintosh:	Winston
Nicholas Rowe:	J
Nick Marg:	Charles
Charles Forbes:	Willie
Vinnie Jones:	Big Chris
Lenny McLean:	Barry the Baptist
Peter McNicholl:	Little Chris
P. H. Moriarty:	Hatchet Harry
Frank Harper:	Dog
Steve Sweeney:	Plank
Huggy Leaver:	Paul
Ronnie Fox:	Mickey
Tony McMahon:	John
Stephen Marcus:	Nick the Greek
Vas Blackwood:	Rory Breaker
Sting:	JD
Jake Abraham:	Dean
Robert Brydon:	Traffic warden
Stephen Callender-Ferrier:	Lenny
Steve Collins:	Boxing gym bouncer
Elwin 'Chopper' David:	Nathan
Vera Day:	Tanya

Jimmy Flint:	Don
Alan Ford:	Alan
Sid Golder:	Phil (as Sidney Golder)
Alex Hall:	Slick
John Houchin:	Doorman
Danny John-Jules:	Barfly Jack
Bal Jusar:	Gordon
Victor McGuire:	Gary
Mark Mooney:	Serg
Suzy Ratner:	Gloria
David Reid:	Samoan Jo
Graham Stevens:	Policeman
Jimmy Tarbuck:	John O'Driscoll
Andrew Tiernan:	Man in pub
Richard Vanstone:	Frazer
Matthew Vaughn:	Yuppie in car
Director and writer:	Guy Ritchie
Producers:	Stephen Marks
	Georgia Masters
	Peter Morton
	Angad Paul
	Sebastian Pearson
	Jan Roldanus
	Trudie Styler
	Steve Tisch
	Ronalda Vasconcellos
	Matthew Vaughn
Original music:	David A. Hughes
	John Murphy (II)
Cinematography by:	Tim Maurice-Jones
Film editing:	Niven Howie
Casting:	Celestia Fox
	Guy Ritchie
Production design:	Iain Andrews
	Eve Mavrakis
Costume design:	Stephanie Collie

SELECT BIBLIOGRAPHY

INTRODUCTION
Eco, Umberto, *Faith in Fakes*, Secker & Warburg, 1986
Peary, Danny, *Cult Movies*, Vermilion, 1982

YOU CAN'T DO THAT: *A HARD DAY'S NIGHT*
Brown, Peter, and Steven Gaines, *The Love You Make*, Macmillan, 1983
Davies, Hunter, *The Authorised Beatles Biography*, Sidgwick & Jackson, 1968
Lewisohn, Mark, *The Complete Beatles Chronicle*, Pyramid, 1992
Lewisohn, Mark, Peit Schreuders, and Adam Smith *The Beatles' London*, Hamlyn, 1994

WE'RE NOT IN KANSAS ANY MORE: *BLOW-UP*
Dreja, Chris, Jim McCarty, and John Platt, *The Yardbirds*, Sidgwick & Jackson, 1983
Green, Jonathon (ed.), *Days in the Life: Notes from the English Underground, 1961–1971*, William Heinemann, 1988
Miles, Sarah, *A Right Royal Bastard*, Macmillan, 1993
Miles, Sarah, *Serves Me Right*, Macmillan, 1994
Sinclair, Iain, *Lights Out for the Territory*, Granta, 1997
Stamp, Terence, *Double Feature*, Bloomsbury, 1989

WILL THEY CARE IN WIGAN?: *IF . . .*
Anderson, Lindsay, and David Sherwin, *If . . . : A film by Lindsay Anderson*, McGibbon & Kee, 1969
Rakoff, Ian, *Inside the Prisoner*, Batsford, 1999

Sherwin, David, *Going Mad in Hollywood*, André Deutsch, 1998
Sussex, Elizabeth, *Lindsay Anderson*, Studio Vista, 1969
Walker, Alexander, *Hollywood, England: The British Film Industry in the Sixties*, Harrap, 1986

THE NOTTING HILL FILM: *PERFORMANCE*
Brown, Mick, *Performance*, Bloomsbury, 1999
Faithfull, Marianne, *Faithfull*, Michael Joseph, 1994
Fox, James, *Comeback: An Actor's Direction*, Hodder & Stoughton, 1983
MacCabe, Colin, *Performance*, BFI, 1998
Raban, Jonathan, *Soft City*, Flamingo, 1974
Scaduto, Anthony, *Mick Jagger*, W. H. Allen, 1974
Vague, Tom, *London Psychogeography: Rachman Riots and Rillington Place*, 'Vague 30', 1998

WHAT WOULD JESUS SAY?: *GET CARTER*
Caine, Michael, *What's It All About?*, Century, 1992
Chibnall, Steve, and Robert Murphy (eds), *British Crime Cinema*, Routledge, 1999
Freeman, Nick, *That was Business – This is Personal: Professions of Violence in English Cinema from Brighton Rock to the Krays* (from 'Close Up: the Electronic Journal of British Cinema', as published on the Internet)
Gallagher, Elaine, and Ian MacDonald, *Candidly Caine*, Robson Books, 1990
Hall, William, *Raising Caine*, Sidgwick & Jackson, 1981
Keeffe, Barrie, *The Long Good Friday*, original screenplay, Methuen, 1984
Lewis, Ted, *Get Carter, aka Jack's Return Home*, Michael Joseph, 1970

SUBWAY NUMBER ONE: *A CLOCKWORK ORANGE*
Baxter, John, *Stanley Kubrick: A Biography*, HarperCollins, 1997
Burgess, Anthony, *A Clockwork Orange*, Heinemann, 1962
Burgess, Anthony, *Little Wilson and Big God*, Heinemann, 1987
Burgess, Anthony, *You've Had Your Time*, Heinemann, 1990

Ciment, Michel, *Kubrick*, Holt Rinehart and Winston, New York, 1980

Giles, Jane, *Scala: Autopsy of a Cinema*, Shock Xpress, Titan Books, 1994

Robertson, James C., *The Hidden Cinema: British Film Censorship in Action, 1913–1975*, Routledge, 1989

THE TRUE NATURE OF SACRIFICE: *THE WICKER MAN*

Ashurst, Gail (ed.), *Nuada*, nos. 1–2 (available from 15 Moor Road, Northern Moor, Manchester M23 9BQ)

Brown, Allan, *Inside the Wicker Man*, Sidgwick & Jackson, 2000

Frazer, J. G., *The Golden Bough*, Macmillan, 1978

Hardy, Robin, and Anthony Shaffer, *The Wicker Man*, Pan, 2000

'JIMMY DID IT HERE': *QUADROPHENIA*

Cohn, Nik, *Ball the Wall*, Picador, 1989

Hamblett, Charles and Jane Deverson, *Generation X*, Four Square, 1964

Marsh, Dave, *Before I Get Old: The Story of the Who*, Plexus, 1983

Montgomery, John, *Battle of Brighton*, (undated)

For future information on Glenda Clarke's walking tours 'Quadrophenia' and 'Brighton on Film' see www.brightonwalks.com/quadrophenia or email info@brightonwalks.com

ALL RIGHT HERE?: *WITHNAIL & I*

Grant, Richard, *Withnails*, Picador, 1996

Hill, John, *British Cinema in the 1980s*, Oxford University Press, 1999

Owen, Alistair, *Smoking in Bed: Conversations with Bruce Robinson*, Bloomsbury, 2000

Robinson, Bruce, *Withnail & I: The Screenplay*, Bloomsbury, 1995

Thompson, Hunter S., *Fear and Loathing in Las Vegas*, Paladin, 1972

MEAN TIMES: *NAKED*

Coveney, Michael, *The World According to Mike Leigh*, HarperCollins, 1996

Leigh, Mike, *Naked and Other Screenplays*, Faber & Faber, 1994

Movshovitz, Howie (ed.), *Mike Leigh Interviews*, University Press of Mississippi, 2000

CHOOSE DIY: *TRAINSPOTTING*

Adams, Billy, *Ewan McGregor*, B&W Publishing, 1998

Brooks, Xan, *Choose Life*, Chameleon Books, 1998

Collin, Matthew and John Godfrey, *Altered State*, Serpent's Tail, 1997

Hodge, John, *Trainspotting* (screenplay), Faber & Faber, 1996

Pendreigh, Brian, *Ewan McGregor*, Orion, 1998

Pendreigh, Brian, *The Scot Pack*, Mainstream, 2000

Welsh, Irvine, *Trainspotting*, Minerva, 1993

THE FOOTBALLER, THE GANGSTER, THE ICON AND HER LOVER: *LOCK, STOCK AND TWO SMOKING BARRELS*

Jameson, Fredric, *Postmodernism or The Cultural Logic of Late Capitalism*, Duke University Press, 1991

Jameson, Fredric, *Signatures of the Visible*, Routledge, 1992

Jones, Vinnie, *Vinnie: Confessions of a Bad Boy*, Headline, 1998

INDEX

INDEX

INDEX